Lecture Notes in Computer Science 12830

More information about this subseries at http://www.springer.com/series/7407

Richard Li · Simon K. S. Cheung ·
Chiaki Iwasaki · Lam-For Kwok ·
Makoto Kageto (Eds.)

Blended Learning

Re-thinking and Re-defining the Learning Process

14th International Conference, ICBL 2021
Nagoya, Japan, August 10–13, 2021
Proceedings

Springer

Editors
Richard Li
Hong Kong Polytechnic University
Hong Kong, China

Simon K. S. Cheung
Open University of Hong Kong
Hong Kong, China

Chiaki Iwasaki
Kansai University
Osaka, Japan

Lam-For Kwok
City University of Hong Kong
Hong Kong, China

Makoto Kageto
Nihon Fukushi University
Nagoya, Japan

ISSN 0302-9743 ISSN 1611-3349 (electronic)
Lecture Notes in Computer Science
ISBN 978-3-030-80503-6 ISBN 978-3-030-80504-3 (eBook)
https://doi.org/10.1007/978-3-030-80504-3

LNCS Sublibrary: SL1 – Theoretical Computer Science and General Issues

This Springer imprint is published by the registered company Springer Nature Switzerland AG
The registered company address is: Gewerbestrasse 11, 6330 Cham, Switzerland

Preface

Welcome to the proceedings of the 14th International Conference on Blended Learning (ICBL 2021). This year, ICBL 2021 was hosted at the Nihon Fukushi University, Nagoya, Japan, during August 10–13 2021.

Blended learning is one of the promising approaches to teaching and learning. It integrates traditional learning with innovative means to create a new learning environment conducive to effective learning. Like the previous conferences in the series, ICBL 2021 provided a platform for knowledge exchange and experience sharing among researchers and practitioners in this field.

The theme of ICBL 2021 was *Re-thinking and Re-defining the Learning Process*. Over the past decade, enabled by educational and technological innovations, the teaching and learning process has been undergoing a lot of changes, not only on instructional design and delivery but also on student advising and assessment. Our focus was on the innovative educational and technological practices of blended learning, and how these practices change the teaching and learning process.

ICBL 2021 attracted a total of 79 paper submissions. After a rigorous review process, 30 papers were selected for inclusion in this volume. The selected papers cover various areas in blended learning, including content and instructional design, enriched and smart learning experience, experience in blended learning, institutional policies and strategies, and online and collaborative learning.

We would like to take this opportunity to thank the following parties who made the conference a success: the Organizing Committee; the International Program Committee; the conference organizers and co-organizer; the conference sponsors, and all of the conference participants.

We trust that you will enjoy reading the papers.

August 2021

Richard Li
Simon K. S. Cheung
Chiaki Iwasaki
Lam-For Kwok
Makoto Kageto

Conference Organization

Organizing Committee

Honorary Chairs

Horace Ip	City University of Hong Kong, Hong Kong, China
Wakio Oyanagi	Kansai University and Japan Association for Educational Media Study, Japan

Conference Chairs

Lam-For Kwok	City University of Hong Kong, Hong Kong, China
Shinichi Sato	Nihon Fukushi University, Japan

Organizing Chairs

John Hui	Education University of Hong Kong, Hong Kong, China
Makoto Kageto	Nihon Fukushi University, Japan

Programme Chairs

Richard Li	The Hong Kong Polytechnic University, Hong Kong, China
Simon K. S. Cheung	The Open University of Hong Kong, Hong Kong, China
Chiaki Iwasaki	Kansai University, Japan

Finance Chairs

Kwan Keung Steven Ng	Hong Kong Society for Multimedia and Image Computing, Hong Kong, China
Mihoko Chiba	Konan University, Japan

Local Arrangement Chairs

Oliver Au	The Open University of Hong Kong, Hong Kong, China
Hiroki Murakawa	Nihon Fukushi University, Japan
Tomomi Sato	Aichi Shukutoku University, Japan

Publicity Chairs

Morris Jong	The Chinese University of Hong Kong, Hong Kong, China
Yinghui Shi	Central China Normal University, China
Hiroyuki Aoki	International Christian University, Japan
Tomomi Takabayashi	Cyber University, Japan

Web Masters

Richard Li	The Hong Kong Polytechnic University, Hong Kong, China
Ryo Yoshikawa	Nagoya Bunri University, Japan

International Program Committee

Chairs

Richard Li	The Hong Kong Polytechnic University, Hong Kong, China
Simon K. S. Cheung	The Open University of Hong Kong, Hong Kong, China
Chiaki Iwasaki	Kansai University, Japan

Members

Oliver Au	The Open University of Hong Kong, Hong Kong, China
Jinnong Cao	The Hong Kong Polytechnic University, Hong Kong, China
C. S. Chai	The Chinese University of Hong Kong, Hong Kong, China
Kan-Kan Chan	University of Macau, Macau, China
Chih-Tsan Chang	National Chung Cheng University, Taiwan, China
Thomas Chiu	The Chinese University of Hong Kong, Hong Kong, China
Mike Chui	Education University of Hong Kong, Hong Kong, China
Tetsuro Ejima	Aichi University of Education, Japan
Rie Emoto	Iwate University, Japan,
Blanka Frydrychova Klimova	University of Hradec Králové, Czech Republic
Gibran Alejandro Garcia Mendoza	Toyo University, Japan
Yoshiko Goda	Kumamoto University, Japan
Wolfgang Halang	Fernuniversität in Hagen, Germany
Owen Hall Jr.	Pepperdine University, USA
Tianyong Hao	South China Normal University, China

Nehal Hasnine	Hosei University, Japan
Andreas Henrich	University of Bamberg, Germany
Yuki Hirai	Shinsyu University, Japan
Yoko Hirata	Hokkai-Gakuen University, Japan
Yoshihiro Hirata	Hokkai-Gakuen University, Japan
Norio Hozaki	Waseda University, Japan
Jenq-Muh Hsu	National Chiayi University, Taiwan, China
John Yan Keung Hui	Education University of Hong Kong, Hong Kong, China
Josef Hynek	University of Hradec Králové, Czech Republic
Ryohei Ikejiri	The University of Tokyo, Japan
Masatoshi Ishikawa	Tokyo Seitoku University, Japan
Jane Geng Jie	The Chinese University of Hong Kong, Hong Kong, China
Morris Jong	The Chinese University of Hong Kong, Hong Kong, China
Akinobu Kanda	Tokyo Metropolitan University, Japan
Gary A. Kirkpatrick	Nihon Fukushi University, Japan
Takayuki Konno	Meisei University, Japan
Kenichi Kubota	Kansai University, Japan
Masayuki Kudo	Fuji Women's University, Japan
Haruo Kurokami	Kansai University, Japan
Reggie Kwan	The Open University of Hong Kong, Hong Kong, China
Lam-For Kwok	City University of Hong Kong, Hong Kong, China
Chiu-Lin Lai	National Taiwan University of Science and Technology, Taiwan, China
Ivan Ka Wai Lai	City University of Macau, Macau, China
Jeanne Lam	The University of Hong Kong, Hong Kong, China
Keith Lee	The Open University of Hong Kong, Hong Kong, China
Min-Hsien Lee	National Taiwan Normal University, Taiwan, China
Victor Lee	City University of Hong Kong, Hong Kong China
Yi Li	Nanjing University, China
Kam Cheong Li	The Open University of Hong Kong, Hong Kong, China
Heng Luo	Central China Normal University, China
Will Ma	Technological and Higher Education Institute of Hong Kong, Hong Kong, China
Takeshi Matsuda	Tokyo Metropolitan University, Japan
Tatsunori Matsui	Waseda University, Japan
Terumi Miyazoe	Tokyo University of Science, Japan
Kousuke Mouri	Tokyo University of Agriculture and Technology, Japan
Masayuki Murakami	Kyoto University of Foreign Studies, Japan
Junko Nemoto	Meijigakuin University, Japan

Xiaohong Zhang	Kumamoto University, Japan
Yunxiang Zheng	South China Normal University, China
Sha Zhu	Central China Normal University, China

Organizers

Nihon Fukushi University

City University of Hong Kong

Co-organizer

香港多媒體及影像計算學會
Hong Kong Society for Multimedia and Image Computing

Hong Kong Society for Multimedia and Image Computing

Sponsors

香港培華教育基金會
Hong Kong Pei Hua Education Foundation

Hong Kong Pei Hua Education Foundation

Springer

Springer Science+Business Media

Keynote Speakers and Panel Chairs

Keynote Speakers

Katsuaki Suzuki	Kumamoto University, Japan
Jimmy H. M. Lee	The Chinese University of Hong Kong, Hong Kong, China
Yekyung Lisa Lee	Sogang University, South Korea
Wenge Guo	Peking University, China

Panel Chairs

Horace H. S. Ip	City University of Hong Kong, Hong Kong, China
Kenichi Kubota	Kansai University, Japan
Youru Xie	South China Normal University, China

Contents

Enriched and Smart Learning Experience

Experience in Blended Learning

Institutional Policies and Strategies

Online and Collaborative Learning

Keynotes

From Nine Events of Instruction to the First Principles of Instruction: Transformation of Learning Architecture for Society 5.0

Katsuaki Suzuki(✉)

Research Center for Instructional Systems, Kumamoto University, 2-40-1, Kurokami, Kumamoto 860-8555, Japan
ksuzuki@kumamoto-u.ac.jp

Abstract. This keynote addresses a needed shift in designing learning architecture for transforming education to meet the needs of Society 5.0, Super Smart Society. *Classroom of the Future Project* is reviewed to image the transformation of education being sought in Japan. The *Nine Events of Instruction*, a traditional instructional design theory proposed by Robert M. Gagne, will be reviewed as a framework for facilitating human learning based on information processing theory. It will then be compared with a more recent framework of the *First Principles of Instruction*, proposed by M. David Merrill, reflecting various theories and models proposed based on constructivist psychology. Similarities and differences will be discussed to suggest how to utilize them as an architectural framework for blended learning design toward a more learner-centered self-directed learning environment, toward so-called Society 5.0.

Keywords: Instructional design · *Nine Events of Instruction* · *First Principles of Instruction* · Society 5.0 · *Classroom of the Future Project*

1 Introduction

Educational Technology has been a field of study that lasted long and has evolved in relation to the advancement of technology, from teaching machines, radio and television, computer-assisted instruction, to Web-based training and online education [1]. It has been anticipated that a super smart society is just around the corner as the next phase of society after information and communication technology (ICT) society. Japanese government selected the term Society 5.0 [2] for such a super smart society, based on Internet of Things (IoT) technology, to make all the services available anytime, anywhere, and to anybody. It is named Society 5.0, because it comes after the hunting society (Society 1.0), the farming society (Society 2.0), the industrial society (Society 3.0), and ICT society (Society 4.0). However, as Marc Prensky [3] suggested, we may still be trying to educate *Digital Natives* who were born with digital technology, and who will become the major actors of Society 5.0, with an outdated way of education. Most current teachers who teach the Digital Natives are *Digital Immigrants* who had grown up in older societies

R. Li et al. (Eds.): ICBL 2021, LNCS 12830, pp. 3–15, 2021.
https://doi.org/10.1007/978-3-030-80504-3_1

without digital technology. We may still be trying to make our children function well in an assembly line of Society 3.0, if not trying to make them function well now, but soon be substituted by Artificial Intelligence. It is the time that major transformation should be brought to education to better meet the new needs of the future, which is not an easy task, but essential to make Society 5.0 a reality.

This paper will discuss how we can prepare such transformation in two ways. First, a recent attempt by Japanese government will be introduced to form a concrete image of what can be done to make a major shift in school curriculum. Second, a shift in the background theories of instructional design will be explained by comparing and making contrast of two well-known models. It is the author's hope that the concrete image can be supported by theoretical architecture so that the transformation will be designed in all and every contexts of education today.

2 MITI's *Classroom of the Future Project*

As an example of efforts to transform current schools to fit the needs of Society 5.0, The Japanese Ministry of International Trade and Industry (MITI) has launched the *Classroom of the Future Project* in 2018 [4]. MITI intends to corporate with The Ministry of Education (MEXT), from the education industry sectors, to make what is written in the K-12 new standard course of study a reality by the alliance (See Fig. 1). *GIGA Schools Initiative*, GIGA as an acronym for *Global and Innovation Gateway for All*, represents such METI/MEXT corporation for innovation in education, in which Tablet PCs are to be provided to all pupils with high-speed network. The initiative has been accelerated due to the school shutdown occurred in 2020 by the COVID-19 pandemic.

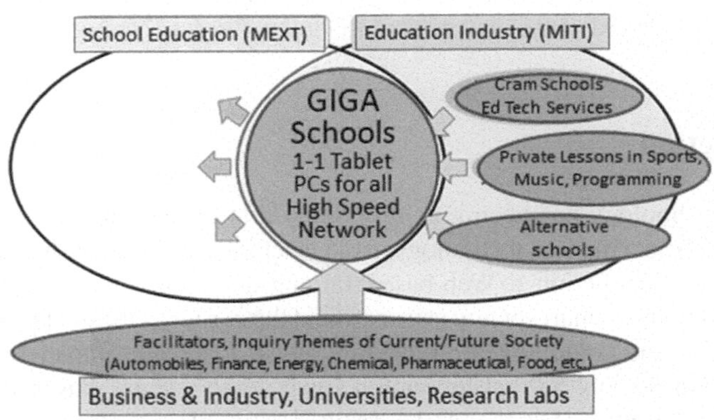

Fig. 1. METI/MEXT Corporation for Innovation in Education in Japan Note: English is provided by the author as unofficial translation.

Figure 2 represents MITI's concept for the *Classroom of the Future Project*. Although MITI deals with Education Industry sectors, its current focus lies in the K-12 schools, with the keywords "Converting school learning to STEAM (Science, Technology, Engineering, Arts, and Mathematics) with personalized and optimized learning." The aim is to form cycles of inquiry-based projects at creation level, with acquisition of necessary basic knowledge and skills, so that interdisciplinary learning can be started from young ages and continued to be at the center of the curriculum. The cycles create the reason to learn basics that could be boring and tedious without clear and immediate needs at hand. Pupils naturally see the reason why they need to learn the basics, because they are to be utilized as the project progresses. Without basics, nobody can create meaningful artifacts in any project. However, basics can be acquired on time and on demand, whenever needed by the project, without spending so much time learning only basics first. This is claimed to be a more exciting way of learning for each pupil, which can be helped by technology managing personal learning plans and learning pathways of all students engaging in different projects.

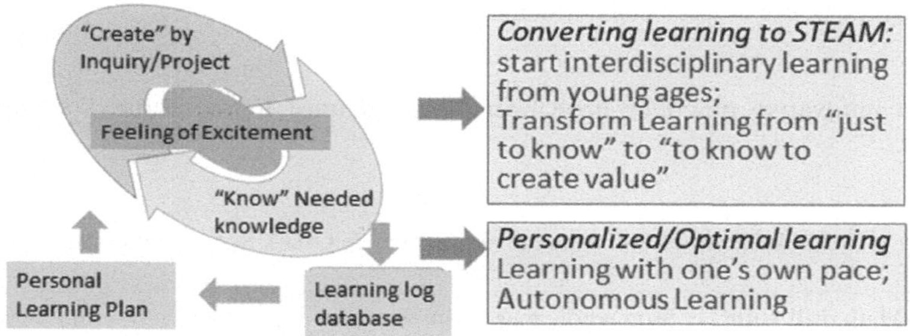

Fig. 2. METI's concept for *Classroom of the Future Project* Note: English is provided by the author as unofficial translation.

In order to assure enough school time for interdisciplinary STEAM education, it is suggested to make learning basic knowledge and skills in all subject matter more personal and optimal, by utilizing EdTech and one-on-one PCs provided by *GIGA School Initiative*. The more efficient it becomes to learn basics, the more time it creates for the STEAM projects. Figure 3 shows such reduction of class time in all subject areas, in addition to currently allocated time for Integrated Study, would be devoted to STEAM education at the central core of the curriculum.

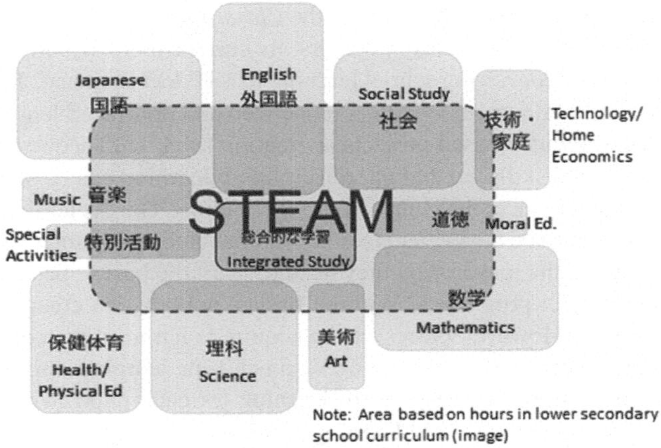

Fig. 3. STEAM at the core of curriculum connected with all subject matters Note: English is provided by the author as unofficial translation.

Many innovative practices have been reported until today. Table 1 shows some examples.

Table 1. Examples of innovative practices in GIGA School Initiative

Adapted Math drill with Robot workshops (Junior High School)	Stop whole classroom teaching and substitute it with AI-based one-on-one math drills to make basic learning more efficient by adjusting to individual math skills. Apply learned math skills to manipulate a robot in a STEAM workshop, making it possible how the acquired math skills are necessary in technology available in society
Individual allocation of learning time to overcome weak subject matters (Junior High Schools)	Utilize individually adapted learning materials to spend time in a weak subject matter, so different students worked on different subjects simultaneously. Created more motivation for learning
Teacher's talk reduced to only 5-min introduction (Elementary school arithmetic)	Utilize one-on-one PCs to learn arithmetic individually as well as cooperatively, to make learning more autonomous and helping each other. More supportive conversation observed
English writing with help of international college students online (High School English)	High school students engage in self-regulated learning with feedback given through online by native college students. More output was produced with more natural composition

(*continued*)

Table 1. *(continued)*

Regional Online Learning Support Center to help pupils with needs	No-one-left-behind concept was introduced to initiate a new Learning Support Center, where monthly interviews were conducted to help all learners create individual learning plan and provide both online (including real-time and on-demand) and offline support to monitor the progress

Source: http://www.kantei.go.jp/jp/singi/kyouikusaisei/jikkoukaigi_wg/syotyutou_wg/dai2/siryou2.pdf.
Note: English is provided by the author as unofficial translation.

Many sample materials for STEAM projects can be found in MITI's STEAM Library Website (https://www.steam-library.go.jp/). They are products created through cooperation of schools, companies and academic institutions, which have been made available for the uses by other schools. Each material is linked to UNESCO's SDGs (Sustainable Development Goals). Table 2 shows some of the examples.

Table 2. Sample titles and related SDGs in STEAM Library

Title	Related SDGs
Is it possible for humans to survive in the universe? (for Elementary Schools)	3, 8, 9
Veggie Meat (business plan, market analysis, plant-based meat)	2, 3, 8, 9
Drone (Society 5.0, design, engineering, presentation)	3, 7, 8, 9
Future Energy (active learning, problem solving)	1, 2, 3, 4
Exploring Comfort (Junior/Senior High School)	1, 2, 3, 6
Disaster Control through Technology (Robot, disaster prevention, natural disaster, inquiry)	9, 11, 13

Source: https://www.steam-library.go.jp/

3 Learning Architecture Models

Until today, various research outcomes have been made available from educational technology research, focusing on how to construct the architecture of learning environment, in the form of various theories and models for instructional design and technology [5–7].

3.1 Gagne's Nine Events of Instruction

The *Nine Events of Instruction* is a traditional instructional design theory proposed in the 1970's by Robert M. Gagne [8]. It was proposed, based on a framework of cognitive psychology, to design nine different kinds of activities (instructional events, in his term)

to be included as components of instruction for facilitating human learning. If instruction is to be structured in such a way to facilitate human learning effectively, it should have distinct features of assisting learners process information with multiple phases. It includes alerting for information processing activities, sensing and selecting relevant information, retrieving already learned basics from one's memory, blending them with newly presented information to make connections with semantic networks within the long-term memory, and practicing retrieval and application of the newly acquired knowledge and skills. Such terms as sensory resister, working and long-term memories, retrieval practice are taken from the information processing theory of human learning, by making an analogy to information processing phases of computers. Table 3 lists the *Nine Events of Instruction*.

Table 3. Nine Events of Instruction

	Events of Instruction	Functions
Introduction (Preparation)	1. Gaining learners attention	Alert for the start of learning
	2. Informing learners of the objectives	Help focusing on the goal of learning
	3. Stimulating recall of entry conditions	Help remembering basics from prior learning
Presentation (Input)	4. Presenting new information	Show the contents of new learning
	5. Providing learning guidance	Help make connections of new items with prior learning to expand semantic network of knowledge and skills
Practice (Output)	6. Giving opportunities to practice	Provide chances to retrieve or apply newly learned knowledge/skills
	7. Providing feedback	Give corrective feedback for mastery
Evaluation	8. Assessing learning performance	Confirm the mastery of new learning
Review	9. Enhancing retention & transfer	Provide review opportunities with intervals and enhance application skills

Since then, Gagne's *Nine Events of Instruction* has been widely used as a framework for designing instruction. It has been one of the most frequently utilized frameworks for designing instruction, together with his categorization known as five learning outcomes (verbal information, intellectual skills, cognitive strategies, motor skill, and attitudes). That is, the nine events are commonly needed for all kinds of learning outcomes, whereas what should be included in each event would be unique for each learning outcome. For example, mnemonics may be effective for remembering verbal information, whereas showing diversity of instances be effective for acquiring intellectual skills. Human models may be effective for learning attitudes, whereas help forming a mental image of execution be effective for motor skill learning. They are the variety to accomplish the same Event 5, Providing Learning Guidance; all other events should also be implemented differently, according to the nature of learning outcome.

If one will design individually adaptive and optimal learning material, as an efficient way of learning the basics in less time, as proposed in MITI's project described above, *Nine Events of Instruction* can be consulted. It will show how much of necessary steps (events) is equipped in each material, whether it is AI-based or not. Any drill-type materials may not have all the events, but mainly consists of Events 6–8. However, if a learner has problem too big to be covered by giving corrective feedback, then some elements of tutorials (Events 4 and 5) may be effective addition to such adaptive learning environment. It may also be beneficial for a learner to be provided a review opportunity (Event 9), based on learning trajectory records of the last attainment date of a mastery. Although Gagne's model is traditional that has been used more than 50 years, it may still be useful to create an adaptive learning architecture for individual learning of the basics. Appendix A shows some sample instructional strategies based on Gagne's model.

3.2 Merrill's First Principles of Instruction

A more recent framework, the *First Principles of Instruction*, was proposed by M. David Merrill in 2002, reflecting various theories and models proposed based on constructivist psychology [9, 10]. It was named the first principles, because the five features consisting of Merrill's model (see Fig. 4) were claimed to be common in most of the constructivist instructional design models proposed at that time.

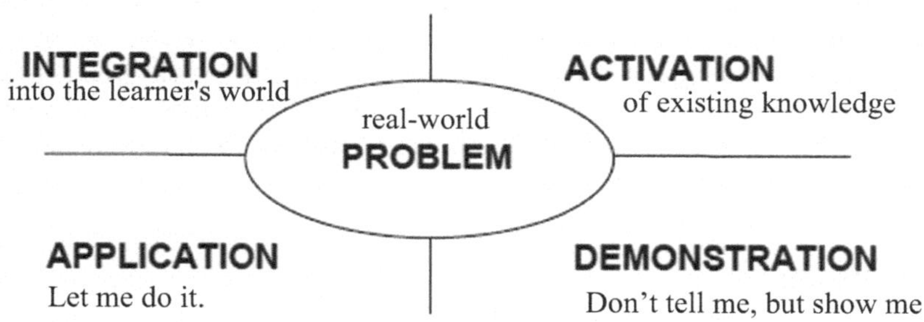

Fig. 4. First principles of instruction diagram

According to Merrill's *First Principles of Instruction*, every instruction should have the following 5 elements to be effective, efficient, and engaging, and to become "5-star instruction":

1. *Real-world Problem*: Learning is promoted when learners acquire knowledge and skill via a problem-solving strategy in the context of real-world problem or tasks.

2. *Activation*: Learning is promoted when learners activate an existing mental model as a foundation for new skills.
3. *Demonstration*: Learning is promoted when learners observe a demonstration of the skill to be learned that is consistent with the type of skill being taught.
4. *Application*: Learning is promoted when learners engage in the application of their newly acquired knowledge and skill that is consistent with the type of content being taught.
5. *Integration*: Learning is promoted when learners reflect on, discuss, and defend their newly acquired skills.

In recent works of instructional design literature, Merrill's *First Principles of Instruction* has been adopted as the foundation for common knowledge base [6], as well as toward creating learner-centered education [7]. More detailed situational design principles have also been proposed to elaborate on Merrill's *First Principles of Instruction* for such diverse sets as discussion approach, experiential approach, problem-based approach, and simulation approach [6]. Another book further elaborated for steps toward learner-centered paradigm of education, in relation to maker-based instruction, collaborative digital multimedia creation projects, gamification and game-based instruction, and instruction for self-regulated learning [7].

If one will design STEAM project as the second core of transformed school education, with adaptive and optimal individual learning, as proposed in MITI's project described above, *First Principles of Instruction* can be consulted. It will be a useful tool to examine if the main features of the 5 principles are covered in the design of STEAM project. How each and every *First Principles of Instruction* can be implemented that fits chosen approach toward problem-based projects? Is there better approach available for a given project to a given set of learners? Those questions can be answered by referring to the *First Principles of Instruction* themselves, as well as more elaborated situational principles proposed later. Merrill's *First Principles of Instruction* can be adopted as the theoretical architecture when designing STEAM projects, with which a firm understanding of human learning can be incorporated in the project design, as well as practical suggestions can be obtained. Appendix B shows some sample instructional strategies based on Merrill's model, with author's interpretations to better fit of them in the context of transformation toward Society 5.0.

4 Conclusion

This paper discussed how we can prepare transformation toward realizing Society 5.0 in two ways. First, *Classroom of the Future Project* was introduced as a recent attempt by Japanese government to form a concrete image of what can be done to make a major shift in school curriculum. Second, a shift in the background theories of instructional design was explained by comparing and making contrast of two well-known models: Gagne's *Nine Events of Instruction* and Merrill's *First Principles of Instruction.* It is the author's hope that the concrete image can be supported by theoretical architecture, so that the transformation will be designed in all and every contexts of education today, in a better and surer way. Society 5.0 needs be proactively designed from transformative efforts in Education sectors, so that children would be able to contribute to shape such a society, not to be struggled in rapid changes of society.

Appendix A: Instructional Strategy Sampler Based on Gagne's Nine Events of Instruction

1. Gaining Learner's Attention
Let the students ready to start learning by:

☐ Start off with some episode, anecdotal, or some issue directly related to the main theme.
☐ Start off your instruction with something unusual, strange, and abrupt.
☐ Seek for something fresh so that the students will not feel "Oh, this one again?"
☐ Use issues, conflict, new fact to override students existing frame of mind.

2. Informing Learner of the Objective
Activate student thinking and let them concentrate key points by:

☐ Make the theme of the lesson visible and clear so the students will not spend time mindlessly
☐ Establish learning contract with students as to what to teach and what to learn
☐ Use plain language of the students to convey the learning objectives clearly
☐ List the checkpoints as to what are the key points of the unit
☐ Help the students find the value by showing how the unit at hand will be useful in their future
☐ Verify where the goal is so that the students themselves can realize when they accomplish it.

3. Stimulating Recall of Entry Conditions (Prior Learning)
Help the students retrieve what they have already learned from their brain by:

☐ Provide a review to refresh students' mind about basics needed for the unit at hand
☐ Specifically identify how the basics of previous learning will relate to today's learning
☐ Embed in the material triggers for remembering the basics, assuming that everything the students have learned in previous unit/lesson is already forgotten
☐ Use small quiz, question, or short review at the beginning of each unit for reviewing the basics.

4. Presenting New Information (Stimulus Materials)
Show the students what are the things they are expected to learn by:

☐ Clearly organize the new information to show the students rules and examples of new learning
☐ Use concrete and familiar examples of new concepts or rules, not just vague statements of concepts or rules themselves

☐ Ask the students to evoke the images that are familiar to their own experiences or environments
☐ Provide a simple, representative case first, then proceed to more complex cases with variations
☐ Use illustrations, figures, and tables to easily capture new materials as a whole, the position of an element, and relationships of that element to other elements.

5. Providing Learning Guidance
Help the students to remember new information/skills in a meaningful way by:

☐ Connect the newly presented information to what the students already know so that they can form a network of information in a meaningful way
☐ Use mnemonic devices, anecdotal, comparisons to more familiar basics, to provide a hint for remembering the new information
☐ Give the students many hints for understanding, and let them accustomed to the use of hints.

6. Giving Opportunities to Practice (Eliciting Performance)
Let the students have opportunities for practicing new contents by:

☐ Give the students enough chances of practice in a risk-free situation so they can find their weak points without punishment
☐ Let them try first, without seeing examples, so they know if they can do it by themselves
☐ Provide cues for earlier stages of practice, and gradually remove them as they master the skill
☐ When application skills are required, have them practices in diverse settings.

7. Providing Feedback
Help the students find weak areas to improve their knowledge/skills by:

☐ Provide informative feedback messages for incorrect answers so the students realize how to fix the problem
☐ Avoid negative feedback to highlight their failures
☐ Give the students appraisals for correct answers, and guidance for incorrect answers.

8. Assessing Learning Performance
Provide tests to verify what the students have become able to do, and feel good about their accomplishment by:

☐ Give the students enough practice opportunities before they are to take a test
☐ Construct a test with enough number of items so that only those who mastered the contents, not the lucky students, can pass the test
☐ Match the test with previously stated objectives and the contents of learning materials, no surprise on the test. Do not test what the students have never been taught.

9. Enhancing Retention & Transfer
Help the student sustain what they mastered and make the new learning applicable to other situations by:

☐ Schedule re-tests when they will be forgotten the new learning, since everyone remembers very little as time goes by
☐ When reviewing, do not let them study the materials that contain answers, but let them try practice items first without seeing the text, to find out how much they remember
☐ Provide application scenarios so that they can use the newly learned knowledge/skills
☐ Provide advanced exercises as an option at the end of each unit, but not as a requirement.

Note: Originally created by Katsuaki Suzuki in 2017.

Appendix B: Instructional Strategy Sampler Based on Merrill's First Principles of Instruction

1. Real-World Problem

☐ Show the task that they will be able to do or the problem they will be able to solve as a result of completing a module or course (i.e., Learning objective).
☐ Challenge the learners if they can solve real-world problems (i.e., Pretest).
☐ Engage the learners with the whole-task problems, not just the basic operation or action level.
☐ Let the learners solve a progression of problems that are explicitly compared to one another.

2. Activation for Diagnosis

☐ Let the learners try to solve the problem by activating relevant previous experiences before teaching. Diagnose missing parts in their solution; if their solution is satisfactory, then no need for training thus finish training without teaching (cf. TOTE model).
☐ Direct the learners to recall, relate, describe, or apply knowledge from relevant past experiences that can be used as a foundation for solving this new problem.
☐ Provide with a relevant experience that can be used as a foundation for the new knowledge.
☐ Give the opportunity to demonstrate their previously acquired knowledge or skill.

3. Demonstration

☐ Demonstrate what is learned, rather than merely telling information about what is to be learned.
☐ Make demonstration consistent with the learning goal: (a) examples and non-examples for concepts, (b) demonstrations for procedures, (c) visualizations for processes, and (e) modeling for behavior.

☐ Provide with appropriate learner guidance including some of the following: (a) learners are directed to relevant information, (b) multiple representations are used for the demonstrations, or (c) multiple demonstrations are explicitly compared.
☐ Make media play a relevant instructional role.

4. Application

☐ Require the learners use their new knowledge or skill to solve similar but new problems.
☐ Make application (practice) and the posttest consistent with the stated or implied objectives: (a) information-about practice – recall or recognize information, (b) parts-of practice – locate, name, and/or describe each part, (c) kinds-of practice – identify new examples of each kind, (d) how-to practice – do the procedure and (e) what-happens practice – predict a consequence of a process given conditions, or find faulted conditions given an unexpected consequence.
☐ Guide the learners in their problem solving by appropriate feedback and coaching, including error detection and correction, and when this coaching is gradually withdrawn.
☐ Require the students solve a sequence of varied problems.

5. Integration

☐ Encourage learners transfer to the new knowledge or skill into their real-life job settings.
☐ Give the learners an opportunity to publicly demonstrate their new knowledge or skill.
☐ Let the learners reflect-on, discuss, and defend their new knowledge or skill.
☐ Let the learners create, invent, and explore new and personal ways to use their new knowledge or skills.

Note: Originally created by Katsuaki Suzuki in 2021.

References

1. Reiser, R.A.: A history of instructional design and technology (Chapter 2). In: Reiser, R.A., Dempsey, D.V. (eds.) Trends and Issues in Instructional Design and Technology, 4th edn., pp. 8–22. Pearson Education (2018)
2. Society 5.0, Cabinet Office, Japan. https://www8.cao.go.jp/cstp/society5_0/index.html
3. Prensky, M.: Digital natives, digital immigrants. In: On the Horizon, vol. 9(5). MCB University Press (2001)
4. Ministry of International Trade and Industry (MITI): Classroom of the Future Project (2018). https://www.learning-inovation.go.jp
5. Reiser, R.A., Dempsey, D.V. (eds.): Trends and Issues in Instructional Design and Technology, 4th edn. Pearson Education, New York (2018)
6. Reigeluth, C., Carr-Chellman, A.A. (eds.): Instructional-Design Theories and Models, Volume III: Building a Common Knowledge Base. Routledge, New York (2009)
7. Reigeluth, C., Beatty, B.J., Myers, R.D. (eds.): Instructional-Design Theories and Models, Volume IV: The Learner-Centered Paradigm of Education. Routledge, New York (2016)
8. Gagne, R.M.: The Conditions of Learning and Theory of Instruction, 4th edn. Wadsworth Pub, New York (1985)

9. Merrill, M.D.: First principles of instruction. Education Tech. Research Dev. **50**(3), 43–59 (2002)
10. Merrill, M.D.: M. David Merrill's First Principles of Instruction, rev. ed. Association for Educational Communications and Technology (2020)

From MOOC to SPOC: Fable-Based Learning

Jimmy H. M. Lee(✉)

Department of Computer Science and Engineering,
The Chinese University of Hong Kong, Shatin, N.T., Hong Kong SAR
jlee@cse.cuhk.edu.hk

Abstract. This presentation gives the pedagogical innovations and experience of the co-development of three MOOCs on the subject of "Modeling and Solving Discrete Optimization Problems" by The Chinese University of Hong Kong and the University of Melbourne. In a nutshell, the MOOCs feature the Fable-based Learning approach, which is a form of problem-based learning encapsulated in a coherent story plot. Each lecture video begins with an animation that tells a story based on a classic novel. The protagonists of the story encounter a problem requiring technical assistance from the two professors from modern time via a magical tablet granted to them by a fairy god. The new pedagogy aims at increasing learners' motivation and interests as well as situating the learners in a coherent learning context. In addition to scriptwriting, animation production and embedding the teaching materials in the story plot, another challenge of the project is the remote distance between the two institutions as well as the need to produce all teaching materials in both (Mandarin) Chinese and English to cater for different geographic learning needs. The MOOCs have been running recurrently on Coursera since 2017. We present learner statistics and feedback, and discuss our experience with and preliminary observations of adopting the online materials in a Flipped Classroom setting.

Keywords: Fable-based learning · MOOC · Flipped classroom

1 Preamble

This short piece of writing is intended to be a narrative of the work done between 2016 and 2020 on the use of Fable-based Learning in designing and teaching a series of Massive Online Open Courses (MOOCs) [3] on the topic of Discrete Optimization. The MOOC contents were later adopted to run as Small Private Online Courses (SPOCs) [6] in the classroom. It serves also as the basis of my Keynote Speech at the Fourteenth International Conference on Blended Learning, August, 2021. The following content is largely based on and revised from Lee [7] and Mavis *et al.* [5].

This is also the story of how the East meets West, and how two very different cultures can synergize to develop novel pedagogies to design and deliver three

R. Li et al. (Eds.): ICBL 2021, LNCS 12830, pp. 16–25, 2021.
https://doi.org/10.1007/978-3-030-80504-3_2

highly acclaimed MOOCs on Coursera. While we shared our common research interests, our work practice and value system are almost at the two ends of a spectrum. After the MOOCs were launched successfully in early 2017, they were later brought into the classroom in a Flipped Classroom setting. The whole thing began in 2015 when The Chinese University of Hong Kong (CUHK) was encouraging research collaboration with other universities.

With a good collaborator, Peter Stuckey, at the University of Melbourne (UniMelb), I applied for a research support from CUHK and spent a week at UniMelb. During that week, we had worked on mainly research of mutual interests. On the day before my departure, we had a casual chat over coffee and started talking about teaching our Discrete Optimization courses at the postgraduate level. Then we discussed about how we can promote our research area to the whole world. The answer was to do a MOOC. I thought I actually knew how to do it well because I had a bit experience in bringing story-telling and game-playing into a learning platform.

The idea is to design the MOOCs in such a way that learners would take the modules while watching a movie. Much to my surprise, Peter bought my crazy idea. Since Discrete Optimization is like magic, I immediately thought about the Harry Potter series of movies. After I returned to CUHK, I mentioned the possibility to our University's Pro Vice-Chancellors in charge of education, she found this a very interesting idea and gave me the full support but suggested that we based our MOOCs on a Chinese classic. Being a person of the West, Peter again bought into the idea. He also mentioned the potential collaboration to UniMelb's Pro Vice-Chancellor and received the same strong support. Then I started regretting since I knew I was getting myself into a tall tall task. It was 2015. The funding was approved after a few months and the project started in 2016. And the rest was history.

2 Massive Open Online Courses

Majoring in Mathematics and Artificial Intelligence, I always teach with many mathematical symbols, definitions, theorems and algorithms to illustrate concepts and methods. Many a times, students do not know why they would see a particular symbol, nor would they know why they would see a definition or theorem when professors teach them to solve problems. It is usually at the very end of a semester when students are told about the areas of application of what they have learned in the entire course.

I did some research and found MOOCs to usually consist of five elements. Basically, MOOCs are large scale public online courses, there should certainly be teaching videos in which teachers can raise interactive questions to gauge the understanding of the learners. Students could also be given reading materials for self-study. A forum should be provided for students to raise questions and for interaction among teachers and students. Some MOOCs would provide an auto-grading system. Others will let students mark assignments for one another.

While I was not certain, I went to the most popular MOOC platform, Coursera, to find out what a MOOC really is. I looked at MOOCs from various top universities and teachers. Most teaching videos are basically slides augmented with voice and some with a small talking head. Of course, some productions are as professional as a TV show and some with animations to explain abstract concepts. After examining a few well-known MOOCs, I started asking myself of what exactly a MOOC is. What are the essentials for a good MOOC? Trying to be controversial, I would argue MOOC is nothing more than a one-way version of classroom teaching, one-way teaching from teacher to students. The teacher who gives lecture in the video would not be able to see the response of the students on the other side of the screen. Do not get me wrong. I believe in classroom teaching, which is the most ancient form of education delivery. In a classroom, however, the teacher can at least see if the students are interested, sleeping, or having any response. If the teacher senses that the students do not understand, the teacher can adjust the explanation and also teaching pace. MOOCs do not allow any of these classroom interactions since teachers cannot see the learners. Besides, learners watch the video asynchronously and at their own pace. Any interactions can take place only on the discussion forum.

My plan was to produce a MOOC that can overcome some barriers of one-way delivery issue. We want to produce a MOOC not because the quality of classroom teaching is not good. We fully support classroom teaching. Face to face teaching is very important. When MOOC teaching is only one-way, the problem of one-way teaching in classroom teaching will be exemplified. A weakness of classroom teaching, as I used myself as an example, is the teacher goes through a lot of mathematical theorems, students do not understand why they have to learn what is being taught. First, students learn without a proper context. In a classroom, they could at least ask the teachers but that is impossible in a MOOC setting. Second, when students get uninterested, they lose focus and will easily get distracted or even give up. I cannot emphasize enough the importance of maintaining students' interest and providing a clear context of learning. These are what we would like to address with Fable-based Learning.

3 Fable-Based Learning

Many MOOCs face a serious problem. Usually we will see a high number of registrations of a course. Students will watch the first one or two lectures and then stop. The common reasons are that they do not have time, not interested or busy. They lost interest all of a sudden. It is of paramount importance for a MOOC to keep learners engaged. I want to produce a MOOC to change students' learning experience.

The MOOCs are on the topic of Discrete Optimization which is a branch of AI, and are at the postgraduate level covering lots of mathematical concepts and computer programming. In order to attract students, we made and put a promotion video[1] for the MOOCs on YouTube. There are many different applications of Discrete Optimization. We base our MOOC content on the plots of a Chinese classic, "The Romance of The Three Kingdoms". Originally, I wanted to use

[1] Promotion video: `shorturl.at/bcvIP`.

"Journey to The West" for this purpose, but my students convinced me that the "Romance of The Three Kingdoms" were very popular in the Mainland China as well as Japan especially in video games. There are many famous battles in "The Romance of The Three Kingdoms" which can be used as the background story and converted to different types of Discrete Optimization problems. For example, we can use teach techniques to help Liu Bei and Guan Yu to solve war related problems. We would go through such famous story scenes as "Oath at the Peach Garden" and "Judging Heroes Cooking Wine". The story is started with a Celestial Wise Guru who considered Liu, Guan and Zhang as heroes of their time, and presented them with a Magical Tablet. When Liu Bei encountered a problem, he could use the Magical Tablet to summon and communicate with two famous AI professors of modern time to help him solve the problem. This is the backbone of the storyline of the course.

Each video lecture of the MOOCs always begin with an animation telling a story to set the stage of a difficult Discrete Optimization problem using a scene from the "Romance of the Three Kingdoms". After the animation, learners would continue with regular lecture and learn some AI techniques from the two professors to solve the posted problem. We made two versions of the MOOCs: one in English and one in Putongua. It is still one-way teaching when students watch our lecture videos, but the animation should help set the stage and engage learners' interest. Each week (a module) is made up of several video lectures. At the end of a week, the two professors would give a debriefing session which is conversational in nature. Learners can see the two professors chatting with each other to discuss the development of the story plots as well as summing up what students should have learned in that week. This dialogue approach takes learners away from the serious one-way delivery mode momentarily every week.

In addition to watching the video lectures, learners would have to attempt two kinds of exercises each week: assignments and workshops. Assignments are for assessment purposes, in which learners would have to solve problem with computer programming using techniques they learn in the module. They also have to attempt a workshop exercise, the setting of which is similar to an assignment. The difference is that we would provide a "solution" video. Students would be encouraged to solve the problems themselves before watching the solution video, in which the two professors would try to analyze and solve the problem on the spot. Students could see how the professors solved the problems. We did not do any rehearsal at all and always attempted the problems afresh. We were conscious not to see the problems and then we solved the problem step by step on the spot, without deleting or editing what and how we did wrong. So the students would be able to see what mistakes we would make and how we would go about rectifying them. This is the process that learners found extremely useful for their learning.

How were these MOOCs designed and produced? Simply speaking, we listed all the knowledge points in the order of teaching needs, and matched them against the *scriptable moments* (or interesting story scenes) of "The Romance of The Three Kingdoms". We needed a scriptwriter/animator who was familiar with the story line of the novel, and were lucky to find one. After a knowledge point was matched with a scene, professors and the scriptwriter just had to sit down and brainstorm to inject a Discrete Optimization problem into the scene. Problem creation sounds easy, but we spent a lot of time on it. Just like polishing a jade stone to perfection, there was no magic or shortcut to speed things up. The episodes were written with countless brainstorming meetings with caffeine injection. When students take our course, their learning experience will be like watching a movie. Therefore, we need to select a good story as the backbone of the movie as we wanted the students to be engaged. People like to identify themselves with heroes. We intend our learners to immerse themselves into the main characters and take the difficult problems as their own. They are motivated to try their best to solve the problems by learning the subject contents to be covered in the remainder of the videos. The story of "The Romance of The Three Kingdoms" serves a good basis for us to inject good stimulation and context into the learning of abstract mathematical concepts and algorithmic thinking.

Fable-based Learning (FBL) is problem-based [1] and immersive, and a form of Anchored Learning [4], in which learners are situated in an interesting and real-life scenario to enhance their learning experience. When students have to learn something new, they know they have to learn the technique to solve a specific problem. So there is a learning context in each lecture. They know what problem they need to solve so they need to learn the specific knowledge. That is, in each lecture, the teacher will give a problem at the beginning. With the story line, we hope to give students an immersive experience. That means students think they have become the characters of the story. For example, in teaching arithmetic, students will be taken to the marketplace to go shopping. So they will be motivated to learn basic addition and subtraction.

Some would say that FBL is essentially traditional case studies, which also provide a realistic and complex context for student learning. However, students usually have to jump from cases to cases. Such context switching can slow down learning. For example, we go to the supermarket when we teach addition today. We need to go to the factory floor to learn multiplication another day. In FBL, we use a single story to connect all learning contexts. In our MOOCs, all problems took place in "The Romance of The Three Kingdoms". This idea is actually not new. Back in the 2000s, we introduced the Folklore-based Learning approach [8], in which we created a prototypical game-based learning platform with story telling for teaching introductory to advanced probability concepts. FBL is essentially Folklore-based Learning without the game component. However, Folklore-based Learning was applied to only a few topics. This project is the first time story-telling is applied coherently in a large scale.

4 MOOCs Status and Learners' Feedback

In the first stage of the project, we created two MOOCs. One MOOC is roughly equivalent to the materials of one month's workload in university teaching. The MOOCs have both an English and a Chinese version. In March, 2016, I led a group of four persons to Melbourne for four months, including one animator/scriptwriter and my two PhD students as my assistants. UniMelb met us with pedagogical experts, project managers and an excellent film and production crew. We finished all videos, assignments, course outline, animation, and logo design, as required by Coursera. I developed all materials in English, and then my assistants translated them into Chinese. As there are two language versions for the MOOCs, Peter and I taught separately the English and Chinese versions respectively. Some videos (the module summaries and the workshop solutions videos) with dialogues between Peter and I would be made in English. Chinese subtitles were added in the post-production phase.

After we returned to Hong Kong, we still spent roughly half a year of post-production work. The two MOOCs were put online on Coursera in January and February in 2017 respectively. In August, 2017, we spent another three months in Melbourne to produce the third MOOC on the subject. The best story scenes of "The Romance of The Three Kingdoms" were used up. The new MOOC was based on selected stories from "The Book of Mountains and Seas" [2], "The Investiture of the Gods" [11] and "Journey to the West" [10], and was launched in May, 2018. Each of the three MOOCs lasts for four weeks, and is running on Coursera on a rolling basis.

The three MOOCs consists of 13 modules/weeks totaling 61 lecture videos, 3 MOOC introduction videos, 12 module summary videos, 14 live coding videos, 14 workshops and 12 assignments. That translates to 23 h 38 m of high quality videos, which were produced in close to two and a half years. The MOOCs, including the grading of assignments, are completely free for learners, unless they want a certificate from Coursera in which case they have to pay a small fee.

Up to April 27, 2021, the MOOCs attracted the following enrollments.

	Visitors	Enrolled	Started	Completed
1	112,075	20,549	10,204	851
2	58,466	15,654	4,781	245
3	50,113	6,321	2,465	87

Learners came from 164 countries in 6 continents. The top 10 countries are USA, India, Germany, Australia, Canada, UK, Brazil, Hong Kong, France and China. We are able to promote Discrete Optimization to thousands of learners around the world, which is impossible by just lecturing in our classrooms alone.

We received top ratings from the learners for each of the three courses:

1. 87% 5 stars, 11% 4 stars and 1% 3 stars
2. 94% 5 stars and 6% 4 stars
3. 88% 5 stars and 9% 4 stars.

Peter and I were rated as *Top Instructors* on Coursera during different period of time in 2020 and 2021. Coursera bestows the Top Instructors title on the top 10 instructors in each domain based on the instructor ratings given by the learner, where the Computer Science domain consists of 627 MOOCs.

Learners leave comments to MOOCs on Coursera. For our MOOCs, some liked our MOOCs because there was a different application in each video. Some found out the techniques taught in the MOOCs allowed them to solve many different types of problems. Some appreciated the story-based examples. Initially, we were a bit worried that we should probably use western stories as background for the English version of the MOOCs, but Peter did not think that there would be any problem since Chinese stories could be amazing too. Therefore, we also used "The Romance of The Three Kingdoms" for the English version.

Amongst all the comments we received, we shared the following one from 2018 with you. He went to a top AI conference in Australia in 2017. He heard of our courses at the conference and then looked them up. He was a key person of the top research funding agency in North America, and responsible for approving funding to AI research projects. It was a long one but we give the following summary.

> "... *I first became interested in MiniZinc when I attended CP/SAT/ICLP in Melbourne. I saw you both there, I think, but I did not have an excuse to meet you (I spent most of my time in ICLP). I am not a researcher in any of those communities.* ... *Your course is excellent and engaging. Thank you for the care you have obviously put into the course design. I think I probably put much more time into this than I had anticipated, and yet I really enjoyed doing that because you managed to keep me on the edge of my abilities and comprehension of the language features, which I believe is really the place to be for learning such a skill.* ... *The workshops were probably the best pedagogical devices for me for most of the course.* ... "

He did not have much computer programming training but thought our MOOCs were truly engaging and challenging. He only planned to spend a little time on the MOOCs, but eventually found himself hooked and ended up spending much more time than anticipated. He liked the design of assignments much. He "felt sorry" after taking the courses since he started noticing his surroundings and found so many things not being optimized. In early 2020, I was attending another AI conference and the learner came looking for me to thank me in person. That was truly a special moment to meet a fellow learner from our MOOCs.

A natural question is whether FBL is transferable to other subject disciplines. We think that story telling can be used in highly technical courses emphasizing problem solving skills in general. The approach is good for students but can be a big challenge for teachers. The first challenge is to develop a story. It sounds easy but we spent a lot of time to match the knowledge point against the scriptable moments of the story which must follow a chronological order. Incorporating problems into the scriptable moments and story scenes naturally is another challenge involving both me and the scriptwriter while making the stories fun. The third challenge is to my teaching method. I had been accustomed to the traditional teaching mode for so many years by teaching the theories before mentioning applications. Now I had to come up with application problems first before teaching the definitions and theorems. This is problem-based approach. It sounds easy but I had to do my lesson planning upside down and inside out. Before a teacher plans to adopt FBL, the teacher must ask whether (s)he can afford the time, labour and monetary cost.

5 Small Private Online Courses and Flipped Classroom

MOOCs allow learners from around the world to learn our subject matter. There are no reasons why we cannot bring the videos back to our classrooms to conduct *Small Private Online Courses (SPOCs)* [6]. With permission of CUHK, I was allowed to use the videos to teach in classrooms in a blended learning, with which classroom contact hours with students can be reduced by half. Many students took the course for the reduction in classroom hours and then some of them would regret.

In our SPOC setting, students have to complete all the learning activities of the MOOCs, which include learning from the videos, attempting the workshops and assignments, and participating in the online forum discussions. We have constructed an automatic grading system, to which students can submit their assignment multiple times. If students are not satisfied with the results, they can try again and resubmit. This motivated our students to improve their assignment submission attempts over and over. This encourages self discovery and self learning.

In addition, every student must also fill in an online "questionnaire" as part of the assessment. Some questions asked if the student had completed the various learning activities of the week. Some asked about simple concepts that they were supposed to have learned. Some would be more involved, requiring students to solve simple problems. These questionnaires serve as reminders and help students to do stocktaking, making sure that students are on track with their learning.

Even when the students were exempted from half of the classroom time, they still needed to come. We do away with traditional lecturing. In the flipped classroom [9], students would be encouraged to raise questions. If they stayed stagnant, I would ask them questions including those in the weekly questionnaire. I hoped to take the opportunity to correct their misunderstanding of some concepts. Also, more problems would be provided for students to solve. Sometimes, students form groups and solve problems together. Since the class size was small, students would have to answer questions and present problem solutions in turn. Students could critique each others' answers. Like other universities, CUHK has a system of course and teacher evaluation at the end of semesters. The score they gave us was quite good. I was particularly happy since students doing well in the course usually gave higher scores in the evaluation. In other words, those who did well in the course tended to like this teaching approach.

Students also gave written comments. In general, they enjoyed all the teacher-student interactions in the classroom, found the explanation clear and the teaching approach interesting, and students were encouraged to learn. However, why would some students regret taking the course? Although the class hours were reduced by half, students had to spend much more time and effort in learning. They had to watch all the videos and then come to the class and answer my questions. They felt they had to spend a lot of time on the course. Some students did indicate that they preferred traditional classroom teaching.

6 Evaluation of SPOC and Limitations

The learning enhancement and research unit of the university (called "CLEAR") was invited to do more in depth analysis of students' responses to the new learning approach when the course was taught in 2018 and 2019. In 2018, CLEAR designed a questionnaire. In 2019, a focused group with students was organized.

Firstly, we wanted to see how students compared flipped classroom teaching and traditional classroom teaching, and which one they would prefer. What did they think of flipped classroom teaching? What did they think of problem-based teaching and story-based teaching? Finally, we would like to see if the weekly questionnaires were useful. The results showed that in general students thought the course brought nice learning experience. Students were also satisfied with the quality of the teaching materials of the MOOCs. To them, quality was of paramount importance as it would affect the learning result significantly. They also found the bi-weekly classroom activity very important. Some students indicated that they preferred traditional classroom teaching. Most of the students thought that they could catch up with the course progress. In particular, they found the weekly questionnaires very useful.

Students had their chance to evaluate the course and the teacher. We evaluate students too by the course assessment, which includes the regular assignments and a final examination. Looking at the marks, I found that students in the class could be roughly put in two bands. Students in the top band are the high achievers and attended 60% or more of the classroom meetings. Students in the low band were the ones attending less than 60% of the class meetings. The results are not surprising since those attending more classes are the ones who (a) spent more time in the subject and (b) were the more motivated to learn.

I understand that this sharing of teaching experience has limitations. I only taught one class every year. In 2018 and 2019, there were 17 and 22 students respectively. In the first class every year, I usually tried to scare students off so that I did not have to mark so many examination papers. However, the enrollment kept on increasing. Another limitation was that students did not take the course for no reason. They took the course because they saw our promotion and liked the approach. They should like the subject too. Thus, the sampling was not random. I did not have a chance yet to implement a research in which I could have both a controlled group and an experimental group. Students in the controlled group would be taught in the traditional approach.

7 Concluding Remarks

The MOOCs have been deployed for only a few years. It might be a bit early to draw any definitive conclusions on the effectiveness of the FBL approach.

In a sense, we are conducting a large scale experiment which is still ongoing. We encountered hiccups during the design and development of the pedagogy and the MOOCs, but the multi-cultural team overcame our differences and resolve the encountered difficulties. Building a high quality FBL course is challenging and requires a great deal of planning and strong communication between scriptwriters and educators. But, at least for us, the process was immensely rewarding, and it continues to attract highly motivated learners of the materials.

References

1. Barrows, H.S.: Problem-based learning in medicine and beyond: a brief overview. New Dir. Teach. Learn. **68**, 3–12 (1996)
2. Birrell, A.: The Classic of Mountains and Seas. Penguin Books, London (1999)
3. Blackmon, S.J., Major, C.H.: Wherefore art thou MOOC?: defining massive open online courses. Online Learn. J. **21**(4), 195–221 (2017)
4. Bransford, J.D., Sherwood, R.D., Hasselbring, T.S., Kinzer, C.K., Williams, S.M.: Anchored instruction: why we need it and how technology can help. In: Nix, D., Spiro, R.J. (eds.) Cognition, Education, and Multimedia: Exploring Ideas in High Technology, chap. 5, pp. 115–142. Lawrence Erlbaum Associates, Hillsdale (2012)
5. Chan, M., Chun, C., Fung, H., Lee, J.H., Stuckey, P.J.: Teaching constraint programming using fable-based learning. In: Proceedings of 10th Symposium on Educational Advances in Artificial Intelligence (EAAI 2020), pp. 13366–13373 (2020)
6. Fox, A.: From MOOCs to SPOCs. Commun. ACM **56**(12), 38–40 (2013)
7. Lee, J.H.M.: Story-based learning in a MOOC course: an experience to share. Res. Educ. Commun. Technol. **122**, 1–9 (2020)
8. Lee, J.H.M., Lee, F.L., Lau, T.S.: Folklore-based learning on the Web - Pedagogy, case study, and evaluation. J. Educ. Comput. Res. **34**(1), 1–27 (2006)
9. Uzunboylu, H., Karagozlu, D.: Flipped classroom: a review of recent literature. World J. Educ. Technol. **7**(2), 142 (2015)
10. Wu, C., Jenner, W.J.F.: Journey to the West. Foreign Language Press, Beijing (2003)
11. Xu, Z.: The Investiture of the Gods. China Zhigong Press, Beijing (2012)

The Meaning of Learner Centeredness in College Online Environments Revisited

Yekyung Lisa Lee(✉)

Sogang University, Seoul, Republic of Korea
ylee5@sogang.ac.kr

Abstract. This paper addresses the meaning of 'learner centered' education at a time when university students and educators all over the world have been thrust into the world of online learning due to the Covid-19 pandemic. Going online for months surely tests the ability of educators to deliver student centered and interactive learning in a challenging environment. Learner centeredness, in general, implies learning in which the learner's responsibilities and activities are emphasized compared to that of the instructor's. This does not mean that the educator's role is weakened. Professors must be active in providing feedback about misconceptions and confusions to help students grow into experts. They should also clarify the relation between class projects with the course objectives and the real world, and help students with low competencies develop strategies for solving open-ended problems. Students want to think like an expert and apply their skills for solving real world problems. They also desire academic growth by modeling deep insight from their professors. The educator's role for providing meaningful guidance has become more critical than ever especially for first or second year students who may need more scaffolding for their intellectual development. However, when online classes are carried out for a prolonged time, students' self-regulation subsides, and the yearn for 'togetherness' rises, making it difficult to maintain learner centeredness. Specific examples and their underlying principles of the support provided to students and educators for overcoming their difficulties are discussed in this paper.

Keywords: Learner-centeredness · Online learning · Intellectual growth · Higher education

1 Introduction

Teaching methods such as problem-based learning or flipped learning have become widely popularized across universities [1, 2]. These methods are considered 'learner-centered' as they provide students opportunities to engage in interactive activities that promote learning at a deeper level. These pedagogical approaches provide a class structure in which the instructor steps down as the 'sage of the stage' and promotes the learner's ownership over his/her learning.

The aim of higher education is to nurture critical and creative thinkers equipped with academic expertise for solving the problems we face in this world. Despite the fact that

R. Li et al. (Eds.): ICBL 2021, LNCS 12830, pp. 26–35, 2021.
https://doi.org/10.1007/978-3-030-80504-3_3

college education is perceived by many as a ticket for better jobs, the aforementioned aim is still relevant, and expected by instructors and students. Thus, student-centered approaches emphasizing learner autonomy are frequently utilized. College students are expected to take more responsibility of their learning, and the depth and breadth of the contents covered during classes are much more than what students experienced in high school. Such being the case, it seems that methods utilizing frequent discussions and problem solving should fit quite well with college classes. However, studies have indicated that although methods promoting active engagement have been effective in transforming classes to become student-centered, students' perceptions and satisfaction about it may not be all that positive as expected [1, 3, 4].

Challenges such as student workload, the gap between students' competencies and the instructional goals, and the lack of effective in-class activities might help classes appear to be student-centered but not necessarily satisfying. That is, since various factors affect the effectiveness of student-centered learning, educators should be perceptive to whether one's teaching methods fulfill the intellectual needs of college students. Perceptiveness can be enhanced by scrutinizing the meaning of learner centeredness and the needs of college students. This paper will explore the meaning of 'learner centeredness' in higher education, and then present relevant cases showing how learner centeredness could be achieved.

2 The Meaning of 'Learner Centeredness'

Learner centered education (LCE) implies that the learner's responsibility and activities are prioritized rather than that of the educator's [5]. McCombs & Whisler [6] specifically defined learner centered education as an approach which strives to find a solution that helps the learner be strongly motivated to learn and achieve his/her best, based on consideration of the learner's qualities including experiences, perspectives, preferences, abilities, and needs. It is an approach that reflects the learner's individuality and includes instructional solutions. While MicCombs & Whisler define learner centered education from a teaching point of view, Lea, Stephenson, & Troy [7] defined LCE from an epistemological point of view and stated that LCE is an approach in which knowledge and its context, personal meaning making exists. This perspective assumes the equal relation between the educator and the learner and emphasizes the power of the learner. Lea et al.'s perspective also implies that it is not about the power of the educator weakening, but that the educator's role as a supporter is actually strengthened.

Conceptually one can analyze LCE from three dimensions: instructional method, educator-learner relationship, and learning outcomes. McCombs & Whisler [6] suggested that in terms of instructional methods, factors such as personalization, autonomy, and self-directedness contribute to higher levels of achievement. Personalization implies finding the optimal conditions for learning based on the learner's experiences, ability, and aptitude. Autonomy implies that the individual's independent decisions and choices are respected. Self-directedness, as opposed to passive knowledge acquisition, implies active meaning making of the learning contents and being responsible for one's learning.

Secondly, as for the relation between educator and learner, mutual trust of the two precedes transition of learning responsibilities from educator to learner [7, 8]. Taking responsibility of one's own learning occurs when the educator recognizes and trusts the learner's experiences, choices, and autonomy. Mutual trust exists on the grounds of respect for the learner's abilities and character. Trust towards the educator stems from expertise, teaching competence, and authority [9].

Thirdly, the outcomes of learner-centeredness include, deep understanding, integration of content and experience, and self-directed learning competencies for lifelong learning [7, 10]. That is, learning is more than achieving the lower levels of learning of Bloom's taxonomy of cognitive learning, such as recall, comprehension, and application, but implies constructing new meaning. Learning in this case is not only a matter of applying knowledge to real world problems, but also of identifying and solving problems at a profound level, a foundation for life.

The elements of learner-centeredness make the boundaries of the role of learner and educator ambiguous as both the educator and the learner must take an active role in learning. Elen [11] proposed that for LCE, the relation between educator and learner could be seen from a balanced, transactional, or independent perspective. Among the three, Elen proposes that it is necessary to view LCE from a transactional perspective. That is, LCE is not merely about distributing responsibilities and tasks to the learner, it is about both instructor and learner taking responsibilities. The instructor must facilitate knowledge construction of the learner in a systematic manner. The level of responsibilities handed on to the learner should be determined based on the learner's will and abilities.

Thus, learner-centeredness is realized through instructional methods, educator-learner relationship, and learning outcomes. It is about redefining the relationship between the two. The role of the instructor does not diminish but is transformed to a guide for constructing knowledge. The learner is responsible for actively constructing meaning. The following section will introduce cases from flipped learning classes before the pandemic and online learning classes during 2020, so as to describe how learner-centeredness may be carried out at universities.

3 Designing Learner-Centered Environments

3.1 Example 1: Promoting Learner-Centeredness in a Flipped Classroom

3.1.1 The Relation of Flipped Learning and Learner-Centeredness

Studies have shown that flipped learning (FL) classes are especially effective for giving back the responsibility of learning to the students. A study by Cheng, Ka Ho Lee, Change, & Yang [12] demonstrated that FL was effective for prompting students to seek people who could help them with their academic problems. McLean, Attardi, Faden, & Goldszmidt [13] pointed out that students appreciated the interactive, creative aspect of FL classes which allowed them to apply what they had learned. Their study results also indicated that students strived for deep learning, by making sure they understood the content well enough, or taking notes rather than typing on their laptops. Studies as such indicate that FL promotes interactive and autonomous learning.

Other than studies which focus on the positive aspects of FL, studies looking at the overall characteristics and perceptions of FL show that comprehending the effectiveness of FL is a complex task. Jensen, Kummer, & Godoy [14] compared a flipped and non-flipped class both using constructivist based active learning methods, and concluded that FL did not produce better gains in learning than non-flipped classes. Their study results also implied that any learning gains might have come from active learning methods rather than FL. Interestingly, students in the FL class students suggested that more lectures should be included, even more than the non-flipped class students. Lou, Yang, Xue, & Zuo [15] compared three classes using FL methods with differing levels of student agency, and revealed that low student agency classes received higher student ratings and achievement scores for objective test items. Their study suggests the need for a more active instructor role during in-class activities. The results of both studies imply that for learner autonomy to benefit learning, the instructor's guidance, scaffolding, and other pedagogical issues must be deliberately incorporated into instruction.

Hao [1] explored FL readiness of undergraduate students and found that, despite a majority (60%) of students recognizing the benefits of FL, many students were not well prepared for FL, with only a small portion (38%) perceiving that their learning needs were met. Khanova et al. [4] conducted a study investigating student experiences of multiple flipped courses in a single curriculum, and demonstrated that issues such as overwhelming workload, the lack of thoughtful design of in-class activities, and the need of faculty development for understanding and designing FL classes existed in college FL. These findings indicate that the combination of college instructors who are generally less prepared for designing learning compared to professionally trained and experienced K-12 teachers, and the belief that giving autonomy to college students will naturally lead to meaningful learning, may have created this discontent.

Poorly designed class activities and/or the lack of informative instructor guidance induce resistance to student-centered teaching in higher education [16]. Wallace, Walker, Braseby, & Sweet [17] emphasized that FL classes should help learners think like an expert, and have them apply their skills to solving real problems. They also suggest that instructors should actively provide feedback about misconceptions and confusions to help them grow into experts. The importance of providing effective guidance to students in student-centered classes has been emphasized as well. For example, instructors should clearly show the relation between class projects with the course objectives and the real world [18], and provide help to students with low competence for developing strategies when solving open-ended problems [3].

3.1.2 Personal Experiences of Learner-Centeredness in FL

If flipped learning should be considered a method for attaining the goals of higher education, it would be necessary to understand in-depth how flipped learning is experienced by students from their own views and see how they perceive their learning outcomes, the type of pre-class lecture/materials and in-class activities benefiting their learning, and the guidance they want from their instructors.

In a qualitative study by Lee [19] which explored students' experiences of learner-centeredness in college flipped learning classes, a phenomenological method was implemented, and the experiences of 19 students attending a total of 7 flipped learning classes were investigated using a half structured interview method. Results of this study viewed learner-centeredness from three categories - educator-learner relationship, instructional methods, and learning outcomes, and derived the following assumptions.

First, in terms of the category of the relation between the instructor and learner, students came to possess a strong sense of responsibility even though the workload was heavy. They believed that it was up to themselves for making classes meaningful. Students said that this feeling was quite unfamiliar to them since they had hardly experienced this in the past. Students also considered the instructor's role as a 'supporter for intellectual growth'. Specifically, they wanted minimum intervention from the instructor, but at the same time, when intervention was necessary it should provide a clear direction.

Secondly, in terms of instructional methods, interviews revealed that flipped classes could be classified into 'closed' and 'open' types. Closed types pertain to classes that present tasks that have a fairly limited boundary in terms of solutions and resources necessary to carry out the task. Open types pertain to tasks that have open ended solutions and a broad range of resources many of which may not be easily accessible or comprehensible to the students within a limited time. The latter required more guidance and information from the instructor. Discussions, which were most evident to the students as a learning method, elicited various emotions. Some were happy with finding their voice, others saw discussions just as an obligation to be fulfilled. Discussions are considered an essential method for learner-centered classes. However, when the bond between discussion and class objectives is weak, or when the instructor does not provide deep academic insight students lose their motivation.

Lastly, in terms of learning outcomes, students perceived internalization of knowledge, finding one's voice, independent decision making, and solidifying knowledge as the main outcomes, and considered these outcomes fit for college learning. The results of this study imply that in order to realize learner-centeredness at the college level, rather than focusing on the technicalities such as developing online lectures, it is more important to focus on developing perspective and understanding of the essential features of learner-centeredness, such as, independence, choice, role, and initiative of the learner.

3.2 Example 2: Supporting Students of Online Classes During the Pandemic

3.2.1 Investigating Students' Needs Using the Learning Experience Design (LXD) Method

In 2020 schools around the world had to make the sudden transition from face-to-face to online classes. As most classes, regardless of their fit with online learning, were forced to go online both educators and students had to adjust to the online paradigm through frequent trial and errors. Educators without enough online experiences found themselves in much confusion regarding online content development and student interaction. As for the students, their satisfaction for online classes differed greatly depending on the online platform or tools that were used. Students were particularly frustrated with the feelings of isolation and loneliness, and had difficulties adopting to college level learning and social relationships with colleagues [20, 21]. Thus, it was necessary to look into students' experiences and understand their needs in order to provide adequate learning experiences in the future.

At Sogang University, the Center for Teaching & Learning (CTL) carried out a study to explore how students were dealing with a semester consisting only of online classes. In order to design learner centered online classes the research method employed in this case was Learning Experience Design (LXD). The term 'experience' implies all aspects of human experiences when interacting with a system. User experience design implies that not only are the needs of the user, but also the user's goals and motivations should be considered to provide satisfaction beyond the user's expectations [22]. LXD, an application of Experience Design in the field of education, is a process for designing pleasant and satisfying learning experiences [23].

Recently this method has been applied to the field of education with the hope of designing highly satisfying learning experiences. This approach focuses on how meaningful learning is to the student rather than the functional features of a program. It involves developing a 'persona', a fictional character representing typical learner types. Specifically, the process of this method consists of 1) collecting data regarding users' needs and behaviors, 2) identifying learner behavioral patterns and deriving persona, 3) identifying needs of the persona, 4) design program, 5) modification, and 6) management [22].

The advantage of LXD is that using personas developed through actual research make it easier to understand behaviors and motives of learners [22]. Since, in reality it is impossible to satisfy everyone's needs, assuming personas provides a concrete image of the learner to work with and develop programs in a more efficient manner.

3.2.2 Experiences of College Students After Total Shift to Online Environments

The study carried out by Lee, Kim, Lim, & Kim [24] for the Center of Teaching & Learning at Sogang University explored the experiences of students who mainly had courses utilizing pre-recorded video lectures or synchronous online lectures using tools such as Zoom. At Sogang University all courses were carried out online in the first semester of 2020. During the second semester a limited number of classes were allowed to carry out face-to-face classes, but that did not go long due the surge of confirmed cases in Korea throughout the fall semester. The goal of this study was to explore what support system would help college students cope with their studies and social life in a situation that runs against their expectations of college life.

This study applied the LXD approach and conducted surveys and in-depth interviews with university students. A total of 336 students participated in the survey, and 11 students were interviewed. Based on the results researchers developed personas and journey maps for each persona.

Analysis of the survey revealed that the dominant form of online learning was 'Asynchronous lecture (e.g., PowerPoint slide with audio recording, video recording of lecture)'. Specifically, the majority of students preferred video lectures in which the instructor would appear. Students had a neutral attitude towards online learning. But answered that negative feelings emerged when they sensed isolation due to lack of communication with instructors. However, students were positive towards the availability of online lectures for repetitive viewing, and efforts made by instructors to improve their classes. Overall, students preferred online classes where instructors provided quick and concise feedback, and frequent interaction among peers and instructors existed. On the other hand, classes that tended to substitute assignments for actual lectures, classes that frequently changed its method, and instructors who gave late or no feedback aroused negative feelings.

Based on the analysis of survey and interview results, researchers elicited three personas representing the students. Criteria for determining personas included years in college, gender, learning style (individual vs. collaborative), major, the dominant type of online classes experienced, preferred online methods, level of self-regulation, motivation, online class satisfaction, academic achievement, needs, and technological environments.

Persona #1: High self-regulation and motivation. Overall satisfied with online classes but gets frustrated when instructor lacks online learning competencies, or consistency. Likely to be junior year student with a major in the humanities and above average GPA.

Persona #2: Low self-regulation and motivation. Overall not satisfied with online classes especially when experiments cannot be carried out at campus and instructor feedback is slow. Likely to be in freshman year majoring in natural sciences or engineering.

Persona #3: Mid-level self-regulation and motivation. Most likely to be in sophomore year with a major in social sciences. Majority of online classes use problem-based learning. Values collaboration and interaction with peers.

Based on the three personas researchers derived a journey map which showed the learning process and emotions experienced by each persona. The journey map depicted how students' attitudes changed before, during, and after the semester in reference to the events that occurred (e.g., notification of semester long online classes, Zoom classes, video lectures, online mid-term test, assignments, etc.)

This study indicates that universities should advise instructors to present themselves in person on online classes, and administrators should consider opening offline classes at least occasionally for experiment-based classes with caution. The personas and their journey maps elucidated that successful offline class strategies might not work for online classes due to its distinctive environment and ways of communication. This implies the need for the CTL to develop novel approaches for increasing online class satisfaction.

Figure 1 is an example [24] of the final journey map. The face icons on the left are present to show how the students' attitudes changed from positive to negative or vice versa. From left to right the circles depict the events or important elements of the class (e.g., announcement to go fully online, Q & A, asynchronous lectures, etc.) throughout the semester, and the text in the boxes show examples of students' accounts of their experiences regarding the events during the semester.

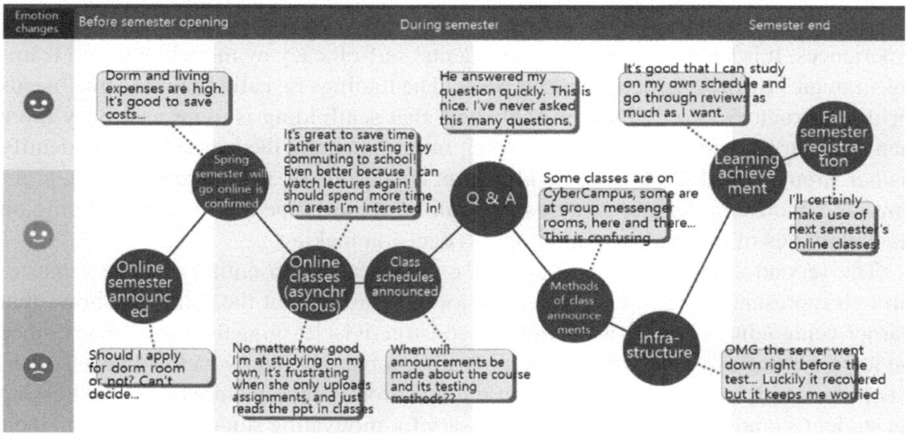

Fig. 1. Journey map of persona 1 [24]

Based on this study, in an effort to increase online learning satisfaction, the CTL designed a new program named ‘Step Up’ which organized students into study groups to provide each other with academic and emotional support. This program was developed based on the study results indicating students’ needs for interaction and support academically as well as emotionally. Students’ needs for practical help when completing assignments, or preparing for tests was also considered. Students who volunteered to participate in this program would meet offline and online using various tools such as Zoom or messenger applications. Applications for increasing productivity and Excel were used to control themselves and monitor their progress. They would report to each other their study plans, schedules, activities, and progress to the group so as to encourage self-regulation to each other. In the beginning, students felt awkward talking to other members whom they have never met in person. But after having weekly meetings, their intimacy grew, and week after week the members helped each other overcome their problems together. Students also mentioned that they could discover their weaknesses and find the optimal method for concentrating on their studies, and that the members had a strong positive influence on themselves for striving through this unusual semester. Researchers believe that this program basically helped students gain control over their learning, a critical factor for learner-centeredness in online environments.

4 Conclusion

The qualitative study investigating students’ experiences in flipped learning classes demonstrate that even with the use of constructive methods such as discussions it is still challenging to promote true autonomy when the topics and activities are determined by the instructor. The format of flipped learning itself does not guarantee a lively, motivated, and satisfying class. Learners were motivated when the discussions were relevant to issues important to them, and when they felt confident that they could accomplish their goals. Although too much liberty may bring confusion, instructors should consider gradually raising the level of self-determination by the students based on their level of experiences. It is necessary to increase students' self-efficacy by modeling useful learning strategies by the instructor or their peers. The findings revealing the students' needs for the instructor's professional insight show that scaffolding is quite necessary more than the instructor might think. Scaffolding implies helping the learner clearly identify his/her strengths and weaknesses, and current conditions for solving challenging problems. In conclusion, learner-centeredness can be achieved better by contemplating on the boundaries of the student's autonomous decision making.

The second study exploring students' experiences of an entirely online semester through representative personas and their journey throughout the semester shows that learner-centeredness is more than applying constructivist learning theories. That is, since the learner's cognitive and affective factors are inseparably interwoven with each other, it is not enough to devise constructivist methods for learner-centeredness. Addressing the student's emotional needs is also necessary for motivating students to focus on their studies. Especially, in 2020 when students were struggling to pull themselves together to focus on all the online classes and at the same time waving aside the temptations interrupting their learning, peer support was helpful. It helped students connect with other students feeling the same way. This is an example demonstrating how schools can lay the grounds of ownership of learning by strengthening students' autonomy and self-regulation which are the basis of learner-centeredness.

Learner-centeredness is achieved through a fine balance of the educator's depth of guidance and the students' readiness to construct meaningful knowledge. It is also based on an interactive relationship with affective factors such as the sense of control over one's study habits or time management which in the end forms the basis of self-directed learning. As it appears that the amount of time students will have to spend on online classes will be more compared to pre-pandemic times and perhaps grow, higher education must make efforts to promote learner-centeredness. Colleges should devise methods for evaluating students' level of readiness in terms of knowledge and affective qualities and identify adequate levels of instructor guidance as well as various learner support systems.

References

1. Hao, Y.: Exploring undergraduates' perspectives and flipped learning readiness in their flipped classrooms. Comput. Hum. Behav. **59**, 82–92 (2016)
2. Lee, J., Lim, C., Kim, H.: Development of an instructional design model for flipped learning in higher education. Ed. Tech. Res. Dev. **65**, 427–453 (2016). https://doi.org/10.1007/s11423-016-9502-1
3. Douglas, E.P., Koro-Ljungberg, M., McNeill, N.J., Malcolm, Z.T., Therriault, D.J.: Moving beyond formulas and fixations: solving open-ended engineering problems. Eur. J. Eng. Ed. **37**, 627–651 (2012)
4. Khanova, J., Roth, M.T., Rodgers, J.E., McLaughlin, J.E.: Student experiences across multiple flipped courses in a single curriculum. Med. Ed. **49**, 1038–1048 (2015)
5. Cannon, R., Newble, D.: A Handbook for Teachers in Universities and Colleges: A Guide To Improving Teaching Methods. Kogan Page, London (2000)
6. McCombs, B.L., Whisler, J.S.: The Learner-Centered Classroom and School: Strategies for Increasing Student Motivation and Achievement. Jossey-Bass, San Francisco (1997)

7. Lea, S.J., Stephenson, D., Troy, J.: Higher education students' attitudes to student-centred learning: beyond 'educational bulimia'? St. High. Ed. **28**, 321–334 (2003)
8. Kang, I., Choo, H.J.: Re-conceptualization of the learner-centered education: the status quo of the in-service teachers. J. Learn. Cent. Curr. Instr. **9**(2), 1–34 (2009)
9. Jeong, E.I., Park, Y.H.: Development and validation of the professor trust scale (PTS). Kor. J. Psy. Gen. **28**(2), 405–426 (2009)
10. Baeten, M., Kyndt, E., Struyven, K., Dochy, F.: Using student-centred learning environments to stimulate deep approaches to learning: factors encouraging or discouraging their effectiveness. Ed. Res. Rev. **5**, 243–260 (2010)
11. Elen, J., Clarebout, G., Leonard, R., Lowyck, J.: Student-centered and teacher-centered learning environments: what students think. Teach. High. Ed. **12**, 105–117 (2007)
12. Cheng, X., Ka Ho Lee, K., Chang, E.Y., Yang, X.: The "flipped classroom" approach: stimulating positive learning attitudes and improving mastery of histology among medical students. Am. Assoc. Anatomists **10**(4), 317–327 (2017)
13. McLean, S., Attardi, S.M., Faden, L., Goldszmidt, M.: Flipped classrooms and student learning: not just surface gains. Adv. Phys. Ed. **40**, 47–55 (2016)
14. Jensen, J.L., Kummer, T.A., Godoy, P.D.: Improvements from a flipped classroom may simply be the fruits of active learning. CBE—Life Sci. Ed. **14** (2015)
15. Luo, H., Yang, T., Xue, J., Zuo, M.: Impact of student agency on learning performance and learning experience in a flipped classroom. Brit. J. Ed. Tech. **50**, 819–831 (2018)
16. Doyle, T.: Helping students learn in a learner-centered environment: a guide to facilitating learning in higher education. Styler, Sterling, VA (2008)
17. Wallace, M.L., Walker, J.D., Braseby, A.M., Sweet, M.S.: "Now, what happens during class?" Using team-based learning to optimize the role of expertise within the flipped classroom. J. Exc. Col. Teach. **25**, 253–273 (2014)
18. Bishop, C.F., Caston, M.I., King, C.A.: Learner-centered environments: creating effective strategies based on student attitudes and faculty reflection. J. Scholarhsip Teach. Learn. 46–63 (2014)
19. Lee, Y.: A phenomenological study on students' experiences of learner-centeredness in college flipped classrooms. J. Ed. Cult. **24**, 329–354 (2018)
20. Lee, Y., Park, Y., Yun, J.: Exploring the "types" through case analysis on operation of distance education in universities responding to COVID-19. J. Yeolin Ed. **28**, 211–234 (2020)
21. Lee, J.M.: An exploratory study on effects of loneliness and Youtube addiction on college life adjustment in the distance education during COVID-19. J. Kor. Cont. Assoc. **20**, 343–351 (2020)
22. Cooper, A., Reimann, R., Cronin, D.: About Face: Interface und Interaction Design. Mitp, Heidelberg (2010)
23. Pardal, S.S.: Learning experience design: what you need to know. https://elearningindustry.com/learning-experience-design-what-need-know.
24. Lee, Y., Kim, S., Lim, Y., Kim, B.: Personas Development based on Students' Experiences of College Online Classes. Sogang University, Seoul (2020)

Seeing the Future of Education: Three-Year Experiment of Digital Reading Online Course

Wenge Guo(✉)

Graduate School of Education, Peking University, Beijing 100871, China
wgguo@pku.edu.cn

Abstract. The history of the evolution of education and media technology from oral to Internet shows that literacy has developed from the Oratory, the print-based literacy, to the digital literacy. In the ecosystem of Internet, the form of reading materials is changing from paper-printed books to digital multi-modal content including e-books, video, audio, VR, games and so on. Meanwhile, the setting of teaching is changing from face-to-face classroom to online classroom mediated by ICT. The change of teaching methods has further brought about the new paradigm of educational research. Based on this background, the Digital Reading Lab of GSE of Peking University initiated an online digital reading courses experiment from 2015 to 2018 cooperated with three middle schools. This paper will introduce this experiment and the findings.

Keywords: Digital reading · Online course · Persona · Behavioral sequential analysis

1 Background

The Ministry of Education of China (MOE of China) issued the *Educational Technology Ability Standards for Primary and Secondary School Teachers (Trial)* [1] in 2004. In the next year, MOE of China initiated the *National Educational Technology Capability Building Plan for Primary and Secondary School Teachers* [2], and entrusted *Peking University* and *East China Normal University* to develop online training courses of educational technology competence Training of K12 school teachers respectively. The author coordinated the design and implementation of *Peking University Educational Technology Capability Building Plan Online Training Course for K12 Teachers.* At that time, I just came back from visiting SUNY at Albany, so I introduced features from the asynchronous online course which is popular in North America, designed *K12 Teachers Online Training Course of Peking University Educational Technology Capability Building Plan*, which featured with small class, activity-centered online learning, and frequent interaction between teacher-student and student-student. This model is so different with

This research was funded by National Social Science Foundation 2016 Education General Project of China "Developing Students' Digital Literacy through Digital Reading" (BCA160056) and Peking University Education Big Data Research Project.

R. Li et al. (Eds.): ICBL 2021, LNCS 12830, pp. 36–49, 2021.
https://doi.org/10.1007/978-3-030-80504-3_4

the video-centered online course in China. The expert group appraised that this model of Online Training Course is outstanding and innovative in China. It is suggested that MOE of China promotes this online training course to the country, and improves it in practice constantly.

From 2007 to 2013, more than 470 thousands Chinese K12 teachers enrolled in Peking University Online Training Course, which became a MPOC [3] online training program. With the development of the project, I visited Guangzhou, Shanxi, Shaanxi, Sichuan and other provinces and interviewed the trainers and the K12 teachers to investigate the effectiveness and satisfaction of this online training program. The research shows that this K12 large-scale online training has two shortcomings. First, there is a gap between the two teaching scenarios of "Trainer-K12 teacher" and "K12 teacher-student". K12 teachers are like setters who get trained from trainers and it would take a whole process of self-learning to transmit the training contents to education practice in actual class. Second, with regard to the challenges brought by Internet, no one, included the officials of education administration and researchers of university, truly knows the path of education reform in future. Thus everyone who stands behind the K12 teachers are trying to transmits their strength to K12 teachers who face the revolution of education directly and hope them to find the answer. The K12 teacher training system became a "pressure transmission system". I figured if there was a possibility to design a "shoulder to shoulder" K12 teacher online training program. The solution is to develop online courses for K12 students, the trainers and teachers work together to teach K12 students online, to study and solve the problems and challenges of the revolution of education.

At the same time, I have been carrying out an interdisciplinary research based on the history of media technology and the history of education, and published the paper *The Outline of Education History: Based on the framework of Media Technology Evolution* [4] in 2011. This research outlines the education history from oral to Internet according to the four attribute dimensions of {symbol, carrier, replication and transmission characteristics}. As shown in Table 1.

Table 1. The outline of education history: based on the framework of media technology evolution

Time	Symbol System	Carrier	Duplicate Tech	Transmission Characteristics
Before BC 387: Oral Poet	oral syllable	human memory	speak and memory	Oral Poets: synchronous, two-way transmission;
From BC 387 – 1453: Manuscript Era	alphabetical language	papyrus, parchment, artificial paper	hand transcription	Transcriber: asynchronous, one-way transmission
From 1450s-now: Printing Press	alphabetical language	artificial paper	print press	Printed Publications: asynchronous, two-way transmission;
From 1830s-now: Electronic Medium – Radio and TV	Express Symbol: oral, alphabet, picture, video and so on. Save and Convey: analog e-signal.	tape, CD etc.	copy	Radio/ TV: one-way transmission
From 1990s: Digital Medium - Internet	Express Symbol: oral, alphabet, picture, video and so on. Save and Convey: digital e-signal.	Internet	download/upload	Internet: synchronous/asynchronous, two-way transmission;

This framework provides a *long-term* and *panoramic* history picture of the revolution of education and technology. The first revolution of educational technology took place in Greece around 4th century BC. Socrates, Plato and Aristotle experienced the revolution from spoken language to alphabetic writing, and founded the school of *Academy* and *Lykeion*. In the middle of the 15th century, Gutenberg invented the printing machine, and triggered the revolution from manuscripts to printing book in Europe, then the textbook and the modern school system were born. Today, we are experiencing the revolution brought by Internet. From the *long-term* perspective of the revolution of education, the meaning of literacy changed with the innovation of media technology, and the new literacy is the cornerstone of new education system.

In 2013, MOE of China launched the "The National Primary and *Secondary School Teachers' Information Technology Application Ability Improvement Project 2.0*" [5], the central government increased the financial support for K12 teachers' training, with more educational institutions participating in the K12 teachers training project. In the spring of 2014, the Open University of China held a meeting, and invited experts to give suggestions for the teacher training program. I introduced the solution of "shoulder to shoulder", OU China didn't support it because of the high investment of R&D and the uncertain returns. Fortunately, Professor Qiang Luo, the vice president of No. 10 Middle School of Suzhou, attended this meeting too, he appreciated this solution, and was willing to carry out this innovation experiment in No. 10 Middle School of Suzhou. This idea was strongly supported by Professor Yuanzhao Liu, the president of No. 10 Middle School of Suzhou. In April, 2015, the project of Digital Reading Online Course initiated in No. 10 Middle School of Suzhou, is aimed to explore cooperatively to develop and implement online courses for students, and reshaped the relationship between universities and middle schools.

2 The Rationale of the Project of Digital Reading Online Course

The *long-term* and *panoramic* history picture of the revolution of education and technology implies that the digital reading will be the cornerstone of the Future Education.

2.1 From Literacy to Digital Literacy

Reading is a common learning behavior of all subjects. Learning to learn actually means learning to read. With the development of Internet-based education ecosystem, reading is changing from paper-based reading to digital reading.

There are two ways for a person to know the world: the first-hand experience and the second-hand reading. Reading makes one's cognition beyond the limitation of time and space of personal experience. From the perspective of communication, reading is a process of transmitting information from one person to the other person. The process of communication is: $Person_1$-Eecode-Channel-Decode-$Person_2$. Writing is encoding; Reading is decoding. Alphabet is one of the symbol system.

From the *long-term* and *panoramic* history picture of the revolution of education and technology, in addition to words, the oral language, Morse code, 01 number code are coding symbols too. With the evolution of media technology, the nature of *Literacy* has changed from listening and speaking (oracy), to reading and writing (literacy), and to digital reading and digital writing (digital literacy). The digital literacy will become the cornerstone of the Future Education, digital reading will become the basic behavior of learning.

2.2 Digitalization of Reading Materials

The concept of reading appeared with the invention of the printing press. Up to now, when reading is mentioned, the first thing people think of is "reading" printe book!

Compared with the print book, digital expression is a multi-modal expression with unique advantages. Multimodal expression promotes the cross-language and cross-cultural flow of content on a global scale. Today, young people can easily read English magazines, watch English TV series, and learn cutting-edge scientific and technological content such as TED and artificial intelligence on the Internet. English textbooks compiled by local experts have been replaced by digital multi-model contents. Digital multi-modal expression has the characteristics of visualization, dynamics, and interaction. The originally *tacit* operation skills can be expressed through dynamic video, so the international students can cook for themselves following the video of food bloggers, and cultivate independent living skills.

In summary, digital reading does not means E-book reading, it is a new cognitive and learning behavior in the Internet ecosystem of education.

2.3 The Pedagogy of Reading Instruction: Online Course

The multi-modal feature of digital reading determines that "reading" is moved away from paper media, and ICT "reading" and "writing" equipment must be used. In addition, the characteristics of personalization of reading content and different speeds of reading progress determine that classroom teaching is not the suitable pedagogy of reading instruction, the suitable pedagogy of reading is online course. However, in the Internet era, the way of getting the latest and most cutting-edge information for people is no longer the "paper printing media", but the mobile devices such as network, mobile phones and pads etc.

By designing sections which can guide students to extract information from multi-modal content and to express in his/her own words with forms of text, sound, pictures, audios, and videos etc., in the online learning courses, we can cultivate students' abilities of identifying information, gathering factual evidence, and building their own cognitive framework. Thus we can develop students' critical thinking ability and digital literacy through the online learning courses.

3 The Design and Implication of Digital Reading Online Course

The digital reading online course employed the pedagogy of K12 teachers online training course, and featured by learning activities, small class sizes, and high-frequency interactions. The two fulcrum of the design of digital reading online course are: (1) high quality video resources to ensure that every minute spent by students is valuable. (2) the interesting and challenging learning activities to make sure the students engaged in the online course.

3.1 High Quality Video Resources

The digital reading regards the abundant video resources online as a type of digital "reading material", which is equivalent to the textbook in the printing era. Since the reviewing and grading system of online content has not yet been formed, the dichotomy between Fiction and Non-Fiction in book publishing was used as a reference, and particularly the Non-Fiction was selected as the "digital reading material" of the course, including documentaries produced by BBC, CCTV, THC, Discovery, NHK, etc., TED lectures, public video courses from world-class universities, and excellent film and television programs. Nevertheless, the data of such content is still huge in size. In the process of sorting out the materials of media history and educational history, the author "read" a large number of historical, media and technical documentary resources, and the final course resources were selected from this "narrow resource pool".

In selecting the digital reading material - the video - the curriculum development team focused on the logic and objectivity of knowledge presentation. The curriculum development team evaluates the value of the video from the following aspects:

1) What evidences does the video provide?
2) What points does the video offer?
3) Is there a rational relationship between evidences and points?
4) What is the educational value of video?
5) Will students be engaged?

Resources of high quality usually have their own narrative perspective, and each course must also have an explicit teaching objective. How to tap the "nutrition" of high-quality resources and utilize them to achieve the training objectives of a course is the principal primary determinant of the success of an online course, with a weight of over 50%.

For example, the seven TED videos from the online course, *Innovative Thinking*, are sifted from more than 100 TED short videos. In designing the course, we did an extensive "reading" and tried multiple options on which TED Talks to select and into which topic to integrate an online course. In the process of repeatedly "watching (reading)" and thinking, one day a sudden inspiration occurred. The curriculum research and development team found a core concept – the complex system thinking. Complexity system thinking is a vital part of innovative thinking. Today's innovation is not about building a Boeing airplane from scratch, but improving one part or local structure of a Boeing airplane with complexity system thinking. This kind of systematic and locally complexity system thinking will break down a large innovation into a series of small components, so that students can feel that they are able to make innovations themselves. Therefore, the theme of this course is determined to be starting with system thinking and opening up students' innovative thinking. Thomas Thwaites: How I Built a Toaster – From Scratch is the first module of this course. The discussion topics designed for this TED Talk are as followed:

Discussion: How to make a toaster from scratch?

The objects of the world can be roughly divided into two categories: the first is the creation of nature, known in manufacturing as "raw materials"; The other is artifact, which is, with the help of knowledge and tools, human beings make different types of raw materials through chemical, physical and other technology processing into practical daily necessities.

Artifact is an important presentation of human civilization, which contains valuable knowledge accumulation. Each artifact involves a different type of raw material which is made step by step. This is a complexity system of large-scale collaboration.

According to the video, please briefly and clearly express the process of Thomas Thwaite making the toaster in the form of concept map. Here are a few aspects to think about the toaster manufacturing process:

1) What materials are used to make the toaster?
2) How did Thomas Thwaite get these materials?
3) Which parts of the toaster did these materials make?

Please upload your concept map to the online learning platform with a brief description. Look at other students' concept maps, choose one of them and comment on the advantages and disadvantages of his or her concept map, and make one suggestion for improvement.

The course Innovative Thinking is structured as 7 + 1 – seven modules of video reading and learning tasks, plus an exploratory research task undertaken by a group. Based on the idea of complexity system, teaching activities such as "Designing a wearable communication tool" and "Why X represents the unknown" are also planned in the later modules of the course, so that students can further understand that the manufacturing of wearable devices and the development of mathematics knowledge are the results of large-scale collaboration of human beings.

The final exploratory task requires students in each study group to choose a commodity, study its manufacturing process, and express it in the form of concept map, story, etc. Through analysis, students' experience and understanding of large-scale collaboration and complex thinking can be further deepened. The above is the structure of the first course and the rest of the courses basically adopt the same idea of design.

As shown in Fig. 1, a total of 9 online courses of "digital reading" have been developed so far:

1) Innovative Thinking
2) BBC: Mapping the World
3) CCTV: Five Thousand Years of Chinese Characters
4) THC: America: The Story of US
5) Grow up to Be a Better Adult
6) Funny Nobel Prize: Rethinking Daily Life from the Academic Perspective
7) Amination: Craftsmanship Behind Innovation
8) Poetry: From Homer to Bob Dylan
9) Poetry: Love and Beauty

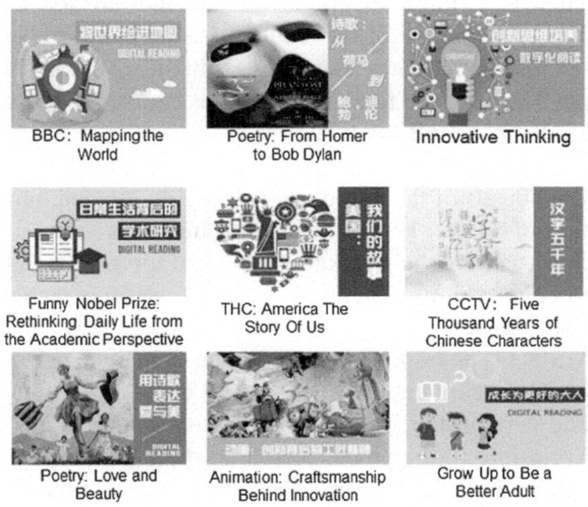

Fig. 1. Digital reading online courses

3.2 A Small-Scale, Highly Interactive Class Centered on Learning Activities

With carefully selected video content and well-designed learning activities, if students are not actively engaged, they will not be able to gain the nutrition of growth. In order to keep students engaged in the online learning, the following activities are designed for this course:

- Reading: Students use tools such as record sheets to learn independently by watching videos.
- Quiz: An examine of the above reading activities to check students' understanding of the basic facts in the video.
- Discussion: Based on the content of the video, students will post a main post according to the task design; Read peer's posts and choose two to reply to. The teaching assistant (TA) will grade each student's main post and provide feedback (Private Information which can only be seen by student him/herself); Check two replies. Discussions are the most important learning activity in the "Digital Reading" program which account for the highest proportion of the grade. In the discussion, there is not only the 1-to-1 interaction between teacher and student, but also student-to-student many-to-many interactions, which provides abundant information for analyzing the social interaction network of the class.

- Assignments: The TAs mark and give feedback on student assignments, which is a private message and can only be viewed by the student him/herself.
- At the end of each module, TAs will make a summary and select excellent student assignments to share with the class. The "summary" is equivalent to a lecture by the TA to the class; Outstanding student work is a kind of generative teaching resource formed in the process of teaching and learning.
- Prior to the formal start of the course, TAs will also set up a class QQ group, which will serve as a bulletin board to issue notices and solve students' technical problems. QQ group functions similarly to WeChat group and is also a product of Tencent. In China, secondary school students often prefer to use QQ groups in order to avoid "encountering" their parents online.

The overall structure of the "Digital Reading" online course is shown in the Fig. 2: the main learning activity flow in the online course module is shown in the middle; The right side reveals the learning behavior and interactive cues corresponding to each learning task; The left side shows the QQ group class discussion area.

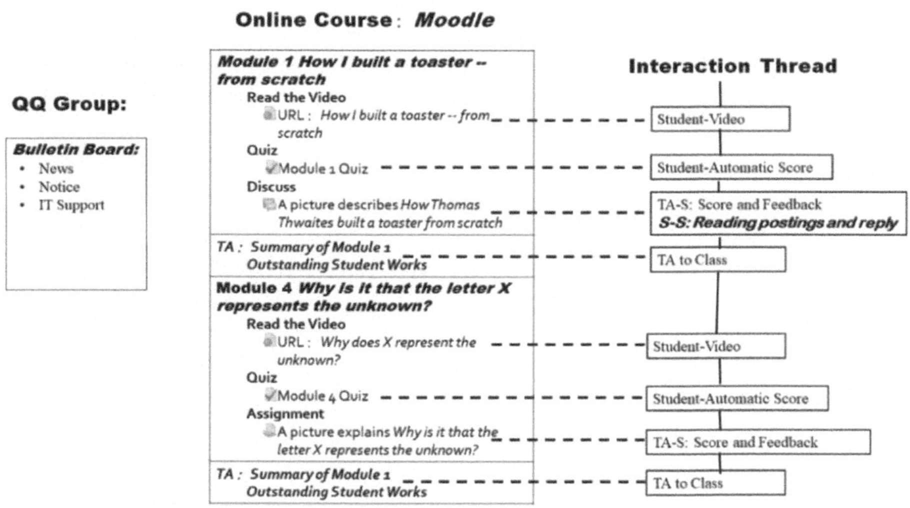

Fig. 2. The template of digital reading online courses

3.3 The Effectiveness of Digital Reading Online Course

From 2015 to 2018, the Lab of Digital Reading of Peking University cooperated with three high schools in Suzhou, Jiaxing and Beijing to offer online course for middle school students. More than 1,500 middle school students enrolled the online course. No. 10 Middle School of Suzhou introduced 9 online courses, and 1,122 middle school students in 33 classes enrolled the digital reading online course. The overall completion rate of high school students was about 82.9%, and the overall completion rate of junior middle school courses was 90.7%.

Online courses implemented in small class with 30–40 students. A Peking University graduate student and a teacher from No. 10 Middle School of Suzhou formed an online tutor team to manage and tutor an online class.

Online courses are offered in winter and summer vacations. Students logged in the LMS and QQ class group at home to study from 19:30 to 21:00 every day. Graduate assistants and teachers of No. 10 Middle School of Suzhou accessed online learning platforms and QQ groups at home to monitor students, and remind students to complete their learning tasks on time, and grade the students' homework, and administrate class affairs. Professor Qiang Luo participated in the online teaching personally. He shared the creative works of students in the Moodle discussion board to the QQ group, praised the students' creative ideas, and further proposed suggestions for improvement. He transformed the QQ class group for Posting notices and delivering technical services into a synchronous teaching scene. Inspired by vice-principle professor Luo, many students revised their work again and again until they thought it is perfect. Because the learning task of course design is open and requires comprehensive ability, students can only complete each task well if they engage in it. "It's impossible to distract during online learning," said one student.

In order to cultivate the multimodal expression ability of middle school students, the online course assignment are designed in the form of multimodal expression. The forms of expression include text, poetry, recitation, animation, design of wearable devices, drawing mind map and other forms. Figure 3 shows an emotional cloth mood dress designed by a student.

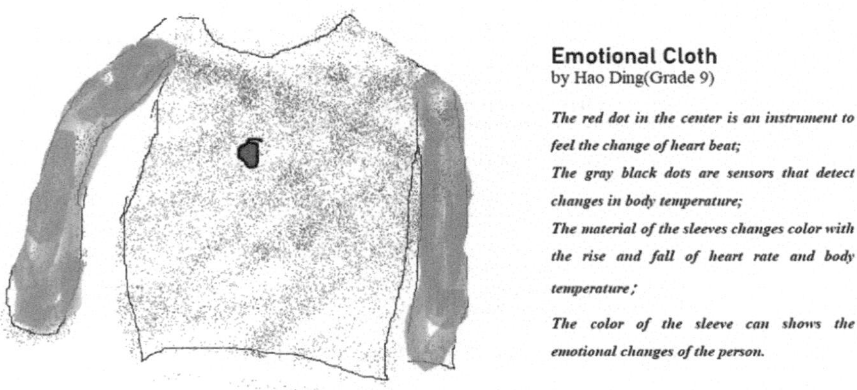

Fig. 3. Emotional cloth by Hao Ding

It found in online teaching that most middle school teachers are not comfortable with this interdisciplinary, online approach to teaching. The teaching assistants are mainly graduate students from the Graduate School of Education, Peking University. When the online course closed, each graduate assistant will analyze the completion rate, excellence rate, etc. In addition, the graduate teaching assistants are required to select 3–6 students (not meet in person) impressed and perform a personalized analysis. The online teaching has become the practical classroom for graduate students.

During the period of 2019–2020, Mengqian Wang interviewed 18 middle school students of No. 10 Middle School of Suzhou, and found that the digital reading online course was the first and only online course they had enrolled in high school. Because the pedagogy of the digital reading online course is so different from that of the school courses, the digital reading online course impressed the high school students even after three years.

4 Learning Behavior Analysis of Digital Reading Online Course

With the development of digital reading online courses, more and more "big data" of the learning process have been accumulated on Learning Management System. It mainly includes three types of data: (1) student academic records, including scores and works; (2) student logs, which record students' online learning behavior; (3) online learning interaction records, including student-student interactions and the students-teacher interaction. These data provide convenience for analyzing the characteristics of students' learning behavior, the status of critical thinking, and the writing style of middle school students.

Since 2016, several graduate students have selected data from digital reading LMS to carry out a series of researches on topics such as student persona, characteristics of critical thinking, social network structure of online class, lag sequence analysis of learning behavior, and so on. This article takes two studies by Mengqian Wang and Han Zhuo as examples to introduce how the big data-based research has increased our knowledge of the dynamic process of teaching and learning.

4.1 The Analysis of Students Persona [6]

Dr. Mengqian Wang selected a log of one class in 2016 and calculated the values of seven items of 37 students: Reading Score, Reading Times, Score of students' posts and assignments, The average number of words in students' postings, The average words number of reply postings, The number of replies, and The learning time. She drew the spider diagram of the whole class. The study found that the characteristics distribution of students H and L is unique, as shown in Fig. 4.

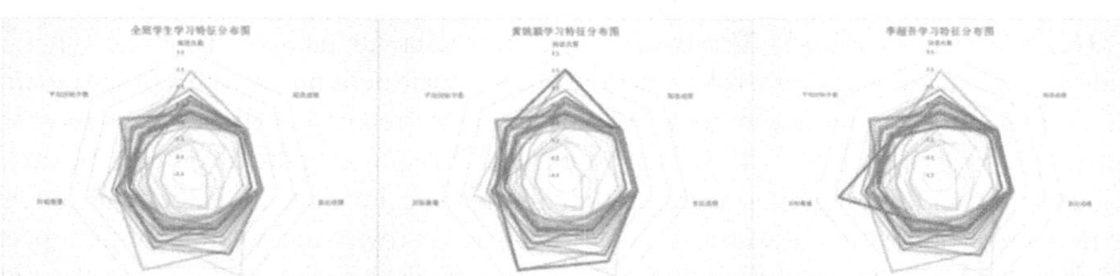

Characteristics Distribution of The Class Characteristics Distribution of H Characteristics Distribution of L

Fig. 4. Characteristics distribution of the class, H, and L

Mengqian Wang further analyzed the positions of students H and L in the social network of the class and the relationship between their learning time investment and the time investment curve of the whole class, as shown in Fig. 5.

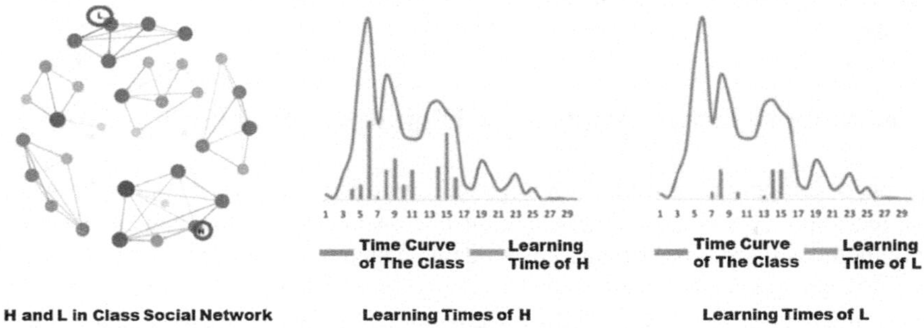

Fig. 5. Positon in the social network and learning time of H and L

Based on the above analysis, Mengqian Wang synthesized the analysis of the previous 7 dimensions, as well as the results of social network analysis and time investment analysis, and visually described the persona of H and L. As shown in Fig. 6.

This preliminary study profile analysis describes the cognitive indicators such as reading performance and writing performance of the two students of H and L; it also describes non-cognitive indicators such as class social network location and time management. It has very important value for reforming the future student evaluation mechanism and improving the college entrance examination system.

4.2 The Learning Behavior Sequence Patterns of Excellent, Medium and Behind Students [7]

Zhuo Han selected 121 grades and log data of 7th grade students, and divided the students into three groups using the cluster analysis technique of their grades: excellent students, average students, and special students. Then, the learning behavior in the log is coded, and the learning behavior sequence patterns of the three types of students was explored using the lag sequence analysis technique.

Her research found: (1) The overall learning behavior path of the three types of students is basically the same, following the order of instructional design. (2) *Discussion* which is the most important learning activity in digital reading online courses have the highest proportion of grades. There is a significant difference in the discussion behavior sequence of excellent students, average students, and special students. Excellent students are the only group who will watch the video again and browse the postings of their peers before publishing their main posts. On the contrast, the special students are the only group who failed follow the requirements of the learning task for posting the main post and distracted to browse student information. The learning behavior sequence of these three types of students are shown in Table 2.

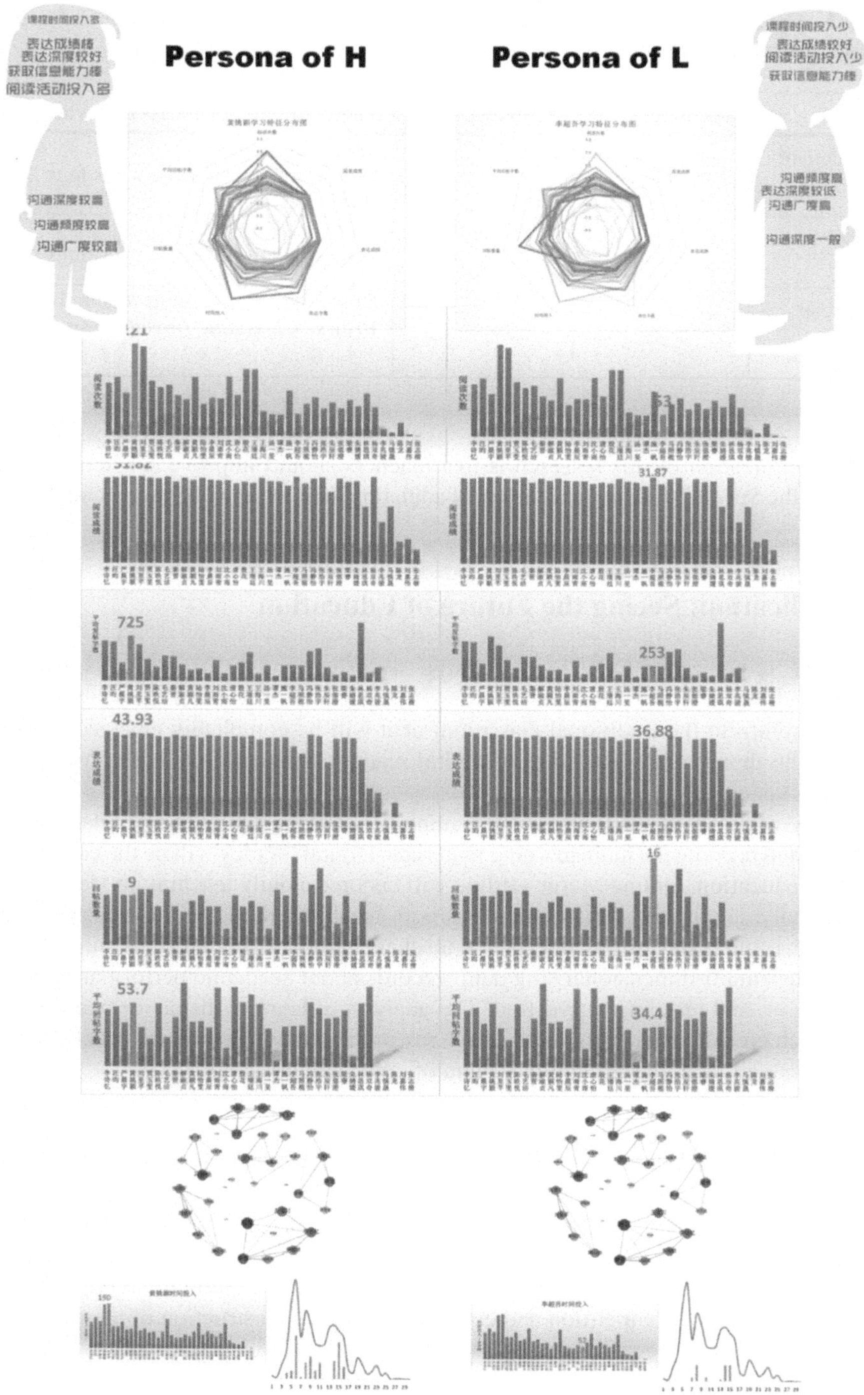

Fig. 6. The persona of H and L

Table 2. The same and different characteristics of the learning behaviors sequence of excellent, average and special students.

Grade	The Same Learning Behavior Path	The Different of Discuss Behavior:
Excellent	↓ Read the Video ↓ Quiz ↓ Discuss ↓	*Read Video Again* Skim through classmate's postings Write and Post
Average		Write and Post Skim through classmate's postings
Special		Do not write and post as required ***Browse Classmate Introduction***

The implication of this research is that teachers should improve academic performance of the Special students by the way of adjusting their learning behavior and develop the ability of time management.

5 Implication: Seeing the Future of Education

Under the sequence of COVID-19, a large scale experiment of online courses are launched globally. In the post-pandemic era, the question of whether the school education will return to the traditional classroom or it will be completely changed is worth asking. The three-year exploration of digital reading online course has shown us the following vision:

Firstly, digital contents such as video, animation, VR, and games will replace printed textbook and become the main learning materials. Digital literacy will be the cornerstone of future education. Online Merge Offline will become a daily teaching mode.

Secondly, compared with offline classroom teaching, the LMS records the teaching and learning behavior of students and teachers automatically and continuously, and accumulates multi-dimensional "big data" records about academic performance, learning behavior, and teaching interaction. The analysis of learning behavior based on big data will change the paradigm of education research, and will reform the mechanism of student evaluation and examination system of college admissions.

Thirdly, digital reading online courses gather teachers and students who are separated by time and space in the Online Classroom to establish a new educational organization and curriculum model that connects between universities and middle schools. During the epidemic, there were also cases of professors from all over the world jointly open a course on ZOOM, ClassIn etc., which shows that the Internet brought a new business model for education entrepreneurs to "collect" global educational production factors and organize education and teaching services. This has brought new development opportunities for global education competition and cooperation, and reconstruction of the traditional education system.

References

1. Notice of the Ministry of Education on Issuing the "Educational Technology Ability Standards for Primary and Secondary School Teachers (Trial)". http://www.moe.gov.cn/srcsite/A10/s6991/200412/t20041215_145623.html
2. Notice of the Ministry of Education on Initiating the Implementation of the National Educational Technology Capability Building Plan for Primary and Secondary School Teachers. http://www.moe.gov.cn/srcsite/A10/s7058/200504/t20050404_81753.html
3. Guo, W.: From SPOC to MPOC - The effective practice of peking university online teacher training. In: 2014 International Conference of Educational Innovation through Technology, pp. 258–264 (2014)
4. Guo, W.: The outline of education history: from the perspective of media technology evolution. Peking Univ. Educ. Rev. **9**(3), 137–157 (2011)
5. The National Primary and Secondary School Teachers' Information Technology Application Ability Improvement Project 2.0. http://www.moe.gov.cn/srcsite/A10/s7034/201904/t20190402_376493.html
6. Wang, M.: Ph.D research proposal (working document). Graduate School of Education. Peking University (2016)
7. Zhuo, H.: An analysis of students' learning behavioral sequences in a middle school online elective course: based on a digital reading course[D]. Peking University (2018)

Content and Instructional Design

Construction of the Teacher-Student Interaction Model in Online Learning Spaces

Youru Xie, Yuling Huang(✉), Yucheng Bai, Wenjing Luo, and Yi Qiu

School of Educational Information Technology, South China Normal University, Guangzhou, China

Abstract. The interaction between teachers and students is key in promoting knowledge generation and improving teaching quality. Exploring the use of online learning spaces in effectively supporting the teacher-student interaction has important theoretical and practical value. Guided by the interaction equivalency theorem and the generative learning theory, this study adopts literature research and design-based research to build the teacher-student interaction model in online learning spaces. We first formed a preliminary model by analyzing the principles behind the interaction between teachers and students and the support features of online learning spaces. Then, we refined the interaction model during two rounds of teaching practice. To further validate the interaction model, we collected teacher-student interaction data from two online courses and conducted two interaction analyses (i.e., S-T curve and Flanders). Results showed that the model significantly fostered students' engagement during the interaction.

Keywords: Teacher-student interaction · Model · Online learning spaces · Construction

1 Introduction

As a support point for effective teaching, teacher-student interaction has a critical impact on the quality of undergraduate teaching. In 2019, the Chinese Ministry of Education issued the *Guiding Opinions on Strengthening the Construction and Application of Online Learning Spaces*, emphasizing the promotion of the deep integration of information technology and educational teaching practices. Moreover, the guidance document encourages the construction and application of online learning spaces to promote the reform of teaching and learning and finally build a new ecology of *Internet + Education*[1]. However, the current teacher-student interaction in the classrooms of colleges and universities generally lacks students' active engagement and in-depth integration of information technology. Therefore, the current study aims to build a teacher-student interaction model in online learning spaces via design-based research. This study will contribute to the engaged teacher-student interaction in higher education and provide theoretical and practical insight into effective undergraduate teaching.

[1] Cross-border integration of information technology in the field of education represented by the Internet.

R. Li et al. (Eds.): ICBL 2021, LNCS 12830, pp. 53–65, 2021.
https://doi.org/10.1007/978-3-030-80504-3_5

2 Literature Review

2.1 Teacher-Student Interaction Models

The research perspectives on teacher-student interaction can be roughly divided into philosophy [1], psychology [2], and pedagogy [3]. The research content mainly includes the connotation and classification of teacher-student interaction, teaching strategies, models, and analysis methods. In terms of connotation and classification, for example, Zhang Jinghua believed that teacher-student interaction actually refers to teachers and students in education and teaching, through different teaching and learning behaviors, so as to perform teachers' duties and perform student roles, thereby generating mutual influence and interaction [4]. Based on the span of interaction time, Xin Namin divided teacher-student interaction into synchronous interaction and asynchronous interaction [5]. In terms of teaching strategies, Phung proposed different stages of interaction strategies based on the interaction model, including strategies for enhancing collaboration and interaction awareness, presentation and analysis strategies, self-assessment and reflection strategies, continuous practice strategies, etc. [6] For models, Mu Su constructed the interactive organization mode and corresponding principles in online synchronous teaching based on the interaction equivalency theorem [7].

In summary, the research on teacher-student interaction is very rich. How to build a teacher-student interaction model according to the characteristics of classroom teacher-student interaction in the "Internet+" era and the analysis of the principle of teacher-student interaction based on previous research needs to be further improved. At the same time, more studies are needed to further improve the effectiveness and efficiency of teacher-student interaction analysis.

2.2 The Application of Online Learning Spaces

There is a wealth of research on the teaching practice and application of online learning spaces. For example, Guo Jiong investigated and studied the space platform used by 381 basic education schools in the 2018 Online Learning Spaces Application Popularization Activity of the Ministry of Education, and proposed the current situation, problems and countermeasures of the construction and application of online learning spaces in the field of basic education [8] ; Liu Yawei and others carried out practical research on teaching models based on different types of online learning spaces such as Sakai [9] ; Hou Ning and others have constructed a hybrid teaching model from the perspective of the online learning platform [10] ; Xiao Zhiguo [11], Guo Mei [12], Guan Yu [13] and others carried out practical research on flipped classroom teaching based on the online learning spaces; Xie Maosen [14], Lei Juncheng [15] and others carried out online and offline learning evaluation design research based on the online learning spaces.

To sum up, as virtual spaces that supports online and offline, synchronous and asynchronous teaching, online learning spaces can effectively support teacher-student interaction, but existing research has paid little attention to the support of online learning spaces to enhance the activity of teacher-student interaction. Therefore, this study will clarify the point of convergence between the online learning spaces and teacher-student interaction. Moreover, we will analyze the functions and application methods of the online learning spaces to support engaged teacher-student interaction.

3 Research Procedures and Methods

This study comprehensively applied a variety of research methods and consisted of four sessions. The specific research processes and methods are shown in Fig. 1.

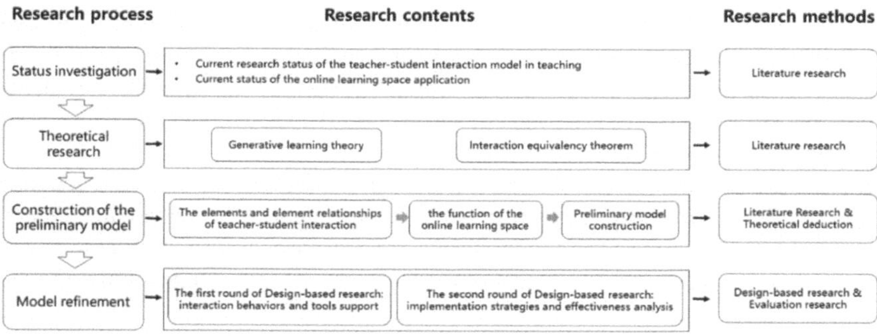

Fig. 1. Research process and methods.

① **Status investigation.** This study adopted the literature research method to systematically analyze the current research status of the teacher-student interaction model in teaching and the status of online learning spaces application, laying the foundation for subsequent research. ② **Theoretical research.** This study adopted the literature research method to clarify the theory of teacher-student interaction, and provide theoretical support for this research. ③ **Construction of the preliminary model.** This study adopted the literature research methods and theoretical deduction methods to clarify the elements and element relationships of teacher-student interaction, analyze the function and application methods of online learning spaces to support the interaction, constructing a preliminary interaction model based on online learning spaces. ④ **Model refinement.** This study adopted design-based research to further analyze the interaction behavior between teachers and students supported by tools, and proposed model implementation strategies.

4 Construction of the Preliminary Teacher-Student Interaction Model

4.1 Theoretical Frameworks

Interaction Equivalency Theorem. The interaction equivalency theorem emphasizes that the interactions between student-teacher, student-student, and student-content have an alternative and complementary effect. The theory believes that when teachers are designing instruction, taking into account factors such as education cost, convenience, technical complexity, and practical limitations, a reasonable design of one of these types of interactions can also effectively support in-depth and meaningful formal learning, and will blow-up the teaching experience [16].

Implications for this study: Based on the teaching of online learning spaces, teacher-student interaction is the most frequently occurring, easier to organize, and effective among the three interactions. Therefore, it can give full play to the role of teacher-student interaction and achieve better teaching results.

Generative Learning Theory. Wittrock's generative learning model includes four main components: generation, motivation, attention and prior knowledge. The theory believes that learning activities can be understood from four aspects: motivation, learning process, generation process and creative process. Among the four elements of generative learning theory, teachers can use some means to control each element and have the most direct impact on students' learning activities.

Implications for this study: Teachers should pay attention to the construction of a dynamically generated learning environment so that students can interact, and construct meaningfully based on the original cognition and presented information materials and teaching content, so as to promote generative learning and improve teaching effects.

4.2 Principles and Analysis of Teacher-Student Interaction

Elements of Teacher-Student Interaction and Their Relationship. This study combines the characteristics of teacher-student interaction in the era of educational informatization 2.0 and proposes four elements of teacher-student interaction: subjects, behaviors, tools, and environment.

Subjects. Including teachers and students, they are the fundamental element of teaching activities.

Behaviors. Including teacher behavior and student behavior. Teachers and students can freely communicate, discuss, and collaborate according to teaching needs, share each other's views, thoughts, and knowledge, and promote knowledge conversion, knowledge discovery and knowledge generation.

Tools. Including live interactive tools, synchronized collaboration tools, discussion and communication tools, information collection tools, classroom management tools, etc.

Environment. Including physical environment, technology and resources that support teacher-student interaction. This study relies on online learning spaces to create a teaching environment to carry out teaching. The resource sharing service, teaching support service, analysis and evaluation service and education management service provided by online learning spaces.

The four elements (i.e., subjects, behaviors, tools, and environment) in the teacher-student interaction mutually affect and cooperate with each other. The relationship of the elements is shown in Fig. 2.

Teacher-Student Interaction Forms. The form of teacher-student interaction is a way to help teachers and students transform interactive behaviors, interactive tools, and interactive environment into specific activities. In this study, the form of teacher-student

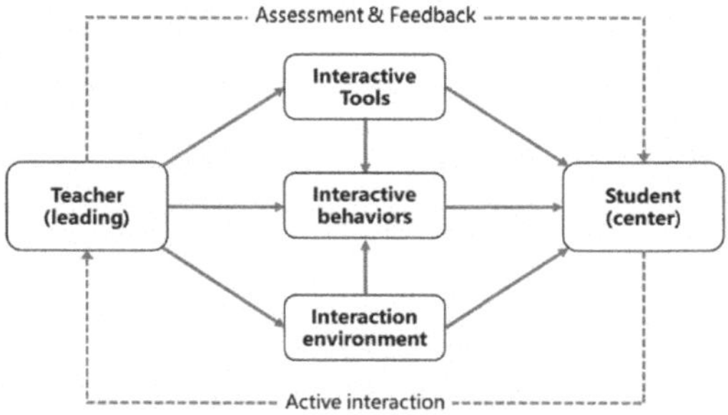

Fig. 2. Elements of teacher-student interaction and their relationship

interaction is divided into online synchronization, online asynchronous, offline synchronization, and offline asynchronous based on spaces and time standards. The typical interactive behavior corresponding to each type of interactive form is shown in Fig. 3.

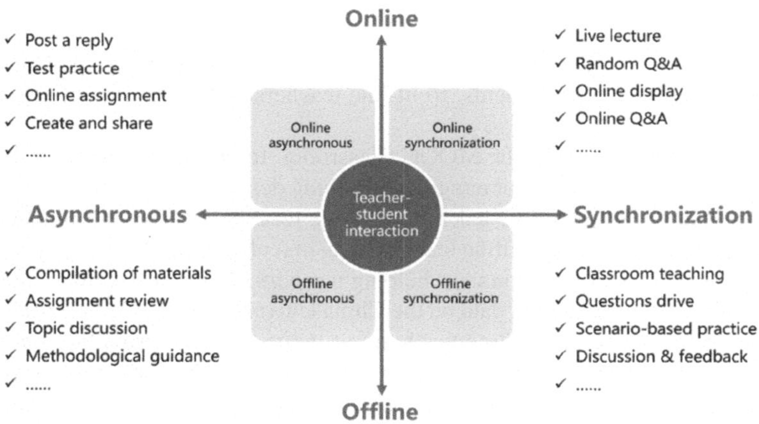

Fig. 3. Four interaction forms and their typical behaviors

4.3 Features of Online Learning Spaces in Supporting Teacher-Student Interaction

Based on online learning spaces, this study proposes an application method for online learning spaces to support teacher-student interaction based on the basic principles of online teaching, the MOOC platform of Chinese universities, Mu classroom and interactive tools, and geared towards the need to enhance the activity of teacher-student interaction in colleges and universities, as shown in Fig. 4.

One course platform is the MOOC platform of China University. In online teaching, teachers rely on the China University MOOC platform to provide students with diverse teaching resources; organize systematic and complete teaching activities; at the same

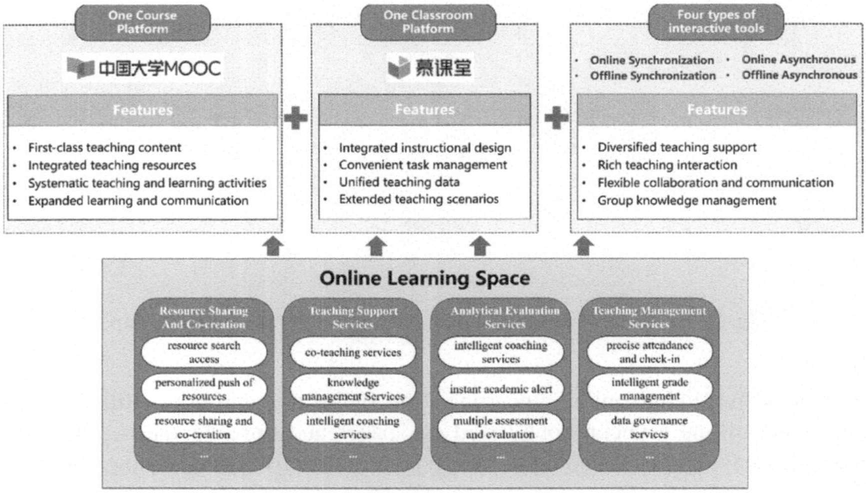

Fig. 4. Application methods of online learning spaces to support the teacher-student interaction

time, expand online multi-party learning and communication, promote equal interaction and communication among students, front-line teachers and education informatization workers.

One classroom platform is the MOOC Classroom. In offline teaching, teachers rely on MOOC Classroom to carry out integrated teaching design, considering before, during and after class, online and offline teaching; helping teachers and students manage tasks conveniently, view online and offline learning data in real-time, and adjust teaching content and methods in a targeted manner; helping teachers synchronize offline interaction data with online course teaching data on the China University MOOC platform, forming a closed loop for online and offline teaching; at the same time, providing on-demand tests, tests and exercises for teacher-student interaction. At the same time, it provides functions for teacher-student interaction such as in-class tests, random roll-calls, class questionnaires and assignments, creating a variety of interactive scenarios.

Four types of interaction tools are online synchronous interactive tools, online asynchronous interactive tools, offline synchronous interactive tools and offline asynchronous interactive tools. The interactive tools complement the course platform and classroom platform, compensate for the functional limitations of the platform, and expand the variety of interaction forms.

4.4 The Preliminary Teacher-Student Interaction Model

This study clarifies the relationship between the elements of teacher-student interaction and the functional support of online learning spaces for teacher-student interaction through the above analysis and constructs a preliminary model of teacher-student interaction based on online learning spaces, as shown in Fig. 5.

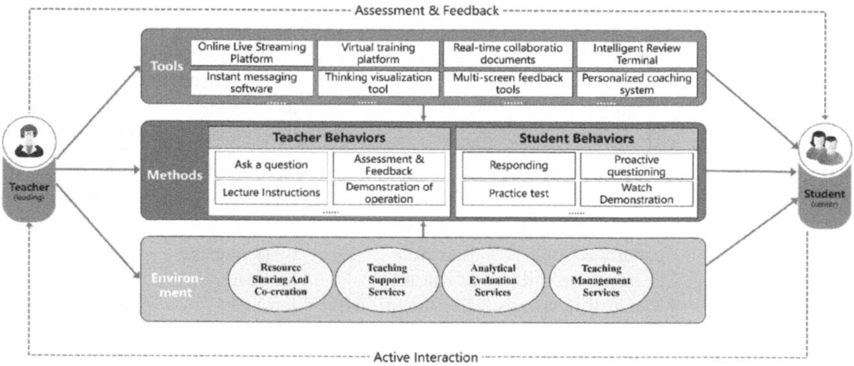

Fig. 5. A model of teacher-student interaction based on online learning spaces

5 Refinement of the Teacher-Student Interaction Model

5.1 Research Design

Participants. This study involved 16 weeks of classroom practice in teaching the *Research Methods in Educational Technology* course in a university's 2018 Educational Technology program. The sample for this study was 31 undergraduate students. The students had blended learning experiences in other prerequisite courses. The course was taught online using the *Educational Technology Research Methods* course on the Chinese University MOOC platform, and offline using the "MOOC Classroom" platform. The course is supplemented by other interactive tools as appropriate.

Research Methods. This study adopted a design-based research method, and after two rounds of iterative modifications, the teacher-student interaction model based on online learning spaces was optimized. The design-based research plan is shown in Table 1.

Instruments. The tool used in this study to analyze classroom interaction behaviors is the "Real-time Dynamic AI Analysis System for Teaching and Learning", which has a sophisticated algorithm for analyzing classroom teaching characteristics, mainly the classroom sound containing textual information, and can automatically collect various teaching data generated in the classroom through AI analysis and computational models to form analysis reports.

5.2 The First Round in Design-Based Research: Interaction Behaviors and Supporting Tools

The first round of design-based research in this study focused on "Overview of Educational Technology Research Methods", "Educational Technology Evaluation Research" and "Online Teaching and Learning in the Epidemic Prevention and Control Era" as in the first round of the study, the design of teacher-student interaction was based on the

Table 1. Design-based research schedule

Design-based research	Purpose of the study	Teaching content	Teacher-student interaction behaviors	Teacher-student interaction tools
First round 2020.9.10– 2020.10.15	Observe and analyze teacher-student interactions based on online learning spaces to refine the interactive behaviors and tools supported in the model	① Overview of educational technology research methods ② Educational technology evaluation research ③ Research on online teaching in the period of epidemic prevention and control	Recorded lectures, posting responses, learning feedback, critique feedback, classroom workshops, data compilation	China University MOOC platform, Mu classroom interactive applet, the WeChat, WeChat public number
Second round 2020.10.22–2020.11.19	Based on the first round of design-based research, the implementation strategy and effect analysis of the model are presented	① Content analysis ② Statistical processing of research data ③ Educational technology action research	Recorded lectures, posting responses, test practice, task management, feedback, face-to-face Q&A, question and answer	China University MOOC platform, The MU classroom interactive applet, WeChat Public, The Sojump, Tencent Document

model of teacher-student interaction in online learning spaces and the implementation of teaching.

After this round of teaching practice, through analysis of the platform data, we found that the learning effect of applying this mode is obvious, but also revealed some problems: ① Pre-learning session. Students were able to respond to the discussion topics posted by the teacher as requested, but most of them copied the textbook content without expressing it through their own understanding and digestion; ② Group discussion. Due to time constraints, teachers can only randomly guide individual groups in class, making it difficult to grasp the progress of the overall discussion and ensure the quality of the overall discussion; ③ Summary and reflection session. The teaching activities are mainly for the teacher to lead students to summarize the class content, which makes it difficult to truly understand the overall mastery; ④ Evaluation of effectiveness. Teachers need to analyze students' online learning and offline classroom performance separately, and the workload and difficulty of analyzing the data are greater.

This study analyses and summarizes typical teacher-student interaction behaviors and tool support in different forms of interaction based on the main problems of teacher-student interaction in online learning spaces, as shown in Fig. 6.

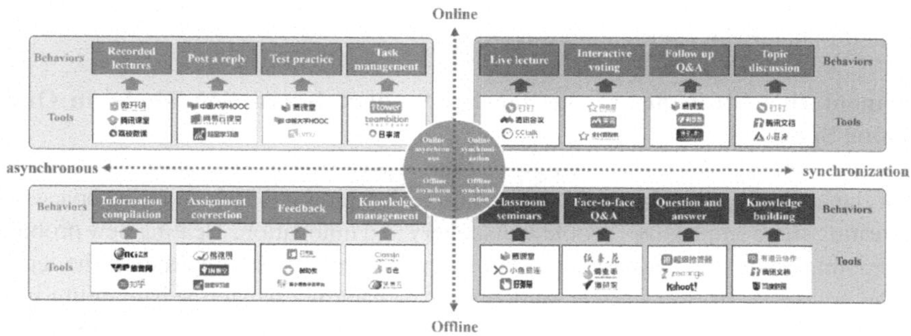

Fig. 6. Teacher-student interaction behavior and tool support based on online learning spaces

This study elaborates on the specific representations of these 16 types of teacher-student interaction behaviors, clarifies how teachers and students interact in each type of teacher-student interaction behaviors, and provides targeted and representative interaction tools for the characteristics and needs of each type of teacher-student interaction behaviors, in order to improve the active level of teacher-student interaction.

5.3 The Second Round in Design-Based Research: Implementation Strategies and Effect Analysis

The second round of design-based research mainly focused on "content analysis", "statistical processing of research data" and "action research on educational technology" as teaching contents. In response to the problems in the interaction between teachers and students in the first round of design-based research, the following improvement measures were taken: ① Pre-learning sessions. Students are not only helped to learn on their own through question guides and topic responses but are also encouraged to ask questions and are guided to learn in a problem-solving manner in class; ② Group discussion sessions. Teachers guide groups to use the online collaboration platform for learning, and monitor and grasp the progress and situation of each group's discussion in real time. On this basis, targeted guidance is given to groups with difficulties; ③ Summary and reflection session. With students as the center, teachers guide students to use multi-screen interactive tools to comprehensively collect and record each student's gains and reflections; ④ Evaluation of effectiveness session. Teachers use the China University MOOC platform and MOOC Classroom to collect students' online learning data and offline interactive data, so as to achieve the interoperability of online and offline, before and after data of class learning.

Based on the application of the teacher-student interaction model based on online learning spaces and the practical experience of two rounds of design-based research, this study proposes implementation strategies for teacher-student interaction based on online learning spaces to help teachers adjust their teaching philosophy and teaching behaviors, promote effective interaction and communication between teachers and students, and enhance the activity of teacher-student interaction. At the same time, the "Real-time dynamic AI analysis system" is used to analyze the effectiveness of the teacher-student interaction model based on e-learning spaces in terms of real-time analysis of the S-T curve and Flanders interaction analysis.

Implementation Strategies of the Teacher-Student Interaction Model in Online Learning Spaces

Generative strategies for pre-learning questions supported by technology. Taking advantage of the technological features of personalized learning in online learning spaces, the pre-learning stage emphasizes problem discovery and innovation, creating new problems from existing contexts or experiences and expressing and presenting them. The teacher uses the course platform to guide students through individualized self-learning in the form of question guides and topic responses before class, while encouraging students to identify, ask and solve problems.

Collaborative thinking visualization strategies supported by technology. Using the web-based learning spaces to perceive contexts and enrich resources, teachers guide students to externalize the state and quality of collaborative knowledge construction, which helps teachers to understand how students communicate, collaborate and negotiate in collaborative knowledge construction activities.

Interactive data integration strategy supported by technology. Based on the technical features of real-time feedback and expanded scenarios in online learning spaces, teachers make use of the connectivity of course platforms and classroom platforms to co-ordinate online learning data and offline interaction data before, during and after class, and view students' online and offline learning data in real-time, forming a closed loop of online and offline teaching and creating a variety of teacher-student interaction scenarios.

Effect Analysis of the Teacher-Student Interaction Model

Interaction S-T curve. The teacher-student interaction curve provides a visual representation of teacher-student interaction, with the line along the horizontal axis representing the teacher speaking and the line along the vertical axis representing the students speaking. When the curve is skewed towards the horizontal axis, teacher activity is pre-leading; when it is skewed towards the vertical axis, student activity is pre-leading. When a segment of the curve is parallel to the 45-degree line as a whole, it indicates that there was sufficient teacher-student interaction during this period. In this study, the ratio of student-teacher speech duration was defined as teacher-student interaction activity, with a lesson sliced into 20 segments and 2 min into one segment, and three variables were constructed to describe student-teacher interaction, as shown in Table 2.

In this study, we sampled and analyzed the videos of teaching activities of two online courses: *Overview of Educational Technology Research Methods* and *Educational Technology Action Research.* The comparison of the teacher-student interaction curves of the two classes is shown in Table 3.

As shown in Table 4, the teacher-student interaction curve in *Overview of Educational Technology Research Methods* tends to be horizontal, which indicates that the teacher leads the class, and the students speak less, and the teacher-student interaction

Table 2. Comparison of teacher-student interaction curves in a typical lesson

Variables	Formula	Definitions
Percentage of student speak time	$\sum_{i=1}^{20} Row(i) \div Total$	The ratio of the length of student speech in a lesson, including discussions, questions, etc
Percentage of teacher speak time	$\sum_{j=1}^{20} Row(j) \div Total$	The ratio of the teacher's speaking time in a lesson, including questions, instructions, etc
Active student-teacher interaction	$\sum_{i=1}^{20} Row(i)\ \sum_{j=1}^{20} Row(j)$	The ratio of student-teacher speaking time in a class

Table 3. Comparison of teacher-student interaction curves in typical class cases

typical class examples	Overview of educational technology research methods	Educational technology action research
Student-teacher interaction S-T curve	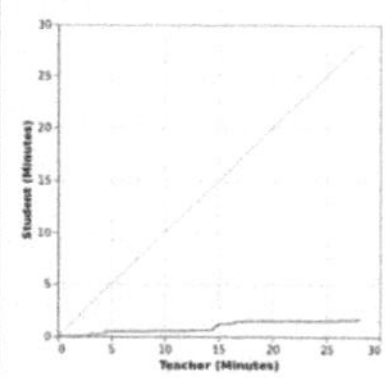	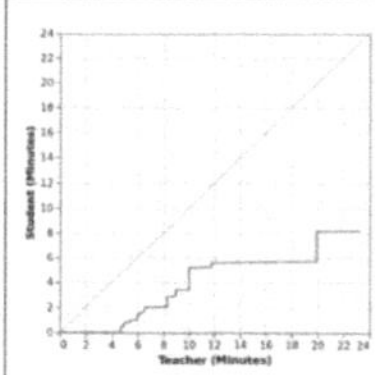

is relatively poor. The teacher-student interaction curve in "Educational Technology Action Research" tends to be stable at the 45-° line from 4 to 12 min and alternates vertically and horizontally in the rest of the time, which indicates that the teacher-student interaction is good and appropriate. Based on this, this study found that the teacher-student interaction curves of two typical lessons, *Overview of Educational Technology Research Methods* and *Educational Technology Action Research* can effectively improve the teacher-student interaction based on online learning spaces model. The study found that the teacher-student interaction model based on e-learning spaces can effectively improve the activity of teacher-student interaction.

The Flanders Interaction Analysis. After two rounds of design-based research, the *Real-time Dynamic AI Analysis System* was used to automatically collect various teaching data generated in the classroom, and the analysis report is shown in Table 4.

The data showed that: (1) the steady state ratio (SSR) values were similar in both rounds of the design-based study, indicating that the teacher-student interaction was relatively stable. (2) compared with the first round of the study, the second round of the study specified the content and form of teacher-student interaction, with a decrease in

Table 4. Flanders teacher-student interaction analysis data

Indicators	1st round	2nd round	Reference	Definitions
TT Percentage of Teacher Talk	0.89	0.72	0.68	The proportion of teacher talk time to all instructional time
PT Percentage of Pupil Talk	0.09	0.26	0.20	The proportion of pupil talk time to all instructional time
TRR Teacher Response Rate	0.42	0.62	0.42	The ratio of the teacher's feedback of the student's time to the teacher's non-teaching time
SSR Stable State Ratio	0.79	0.82	0.50	The ratio of discourse time in which teacher-student talk stays for more than 3 s to the total instructional time
PSSR Pupil Stable State Ratio	0.04	0.21	0.35	The percentage of the student's discourse time that lasts for more than 3 s as a percentage of the student's discourse time

the percentage of teacher talk (TT) and an increase in the percentage of pupil talk (PT) and pupil steady state ratio (PSSR), indicating that the teacher paid more attention to the students' learning experience and returned the initiative to the students. This indicates that teachers pay more attention to students' learning experience and give the initiative back to students. (3) teachers coordinate the cooperative learning status of each group and make targeted suggestions more efficiently, resulting in an increase in teacher response rate (TRR).

6 Conclusion

The engaged interaction between teachers and students is key in promoting knowledge generation and improving teaching quality. Guided by the interaction equivalency theorem and the generative learning theory, this study adopted literature research and design-based research to build the teacher-student interaction model in online learning spaces. We first formed a preliminary model by analyzing the principles behind the interaction between teachers and students and the support features of online learning spaces. Then, we refined the interaction model during two rounds of teaching practice. Results from two teacher-student interaction analyses (i.e., S-T curve and Flanders) showed that the model significantly fostered students' engagement during the interaction. We hope that the model can provide new ideas and methods for the integration and innovative application of online learning spaces in the era of education informatization 2.0.

References

1. Smith, F., Hardman, F., Higgins, S.: The impact of interactive whiteboards on teacher-pupil interaction in the national literacy and numeracy strategies. Br. Educ. Res. J. **32**(3), 443–457 (2006)
2. Valenzeno, L., Alibali, M.W., Klatzkya, R.: Teachers' gestures facilitate students' learning: a lesson in symmetry. Contemp. Educ. Psychol. **28**(2), 187–204 (2003)
3. Steinbring, H.: Epistemological investigation of classroom interaction in elementary mathematics Teaching. Educ. Stud. Math. **32**(1), 49–92 (1997)
4. Jinghua, Z.: The current situation and effect of teacher-student interaction in college teaching. Res. Educ. Dev. **39**(23), 10–17 (2019)
5. Namin, X., Lixun, W., Weiyuan, Z.: A review of the concepts and factions of interaction in distance education. Dist. Educ. China **17**, 27–33+7 (2003)
6. Dao. P.: Effect of interaction strategy instruction on learner engagement in peer interaction. System **91,** 102244 (2020)
7. Su, M., Xiaojin, W., Guanchao, F., Han. Z.: Interaction design and implementation in online synchronous teaching. China Educ. Technol. **11**, 52–59+66 (2020)
8. Jiong, G., Xiaojun. Z.: Research on current situation, problems and countermeasures of construction and application of e-learning space in the field of basic education. e-Educ. Res. **40**(10), 89–95 (2019)
9. Yawei, L., Linjiang, Z., Zhilong, L.: Research on the hybrid teaching mode of applied colleges and universities based on network learning space. Educ. Modern. **4**(44), 62–63 (2017)
10. Ning, H.: Hybrid teaching design and practice exploration from the perspective of network learning space——taking the course of "electrical and mechanical equipment installation and commissioning" as an example. J. Shandong Radio TV Univ. **04**, 39–42 (2019)
11. Zhiguo, X., Ting, Q.: Mode and strategy of supporting the flipped classroom using the network learning space. J. Jiamusi Vocat. Inst. **08**, 189 (2016)
12. Mei, G., Min. X.: Research on flipped classroom teaching based on online learning space——taking data structure course as an example. China Educ. Technol. Equip. 3:76–77+80 (2019)
13. Guan, Y., Youshun, P., Jie, L.: Research on the application of network learning space teaching based on flipped classroom——a case study of Yuketang and "University Computer" Courses. Modern Inf. Technol. **4**(08), 192–195 (2020)
14. Maosen, X., Wenwu, Z.J.: On Learning effectiveness of blended learning model based on learning network. J. Sichuan Minzu College **24**(05), 101–108 (2015)
15. Juncheng, L.: Learning evaluation design of mixed teaching mode based on MOOC. Comput. Era **12**, 82–84 (2015)
16. Anderson, T.: Getting the mix right again: an updated and theoretical rational for interaction. Int. Rev. Res. Open Distrib. Learn. **4**(2), 1–16 (2003)

The Influence of Different Partnerships on Learning Motivation and Social Network in Peer Assessment

Yuru Lin(✉), Yi Zhang, and Yichi Wang

Central China Normal University, Wuhan 430079, China
linyuru@mails.ccnu.edu.cn

Abstract. This study explored the influence of different partnerships on learners' learning motivation and social network in online peer assessment, designed a single-factor experiment with 93 students from Central China Normal University as the research object. Students in one experimental group are in a one-to-one fixed partnership peer assessment, while students in the other experimental group are allowed to freely and dynamically invite their peers in assessment and discussion. This study confirmed that the free inviting partnership between students had a positive impact on their learning motivation in the peer assessment. Social network analysis found that the interactive network formed by the dynamic invitation partnership is closer, and student participation is higher. However, the interactive network formed by the fixed partnership is looser, student participation is lower, and the level of student participation varies greatly. Furthermore, the students who occupied the central position in the out-degree centrality perceived higher-level learning motivation. For in-degree centrality, the students who occupied the central position in the in-degree centrality perceived higher-level learning motivation in the dynamic invitation partnership, while there is no significant difference between learners in the fixed partnership. Based on this, the study suggests that educators could take advantage of the dynamic pairing or inviting mechanism to sustain students' motivation in networked peer assessment. Meanwhile, educators could use out-degree centrality and in-degree centrality to monitor students' engagement in online collaborative learning activities.

Keywords: Peer assessment · Partnership · Learning motivation · Social network

1 Introduction

With the advancement and deepening of educational informatization, learning space has been extended and expanded beyond the limitation of time and space, and diversified teaching models have sprung up in the field of practice. The 13th Five-Year Plan clearly points out that it is necessary to continue to promote online and offline blended teaching in colleges and universities. Peer assessment, as one of the commonly used formative assessment methods in blended teaching, is to organize learners to determine the quality or value of peer learners' works or performances [1]. The expectancy-value theory of

R. Li et al. (Eds.): ICBL 2021, LNCS 12830, pp. 66–77, 2021.
https://doi.org/10.1007/978-3-030-80504-3_6

motivation holds that learning motivation as a dynamic factor has a positive effect on individual behavior [2]. In the process of peer assessment, how to stimulate students' learning motivation and make learners actively participate in peer assessment is the basis of meaningful learning. Recently, most of these studies focused on perceptual engagement, such as motivation, confidence, perceived usefulness, and sense of enjoyment in blended learning [3, 4]. At the same time, some scholars pointed out that attention to individual psychological traits such as motivation, emotion, and confidence is the trend of peer assessment research [5]. In the process of peer assessment, students conduct interact with peers and constantly deepen the learners' understanding of what they have learned. In the field of interactive research, social network analysis has gradually become one of the effective analysis methods with the development of big data. Researchers generally believe that social network analysis methods provide some effective and important information and ideas for discovering and explaining the relationship and structure of learning interaction among students [6, 7].

Following these research development trends, this study is based on the SPOC Forum of Central China Normal University, focusing on the individual psychological trait of learning motivation, and exploring the impact of different forms of peer assessment on learning motivation and social networks. Using social network analysis to further analyze whether there are significant differences in learning motivation among students with different social network positions. It aims to provide practical suggestions and empirical evidence for teaching practitioners to design and implement peer assessment activities.

2 Literature Review

After exploring different types of blended learning, researchers happen to coincide peer assessment as the main form of formative assessment [8, 9]. The use of an online learning platform to carry out peer assessment also fully reflects the basic requirements of hybrid teaching resources online, guidance offline, and assessment throughout the process, which is helpful for students' in-depth interaction [10].

2.1 Influencing Factors of Peer Assessment Learning Motivation in Blended Teaching

Learning motivation can stimulate the persistence of learning, and related researchers have paid attention to the factors that affect learning motivation in peer assessment. For example, Miyazoe and Anderson tried to study the impact of real-name and anonymous peer assessment teaching strategies on writing in a blended learning environment and found that students have higher internal motivation and learning participation in an anonymous peer assessment [11]. The findings of Nadine et al. showed that peer assessment can improve the learning motivation of the girls-only learning group [12]. Coutts et al. explored the motivation and mood of freshmen to participate in peer assessment and found that in the 7th week, as students' negative emotions increased significantly, positive emotions reduced, and students' internal motivations decreased significantly

[13]. It can be seen that most of the relevant studies analyze the factors that affect students' learning motivation in online peer assessment from individual factors such as anonymity, gender, and emotion. However, online peer assessment is also a process of social interaction between learner groups. Social capital theory points out that the resources an individual possesses do not only exist in his/her personal properties, but also in the links and interactions between which he/she connects to others [14]. Such a thesis suggests that partnership and interaction play an important role in their participation in group work. Studies have paid more attention to the influence of individual factors on motivation in peer assessment, and how peer partnerships affect learners' learning motivation were not clearly addressed in the literature.

2.2 Interactive Behavior of Peer Assessment in Blended Teaching

Online peer assessment is conducive to the formation of learning communities. Learners of online peer assessment are driven by the common learning purpose of peer assessment and conduct community activities such as discussion, communication, interaction, and feedback on the Internet. Has formed a general learning community [15]. At present, the research of peer assessment on the Internet is mainly carried out from two aspects of the process and effect of peer assessment. In terms of the interactive process, researchers such as Hou used content analysis to describe the process of peer assessment and discussion on the Internet, revealing the level and proportion of learners' interactive knowledge construction in mutual assessment activities. In addition, the study also analyzed the behavioral patterns and characteristics of peer assessment discussions [16]. In terms of interactive effects, Cai et al. found that peer feedback, especially encouraging and appreciative comments, can make learners feel community belonging [17]. It can be seen that the interactive behavior of peer assessment in a blended teaching environment is more inclined to qualitative analysis of the comments. However, how students conduct assessments and discussions around peers' works in the learning community, and what kind of social networks are formed through peer assessment and interaction on the Internet are rarely involved in the current literature.

Based on the above literature review, it is worthwhile to investigate students' online peer assessment activities to better understand their motivation and engagement in the learning community. In order to explore the influence of different partnerships on the assessment effect, and to ensure that the work of each group can be assessed by peers every time. At a general level, this study intended to compare students' learning motivation and interactive network structure in two settings. One of the settings is to form a one-to-one fixed partnership in peer assessment and the other allows students to freely invite peers to evaluate each week. At a detailed level, this study analyzed what kind of influence does the student's position in the social network has on the learner's motivation? In sum, this present intended to answer the following three research questions:

RQ1: Will the one-to-one fixed partnership and dynamic invitation partnership affect the learning motivation of the students in their peer assessment?

RQ2: What is the learner interaction network in two settings of peer assessment?

RQ3: Do students in different network positions in social networks have significant differences in learning motivation?

3 Method

3.1 Participants

The participants of this study are based on 93 students who had peer assessment experience of a compulsory course in Educational Technology at Central China Normal University. The course is divided into two classes, both taught by the same teacher, one of which has 48 students and the other has 45 students. The participants in both classes are equally divided into eight groups freely. Students can collaborate and complete weekly course tasks in groups.

3.2 Instruments

SPOC Forum and Social Networking. The SPOC forum serves as a platform for students to conduct online peer assessment and discussion. After a semester of study, Class 1 and Class 2 completed 13 weeks of online peer assessment and discussion, producing 1021 and 1319 discussion posts respectively. This study collected their online interaction data to form an interaction matrix and used the social network analysis method and UCINET to analyze the social network of the two classes.

Motivated Strategies for Learning Questionnaire (MSLQ). The Motivated Strategies for Learning Questionnaire (MSLQ) [18] was conducted to uncover the impact of the online interaction on participants' motivation associated with the fixed relation and dynamic peer-assessment. MSLQ was adapted according to the context in this study. The questionnaire includes twenty-three 5-point Likert items asking students' motivation in the dimensions of intrinsic/extrinsic goal orientation, task value, self-efficacy, and peer learning, as these dimensions were directly related to the context of the study. The questionnaire is found to be adequately reliable as the Cronbach reliability (alpha) is 0.89. The alpha of intrinsic/extrinsic goal orientation, task value, self-efficacy and peer learning are 0.83, 0.76, 0.87, 0.84, 0.73.

3.3 Procedure

Online peer assessment is implemented in a semester's course. The course is offered in the form of blended teaching based on SPOC. The research procedure is shown in Fig. 1. Before class, learners independently preview learning resources online and complete the learning of basic knowledge. In the class, the teacher uses face-to-face instruction in the smart classroom, which mainly includes knowledge explanation, cooperative inquiry, a display application, and a summary. It helps students systematically sort out knowledge, deepen their understanding of knowledge and provide personalized guidance. After class, the group work is completed and uploaded to the SPOC forum, and students conduct an online peer assessment and discussion weekly.

Class 1 and Class 2 adopt two different ways of mutual assessment. Class 1 adopts one-to-one peer assessment, and each group of learners assessments the works of fixed other groups in each peer assessment, such as Group 1 assessment Group 2, Group 2 assessment Group 3……..Group 8 assessment Group 1, forming a fixed partnership. Class 2 adopts the free invitation method of mutual assessment. Each student is free to invite other group members to assess or comment on their group assignments. The invited learners can choose whether to respond to the invitation and complete the evaluation of the group's work. At the same time, learners who are not invited can freely choose the works of other groups for evaluation. Therefore, the learners invited by each group can be different each time, and the groups that learners can freely choose to evaluate can also be different, so that there is a dynamic relationship in the peer evaluation of Class 2. Participants in both classes can post responses to other students. Weekly interactive data are collected and an interactive matrix is formed, and then the social network analysis method is used to analyze the interactive network of two classes.

The students went through a total of 13 weeks. The empirical sampling method can more accurately examine the trajectory of learning motivation changing with time and context and help to accurately analyze relevant influencing factors [19]. Therefore, fixed sampling was used to measure students' learning motivation in this study. The MLSQ was distributed to all participants in the first week, seventh week, and the thirteenth week of the semester. Participants' learning motivation in these three times was averaged to obtain an overall motivation. The participants' feedback to the MSLQ is analyzed to understand their motivation associated with the two networked peer assessments.

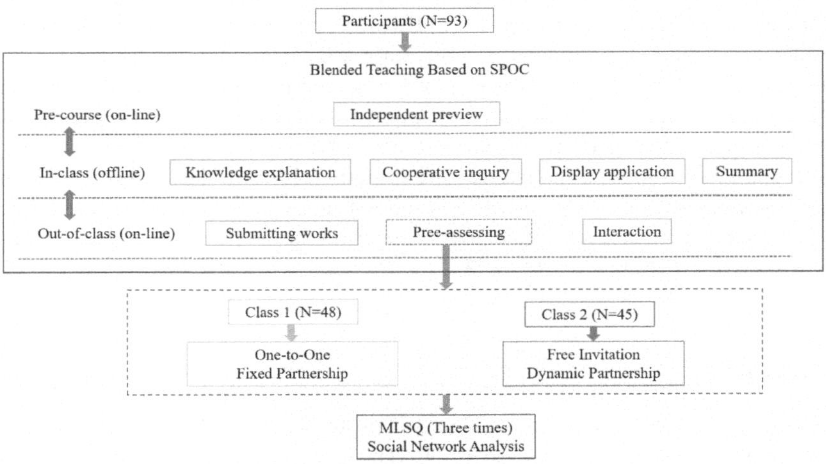

Fig. 1. Research process of this study.

4 Results

4.1 Learning Motivation in Fixed Partnership and Invitation Peer Assessment

Participants' motivation in the two settings was analyzed with independent samples t-test. As shown in Table 1, the t-test results of students' average motivation indicated that it was significantly associated with the two different types of online peer assessments.

The average learning motivation of the students who dynamically invite peer assessment in Class 2 is 3.87, which is significantly higher than the peer assessment of 'one-to-one' fixed learning partnership in Class 1 (3.63) ($t = -2.84^{**}$, $p = .006 < .01$). A closer analysis of the learning motivation dimensions found that students perceived a higher level of intrinsic motivation ($t = -4.55^{**}$, $p = .000 < .01$), task value ($t = -2.70^{**}$, $p = .008 < .01$) and self-efficacy ($t = -3.19^{**}$, $p = .002 < .01$) associated with the Class 2 than with the Class 1. It indicated that students showed an enhanced learning motivation when they were able to dynamically invite or be invited to participate in online peer assessment and discussion.

Table 1. The t-test results of learning motivation of Class 1 and Class 2 students

Dimensional	Class 1		Class 2		T	p
	M	SD	M	SD		
Overall	3.63	.37	3.87	.46	−2.84**	.006
Intrinsic	3.61	.46	4.03	.41	−4.55**	.000
Extrinsic	3.67	.49	3.77	.61	−.93	.358
Task value	3.61	.48	3.89	.55	−2.70**	.008
Self-efficacy	3.67	.35	3.94	.46	−3.19**	.002
Peer learning	3.56	.50	3.73	.66	−1.22	.227

$^{**}p < .01$; $^{*}p < .05$

4.2 Social Network Analysis

After 13 weeks of learning, learners have established a certain online connection. The network density of Class 2 is higher than that of Class 1, which indicates that the online interaction of Class 2 learners is closer than that of Class 1. Network density is the most commonly used measure of network connectivity, which indicates the closeness of learners' online interaction [20]. When the network density is higher, it shows that there is a closer relationship between learners in the network, and the network may have a greater impact on learners ' attitudes and behaviors. This study collects the interactive data generated by online peer assessment of two classes, and the data matrix is established according to the requirements of the UCINET social network analysis tool. Then, UCINET is used to draw the interactive network of two classes and calculate the social network density. The social networks of Class 1 and Class 2 are shown in Fig. 2 and Fig. 3. The overall network density of Class 1 is 0.27, which is smaller than that of Class 2 (0.41), which shows that the free invitation dynamic relationship can make Learner interaction is more adequate and promote more interactive peer review. However, the standard deviation of the interaction network of Class 1 is 1.38, which is higher than that of Class 2 (1.17). This reveals that the level of students' participation in online interaction is more uneven.

In Fig. 2 and Fig. 3, learners with the same color nodes show a closer connection. The connections between students become looser as the network center moves toward the edge. The network position of learners in two classes is analyzed through degree centrality. The position of students is analyzed from the perspective of learners to grasp the interaction structure, understand the overall interaction between learners, and discover the position and importance of different roles [21]. In-degree centrality shows the number of responses received by other learners, indicating the degree to which other learners search for the learner to establish a connection. If the student has a high in-degree centrality, it means that he is more popular and prestigious in the online community. By observing the interaction between the two classes, it is decided to determine the prestigious learners with an In-degree centrality of 10 or more, and it is found that Class 1 has 11 prestigious learners (in-degree centrality $\geq$ 10), Class 2 has 14 prestigious learners (in-degree centrality $\geq$ 10).

The out-degree centrality represents the number of replies learners post to other learners, which shows the students' ability to contact others in the network. High out-degree centrality indicates that the learner is more active and influential. The out-degree centrality of learners in the two classes is calculated, and the top 30% of the learners in the class are regarded as influential learners. Statistics show that Class 1 has 12 influential learners (out-degree centrality $\geq$ 24), Class 2 has 16 influential learners (out-degree centrality $\geq$ 31).

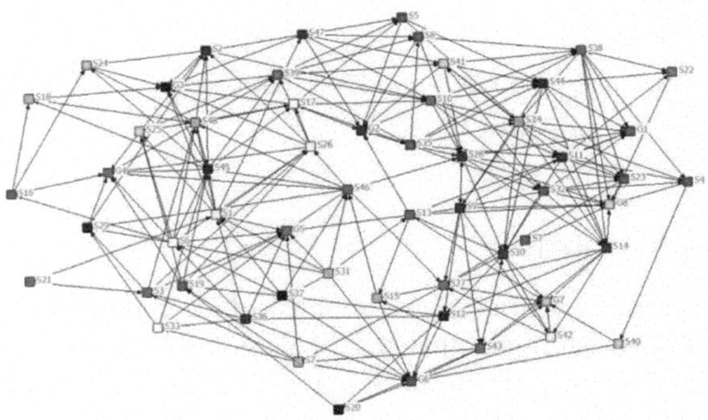

Fig. 2. The social network with the Class 1 one-to-one fixed partnership peer assessment.

4.3 Impact of Social Network on Learning Motivation

Students' learning motivation was analyzed in relation to their in- and out-degree centrality with the t-test. Table 2 displays the results of the t-test analysis of the two classes regarding the in-degree centrality. In Class 1, the 11 students who showed higher in-degree centrality (centrality $\geq$ 10) perceived no significant difference in learning motivation between the other 14 who showed lower in-degree centrality (centrality $<$ 10). However, the 14 students who showed higher in-degree centrality (centrality $\geq$ 10) perceived a significantly higher level of learning motivation than the other 31 students (centrality $<$ 2) in Class 2. Such significant difference was found in the level of overall motivation (t = 2.64*, p = .011 $<$ .05), intrinsic (t = 2.05*, p = .046 $<$ .05), extrinsic (t = 2.80**, p = .008 $<$ .01), task value (t = 2.59*, p = .013 $<$ .05), and the self-efficacy (t = 3.50**, p = .001 $<$ .01).

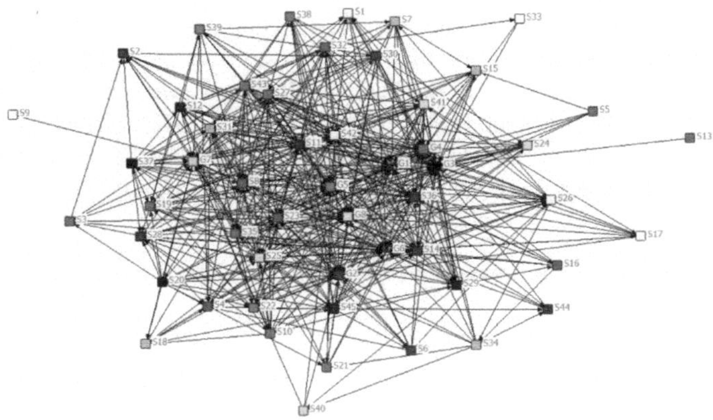

Fig. 3. The social network with the Class 2 dynamic invitation partnership peer assessment.

Table 2. The t-test results of learning motivation for different levels of in-degree centrality.

Dimensional	Centrality	Class 1			Class 2		
		M	T	p	M	T	p
Overall	High	3.76	1.381	.174	4.13	2.64*	.011
	Low	3.59			3.76		
Intrinsic	High	3.77	1.24	.222	4.21	2.05*	.046
	Low	3.57			3.95		
Extrinsic	High	3.79	.94	.353	4.13	2.80**	.008
	Low	3.63			3.61		
Task value	High	3.76	1.04	.318	4.19	2.59*	.013
	Low	3.56			3.76		
Self-efficacy	High	3.71	.52	.608	4.26	3.50**	.001
	Low	3.65			3.79		
Peer learning	High	3.78	1.46	.151	3.85	.785	.437
	Low	3.53			3.68		

**$p < .01$; *$p < .05$

The out-degree centrality also had a significant influence on learning motivation. As shown in Table 3, the 12 students who showed higher out-degree centrality (centrality $\geq$ 24) perceived significantly higher learning motivation than the other 36 students in the lower out-degree centrality (centrality $<$ 24) in Class 1. It was shown that the significantly higher in the level of overall motivation ($t = 2.32$*, $p = .025 < .05$), intrinsic ($t = 2.11$*, $p = .047 < .05$), task value ($t = 2.07$*, $p = .044 < .05$), and the self-efficacy ($t = 2.48$*, $p = .017 < .05$).

In Class 2, 16 students with higher out-degree centrality (centrality $\geq$ 31) had significantly higher learning motivation than the other 29 students (centrality < 31). Such significant difference was shown in the level of all dimension: overall motivation (t = 3.96**, p = .000 < .01), intrinsic (t = 2.76**, p = .009 < .01), extrinsic (t = 3.45**, p = 0.001 < .01), task value (t = 3.52**, p = .001 < .01), self-efficacy (t = 5.13**, p = .000 < .01) and peer learning (t = 2.11*, p = .041 < .05).

Table 3. The t-test results of motivation for different levels of out-degree centrality.

Dimensional	Centrality	Class 1			Class 2		
		M	T	p	M	T	p
Overall	High	3.83	2.32*	.025	4.22	3.96**	.000
	Low	3.56			3.71		
Intrinsic	High	3.84	2.11*	.047	4.26	2.76**	.009
	Low	3.54			3.92		
Extrinsic	High	3.81	1.56	.235	4.19	3.45**	.001
	Low	3.62			3.58		
Task value	High	3.84	2.07*	.044	4.28	3.52**	.001
	Low	3.53			3.72		
Self-efficacy	High	3.87	2.48*	.017	4.36	5.13**	.000
	Low	3.60			3.75		
Peer learning	High	3.80	1.71	.094	4.03	2.11*	.041
	Low	3.52			3.60		

**p < .01; *p < .05

5 Conclusions and Discussion

This study examining students' learning motivation and their participation in the social network for the 13-week networked peer assessment, the main conclusions reached are as follows:

5.1 Learners Have Higher Learning Motivation in Freely Invited Partnership

Aiming at the first research question, this study analyzes and compares the learning motivation of learners in the one-to-one fixed partnership and dynamic invitation online peer assessment. It is can be found that the students demonstrated improved motivation as they could freely invite peers to online assessment and discussion. Related studies have confirmed pairing or grouping schemes impacted students' motivation and engagement in collaborative learning activities [22, 23]. The long-term fixed partnership is more likely to cause uneven relationships [24]. The uneven roles largely decreased students' motivation in the collaborative learning activity. This study found that the students perceived an enhanced motivation when they were able to dynamically invite learners in online comments and discussions. Some learners in Class 2 mentioned that they are willing to participate more actively in the discussion forum to obtain invitations from others in the reflection report. The invited students also said that they felt very happy to be invited. Being invited to participate in assessments will make them read other group assignments more seriously to make more valuable suggestions. Most of the learners in Class 2 also expressed that this kind of online peer assessment allows them to gain and learn a lot. This explained why students perceived a higher level of learning motivation than Class 1 learners who form a one-on-one fixed partnership peer assessment. In other words, educators could take advantage of the dynamic pairing or inviting mechanism to sustain students' motivation in other networked collaborative learning activities.

5.2 Learners Are More Connected in Freely Invited Peer Partnerships

For the second research question, this research collects interactive data of two classes and analyzes the formed interactive network. It is found that learners are more closely connected in the dynamically invited partnership. This further indicates that learners with higher learning motivation can participate more actively in online peer assessment. Therefore, in the process of conducting peer assessment or organizing blended teaching, teachers can take certain interventions to enhance students' learning motivation, which is to support and help students participate more in learning activities and achieve the purpose of enhancing learners' own enthusiasm and initiative.

An interesting phenomenon was also found through social network analysis. The standard deviation of the interactive network of Class 1 was greater than the standard deviation of Class 2 interactive network, which indicated that there is a greater difference in the participation of class 1 learners in the process of online peer assessment. Analyzing the interactive data, it is found that the same part of the learners participates in the comments and discussions during the group one-to-one fixed peer assessment. Through the reflection report of some learners in class 1, they are reluctant to post repeatedly when they found other members of the group are consistent with their own ideas and have already put forward them, which has caused the enthusiasm of participating in peer assessment to gradually weaken. This further confirmed that long-term fixed partnerships have the tendency to cause uneven relationships. With the opportunity for freely inviting peer assessment, students had full control during the assessment process and avoided the risk of the long-term uneven role.

5.3 Learners with High Degrees of Centrality Are More Motivated

Finally, for the third research question, it is found that there is an interesting relationship between students' learning motivation and their social network position. The students' out-degree centrality had a positive impact on students' motivation. In other words, the students who occupied the central position in the out-degree centrality had higher-level learning. From the perspective of in-degree centrality, learners with higher in-degree centrality also have higher learning motivation in the peer assessment partnership of dynamic free invitation, while class 1 has no such relationship. This shows that in-degree centrality represents the popularity of students [25] but did not imply a high level of motivation in the fixed partnership network peer assessment. On the contrary, the out-degree centrality may appropriately represent the students' participation in the online peer assessment activity as it had a positive relationship with students' motivation. Therefore, educators could use out-degree centrality and in-degree centrality to monitor students' motivation in online collaborative learning activities.

In a word, the results of this study contributed to a sound understanding of students' learning motivation and social network in online peer assessment and advised that free invitation or dynamic partnership strategy among students had a positive impact on their motivation and engagement. Further, The study will be repeated to prove the findings can be generalized cohort after cohort. At the same time, the qualitative analysis will be integrated to explore the influence of different partnerships on the quality of peer assessment from the perspective of the quality of comments. Hoping to obtain a more thorough understanding of student engagement in networked peer assessment, which would help educators and teachers implement effective blended learning activities.

References

1. Topping, K.: Peer assessment between students in colleges and universities. Rev. Educ. Res. **3**, 249–276 (1998)
2. Wigfield, A., Eccles, J.S.: Expectancy-value theory of achievement motivation. Contemp. Educ. Psychol. **25**(1), 68–81 (2000)
3. Miyazoe, T., Anderson, T.: Learning outcomes and students' perceptions of online writing: Simultaneous implementation of a forum, blog, and wiki in an EFL blended learning setting. System **38**(2), 185–199 (2010)
4. Woo, M., Chu, S., Ho, A., Li, X.: Using a wiki to scaffold primary-school students' collaborative writing. Educ. Technol. Soc. **14**(1), 43–54 (2011)
5. Han, Q., Bai, H., Yang, X.: Effect of peer review on college students' learning motivation in mobile learning environment. Dist. Educ. China **000**(011), 34–40 (2018)
6. Lin, X., Hu, X., Hu, Q., Liu, Z.: A social network analysis of teaching and research collaboration in a teachers' virtual learning community. Br. J. Edu. Technol. **479**(2), 302–319 (2016)
7. Moolenaar, N.: A social network perspective on teacher collaboration in schools: theory, methodology, and applications. Am. J. Educ. **119**(1), 7–39 (2012)
8. Liang, Y.: Study on influence of rubric-based peer assessment of cognition, emotional engagement and learning outcomes on online learning. E-educ. Res. **9**, 66–74 (2018)
9. Huang, Z., Zhou, R., Wan, L.: Design and empirical research on interactive classroom ecosystem in blended learning environment. E-educ. Res. **4**, 78–85 (2020)
10. Bi, Q., Dong, Y., Han, Y.: An empirical study on the development of critical thinking of junior high school students: from the perspective of learning activity design. E-educ. Res. **39**(7), 83–90 (2018)
11. Miyazoe, T., Anderson, T.: Anonymity in blended learning: who would you like to be? Educ. Technol. Soc. **14**(2), 175–187 (2011)
12. Nadine, J., Mark, W.: Supporting girls' motivation in science: a study of peer- and self-assessment in a girls-only class. Educ. Stud. **37**(37), 391–403 (2011)
13. Coutts, R., Gilleard, W., Baglin, R.: Evidence for the impact of assessment on mood and motivation in first-year students. Stud. High. Educ. **36**(3), 291–300 (2011)

14. Nahapiet, J., Ghoshal, S.: Social capital, intellectual capital, and organizational advantage. Acad. Manag. Rev. **23**(2), 242–266 (1998)
15. Li, H., Liu, M.: An applied study of peer assessment of composition in blended teaching. E-educ. Res. **41**(06), 83–90 (2020)
16. Hou, H., Chang, K., Sung, Y.: An analysis of peer assessment online discussions within a course that uses project-based learning. Interact. Learn. Environ. **15**(3), 237–251 (2007)
17. Cai, G.: A contrastive study of online peer feedback and online teacher feedback on Chinese college students' English writing. Foreign Lang. Circle **2**, 65–72 (2011)
18. Pintrich, P., Smith, D., Garcia, T., McKeachie, W.: A manual for the use of the motivated strategies for learning questionnaire (MSLQ). College Stud. **48109**, 76 (1991)
19. Wan, L.: Learner engagement in digital learning: linking learning motivation and learning performance——an interview with professor Xie Kui. Modern Dist. Educ. Res. **31**(04), 11–18+46 (2019)
20. Lee, J., Bonk, C.: Social network analysis of peer relationships and online interactions in a blended class using blogs. Internet High. Educ. **28**, 35–44 (2016)
21. Saqr, M., Fors, U., Nouri, J., Gruebner, O.: Using social network analysis to understand online Problem-Based Learning and predict performance. PLoS ONE **13**(9), 1–20 (2018)
22. Huang, Y., Liu, C., Wang, Y., Tsai, C., Lin, H.: Student engagement in long-term collaborative EFL storytelling activities: an analysis of learners with English proficiency differences. Educ. Technol. Soc. **20**(3), 95–109 (2017)
23. Liu, C., Tsai, C.: An analysis of peer interaction patterns as discoursed by on-line small group problem-solving activity. Comput. Educ. **50**(3), 627–639 (2008)
24. Liu, C., Chen, Y., Tai, S.: A social network analysis on elementary student engagement in the networked creation community. Comput. Educ. **115**, 114–125 (2017)
25. Rabbany, K.R., Takaffoli, M., Zaiane, O.R.: Social network analysis and mining to support the assessment of on-line student participation. ACM SIGKDD Explor. Newslett. **13**(2), 20–29 (2012)

Re-thinking and Re-defining the Learning Process? Students' Feedback on Online Distance Instruction

Ludmila Faltynkova, Ivana Simonova(✉), Katerina Kostolanyova, and Slavomira Klimszova

University of Ostrava, Ostrava, Czech Republic
faltynkova@epol.cz, {ivana.simonova,katerina.kostolanyova, slavomira.klimszova}@osu.cz

Abstract. The paper deals with the re-thinking and re-defining the process of online distance instruction. The main objective of the presented research is to detect crucial features of the process of online distance instruction and propose didactic recommendations towards improving the quality. Data were collected via a questionnaire consisting of 18 items requiring both multiple-choice and open answers. The research sample included 272 respondents attending upper secondary and higher education institutions in the xxx Republic. Each respondent provided feedback on two courses taught within the winter semester (Sept 2020–Jan 2021). First, they reflected on the course they appreciated, liked the learning in it, and learned as much as possible. Second, they described the course which was designed and conducted in an inappropriate and unsatisfactory manner from their point of view, a course which did not suit their learning. Courses were assessed using four criteria: (1) First contact and communication, (2) Learning content acquisition, (3) Learning content delivery, (4) Student's final feedback on online distance instruction, including teachers' and learners' effort devoted to teaching and learning, and the quality of learning outcomes. Based on the collected data, didactic recommendations were defined towards designing and conducting helpful online distance courses.

Keywords: Online instruction · Distance instruction · Upper secondary · Higher education

1 Introduction

During the past two decades, information and communication technologies (ICT) provided a chance to change the way of teaching and learning in all subjects and types of schools. The exploitation of ICT, particularly mobile and smart devices and applications, has been widely used by large amounts of young people attending educational institutions of any level. At the same time, the exploitation of technologies for education has been considered standard [1].

In 2012, Crawford-Ferre and Wiest [2] defined online education as a popular alternative to face-to-face classroom instruction, which provides educational opportunities

R. Li et al. (Eds.): ICBL 2021, LNCS 12830, pp. 78–91, 2021.
https://doi.org/10.1007/978-3-030-80504-3_7

to learners with geographic, time, or other constraints that make it difficult or impossible, or to those having individual preferences in learning. A few years later, the state is completely different. Under the current conditions caused by the covid-19 pandemic, new ways of instruction are the topic of the day. In many cases, distance education conducted through online tools is the only way in which lessons can be held. In relation to this approach, however, questions may appear dealing with the quality of distance education, both of teaching and learning, particularly what the level of teachers' didactic skills is to conduct distance education via the latest technologies, whether students know how to learn efficiently in this manner, what the learning outcomes are etc. To some extent, all questions are interconnected. However, the crucial question is whether the process of online distance instruction should be re-thought, and/or re-defined, and thus improved. To get answers, numerous attempts have been made to investigate the process and potential of online distance education, e.g. [3–5].

In this paper, we focused on students' satisfaction with online distance instruction. The main objective is to introduce the results of the research, the aspiration of which was to discover features of online distance instruction that are typical for courses students appreciate, and for those not appreciated. Data collected within both types of courses were compared and discussed. Didactic recommendations were proposed towards improving the quality of future online distance instruction.

2 Theoretical Background

2.1 Principles and Knowledge

To make learning easy, fast, and open to all learners is a general target which is proclaimed for ages, e.g. by Comenius [6]. In the 17th century, Johann Amos Comenius, an international educator of Czech origin, defined methodological principles which largely contribute to this target and have been implemented in various theories [7]. To sum up briefly, he stated that study materials of any type should be illustrative, appropriate to learners' age and level of knowledge, learners should acquire the learning content step-by-step, in a systematic manner so that the retention period of learning outcomes was life-long. Currently, these principles do not sound new, but in that period, they were revolutionary, and if applied they had the potential to change the then education. However, even now they are missing in some lessons.

Moreover, these days teachers are expected to be competent in ICT implementation in education, as required by the technological pedagogical content knowledge (TPCK) framework designed by Mishra [8]. Teacher's competency is expressed as the intersection of all types of knowledge. Later on, the acronym was changed to TPACK by Thompson and Mishra [9] emphasizing the fact that knowledge and skills in technology do not transfer automatically into efficient teaching, but teachers have to be trained in using them.

2.2 Online Distance Process of Instruction

The above-mentioned didactic principles and TPC(A)K framework are to be applied in any process of instruction, either conducted in the face-to-face or distance manner.

The process of online distance instruction in the xxx Republic, which is under the focus of this research, was conducted from September 2020 to January 2021. Reflecting the entire learning content of each course, it was designed to follow both the principles and framework. Moreover, the approach to learning defined by Gagne [10] was implemented. He identifies five major categories of learning: verbal information, intellectual skills, cognitive strategies, motor skills, and attitudes. Each category requires a different type of instruction. Gagne suggests a learning hierarchy when sequencing the process of instruction into nine instructional events and corresponding cognitive processes: (1) Gaining attention – reception, (2) Informing learners of the objective – expectancy, (3) Stimulating recall of prior learning – retrieval, (4) Presenting the stimulus – selective perception, (5) Providing learning guidance – semantic encoding, (6) Eliciting performance – responding, (7) Providing feedback – reinforcement, (8) Assessing performance – retrieval, (9) Enhancing retention and transfer – generalization. These events should satisfy or provide the necessary conditions for learning and serve as the basis for designing instruction and selecting appropriate media [11]. In each researched course, the following phases were covered in the appropriate order, and adequate methods and forms of instruction were exploited for motivation, learning content explanation, practising, fixing, and assessing the newly acquired knowledge.

Online distance instruction was conducted in MS Teams. All monitored courses were taught 2–3 times per week (90–135 min) by qualified teachers, i.e. the teachers had qualification in the field and in teaching. Compared to the spring period (from March to June 2020), when all schools were closed promptly, another closure was expected after the summer holidays (July–August 2020). Therefore, there was time before the winter semester to make didactic preparation on how to teach and learn in an online distance manner. Didactic training in using MS Teams was available to the teachers in late August before the semester started, and all of them were trained (10 h, 45 min each). Students were instructed during the first lessons in September 2020. Before the research started, we were aware that the level of teachers' knowledge differs, as well as their motivation, willingness, and efforts towards online distance instruction. Identical features could be seen in learners. Moreover, we also took into consideration that each course differs in its appropriateness for online distance instruction. However, in August 2020, a new act was introduced defining this way of instruction as compulsory for each learner [12], whereas in the spring period 2020, learners' participation was voluntary for various reasons, e.g. lack of hardware, software in socially weak families, small schools not fully equipped with hardware, insufficient Internet signal etc. During the summer months, didactic recommendations for teachers were published by the Ministry of Education providing principles and rules of successful distance education [13]. Unfortunately, they were rather general and schematic, neither distinguishing learners' age, nor other criteria, e.g. applying the Comenius' principles mentioned above. They rather reminded of promotional slogans: Join every learner, Communicate, Follow the rules, Support others, Monitor and appraise the process. Therefore, schools organized the training by themselves, being aware of all related negatives to the future quality of education which the lack of competency in this area can cause. In February 2021, another semester started with online distance instruction. A few exceptions were allowed for study programmes requiring practical lessons, but all-country solution has not been proposed. Therefore, researching online distance instruction is a kind of help to teachers and learners.

3 Methodology

3.1 Research Problem, Question, Objective

As Mishra states, world-wide education has been disrupted by the covid-19 pandemic at an unprecedented scale. On the other hand, we are living through the largest educational social experiment in history! [14, not paged]. There will be no pedagogical experiments any more with an experimental group exploiting ICT in the process of instruction compared to a control group taught without technologies. Now, all learners are in the experimental group. As the requirement for online distance instruction appeared rather unexpectedly and neither in-service, nor pre-service teachers had time to undergo deep training, there is a high demand for information on how this process is conducted, what teaching and learning methods and forms are most efficient, and whether/how learning outcomes of high quality and retention can be built. Considering all these questions, *the main objective of our research is to detect the principal features of the process of online distance instruction; based on the collected data, to propose didactic recommendations towards improving the quality of future online distance instruction.*

3.2 Expectations

We expect that if the process of instruction is designed and conducted in accord with didactic principles by qualified teachers, an appropriate level of new knowledge is developed in learners. This approach is valid both for face-to-face and online distance instruction. Therefore, the following four criteria were set for online distance instruction consideration:

(1) *First contact and communication.* The earlier the contact is, the earlier the instruction starts and the less time is lost. If early contacted by teachers, students feel their online distance instruction is directed as it used to be in face-to-face lessons. Moreover, the regularity and frequency of contacts are important. If contacts are regular, scheduled in preset times, and their frequency follows the amount of lessons per week, they are helpful.

(2) *Learning content acquisition.* The more similar the online distance process of acquiring the new learning content is compared to the previously conducted face-to-face instruction, the less it is disrupted and negatively impacted. If students have available identical types of study materials, exercises, and (online) tests, they are able to study in the most similar manner and reach learning outcomes of the same quality and level as in the face-to-face process of instruction. Teachers' support and advice on how to study online and teacher-student and student-student communication, particularly asking/answering questions and discussions during the whole course, bring the online distance instruction closer to the face-to-face manner and help build learners' feelings of real learning.

(3) *Learning content delivery.* The more channels are through which learners are exposed to the new learning content, the higher the chance is that it captures their attention and starts and keeps the process of online distance learning. However, if too many ways are exploited for delivering the learning content, learners' attention is distracted. Having all study materials, exercises, and tests at one place is more convenient, we think.

(4) *Student's final feedback on online distance instruction.* At the end of the course, students automatically assess whether the courses brought them the expected learning outcomes. They assess subjectively how much effort teachers and they themselves devoted to teaching and learning. In close relation to this aspect, their final decision is whether they appreciate (or not) the online distance learning in a course and whether they learned much (or not) in this manner.

3.3 Research Methods and Tools

The comparative analysis exploiting the questionnaire method was applied on data collected in the process of online distance instruction. Totally, 18 items were included in the questionnaire. Thirteen of them were of multiple-choice type, providing from four to twenty choices: one choice in items 1, 3, 4; four choices in items 9–14; eleven choices in items 6–8; twenty choices in one item; an open answer was required in five items (2, 15–16). The collected data monitored using the following criteria: (1) first contact and communication (first contact and the tool used, regularity, frequency of contacts within the whole semester), (2) learning content acquisition (materials and methods for explanation, practising, fixing, assessment of newly acquired knowledge), (3) learning content delivery (tools used for the delivery of study materials, exercises, tests, exams), (4) students' final feedback on the whole process of online distance instruction (Teacher invested much effort in online distance teaching, Student invested much effort in online distance learning, I appreciate online distance learning, I learned much through online distance learning). Last four items were in the form of statements and were considered on the four-level Likert scale (Fully agree, Rather agree, Rather disagree, Fully disagree).

Each respondent provided their individual feedback on two courses taught in an online distance manner. First, respondents described a course the learning in which they appreciated, liked, enjoyed, and considered efficient. Second, they depicted a course which caused discomfort in learning, i.e. which was conducted in a way that did not suit them, and which did not bring the expected learning outcomes. In other words, they provided positive and negative feedback on online distance instruction through the evaluation of learning in the two courses. The courses receiving a positive feedback are called courses A, the courses having a negative feedback are called courses B further on. The feedback on courses is not compared; it serves as a basis for defining didactic recommendations.

3.4 Research Sample

Totally, we collected data from 272 respondents. They provided their opinions on 64 online distance courses taught by 72 teachers. Students attended three institutions: upper secondary school for medical staff (N = 131), advanced studies for higher medical staff

(N = 69), and the University of Ostrava, Faculty of Education, Department of Information Technologies and English Language and Literature (N = 72). Upper secondary students formed the sample group of secondary students; students of advanced studies and university students were included in the sample of higher education (HE). More respondents were of female gender (F = 178; M = 94). The institutions were intentionally selected from the following reasons: (1) They were authors' home institutions so that the conditions for conducting online distance courses were firmly set. Moreover, the authors also participated in teacher training in online distance instruction and continuous consultations as mentioned above. (2) All researched courses included both theory and practice (in hospitals, laboratories, schools), however, only theoretical courses taught in the online distance manner were under the focus of research. (3) The preparation of medical staff, higher medical staff, prospective teachers of Informatics and English language belongs to the profile fields of graduation exams which have been under the focus of the Czech system of education since 2008 [15]. The structure of the research sample is displayed in Table 1.

Table 1. Research sample: structure.

Institution	Male	Female	Total
Upper secondary school	22	109	131
HE: Advanced studies	30	39	69
HE: University	42	30	72
Total	94	178	272

4 Results

Collected data were compared, presented in figures, and described. They follow criteria 1–4 described above.

4.1 The First Contact and Communication

Contacts between teachers and students were monitored from four views: (1) when students in the described course were contacted by their teachers for the first time, (2) which tool was used for the first and further teacher-student contact, (3) whether the contacts were regular or not, (4) how frequent the contacts were. In this section, contacts initiated by teachers are included only. Those started by students are described within the learning content acquisition. Results are displayed below (see Fig. 1).

For the first teacher-student contact, a period of four weeks from the beginning of the semester was detected. The data show that early contact (i.e. within the first two weeks of the semester) was frequently monitored in courses A. In courses B, nearly one third of the first contacts appeared in weeks 1 and 2. However, later contacts (in weeks 3 or 4) were detected in courses B only. The first contacts initiated by students, not by teachers, in weeks 1 or 2 were also made both in courses A and B.

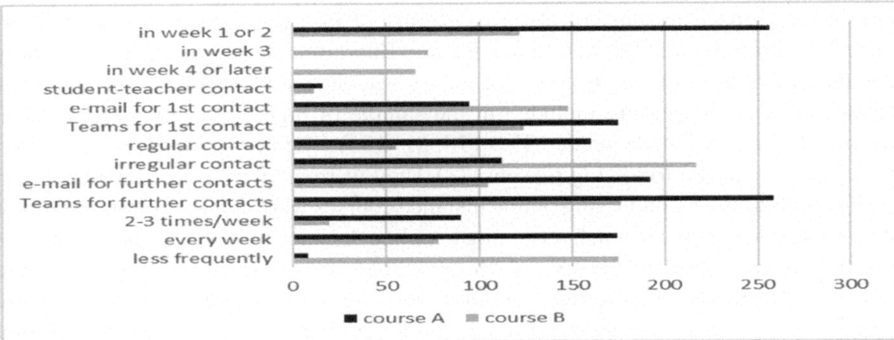

Fig. 1. The first contact and communication: the first contact, tool, regularity, frequency.

Then, the tools exploited for the first contact were monitored. From the choice of eleven tools (*e-mail, Skype, MS Teams, Zoom, Hangouts, Facebook, Instagram, Twitter, Another social network, online course, e.g. in LMS Moodle, Others*) only two of them were exploited (e-mail, MS Teams). These tools are used repeatedly in various other steps in online distance instruction. The reason is that both are easily available and widely used by students in private communication. Moreover, the use of MS Teams was recommended by the xxx Ministry of Education for online distance instruction. Data show that e-mail contact was more frequently exploited in courses B, whereas MS Teams was more used in courses A. This fact suggests the e-mail service was chosen by those teachers who were not so good (despite all teachers were trained) at using MS Teams whereas the others who were capable in using it, contacted their students via MS Teams.

Then, the regularity/irregularity of further contacts during the semester was considered. It is clearly visible that regular contacts are in favour of courses A; in courses B twice more irregular contacts were monitored compared to courses A.

E-mail and MS Teams were the tools used for contacting students during the semester; both were exploited more frequently in courses A.

Frequency of contacts was considered on a five-level scale (*Every day, Every other day, 2–3 times per week, Every week, Less frequently*). Choices *Every day* and *Every other day* were not selected by any respondent. Choices *2–3 times per week, Every week* were frequently detected as they refer to the frequency of courses – at upper secondary school, lessons are mostly taught 2–3 times per week (45 min each), in higher education institutions the frequency of courses mostly is once per week (90 min each). However, the choice *Less frequently* was detected very often in courses B, it was rather identical with *Every week* in courses A. In rare cases, Zoom and Facebook were used by teachers for contacting students.

4.2 Learning Content Acquisition

The online distance process of acquiring new knowledge is reflected through twenty choices; through data processing, some of them were joined, and finally, seventeen criteria were exploited for evaluation of the online distance process of instruction from the view of acquiring new knowledge. First, promoting *motivation* and providing support (both didactic and technical) on *how to study online* from teachers to students was under focus. As expected, in courses A students were aware that the teachers motivated them to start learning online, continued with motivating them through other lessons, and were helpful with solving technical problems (if the teachers themselves were able to do so). In courses B teachers' motivation of students towards online distance learning was weak. In both courses A and B students received some (not much) information how to study in the online distance manner. However, this is the crucial step in conducting online distance instruction successfully, so it was expected to appear much more frequently, at least in courses A.

Other four criteria focused on *oral communication* and *discussion* over the learning content in MS Teams, mainly *asking and answering questions* when explaining mistakes made in exercises and online tests etc. These online distance activities were similar to the maximum extent to those conducted in face-to-face lessons. Of course, all of them were much more frequently detected in courses A. In some cases, the communication was initiated by students (*S-T communication*).

Further on, the types of study materials (SM) were monitored, particularly *texts* and links (URLs) to them, *presentations* (most of them prepared by teachers), *video-recordings* (a few of them recorded by teachers), and *other sources*. In all criteria, the occurrence was multiple higher in courses A, as expected.

The process of practicing, fixing, and assessment of newly acquired knowledge was monitored through four criteria: *Exercises, Online tests with feedback* (i.e. with automatic feedback stating correct, or incorrect answer), *Online tests with feedback+* (i.e. with automatic feedback stating correct, or incorrect answer, and a written explanation why the answer is incorrect and where the topic is available in the study materials – showing the page, or link to the page, so that it could be studies again). Despite a certain part of teacher training in working with MS Teams was devoted to skills how to create or upload exercises and online tests, these tools were rather frequently exploited in courses A; a very low occurrence was detected in courses B. Results are displayed below (see Fig. 2).

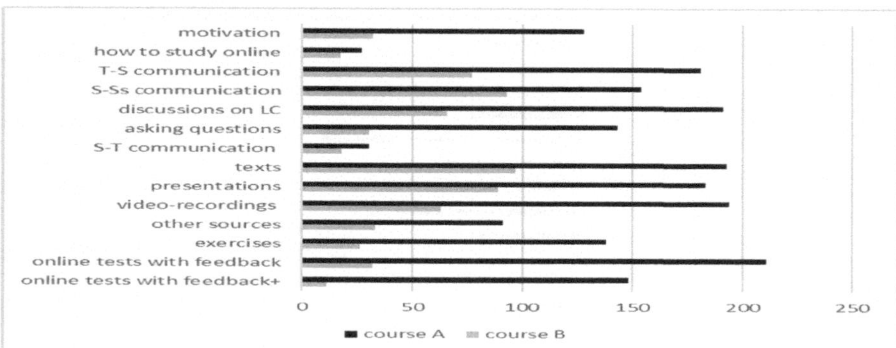

Fig. 2. Learning content acquisition. (T: teacher; S: student)

4.3 Learning Content Delivery

Identically to the process of acquisition, there were eleven tools for monitoring the delivery of study materials, exercises, and online tests (*e-mail, Skype, MS Teams, Zoom, Hangouts, Facebook, Instagram, Twitter, Another social network, online course, e.g. in LMS Moodle, Others*). As in previous cases, e-mail, MS Teams, and in a few cases LMS Moodle were used from all the tools. Occurrence was always higher in courses A, except some exercises and online tests which were delivered via e-mail. Similarly to the above presented results, MS Teams was most frequently exploited for the delivery of study materials (SM), exercises and online tests (OT) in both courses A and B. However, in courses A the frequency was higher in study materials, exercises, and online tests. A few occurrences were detected in using e-mail services for delivering study materials in both courses, hardly any use was detected for delivery of exercises and online tests in course A. The LMS Moodle was used for the delivery of study materials, but not for exercises and online tests.

For delivering exercises for practising and online tests for assessment of the newly acquired knowledge, MS Teams was exploited in most courses A and B.

Regarding the final exam, nearly half of teachers proclaimed at the beginning of courses A the graduation from the course in the form of oral online distance exam, and they really hold the exams at the end. In courses B, about 12 per cent of teachers announced the exam and they held it.

Moreover, other tools were exploited for the evaluation of students' progress at the end of semester: Student's progress, Further learning development, Other activities. The last criterion means that mere online tests were used for graduation from the course only. This is questionable whether it is sufficient for meeting the didactic requirements expressed in the principles stated above. As in other criteria, higher occurrence was detected in courses A, particularly steps for further development were proposed to students, while student's progress in learning was not defined so often. Results are displayed below (see Fig. 3).

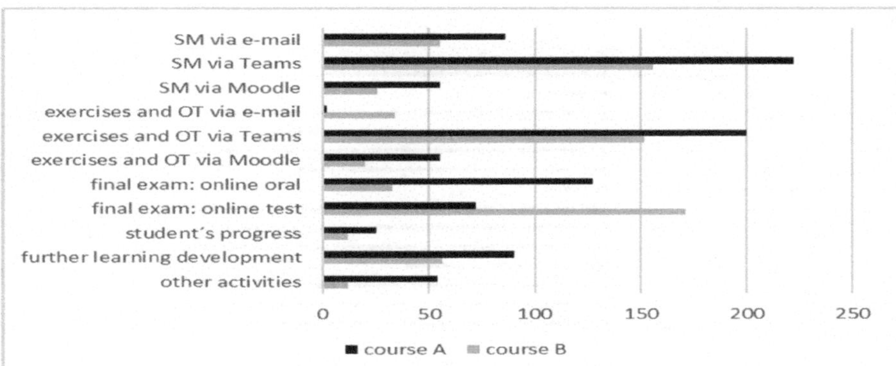

Fig. 3. Learning content delivery: study materials, exercises, final exam. (SM: study materials; OT: online tests)

4.4 Students' Final Feedback on Online Distance Instruction

For the final consideration of online distance instruction, students provided their feedback on four statements: *(1) Teacher invested much effort in online distance teaching, (2) Student invested much effort in online distance learning, (3) I appreciate online distance learning, (4) I did not learn much through online distance learning.* They expressed themselves on four-level Likert scale (from Fully agree to Fully disagree). Results are displayed below (see Fig. 4).

In statement 1, high amounts of students in courses A expressed full agreement with the statement on teachers' effort invested in online distance teaching. Contrary to this, most students in courses B rather or fully disagreed with this statement, and logically, only a few of them expressed their agreement.

In statement 2, students appreciated their own effort devoted to online distance learning. As expected, more of them were from courses A; however, a few students honestly confessed they did not study much. And, even two thirds of students declared their effort when studying in courses B.

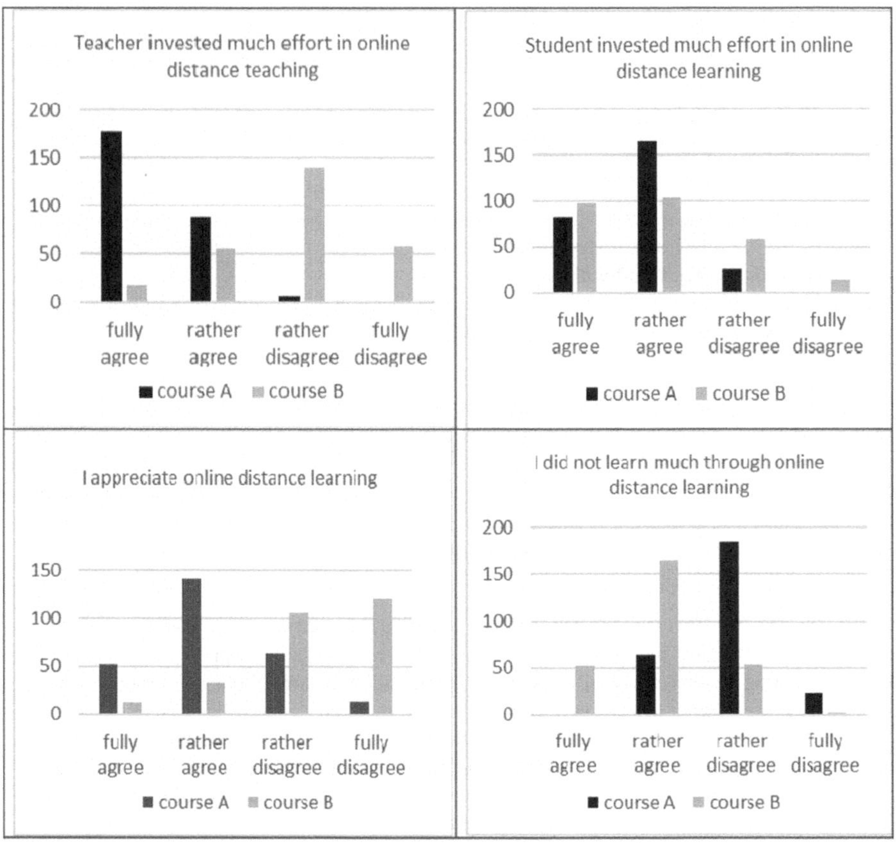

Fig. 4. Students' final feedback on online distance instruction.

In statement 3, the data clearly showed that two thirds of students in courses A appreciated online distance learning, whereas nearly the same amount did not in courses B. However, some students in courses A did not like online distance learning either.

In statement 4, most students in courses A expressed their disagreement on how much they learned, contrary to those stating their full or partial agreement in courses B.

5 Conclusions

5.1 Summary of Results and Didactic Recommendations

Research findings are summarized according to four criteria. Main differences between courses A and courses B are displayed in Table 2.

Table 2. Courses A and courses B: characteristic features and differences.

Criteria - Characteristic features
Ad 1) First contact and communication
Courses A: Early contact (weeks 1 + 2), mostly via MS Teams, regular contacts, every week or lesson, MS Teams for further contacts *Courses B:* Later contact (weeks 3 + 4), mostly via e-mail, however, MS Teams were also rather widely exploited, irregular, less than weekly further contacts
Ad 2) Learning content acquisition
Courses A: Motivation, support on how to study online, T-S, S-Ss, S-T communication, discussion, asking questions, texts, presentations, video-recordings, other sources, exercises, online tests with feedback and with feedback+ *Courses B:* half occurrence in S-Ss and S-T communication and using texts and presentations, much lower exploitation of exercises and both types of online tests
Ad 3) Learning content delivery
Courses A: Study materials via MS Teams and e-mail, exceptionally via LMS Moodle, exercises and online tests via MS Teams, exceptionally via LMS Moodle, final exams in an oral online distance manner, student's progress summarized and further development proposed *Courses B:* Study materials via e-mail, exercises and online tests via MS Teams and e-mail, hardly any final exams in an oral online distance manner but frequent exploitation of online testing only, student's further development proposed in a few courses
Ad 4) Students' final feedback
Courses A: Teachers investigated much effort in online distance teaching; students rather investigated much effort in online distance learning; students (rather) appreciated online distance learning (however, one fifth did not); most students learned much through online distance learning (with a few exceptions) *Courses B:* Teachers (rather) did not investigate much effort in online distance teaching; students (rather) did not investigate much effort in online distance learning; most students (fully, or rather) did not appreciate online distance learning; most students did not learn much through online distance learning (with a few exceptions)

Reflecting the above presented findings, we suggest the following rules to be kept in conducting online distance instruction:

- Teachers should start contact with students as early as possible at the beginning of the semester so that time for learning was not wasted.
- Teacher-student contacts should be on a regular basis so that students know what is in front of them to make individual schedules for learning. If they share computers, notebooks with siblings, this helps them plan their activities.
- Teacher-student contacts should be frequent enough, ideally following the frequency of lessons per week.
- For enhancing and keeping students' motivation during the whole online distance process of instruction, permanent technical support, e.g. from a school administrator, is required.
- Various types of study materials are welcome – students may select those types which meet their learning preferences.
- Online tests with feedback+ are highly recommended, i.e. those not only detecting in/correct answers but making explanations why the answer is not correct and providing a link to sources where the learning content can be learned again.
- Teachers should exploit minimum ways to conduct the online distance instruction, e.g. a platform or LMS (MS Teams in this case, but others also offer similar services – Zoom, Moodle, Blackboard etc. Incessant searching makes students tired and demotivated before they start learning.
- Students' knowledge should be assessed in the same manner as in face-to-face instruction, even though we are aware that conducting e.g. oral online distance exams with numerous students is demanding and time consuming.
- Students should be aware that learning is a demanding activity even if conducted in a face-to-face manner. In the online distance manner, much more effort is required both from them and from their teachers. Online distance learning requires autonomy from them as minimum. Whether they learn much or not is in their hands to a large extent. If online distance instruction is a long-time process, the role of teachers' motivation to students is crucial. The question is who motivates the teachers – therefore, strong support is expected from school management, Ministry of Education, and local authorities to them. Teachers will definitely appreciate any support.
- Finally, teacher preparation in using technology and exploiting it for educational purposes is the first precondition if we expect the process of online distance instruction is successful.

5.2 Limits and Further Research Activities

Results of this research are limited mainly by the sample. First, it is not gender-balanced (more female respondents participated); second, data were collected from students of several selected study programmes. Despite the sample being formed intentionally in the way explained above, it opens doors to other researches.

Since 2019, numerous researches have been made in the field of online distance instruction, e.g. on the rise, on the efficiency, challenges. Various methods, platforms, tools were recommended, students' and teachers' perception was monitored, several conferences were held, fully or partially dealing with the problems, and providing didactic, technical, and technological recommendations (to get a long list of articles, use combinations of key words covid-19 pandemic, online distance instruction/education, research).

Thus, we can see that there is a wide range of problems which deserve the attention of researchers. For further researches, we would propose to focus on how students of various learning styles or motivation types cope with online distance learning, whether/how learners with special educational needs can be educated in this manner, and many others. To answer the question asked at the beginning – re-defining of learning is not the question of the day. Identical principles and rules should be implemented in the process of instruction (see Comenius' principles and rules [6, 7]), regardless it is conducted face-to-face or in an online distance manner. Moreover, other authors or models adapted the principles for the conditions of the computer age (see Mishra [14], SAMR model [16], as Cerna [17] mentions). However, strong changes must be made in re-thinking of online distance instruction, both in students' and teachers' perception of the process. Technologies are here to serve, both for private and educational purposes.

Acknowledgement. The paper is supported by SGS02/PdF/2021 project Online distance education. Optimization reflecting students' and teachers' experience.

References

1. Simonova, I., Prochazkova, Z., Lorenc, V.: Smart and/or mobile: an investigation within Czech University students. In: Raj, J.S. (ed.) ICMCSI 2020. EICC, pp. 361–372. Springer, Cham (2021). https://doi.org/10.1007/978-3-030-49795-8_35
2. Crawford-Ferre, H.G., Wiest, L.R.: Effective online instruction in higher education. Q. Rev. Distance Learn. **13**(1), 11–14 (2012)
3. Peng, H., Ma, S., Spector, J.M.: Personalized adaptive learning: an emerging pedagogical approach enabled by a smart learning environment. Smart Learn. Environ. **6**(1), 1–14 (2019). https://doi.org/10.1186/s40561-019-0089-y
4. Simonova, I., Prochazkova, Z., Lorenc, V., Skoda, J.: Smart approach to ESP instruction. In: Cheung, S.K.S., Li, R., Phusavat, K., Paoprasert, N., Kwok, L. (eds.) ICBL 2020. LNCS, vol. 12218, pp. 163–174. Springer, Cham (2020). https://doi.org/10.1007/978-3-030-51968-1_14
5. Faltynkova, L., Simonova, I., Kostolanyova, K.: Perspectives on distance education in secondary and tertiary education. In: Busch, C., Steinicke, M., Wendler, T. (eds.) Proceedings of the 19th European Conference on e-Learning, ECEL 2020, pp. 556–562. Academic Conferences & Publishing International (2020)
6. Comenius, J.A.: Didaktika velka [The Great Didactics], 3rd edn. Komenium, Brno (1948)
7. Comenius, J.A.: Selections From His Works. SPN, Praha (1964)
8. Herring, M., Koehler, M.J., Mishra, P.: Handbook of Technological Pedagogical Content Knowledge, 2nd edn. Routledge (2016)
9. Thompson, A.D., Mishra, P.: Breaking news: TPCK becomes TPACK! J. Comput. Teach. Educ. **24**(2), 38–64 (2007)
10. Gagne, R.: The Conditions of Learning, 4th edn. Holt, Rinehart & Winston, New York (1985)
11. Gagne, R., Briggs, L., Wager, W.: Principles of Instructional Design, 4th edn. HBJ College Publishers, Fort Worth (1992)

12. Act N. 349/2020 Coll. Accessed 26 Feb 2021
13. Ministry of Education: Principy a zásady úspěšného vzdělávání na dálku_podrobný materiál_A3.pdf, MŠMT ČR (msmt.cz) [Principles and rules of successful distance education]. Accessed 26 Feb 2021
14. Punya Mishra's Web: Living at the junction of education, creativity, technology & design, 13 April 2020. Accessed 22 Feb 2021
15. Act N. 242/2008 Coll., pp. 78–79 [Zákon, kterým se mění zákon č. 561/2004 Sb., o předškolním, základním, středním, vyšším odborném a j... (zakonyprolidi.cz)]. Accessed 24 Feb 2021
16. Puentedura, R.: SAMR model. SAMR Model - Technology Is Learning. google.com. Accessed 28 Feb 2021
17. Černá, M.: Johann Amos Comenius and his legacy at the information age. In: Cheung, S.K.S., Lee, L.-K., Simonova, I., Kozel, T., Kwok, L.-F. (eds.) ICBL 2019. LNCS, vol. 11546, pp. 46–56. Springer, Cham (2019). https://doi.org/10.1007/978-3-030-21562-0_4

Technological Barriers and Learning Outcomes in Online Courses During the Covid-19 Pandemic

Xiangyang He[1](✉) and Harrison Hao Yang[2]

[1] Hunan First Normal University, Changsha 410205, Hunan, China
sunhexy@163.com
[2] State University of New York at Oswego, Oswego 13126, USA

Abstract. Covid-19 pandemic has triggered the popularity of online instruction, a large-scale college students have been forced to convert in-person learning to online instruction at the first time. In this study, 226 students were selected to find out what are beginners' perceptions of online learning outcomes and technological barriers, and what are the technological barriers affecting online learning outcomes. The results showed that the beginners had positive attitude on the outcomes of online learning. Belief was the main second-order barrier of online instruction. Training was the main first-order barrier, and access and vision had impact on part of online learning outcomes.

Keywords: Technological barriers · First-order barriers · Second-order barriers · Learning outcomes

1 Introduction

Technologies have been used in schools since the end of 20th century [1]. Technology can enhance students' learning [2], motivation, attitude, engagement, and self-confidence [3]. Students who learned in a digital environment can performed better when given a complex, computer-based learning task [4]. Online learning, which is derived from distance education, is an important method of technology integration with a long history, but its application in colleges is always limited. Even in the very period of MOOC blooming, most universities carry out online learning within a limited scope. However, a large-scale college students have been forced to convert in-person learning to online instruction due to the COVID-19 pandemic. While so many courses have been moved from traditional in-person instruction to online learning, and most students haven't taken any online course before, two questions have been widely raised: 1) what are the main challenges faced by students taking online course for the first time, and 2) how effective are online classes?

R. Li et al. (Eds.): ICBL 2021, LNCS 12830, pp. 92–102, 2021.
https://doi.org/10.1007/978-3-030-80504-3_8

Therefore, the presented study aims to investigate technical barriers and learning outcomes among college students who were taking online for the first time (beginners). The specific research questions driving this study are:

RQ1. What are beginners' perceptions of online learning outcomes and technological barriers?
RQ2. What are the technological barriers affecting online learning outcomes?

2 Related Work

2.1 Barriers to Technology Integration

Previous research identifies the possible problems of technology integration as first- and second-order technological barriers [5–7]. First-order barriers are extrinsic to participants—problems such as lack of access to computers and software, insufficient time to plan and development, and inadequate training and support [7–10]. Second-order barriers are intrinsic to participants and include the lack of vision and belief in technology integration into teaching and learning, and unwillingness to change [6, 11–13].

Either order of barrier alone can halt students' efforts and learning outcomes. First-order barriers can affect the realization of personal belief, and second-order barriers may impede the meaningful use [7, 12, 14–17]. First-order barriers can prevent the technology integration, but second-order barriers may exacerbate or ameliorate their effects to some degree [7, 18, 19].

2.2 Learning Outcomes

The easiest way to measure the outcomes of the instruction is the score in the test such as GPA [20, 21]. However, the test results cannot fully reflect the learning outcomes. Previous research suggests that some else aspect always used to measure the result of the learning such as satisfaction, perceived progress [22–24], engagement [23], and high-order thinking [25], Perceived progress [26] are related to the perception of learning progress of the course objectives and subject matter. Satisfaction [24] are about the objective perception of the class contribution. Engagement [27] focus on motivation and engagement of the class. High-order thinking [28] focus on the thinking ability such as synthesis, critically analyze, self-confident, communication, evaluate other's view.

2.3 Research Model

Based on the literature list before, we propose that first-order technological barriers (access, support, time, training) and second-order technological barriers (vision, belief) will influence learning outcomes (perceived progress, satisfaction, engagement, high-order thinking), as shown in Fig. 1.

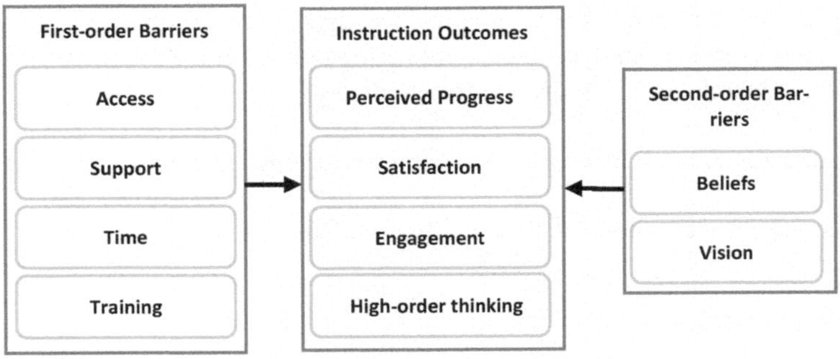

Fig. 1. Theoretical framework and research model.

3 Methodology

3.1 Participants

297 Chinese students from a university in central and southern region participated in this study, who were the beginners taking online courses during the Covid-19 pandemic. Participations in this study were voluntary. 71 students failed to pass the questionnaire's consistency test. As a result, 226 students were finally selected as the participants. Table 1 shows the number and gender of the participants.

Table 1. Number and demographics of participants.

Gender	N	%
Male	34	15
Female	192	85

3.2 Instrumentation

The survey of this study contains three parts: learning outcomes, technological barriers, and demographic information. All items were evaluated based on a five-point Likert scale from one (strongly disagree) to five (strongly agree). The survey used to assess beginners' perceptions of online courses contains two main sections: learning outcomes and technological barriers. In total, 45-items were based on and adopted from previous research.

The section of learning outcomes included: perceived progress (4 items) [25], satisfaction (5 items) [24], Engagement (3 items) [27], and high-order thinking (6 items) [28].

The section of technological barriers contained the first order and second order technological barriers. The first-order technological barriers of the online learning included: access (4 items) [14], time (5 items) [14], support (5 items) [14], and training (3 items) [12]. The second-order technological barriers of the online learning included: vision (3 items) [12] and belief (3 items) [12].

In addition, a participant inventory form was designed to collect demographic information, including gender, grade, experience of online learning before and during Covid-19 pandemic.

3.3 Data Collection and Analysis Procedure

All the items were parallel translated [30] by 3 researchers, and the translated questionnaires received bilingual assessment [31] from two experts who specialized in instructional technology and language. Both expert had more than 10 years of experience in the field. Feedback was collected to adjust the wording to make the questionnaires more readable.

After permission was granted to conduct the research, the questionnaires were put on the website, the link of the survey were sent individually to the students to fill in the survey. Participation in the survey was voluntary and anonymous, and 5 to 10 min are needed to complete the survey. The survey begun at 20th Dec, 2020, and lasted for one week. When finished, all responses were put into SPSS22 for statistical analysis.

4 Results and Analysis

4.1 Reliability and Validity of the Instruments

As shown in Table 2 and Table 3, the instrument was confirmed by reliability, and discriminant validity. The results of the analysis indicated that the composite reliability coefficients were all above 0.67 [32], Cronbach's alpha values were all above 0.74 [33], the AVE values were all above 0.63, which was acceptable [34]. Results showed the acceptance and reliability of the survey results (Table 2, 3 and 4).

Table 2. The factors on the learning outcomes.

Factor	Item	Factor loading				Cronbach's alpha	AVE
		1	2	3	4		
Perceived progress	1	0.895				0.872	0.724
	2	0.876					
	3	0.847					
	4	0.781					
Satisfaction	1		0.875			0.911	0.739
	2		0.878				
	3		0.892				
	4		0.802				
	5		0.848				

(*continued*)

Table 2. (*continued*)

Factor	Item	Factor loading				Cronbach's alpha	AVE
		1	2	3	4		
Engagement	1			0.860		0.824	0.738
	2			0.835			
	3			0.882			
High-order thinking	1				0.878	0.933	0.749
	2				0.876		
	3				0.859		
	4				0.838		
	5				0.849		
	6				0.891		

Table 3. The factors on the technological barriers.

Factor	Item	Factor loading						Cronbach's alpha	AVE
		1	2	3	4	5	6		
Access	1	0.798						0.817	0.652
	2	0.870							
	3	0.866							
	4	0.679							
Time	1		0.868					0.909	0.732
	2		0.865						
	3		0.856						
	4		0.864						
	5		0.825						
Support	1			0.715				0.856	0.630
	2			0.819					
	3			0.803					
	4			0.845					
	5			0.781					
Training	1				0.867			0.828	0.742
	2				0.844				
	3				0.873				

(*continued*)

Table 3. (*continued*)

Factor	Item	Factor loading						Cronbach's alpha	AVE
		1	2	3	4	5	6		
Vision	1					0.844		0.824	0.736
	2					0.830			
	3					0.899			
Belief	1						0.754	0.748	0.668
	2						0.813		
	3						0.880		

Table 4. Analysis of discriminant validity.

	Perceived progress	Satisfaction	Engagement	High-order thinking	Access	Time	Support	Training	Vision	Beliefs
Perceived progress	0.851									
Satisfaction	0.753	0.860								
Engagement	0.731	0.804	0.859							
High-order thinking	0.675	0.661	0.769	0.865						
Access	0.300	0.361	0.360	0.344	0.807					
Time	0.282	0.270	0.281	0.341	0.670	0.856				
Support	0.293	0.241	0.304	0.343	0.593	0.660	0.794			
Training	0.516	0.450	0.491	0.487	0.467	0.433	0.417	0.861		
Vision	0.452	0.427	0.431	0.505	0.230	0.289	0.320	0.373	0.858	
Beliefs	0.592	0.577	0.550	0.574	0.355	0.324	0.341	0.507	0.638	0.817

4.2 Statistical Description

To answer Q1, single-sample-repeated measures and single-sample T test was used to investigate the outcomes and barriers of online instruction.

The result showed that all the scores from the survey on online learning outcomes were much higher than 3 (3 means the evaluation of online learning was same to that of in-person instruction), which indicated that, students felt the learning outcomes of online learning were better than that of in-person instruction. The result also shows that there were differences between the online learning outcomes. High-order thinking was significantly higher than perceived progress and engagement, while perceived progress and engagement were significantly higher than satisfaction ($F = 22.4$, $P = 0.000 < 0.001$).

The results showed that there were significant different between the scores of first-order technological barriers. Support was significantly higher than access and time, while access and time is significantly higher than training ($F = 98.537$, $P = 0.000 < 0.001$). The scores of access, time, and support were significantly higher than 3 (3 means the evaluation of barriers was neutral), and the score of training was significantly lower than 3.

The paired-sample t test shows that there was significant difference between second-order technological barriers ($T = 6.028$, $P = 0.000 < 0.001$), the score of vision was significantly higher than the score of belief. And both of vision and beliefs scores were significantly higher than 3 (3 means the evaluation of barriers was neutral).

Table 5. The evaluation results on instruction comes.

	M	SD	T
Perceived progress	3.41	0.62	9.81**
Satisfaction	3.34	0.71	7.25**
Engagement	3.46	0.69	9.97**
High-order thinking	3.60	0.67	13.42**
Access	3.52	0.67	11.81**
Time	3.55	0.67	12.50**
Support	3.67	0.59	17.05**
Training	2.50	0.62	−12.00**
Vision	3.91	0.60	22.76**
Belief	3.69	0.61	17.03**

*$p < 0.05$. **$p < 0.01$

4.3 The Effects of Online Instruction Barriers

To answer Q2, regression analysis was used to investigate the relationship between first & second-order barriers and the instructional outcomes. As shown in Table 6, the dependent variable was online instruction outcomes, including perceived progress, satisfaction, engagement, and high-order thinking; whereas the predictors were first and second-order technological barriers, including access, time, support, training, vision, and belief.

Belief was significant and positive in predicting perceived progress, while training was significant and negative in predicting perceived progress. Together, they explain 39.5% of the variance.

Access and belief were significant and positive in predicting satisfaction, while training was significant and negative in predicting satisfaction. Together, they explain 36.5% of the variance.

Vision and belief were significant and positive in predicting engagement, while training was significant and negative in predicting engagement. Together, they explain 35.5% of the variance.

Vision and belief were significant and positive in predicting high-order thinking, while training was significant and negative in predicting high-order thinking. Together, they explain 39.5% of the variance.

Table 6. The results on linear regression

Dependent variable	Predictors	B	SE	β	t	R2
Perceived progress	Access	.016	.069	.017	.233	0.395
	Time	.001	.074	.001	.010	
	Support	−.003	.076	−.003	−.034	
	Training	−.276	.066	−.275	−4.197**	
	Vision	.125	.069	.121	1.808	
	Belief	.369	.073	.364	5.030**	
Satisfaction	Access	.214	.081	.202	2.654**	0.365
	Time	−.030	.086	−.028	−.353	
	Support	−.127	.089	−.107	−1.436	
	Training	−.182	.077	−.159	−2.372*	
	Vision	.126	.081	.106	1.559	
	Belief	.460	.086	.398	5.373**	
Engagement	Access	.154	.080	.149	1.934	0.355
	Time	−.068	.085	−.065	−.803	
	Support	.005	.087	.005	.061	
	Training	−.254	.075	−.228	−3.362**	
	Vision	.167	.079	.144	2.099*	
	Belief	.345	.084	.306	4.090**	
High-order thinking	Access	.051	.075	.050	.677	0.395
	Time	.047	.080	.046	.589	
	Support	.026	.083	.023	.314	
	Training	−.222	.071	−.204	−3.114**	
	Vision	.246	.075	.219	3.279**	
	Belief	.317	.080	.288	3.986**	

*$p < 0.05$. **$p < 0.01$

The results imply that people with higher belief are those more likely to gain higher outcomes in online learning; people with higher vision are those more likely to gain higher engagement and high-order thinking; the more one thinks training as a barrier, the less one achieves higher outcomes; the more one thinks access a barrier, the more one achieves a better satisfaction.

5 Discussion and Conclusion

The Covid-19 pandemic drove many courses to move from in-person instruction to online learning, and some students started online learning as beginners. This study investigates technological barriers and online learning outcomes of beginners who have no experience before. As we have found, little research has attempted to focus on these beginners. The results of this study provide new evidence for decision-making with both practical and theoretical contributions.

The most important findings of the survey attached to research question two are that we found that some technological barriers can predict the learning outcomes. Training and belief can predict all the outcomes, access can predict the satisfaction, and vision can predict engagement and high-order thinking. This finding aligns with previous studies, first-order barriers will make efforts only when classrooms are insufficiently equipped [19, 33, 35, 36]. Second-order barriers may also play a more important role when the schools are well equipped and technology is under-use [7]. The R square value is above 0.35, which means the factors we discussed in the survey might explain most changes of online learning outcomes.

The first research questions deal with students' perceptions of online learning outcomes and technological barriers. Students give a high score on online learning outcomes, but regard access, time and support as the barriers in online instruction, and have a good vision and belief of online learning. All the perceived progress, satisfaction, engagement, and high-order thinking gains a more positive evaluation on online learning than in-person instruction. It may because online learning is more flexible and student-centered than traditional in-person instruction, and students have a strong sense of interaction and participation in learning activities. Especially, due to the COVID-10 quarantine, face-to-face communication and in-person meetings have been greatly restricted.

Covid-19 pandemic is an opportunity for the development of online instruction. Online instruction is likely to become a new fashion in the post-epidemic era. Therefore, it is time to focus on how to effectively improve the outcomes of online education by changing the research focus from behavioral intention to outcomes. According to the survey results, the key factors to improve the effectiveness of online teaching focus on relevant factors such as training, vision, and belief. How to apply the training, providing teachers with a strong vision and higher value belief to use technology to support content objectives, and apply student-centered learning, will be a key issue that educators must pay attention to.

The factors that influence online learning outcomes may come from a wide variety of perspectives, but we cannot completely capture all the dynamics. Some other potential factors (e.g., teachers' capacity) may be important and have yet to be analyzed. Cultural differences [37], educational levels, and ICT uses are not included here either. These factors may be considered in our future research.

To conclude, this study identified that belief, training and vision were the most important factors influencing beginners' online learning outcomes in China. Researchers and practitioners should consider the critical influence that first-order and second-order technological barriers, which contribute towards students' online learning outcomes.

Acknowledgements. The work was supported by the National Natural Science Foundation of China (61877017).

References

1. Education Development Center: National study tour of district technology integration summary report (CCT reports, no. 14). Center for Children and Technology, New York (1996)
2. Ottenbreit-Leftwich, A.T., Glazewski, K.D., Newby, T.J., Ertmer, P.A.: Teacher value beliefs associated with using technology: addressing professional and student needs. Comput. Educ. **55**(3), 1321–1335 (2010)
3. Warschauer, M.: Laptops and Literacy: Learning in the Wireless Classroom. Teachers College Press, New York (2006)
4. Spektor-Levy, O., Granot-Gilat, Y.: The impact of learning with laptops in 1:1 classes on the development of learning skills and information literacy among middle school students. Interdisc. J. E-Learn. Learn. Objects **8**(1), 83–96 (2012)
5. Ertmer, P.A.: Addressing first- and second-order barriers to change: strategies for technology integration. Educ. Technol. Res. Dev. **47**(4), 47–61 (1999). https://doi.org/10.1007/BF02299597
6. Ertmer, P.A., Ottenbreit-Leftwich, A.T.: Teacher technology change: how knowledge, confidence, beliefs, and culture intersect. J. Res. Technol. Educ. **42**(3), 255–284 (2010)
7. Ertmer, P.A., Ottenbreit-Leftwich, A.T., Sadik, O., Sendurur, E., Sendurur, P.: Teacher beliefs and technology integration practices: a critical relationship. CAE Comput. Educ. **59**(2), 423–435 (2012)
8. Ryan, T., Bagley, G.: Nurturing the integration of technology in education. J. Theory Pract. Educ. **11**(1), 33–50 (2015)
9. Hsu, S., Kuan, P.Y.: The impact of multilevel factors on technology integration: the case of taiwanese grade 1–9 teachers and schools. Educ. Technol. Res. Dev. **61**(1), 25–50 (2013). https://doi.org/10.1007/s11423-012-9269-y
10. Lim, C.P., Khine, M.: Managing teachers' barriers to ICT integration in Singapore schools. J. Technol. Teach. Educ. **14**(1), 97–125 (2006)
11. Hew, K., Brush, T.: Integrating technology into K-12 teaching and learning: current knowledge gaps and recommendations for future research. Educ. Technol. Res. Dev. **55**(3), 223–252 (2007). https://doi.org/10.1007/s11423-006-9022-5
12. Kopcha, T.J.: Teachers' perceptions of the barriers to technology integration and practices with technology under situated professional development. Comput. Educ. **59**(4), 1109–1121 (2012)
13. Ertmer, P.A.: Teacher pedagogical beliefs: the final frontier in our quest for technology integration? Educ. Technol. Res. **53**(4), 25–39 (2005). https://doi.org/10.1007/BF02504683
14. Hechter, R.P., Vermette, L.A.: Technology integration in K-12 science classrooms: an analysis of barriers and implications. Themes Sci. Technol. Educ. **6**(2), 73–90 (2013)
15. Yu, C.: The integration of technology in the 21st century classroom: teachers' attitudes and pedagogical beliefs toward emerging technologies. J. Technol. Integr. Classroom **5**(1), 5–11 (2013)
16. Xie, K., Kim, M.K., Cheng, S.L., Luthy, N.C.: Digital content evaluation as technology professional development. Educ. Technol. Res. Dev. **65**(4), 1067–1103 (2017)
17. Kim, M.K., Cheng, S.L., Xie, K.: The validation of a systemic evaluation framework to investigate the multi-layered impacts of technology integration projects. Paper Presented the Annual Meeting of the American Educational Research Association, San Antonio, TX (2017)
18. Ertmer, P.A., Addison, P., Lane, M., Ross, E., Woods, D.: Examining teachers' beliefs about the role of technology in the elementary classroom. J. Res. Comput. Educ. **32**(1), 54–72 (1999)
19. Miller, L., Olson, J.: Putting the computer in its place: a study of teaching with technology. J. Curric. Stud. **26**, 121–141 (1994)

20. Zhoc, K.C.H., King, R.B., Chung, T.S.H., Chen, J.: Emotionally intelligent students are more engaged and successful: examining the role of emotional intelligence in higher education. Eur. J. Psychol. Educ. **35**(4), 839–863 (2020). https://doi.org/10.1007/s10212-019-00458-0
21. Hsiao, C.C., Huang, J.C.H., Huang, A.Y.Q., Lu, O.H.T., Yin, C.J., Yang, S.J.H.: Exploring the effects of online learning behaviors on short-term and long-term learning outcomes in flipped classrooms. Interact. Learn. Environ. **27**(8), 1160–1177 (2019)
22. Lin, C.H., Zheng, B., Zhang, Y.: Interactions and learning outcomes in online language courses. Br. J. Edu. Technol. **48**(3), 730–748 (2017)
23. Chen, K.C., Jang, S.J., Branch, R.M.: Autonomy, affiliation, and ability: relative salience of factors that influence online learner motivation and learning outcomes. Knowl. Manag. E-Learn. Int. J. **2**(1), 30–50 (2010)
24. Kuo, Y.-C., Walker, A.E., Schroder, K.E.E., Belland, B.R.: Interaction, Internet self-efficacy, and self-regulated learning as predictors of student satisfaction in online education courses. Internet High. Educ. **20**, 35–50 (2014)
25. Lim, D.H., Morris, M.L., Yoon, S.-W.: Instructional and learner factors influencing learning outcomes within online learning environment (2006). Online Submission
26. Lim, D.H., Morris, M.L., Kupritz, V.W.: Online vs. blended learning: differences in instructional outcomes and learner satisfaction. J. Asynchronous Learn. Netw. **11**(2), 27–42 (2007)
27. Oliver, B., Tucker, B., Gupta, R., Yeo, S.: eVALUate: an evaluation instrument for measuring students' perceptions of their engagement and learning outcomes. Assess. Eval. High. Educ. **33**(6), 619–630 (2008)
28. Alavi, M.: Computer-mediated collaborative learning: an empirical evaluation. MIS Q. **18**, 159–174 (1994)
29. Guillemin, F., Bombardier, C., Beaton, D.: Cross-cultural adaptation of health-related quality of life measures: literature review and proposed guidelines. J. Clin. Epidemiol. **46**(12), 1417–1432 (1993)
30. Harkness, J.A., Schoua-Glusberg, A.: Questionnaires in translation. In: Harkness, J.A. (ed.) Cross-Cultural Survey Equivalence, pp. 87–126. Wiley-Interscience, Mannheim (1998)
31. Nunnally, J.C., Bernstein, I.H.: Psychometric Theory. McGraw-Hill, New York (1994)
32. Helmstadter, G.C.: Principles of Psychological Measurement. Appleton-Century-Crofts, New York (1964)
33. Segars, A.H.: Assessing the unidimensionality of measurement: a paradigm and illustration within the context of information systems research. Omega Int. J. Manag. Sci. **25**(1), 107–121 (1997)
34. Framework for 21st Century Learning. http://static.battelleforkids.org/documents/p21/P21_Framework_Brief.pdf. Accessed 30 Sept 2019
35. Hannafin, R.D., Savenye, W.C.: Technology in the classroom: the teachers new role and resistance to it. Educ. Technol. **33**(6), 26–31 (1993)
36. Office of Technology Assessment: Teachers and technology: Making the connection. U.S. Government Printing Office, Washington, DC (1995)
37. MacLeod, J., Yang, H.H., Xiang, Z.: Understanding college students' intrinsic motivation and social interdependence in intercultural computer-supported collaborative learning between USA and China. Asia Pac. Educ. Res. **26**(3), 205–217 (2017). https://doi.org/10.1007/s40299-017-0341-6

A Study on the Application of AI Experiential Learning in the Architecture and Design Courses of a Taiwan University

Shao-Fu Li[1], Kwan-Keung Ng[1](✉), and Lap-Kei Lee[2]

[1] Chung Hua University, No. 707, Section 2, Wufu Road, Xiangshan District, Hsinchu, Taiwan, China
shaofu@chu.edu.tw

[2] School of Science and Technology, The Open University of Hong Kong, Ho Man Tin, Kowloon, Hong Kong, China
lklee@ouhk.edu.hk

Abstract. With the advent of the new digital era, artificial intelligence (AI) has been developing rapidly in recent years and has become a new phenomenon in the industry and academia. A university in Taiwan's Hsinchu City educates students' AI technological knowledge and enhances their AI capabilities by establishing the first "AI+ Experience Centre" in Taiwan's academia and combining AI with her five colleges' professional fields. Undoubtedly teachers will be happy to use AI as their new teaching platform if AI may improve communication and interaction with students. Students who study design will focus on computer-aid design technology; those who study hotel management will use conversational AI technology to enhance their service level; and those who study business management will apply natural AI language processing to improve their language skill. The authors will share the development, implementation, and reflection details, and the findings will provide strategies for applying AI experiential learning in higher education institutions.

Keywords: Artificial Intelligence (AI) · AI learning · Experiential learning · Computer-Aided Design (CAD) course · Higher Education Institutions (HEI)

1 Introduction

Artificial Intelligence (AI) has been developing rapidly in recent years and has become a new phenomenon in the industry and academia. As all major industries urgently need AI talents to promote industrial AI, a university in Taiwan combines AI with the professional fields of her five Colleges, namely, College of Humanities and Social Sciences, College of Architecture and Design, College of Computer Science & Electrical Engineer, College of Tourism, and College of Management. Besides cultivating the AI concept in students' major studies, the University educates students' AI technological knowledge and enhances their AI capabilities by providing the most updated AI applications and insights into their related industry trends. The University expects every student to become

R. Li et al. (Eds.): ICBL 2021, LNCS 12830, pp. 103–115, 2021.
https://doi.org/10.1007/978-3-030-80504-3_9

an AI talent in the industry through the three-stage learning design of experience, i.e., experience, application, and implementation during students' studies at these five Colleges. The University also establishes the first "AI$^+$ Experience Centre" in Taiwan's academia; the Centre brings the world's latest AI applications to the campus to create contextual experiences in the five colleges, such as smart access control, smart restaurants, smart retail, and smart buildings. To provide students with a certain level of AI application ability, the University applies AI education with the major courses to create application fields and customized practical exercises in the five colleges, as shown in Fig. 1.

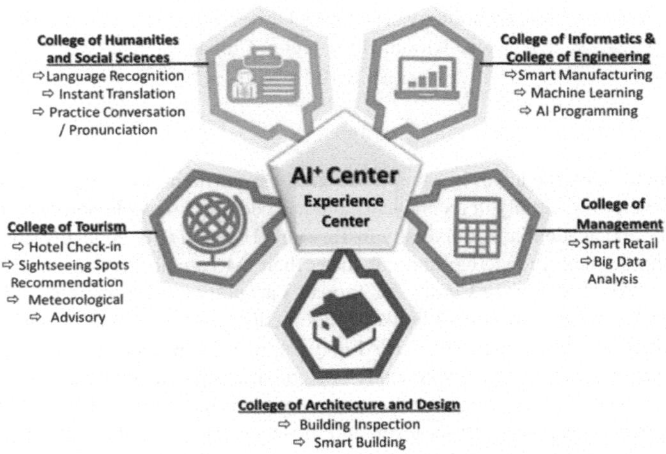

Fig. 1. Service architecture diagram of AI$^+$ Experience Centre.

With the advent of the new digital era, the software engineering talent gap reaches 27,000 vacancies in Taiwan. On average, each engineer has more than three job opportunities. They adopt a three-level curriculum design [1] to cultivate cross-field digital talents, i.e. basic-level, advanced-level, and lean-level. Thus, the University specially appointed AI technical directors from the industry to develop a 600-h "Interdisciplinary Hacker Programming Talent Training Course" to nurture practical-oriented learning to students' information technology. Besides, the University also adopts popular apps like Facebook and Uber as implementation projects to cultivate software design talents. Students, regardless of colleges and departments, can participate in the training for free.

Therefore, since the beginning of 2019, the University has vigorously invited interested academic staff of the five colleges for cognitive training, especially for those who do not have related AI or informatics background, to become the first batch of AI seed teachers. At the same time, in the form of financial subsidies, teachers are encouraged to introduce AI knowledge in their current courses to students. This paper aims to analyze the current AI-practices in a university in Hsinchu City in Taiwan through a review of architecture and design courses in the College of Architecture and Design which the focus is placed on experiential learning and interaction among the students. The authors will share the development, implementation, and reflection details; and the findings will provide strategies for applying AI experiential learning in higher education institutions.

2 The Motivation of the Study

As the first batch of seed teachers selected, one of the authors of this paper carried out the AI experiential learning in the architecture and design courses with a feeling of temptation. It is hoped that students will not resist such experimental teaching. The university requires teachers to teach at least 10 to 15 h in a semester and submit 3 homework assignments in terms of the course subsidies. In fact, the school and teachers are still exploring how to promote AI teaching and learning as of today.

Since mid-2018, the University's AI^{+} Experience Centre has opened various AI cognition courses for the Colleges, staff and students in the University, and all courses are free to participate. These seminars are an application course of AI and/or interdisciplinary technology, suitable for those who are not informatics experts or not deeply involved in the AI field but have enthusiasm in this topic for learning. The software providers in Taiwan, including Microsoft, Google, Asus, and Oracle Academy, are the partners of the AI cognition courses. Most of the courses are about applying artificial intelligence technology to different industries, which is a profound and urgent topic for experts in commerce. These courses would introduce the application status of artificial intelligence technology through practical interdisciplinary AI application examples.

The purpose of the University is to train professional programming talents and popularize teachers and students' awareness of the use of AI technology. The Ministry of Education in Taiwan often emphasizes that the process of learning is more important than the result. American educator John Dewey once said that the "learning by doing" action teaching method could effectively help students absorb richer and more profound learning due to their own learning experience [2]. The University also hopes to cultivate students' self-learning ability and to build confidence in the pursuit of ideals in life, though examinations are only a tiny part of the learning path.

According to Kolb's research [3], mastery of expertise is a continuous process of experience, reflection, conceptualization and experimentation. These elements make up the experiential learning cycle which shows the relationship between each phase. It is the process of learning through experience, and is more specifically defined as "learning through reflection on doing". Effective learning is seen when a person progresses through a cycle of four stages: (1) having a concrete experience followed by (2) observation of and reflection on that experience which leads to (3) the formation of abstract concepts (analysis) and generalizations (conclusions) which are then (4) used to test a hypothesis in future situations, resulting in new experiences [3–5].

Lewis and Williams [7] also demonstrated ways in which experiential learning theory provides a valuable framework for strengthening the critical linkages that can and must be developed among education and work. The AACSB Memorandum [8] has used the following quote to express that such learning is effective, i.e. "*Tell me and I'll forget, Show me and I'll remember, Involve me and I'll understand*" [9].

At present, relevant studies of experiential learning mainly focus on the learning styles and cycle, as well as the factors influencing the effectiveness [10]. There is a lack of study on analyzing the self-growth of teachers. On the other hand, many higher education institutions in Taiwan have been facing the same challenge that students' learning motivation is low as the education opportunities are oversupplied in recent years [11, 12]. Thus, it motivates the authors to investigate how AI technology can effectively reinforce the interaction with the non-IT teachers and students and enhance students' learning motivation via AI experiential learning.

Summarizing the findings from the captioned pieces of literature, external factors and internal factors affect the effectiveness of AI learning implementation in general courses. [13]. External factors include the learning contents, management, and environment, and internal factors mainly focus on students' major studies. According to the University's current strategy, it is hoped that selected seed teachers of various Colleges will start with a fundamental introduction to let students experience the fun of AI. Of course, the University has specific requirements in the curriculum, but basically, it does not interfere with the teachers' teaching methods. Teachers who are willing to apply for the "Interdisciplinary AI Professional Course" in their courses must apply to the University for launching the AI-related courses one semester in advance.

3 Research Design and Implementation

In the process of promoting AI experiential learning, notwithstanding the University's policies are of course important, the cooperation of teachers is the key to success or failure. In the beginning, the University has organized training seminars for the teaching staff of all five Colleges, each seminar will have 30 to 50 teachers participated, and there will be at least 4 to 5 sessions a year on average. At present, the University plans to have 40 courses to incorporate AI experiential learning in each semester and become an "Interdisciplinary AI Course". Table 1 shows the number of applications on launching the AI experiential learning in the six Colleges from the academic year 2019–20.

Table 1. Number of courses applied and approved as the Interdisciplinary AI Course in the recent two academic years. (Source: AI+ Experience Centre, 2021)

College	2019-20		2020-21	
	1st	2nd	1st	2nd
Computer Science & Electrical Engineer	9 (1⅄)	11	8 (1⅄)	7 (2⅄)
Management	4	3 (1⅄)	7	6
Architecture and Design	4	1	3	2
Humanities & Social Sciences	0	1	0	1
Tourism	1	0	2 (1⅄)	1
Total	18	16	20	17

Remark: ⅄ = Rejected application(s) due to the teaching plan(s) unrelated to AI subject

In this study, the University's promotion strategy and the responses from the learners, and the teachers' learning process would be introduced and analyzed; and the current Computer-Aided Design (CAD) courses' teaching practices in the College of Architecture and Design would be reviewed and analyzed.

3.1 AI+ Experience Centre and the Recent Performance

The University combines AI with the professional fields of the Colleges and cultivates students for having the AI technology ability to insight into the industry trends in addition to their major studies. According to the University's teaching strategy [1], every student can become a talented person in the industry through the three-stage learning design of experience, application, and implementation during their studies at the University. The mission of the Centre is to provide various courses for students as described below:

(1) Inter-Academic Experience Micro-Credit Related Courses: A micro-credits[1] course for three weeks to explain the AI content fundamentally and group projects are given as a part of the AI experiential learning. All courses are free, and the content and time arrangement is flexible with a specific learning objective which is to achieve the cognition or skill acquisition of the AI theme.
(2) AI Application Related Courses: It is for students who are interested in learning AI practical skills. The courses are taught by the external professional leaders of the Computer Science & Electrical Engineer industries in Taiwan. Due to the distribution of teaching resources, these courses can only be offered every other semester.
(3) Interdisciplinary AI Related Courses: The University's extensive promotion of these courses are all about creating an AI learning environment, cultivating and enhancing students' AI application ability and employment advantage. The course content includes the subject of big data processing, smart manufacturing, smart building, smart marketing, smart retail, smart finance, robot applications, and AI algorithm.

Since 2018, 578 teachers and staff have participated in nearly 100 AI-related seminars in the University; and more than 3,800 students have so-called AI experience. The seminar offered by the Centre is open to the public. The staff and students of this University are free to join, but people from outside the University would be charged a market price.

3.2 AI-Related Seminars for the Teachers and Staff

In the planning of various AI seminars, the University firstly trains teachers and staff in each College and then open it to outsiders if vacancies available. In addition, training camps for middle school students are held during the winter and summer vacations. The current seminar still focuses on the teaching staff. Table 2 shows the major types of AI seminars launched in the AI^+ Experience Centre since 2018.

3.3 Interdisciplianry AI Courses

In addition to the courses shown in Table 2, a large number of small-scale seminars were offered from early 2017. One of the authors of this paper has participated in nearly ten courses since the seminars started, and recently passed the AI-900 Examination

[1] 6 micro-credits courses are equveliented to one FULL course (2 credit units) in the University.

Table 2. Number of seminars or courses provided by the AI+ Experience Centre

Year	Series of seminars	Number of attendants	Hours per class (no. of class)	Type of attendants
2021	Microsoft AI International License Training Camp*	50	14 h (6 classes)	Schools/Staff/Students
	Enterprise AI Practical Training Course	25	248 h (1 class)	Public
2020	Digital Transformation – What, Why and How	48	7 h (1 class)	Students
	Microsoft AI Innovation Academy Azure Cloud Lab*	25	7 h (2 classes)	Schools
	AI Interdisciplinary Application Seminar*	35	7 h (1 class)	Schools/Public
	Microsoft AI Seminar	35	7 h (4 classes)	Schools/Public
	Google MLCC Physical Course	50	7 h (3 classes)	Schools/Public
	CHU Executive AI Seminar*	40	7 h (2 classes)	Schools
	ASUS & Oracle Course*	40	7 h (6 classes)	Schools/Staff/Students
2019	Microsoft x CHU AI High School Summer Camp	35	14 h (3 classes)	High School Students
	AI Fundamental	35	7 h (2 classes)	Schools/Staff/Students
2018	AI Fundamental*	35	7 h (2 classes)	Schools

Remark: * The courses which the author has participated in.

(Microsoft Azure AI Fundamentals). However, as a reflection of a trained teacher, how much of the AI knowledge has the author learned can be applied to computer graphics or architectural design? Does the author have such an ability to introduce AI to the students?

The University emphasizes such courses to cultivate students' understanding of common AI practices and identify and support everyone's ability to provide AI services in their professionalism. Based on the enthusiasm and support of the University, the author is one of the first batches of trained academic staff to apply the captioned AI experiential learning in the architecture and design courses. Fortunately, the financial subsidy was approved on the first application. Three semesters have been completed since 2019, and the fourth semester is currently being implemented. The applied course is based on the

Computer-Aided Design Class of the first and second year of the Department of Architecture and Urban Planning as the experimental object. Table 3 presents the teaching content and changes in each semester.

As mentioned above, the University is constantly accumulating implementation experience in the promotion process. In the first academic year, 2019–20, a rigorous survey of student satisfaction has not yet been made. However, a systematic questionnaire has been developed since the first semester in 2020–2021, and all courses can only be completed after students filled in the questionnaire.

4 Discussion, Reflection, and Recommendation

Refer to the study schedule in Table 2, in a period of two academic years, the University provides a lot of opportunities for learning new AI skills, and all the courses are free of charge. It is because the University proposes six forms of special learning [1], and AI Experience & Information Education is one of them, and each individual form of special learning has a complete plan and progress, and teachers are required to apply these six forms of special learning in their courses.

4.1 The Willingness to Learn AI of the Academic Staff

Regarding the degree of enthusiasm of teachers enrolling in AI courses, it may be known how teachers apply their AI knowledge in their courses. According to the University's request, each department of the College needs to send two teachers to participate in the AI training, and the Department of Architecture and Urban Planning (DAUP) has three teachers to participate voluntarily. However, not all teachers will apply what they have learnt from the AI classes in their regular teaching since they do not have the incentive to revise their course syllabus and course structure. Besides, not all the courses could be conducted in the computer classroom or AI environment, and teachers have yet to figure out how to apply the AI experiential learning in their regular teaching and course content.

As a reflection after attending the University's AI training classes for non-IT teachers, the author found that there are several reasons behind those teachers who are not so enthusiastic about AI experiential learning. Firstly, those teachers were involuntarily selected to attend the training classes by their department heads. Secondly, some teachers have been teaching at the University for over 30 years, and they are quite resistant to new technology to interfere with their traditional teaching. Thirdly, the AI training classes are very intensive, and the AI concept is too advanced and complicated for a non-IT teacher to learn. Fourthly, as the AI training classes were taught by the external professional leaders of Computer Science & Electrical Engineer industries in Taiwan, they have given a lot of new technology information and examples from their industries but there is no clue how these may apply to their regular teaching courses and subjects. As a result, not many teachers are willing to spend extra effort and time to apply AI experiential learning in their teaching courses.

Notwithstanding the above setbacks, the University is still vigorously seeking the possibility of starting the AI courses in various courses and majors. And the University

Table 3. AI teaching content of the Department of Architecture and Urban Planning

Semester	Course title and course content	Teaching hours	Status
2nd Semester 2020–21	Yr.1 Computer graphic II/Yr.2 Computer-aided design II 1. Concepts of deep learning 2. Microsoft Azure AI services: Exam AI-900; Customvision.AI; AML Studio 3. Case study: Lobe.AI and ArchiGAN	16 (for Year 1 students) 10 (for Year 2 students)	On-going
1st Semester 2020–21	Yr.1 Computer graphic I 1. Concepts of machine learning and big data 2. Case study: ArchiGAN 3. Big data algorithm: Space Syntax depthmapX	16	Completed with student surveys
2nd Semester 2019–20	Yr.2 Computer-aided design II 1. Concepts of machine learning and big data 2. Case study: ArchiGAN 3. Big data algorithm: Space Syntax depthmapX	15	Completed without student surveys
1st Semester 2019–20	Yr.1 Computer graphic I 1. Concepts of machine learning and big data 2. AI in graphic design: Auto Draw; Quick Draw; Scrying Pen; Deep Art; and SketchAR	14	Completed without student surveys

has been repeatedly advocating that the AI$^+$ Experience Centre will provide all necessary teaching materials for the teachers to provide basic and fundamental AI experiential learning to their classes with extra patience.

4.2 Teaching Implementation of AI Experiential Learning in the Courses

Based on the above encouragement and funding subsidies from the University, the author mustered up the courage to participate in the first batch of AI teaching since the first launch of the AI project. Therefore, using the existing compulsory CAD Courses by adding elements of AI seems to be a good start in the architecture and design courses. Regarding the teaching hours allocation of the courses, in principle, it is divided into two parts: 1/4 and 3/4. The first 1/4 series of general AI concepts, the teaching materials are coming from the AI+ Experience Centre, and the 3/4 content of the latter series is the so-called customization in the regular course and assessments.

In the first semester of the 2019–20 academic year, a series of online drawing tools of Google became a natural choice, including Auto Draw, Quick Draw, and Scrying Pen. These online drawing games developed by Google's AI Experiment challenge players to draw a picture of an object or idea and then use a neural network AI to guess what the drawings represent [14, 15]. The other tools, Deep Art and SketchAR are about the experience of recalculating complex graphics [16, 17]. Students must submit a comprehensive report in PDF format, which is the experience of all five captioned tools after use, and attached with screenshots. Students generally find the captioned Google tools are novel and exciting after more than ten hours of experience. However, according to the author's observation, the student will quickly lose patience in such repeated operations, and students find it is not easy to draw attractive artworks from such experiential AI drawing tools. From the author's perspective, the problem may lie in the difference between mouse manipulation and hand-drawn pictures. Unless the University provides touch-panel screen computers in the lab, it is quite difficult to draw computer graphics satisfactorily via a mouse or writing pad. Such negative AI experiential learning will then dwindle students' learning motivation if they lose interest in practising their digital drawing through such primitive drawing tools.

When the author made application to the University introduce AI experiential learning in his architecture and design courses, several AI elements are clearly listed in the teaching plan, namely: big data processing, smart manufacturing, smart building, smart marketing, smart retail, smart finance, robot application, and related AI algorithm-themed content. According to the above eight teaching requirements, we found that University College London's (UCL) Space Syntax analysis software may have the opportunity to meet the purpose of the AI^+ Experience Centre. Space Syntax develops digital modelling tools to forecast the social, economic and environmental performance of buildings and urban places [18–20]. Their works address the "smart cities" technology challenges of delivering low carbon performance, healthy living and access to opportunities [21]. This kind of graphical tools that use AI algorithms may directly correspond to the professional training of architecture, students are required to have advanced CAD drawing skills and experience in architecture and urban design to understand the meaning of spatial analysis. Though this is a challenging learning objective, the author appreciates most students are still willing to learn.

4.3 Performance Evaluation of the AI Applied Courses

In response to students' interests and demands, the captioned UCL spatial analysis tool was applied to two semesters, up to the first semester of 2020–21; and they are most interested in the 3D Animated Agent Analysis. However, the learning requirements of this kind of analysis software are relatively high; most of the students' performance in assignments cannot reach such a high standard even though students were given a passing grade in the course.

Moreover, the University has developed a "Teaching Resource Library" at the AI$^+$ Experience Centre, and required teachers to send a teaching folder for their respective AI applied course to the AI$^+$ Experience Centre, including teaching material, AI course handouts, student homework, and 6 to 8 photos of students in the class. In terms of student homework, the University required the teacher to collect at least 80% of students' homework; however, the author's AI applied courses have failed to meet this requirement for the past three semesters. After reviewing this issue, the author believes that in other regular courses, there were around 10% of students did not submit their assignment on average. For the new AI applied courses, authors observed that some students found difficulties understanding the AI-knowledge and applying the AI-concept in their assignments which demotivate more students who did not submit their assignments. With additional and brand new AI content in the courses, authors found that roughly 30% of students do not submit the assignments and eventually fail. Table 4 shows the status of the AI homework submissions in the last three semesters.

Table 4. AI homework submission status

Semester	No. of students	No. of assignment with a PASS grade	No. of assignment with a FAIL grade	No. of incompleted assignment (ungraded)	Total Submission rate (%)
1st, 2020–21	80	23	15	7	56.3
2nd, 2019–20	98	40	10	20	70.4
1st, 2019–20	96	12	17	32	63.5

5 Recommendation and Conclusion

For the learning of AI applications with the professional fields of all the five Colleges, both students and teachers are beginners. This study primarily focuses on the perspectives of teaching faculties from the CAD courses of the architecture and design department. In fact, in order to enrich the teaching content and enhance the learning motivation, it is recommended that teachers must continue to learn new computer and related AI knowledge, especially the various applications of information technology.

Even though the University fully commits to allocating extra learning and teaching resources, the hardware facilities for teaching also need to be improved simultaneously. Besides, the University is recommended to render extra incentive and support to those non-IT-teachers to apply the AI experiential learning in their regular courses, such as hiring additional IT technicians and teaching assistants to assist teachers in implanting new AI teaching material in their traditional teaching courses.

In the case of the current school, the Computer Vision was first considered for inclusion in the curriculum. It is primarily because such teaching requires constant judgment. The development of architectural design will produce a large number of hand-drawn sketches. Through AI analysis, students can be informed of the circumstances in which this would be a more appropriate choice. Another example is the study of architectural history. In addition to the development of Western Europe, there are also a large number of residential houses in the traditional architecture of the East. The authors will consider how to apply to students' self-experience in the future.

In the case of the College of Tourism, teachers will hope to use the Conversational AI to assist students in training for enhancing their service level to the customer. And Natural Language Processing is of interest to the College of Management for improving their language skill. All teachers focus on how to improve communication with students. Though there is always room for improvement in future work, future research work and directions are suggested in the following two perspectives.

Firstly, in order to enhance the quality of AI teaching and learning, it may be necessary to reconsider the practicality of team teaching in classes. As non-IT teachers teach all AI content, mistakes may inevitably be made without knowing it. Davis [22] provides this succinct definition of team teaching: "*All arrangements that include two or more faculty in some level of collaboration in the planning and delivery of a course*" [23, 24]. The approach of interactive team teaching is suggested, i.e. two faculty members present in front of the class simultaneously. As for the AI experience, teachers with non-information technology backgrounds need to receive experiential training continuously.

Another perspective is the way to stimulate students' learning motivation. For the concerns on the architectural design courses, it is a challenging task. Many aspects cannot be distinguished as right or wrong, for instance, aesthetics; what might be naturally beautiful to someone may just seem too artificial to another one. Thus, students should understand the importance of architecture criticism. Regarding the students of the DAUP, they are accustomed to this kind of AI experiential training gradually, and therefore they can try to use the method of peer assessment to stimulate students' learning motivation. This method describes a range of activities in which students evaluate and provide feedback on the work of their peers [25, 26]. Such practice is employed to save teachers time and improve students' understanding of the course materials as well as improve their metacognitive skills.

In conclusion, looking to the future, authors believe that AI technology on architectural design can be beneficial to architects and/or spatial designers. The new AI technology can save the designers time on their routine works and focus on creative development. Higher education institutions are encouraged to educate students' AI technological knowledge and enhance their AI capabilities by combing AI with professional fields with other non-information technology courses and subjects. The authors hope this reflection report may share a practical example of the development and implementation of AI experiential learning in the non-information technology courses for other higher education institutions reference. The authors believe that AI experiential learning and development will become more mature and advance by having more application examples and researches in the higher education sector.

Acknowledgements. These interdisciplinary AI courses, the first three semesters and the on-going one in 2021 are supported by Chung Hua University. All data are revealed on the official website of the AI+ Experience Centre. The authors thank all the teachers and students who have participated in this study.

References

1. AI+體驗與資訊教育 - 中華大學 Chung Hua University. http://www1.chu.edu.tw/p/412-1000-490.php?Lang=zh-tw. Accessed 13 Mar 2021
2. John Dewey: Portrait of a progressive thinker. https://www.neh.gov/article/john-dewey-portrait-progressive-thinker. Accessed 13 Mar 2021
3. Kolb, D.A.: Experiential Learning: Experience as the Source of Learning and Development. FT press (2014)
4. Kolb, D.A., Boyatzis, R.E., Mainemelis, C.: Experiential learning theory: previous research and new directions. Perspect. Think. Learn. Cogn. Styles **1**, 227–247 (2001)
5. Patrick, F.: Handbook of Research on Improving Learning and Motivation Through Educational Games: Multidisciplinary Approaches. IGI Global (2011)
6. Stremba, B.: Teaching Adventure Education Theory: Best Practices. Human Kinetics (2009)
7. Lewis, L.H., Williams, C.: Experiential learning: Past and present (1994). https://doi.org/10.1002/ACE.36719946203
8. Williams, R.: Experiential-learning in sport management: getting students involved in their community. VAHPERD J. **35**, 20–24 (2014)
9. Tell me and i forget; teach me and i may remember; involve me and i learn – quote investigator. https://quoteinvestigator.com/2019/02/27/tell/. Accessed 13 Mar 2021
10. The out of eden walk: an experiential learning journey from the virtual to the real. https://www.edutopia.org/blog/out-of-eden-experiential-learning-homa-tavangar. Accessed 6 Mar 2021
11. 大學生自我效能及學習成效提升計畫. https://tpr.moe.edu.tw/displays/downloads/4b1141f2737e5a9d01739478946b20eb. Teaching Practice Research Program Achievement Report, published by the Ministry of Education in Taiwan. Accessed 13 Mar 2021
12. 提升學生學習動機之策略. http://www.ater.org.tw/journal/article/7-9/free/20.pdf. Journal of Taiwan Educational Review Monthly, published by Association for Taiwan Educational Review, Accessed 13 Mar 2021
13. Marketing: 三分鐘了解機器學習的四個學習方式, https://www.ecloudvalley.com/zh-hant/machine-learning/. Accessed 13 Mar 2021
14. Let A Computer Guess What You're Drawing In This High-Tech Pictionary Game | HuffPost. https://www.huffpost.com/entry/quick-draw-google-doodling_n_58331234e4b099512f83caca. Accessed 13 Mar 2021
15. How Does Google "Quick, Draw!" Work? This Game Makes Learning About Artificial Intelligence Fun. https://www.bustle.com/articles/196717-how-does-google-quick-draw-work-this-game-makes-learning-about-artificial-intelligence-fun. Accessed 13 Mar 2021
16. AI makes photos look like famous paintings. https://www.businessinsider.com/ai-makes-photos-look-like-famous-paintings-2015-9?r=US&IR=T. Accessed 13 Mar 2021
17. Bulu, M., Önder, M.A., Aksakalli, V.: Algorithm-embedded IT applications for an emerging knowledge city: Istanbul Turkey. . Expert Syst. Appl. **41**, 5625–5635 (2014)
18. Al-Sayed, K., Turner, A., Hillier, B., Iida, S., Penn, A.: Space syntax methodology (2014)
19. Maina, J.: Discovering hidden patterns: an overview of space syntax methods in architecture and housing research
20. Fathy Alagamy, S., Al-Hagla, K., Anany, Y., Raslan, R.: An integrated approach for analyzing connectivity in atria. Alex. Eng. J. **58**, 315–324 (2019). https://doi.org/10.1016/j.aej.2018.12.005

21. Lee, S.-J., Lee, K.-H.: Suggestion for a visual dynamics analysis model using a natural movement model. J. Asian Architect. Build. Eng. **13**, 381–388 (2014). https://doi.org/10.3130/jaabe.13.381
22. Warwick, D.: Team Teaching (1971)
23. Carpenter, D.M., Crawford, L., Walden, R.: Testing the efficacy of team teaching. Learn. Environ. Res. **10**, 53–65 (2007)
24. Shibley, I.A.: Interdisciplinary team teaching: negotiating pedagogical differences. Coll. Teach. **54**, 271–274 (2006)
25. Van Zundert, M., Sluijsmans, D., Van Merriënboer, J.: Effective peer assessment processes: Research findings and future directions. Learn. Instr. **20**, 270–279 (2010)
26. Topping, K.: Peer assessment between students in colleges and universities. Rev. Educ. Res. **68**, 249–276 (1998)

Enriched and Smart Learning Experience

Supporting Students' Reflection in Game-Based Science Learning: A Literature Review

Xiaotong Yang[1(✉)] and Yang Liu[2]

[1] College of Education, Florida State University, 1114 W Call St, Tallahassee, FL 32306, USA
xy18d@my.fsu.edu

[2] School of Education, Syracuse University, 230 Huntington Hall, Syracuse, NY 13210, USA

Abstract. Students' reflection on their gameplay is necessary for a meaningful game-based learning experience, especially in science education. This study reviewed the literature on the design and effects of students' reflection support in game-based science learning. Fourteen empirical and theoretical articles out of 131 identified articles from four databases were included after the searching and screening process. Findings revealed that reflection support varied in the support type (e.g., in-game prompts or instructor guidance), support triggered time (e.g., during or after gameplay), and response type (e.g., no response, written or spoken). Both in-game reflection prompts and instructor guided-reflection are promising in facilitating students' science learning, and the effects varied based on the design and implementation of the support. Implications on future studies and design of reflection support in game-based science learning are discussed.

Keywords: Game-Based Learning · Science Education · Reflection · Learning Outcome

1 Introduction

According to the Next Generation Science Standards [1], science education is more than memorizing scientific facts and concepts. Science education should engage students in science and engineering practices, e.g., planning and carrying out investigations, hypothesis testing, analyzing and interpreting data, and arguing based on evidence [1]. Game-based learning, i.e., learning through playing games designed for educational purposes [2], is a promising method to help students gain conceptual understanding by applying science knowledge in solving game problems [3, 4].

Learners' reflection on their gameplay is necessary for a meaningful game-based learning experience [5–8]. Derived from Dewey's pragmatism theory, reflection refers to a metacognitive process that allows one to be cognitively aware of one's actions [6, 8, 9]. Moreno and Mayer [7] have argued that meaningful learning in multimedia learning environments (e.g., game-based learning) occurs when students select relevant information and organize and integrate it with prior knowledge. Students' reflection contributes to the organizing and integrating process [7], thus making it essential to the game-based

R. Li et al. (Eds.): ICBL 2021, LNCS 12830, pp. 119–131, 2021.
https://doi.org/10.1007/978-3-030-80504-3_10

learning outcome. Kiili [5] has further asserted that reflection enhances students' conceptual understanding by connecting gameplay with learning. According to the experiential gaming model [5], both direct experience and reflective observation are critical to game-based learning. By reflecting on their previous direct experience and corresponding feedback, learners conceptualize their previous gameplay experience to propose a new hypothesis concerning game problems [5]. Moreover, Kori et al. [6] have noted that reflection is especially important for exploratory science learning environments (e.g., game-based science learning) because students tended to hold misconceptions and misunderstandings in their initial explaining of natural phenomena.

Despite the necessity of reflection, few students proactively conducted reflection in game-based learning without extra guidance [4, 10, 11]. Students may solve game problems by guessing or trial-and-error without being metacognitively aware of underlying content knowledge [4, 11], thus impairing their game-based learning outcome [2, 5]. Moreover, reflection is a high-level metacognitive process where students rarely practice in traditional teaching settings [6, 8, 9, 12]. Therefore, it is valuable to investigate how to support students' reflection in game-based science learning to enhance their science understanding. Such research can provide educators and game designers with insights on the design of reflective game-based learning experience to facilitate students' science learning outcome.

A few research papers reviewed the literature on reflection support in game-based learning, but none of them focused specifically on supporting students' reflection in science education. For example, Wouter and Van [9] conducted a meta-analysis to assess the effects of instructional support (e.g., reflection support) on game-based learning outcome based on relevant empirical studies from 1990 to 2012. Results showed that students significantly learn better by playing educational games with reflection support than those without such support ($d = .29$, $p < .01$). Additionally, Taub et al. [8] reviewed studies concerning embedded reflection prompts in game-based learning. They analyzed when reflection was prompted (e.g., time-based, activity-based), how students were prompted (e.g., written, spoken, menu-based), and how students responded to the prompts (e.g., spoken, written). Taub and colleagues found that embedded reflection prompts were effective in improving students' game-based learning outcome. But the researchers did not include out-of-game reflection support in game-based learning, such as teacher guidance.

This literature review is inspired by Wouter and Van [9] and Taub et al. [8]. In the current study, we review the literature regarding the design and effects of students' reflection support in game-based science learning to shed light on the effective game-based science learning design. But unlike Taub et al. [8], we will focus on both in-game (e.g., embedded prompts) and out-of-game reflection support (e.g., instructor guidance). The findings will help educators and game designers gain a better understanding of how to support students' reflection in game-based learning to facilitate their science learning outcome. We will answer the following research questions:

1. How is reflection support designed in game-based science learning?
2. What is the effect of the reflection support on students' game-based learning outcome?

2 Methods

2.1 Database and Search Terms

We used four databases through ProQuest: ERIC, APA PsycINFO, Sociological Abstract, and Education Database. ERIC is sponsored by the U.S. Department of Education to provide extensive access to educational-related literature. PsycINFO is a ProQuest online version of Psychological Abstracts, covering journal articles, book chapters, books, technical reports, and dissertations in psychology and psychological aspects of related disciplines from 1887 to the present. Sociological Abstract covers sociology-related topics including education, social psychology, urban studies, and so on. Education Database supports the study and application of education across all education levels, including early childhood education, primary and secondary education, and higher education.

We used search terms related to game-based learning, science education, and reflection. We identified similar terms using the thesaurus function of the above four databases. The final search terms we used were: ("Game-based learning" OR "educational games" OR "learning games" OR "serious games" OR "video games" OR "computer games" OR "digital games") AND ("science") AND ("reflect*"). The asterisk in the ProQuest platform means searching for words starting with the letters before the asterisk. We set the searching range as abstract and limited the searching results to English peer-reviewed scholarly journals.

2.2 Inclusion and Exclusion Criteria

We identified 131 papers after the database searching process. Then we screened their titles and abstracts to determine the papers included in the current literature review based on the inclusion and exclusion criteria. Our inclusion criteria were:

- Games discussed should be digital or computer games that were used for educational purposes. We focused on digital or computer games instead of board games because the former could have multimedia in-game reflection support.
- Subjects should be natural science, e.g., physical sciences, life sciences, and earth and space sciences.
- Participants should be secondary school students to college students.
- The paper should discuss students' reflection on game-based science learning.

Theoretical or review articles that did not meet items 2 and 3 were also included to enhance the current research topic's theoretical foundation.

Our exclusion criteria were:

- Games were board games.
- The paper discussed researchers' or teachers' reflection instead of students' reflection.

After the screening process, a total of 14 studies were included in the literature review. Among them, ten were empirical studies and four were theoretical or review articles. We conducted systematic analysis mainly based on the empirical studies, while the theoretical or review articles were used to discuss the results.

3 Results

In this section, we first synthesize researchers' definitions of students' reflection in game-based learning. Then, we identify two types of reflection support in the literature: in-game prompts and instructor guidance. We discuss the design and effects of these two types of reflection support on students' game-based science learning.

3.1 Definition of Reflection in Game-Based Learning

Overall, researchers shared the basic understanding of students' reflection in game-based learning: students looking back to their prior experience for new understanding [6–8, 13]. However, researchers focused differently on what "prior experience" students reflected on and what "new understanding" they were supposed to gain from the reflection. Most researchers investigated reflection on students' game strategies or solutions to game problems [5, 7, 9, 10, 13–16]. For example, Wounter and Van [9] and Moreno and Mayer [7] defined reflection as students thinking about and explained their answers or solutions. And the purposes of such reflection were to help students be cognitively aware of their game actions, connecting game problem solving with underlying content knowledge, and detecting potential misconceptions [7, 9, 10, 13, 14].

Other researchers (e.g., [8, 17–19]) held a broad understanding of students' reflection. They focused on reflection on students' whole game-based learning experience, including game information, game environments, students' perceived learning gains and feelings. For example, Nelson [18] investigated students' reflection on evidence or clues they gathered in the game. Nilsson and Jakobsson [19] asked students to reflect on what they have learned from the intervention. In addition to facilitating learning, such reflection was designed to contribute new hypotheses or solutions to game problems and students' self-reported assessment of their learning experience [17, 18]. The next section describes the design and effects of two types of reflection support in game-based science learning.

3.2 Reflection Support Design and Effects

For the empirical studies, we coded their research method (e.g., quantitative and qualitative), participants, reflection support design (e.g., in-game prompts and instructor guidance), reflection support time (i.e., when was the reflection support triggered), students' response type (i.e., how did students respond to the reflection support), and effects of such supports on students game-based learning outcome (e.g., not discussed, positive effects, non-significant effects). Results are shown in Table 1.

Results indicated that most (70%) empirical studies adopted the quantitative research method and two were qualitative research (design-based research, to be specific). The sample size ranged from 22 to 272. Most participants were in the U.S., while three studies were conducted in Europe and one was in Asia.

There were overall two types of reflection support: in-game prompts and instructor guidance. The in-game reflection prompts varied in presentations: textual or pictorial. And instructor guidance varied in implementation forms: individually and collectively.

Table 1. Description of the empirical articles analyzed in this study

Article	Method	N	Participants	Support type	Support time	Response type [a]	Effects [b]
Barab et al., 2009	quantitative	51	Undergraduate students in the U.S.	In-game prompts: textual	After completing each quest	NA	NA
Huang, 2016	quantitative	83	6th-8th grade students in the U.S.	In-game prompts: textual and pictorial	After completing each level	No	+
Geden et al., 2020	quantitative	118	Middle school students in the U.S.	In-game prompts: textual	After finishing a key task or collecting a piece of important evidence	Written	+
Nelson, 2007	quantitative	272	Middle school students in the U.S.	In-game prompts: textual	After interacting with certain characters or digital subjects	No	+
Moreno & Mayer, 2005	quantitative	254	Undergraduate first-year students in the U.S.	In-game prompts: textual	After answering each game questions	Spoken	+
Koops & Hoevenaar, 2013	quantitative	41	High school students in the Netherlands	Instructor guidance: individual	When students seek help	Spoken	-
Anderson & Barnett, 2013	mix-method	91	Middle school students in the U.S.	Instructor guidance: collective	After the whole gameplay	Written and spoken	NA
Namgyel & Bharaphan, 2017	quantitative	31	12th-grade students in Bhutan	Instructor guidance: individual	After the whole gameplay	Written	NA
Nilsson & Jakobsson, 2011	qualitative	42	Secondary students in Sweden	Instructor guidance: collective	After the whole gameplay	Spoken	+
Herrero et al., 2014	qualitative	22	Secondary students in Spain	Instructor guidance: collective	After the whole gameplay	Spoken	+

All in-game reflection prompts were triggered within gameplay (e.g., after students completing a game level or task), while instructor-guided reflection was mostly conducted after the whole gameplay. Moreover, some in-game prompts did not require students to respond, neither spoken nor written, but all instructor-guided reflection required students' response. Findings of six studies indicated that reflection support tended to positively affect students' learning outcomes, while one study yields non-significant results.

In-Game Prompts

In-game reflection prompts were predefined questions in a game to help students reflect on their previous game experience. Researchers designed textual or pictorial in-game prompts triggered when students completed a game level, finished a key game task, or collected an important clue in gameplay. For example, Geden et al. [14] designed a 3D video game to help middle school students learn microbiology knowledge. Students role-played as microbiologists to explore the transmission source and treatment of a pandemic in a virtual island. In-game reflection prompts were presented as the message in the students' in-game cellphone asking them to reflect on their game progress and upcoming plan (e.g., "In your own words, please describe the most important things that you've learned so far, and what is your plan moving forward?", other examples of predefined reflection prompts are showed in Table 2). Such prompts were triggered at five milestones in the game (e.g., after finishing a critical task or collecting a piece of important evidence). Students were asked to type in and send their responses via the in-game cellphone. A total of 118 middle school students in the U.S. played the game for two to three class periods and spent approximately 6 min on writing reflection. Results showed that their responses to the reflection prompts varied significantly in length and quality.

Table 2. Examples of predefined reflection prompts

Article	Predefined reflection prompts
Huang 2016	When you chose the middle-size block, what did you expect to see?
Geden et al. 2020	In your own words, please describe the most important things that you've learned so far, and what is your plan moving forward?
Nelson 2007	Is there anything about this hospital that is different than the ones you have seen?
Koops and Hoevenaar 2013	Did you notice what happened when you did not apply any force?
Nilsson and Jakobsson 2011	How was the design work conducted? What determined your design choices? Did you learn anything from playing the game?
Moreno and Mayer 2005	Justify your planting choices/Justify the correct choice

Similarly, Moreno and Mayer [7] designed textual prompts delivered by a game agent. Moreno and Mayer [7] adopted a multimedia botany game called Design-A-Plant. The game took students to travel around five alien planets with different weather conditions. Students had to choose suitable plants for each planet based on their certain weather conditions to win the game. After making planting choices, a pedagogical agent asked students to justify their planting choices or the correct choice. However, unlike the written responses in Geden and college's [14] study, students in Moreno and Mayer's [7] research were asked to give an oral explanation to the prompts. Researchers recorded the audio and analyzed if students applied correct knowledge in their explanations. Barab et al. [3] also designed three textual in-game prompts to facilitate students' reflection when they played a multiple-user virtual game called Taiga Virtual Park. However, researchers did not report which reflection questions they asked and how students were required to respond to the prompts.

Other researchers [16, 18] only presented the in-game reflection prompts but did not require students to respond. For example, Nelson [18] designed voluntary reflection prompts customized to students' gameplay progress. In a biology game called River City, students interacted with predefined characters and digital agents in a virtual town to investigate why its residents were getting ill. After interacting with certain characters or digital subjects, one or three hint buttons were enabled on the screen. Students were voluntary to click the button(s) to get reflective guidance messages. Each hint contained one message. The messages asked students to reflect on clues they gathered about solving the game problems. For example, after visiting a hospital in the virtual town, a student received a message: "Is there anything about this hospital that is different than the ones you have seen?".

All the above research focused on textual in-game prompts, but Huang [16] designed both textual and pictorial reflection prompts in a physics game to help students learn Newton's Second Law of Motion. The in-game prompts asked students to reconsider the particular game level. For example, a game level required students to choose among three different sizes of blocks to create different forces to a lever. The corresponding textual reflection prompt showed up after students completed this level and asked, "When you chose the middle-size block, what did you expect to see?" For the pictorial version, researchers translated the same content into graphs and icons. In their study, 83 6th–8th grade students were randomly assigned into four conditions: gameplay without reflection support, gameplay with textual support only, gameplay with pictorial support only, and gameplay with both textual and pictorial support. To alleviate the interruption of the support to students' gameplay, the textual or pictorial prompts froze on the screen for specific seconds to trigger students' reflection, but students were not required to answer these questions.

All five papers on reflection support as in-game prompts found positive relationships between using of such prompts and students' learning outcome (e.g., scientific skills, scientific knowledge, retention), except Barab et al. [3], who did not discuss the effects of the prompts.

However, the effects of in-game prompts varied based on their content [7], number [18], and formats [16]. For example, in Moreno and Mayer's [7] study, a total of 78 fresh undergraduate students were randomly assigned into self-reflection group (i.e., students were prompted to justify their answers), program-reflection group (i.e., students were prompted to justify the correct answer), and no-reflection group. Results showed that students from self-reflection and program-reflection groups recalled significantly more focal scientific knowledge than those in the no-reflection group (effect size =

0.81). Further, students in the program-reflection group outperformed those in the self-reflection and no-reflection groups in the far-transfer test (effect size = 0.80). Students' spoken explanation was recorded and analyzed. Results showed that students reflecting on the correct answers generated a higher proportion of correct explanation than those reflecting on their own answers (effect size = 1.10).

Moreover, Nelson [18] suggested that the number of in-game prompts might impact the effects of such prompts on students' learning. In his study, 272 public middle school students were randomly assigned to three conditions: no guidance, extensive guidance (i.e., receiving three reflection messages after each interaction), and moderate guidance (i.e., receiving one reflection message after each interaction). All students played the game over three weeks and completed the pre-and post-content test to measure their science inquiry skills and content knowledge. Results showed no significant difference in the pretest scores across the three groups after accounting for their pretest score. However, results indicated a significant positive relationship between guidance message views and posttest score for students in the extensive guidance group, after accounting for their socio-economic levels, prior science grades, and computer game experience. But the benefit of guidance viewing on learning did not show in the moderate guidance group.

Furthermore, Huang [16] indicated that prompts in both textual and pictorial formats were more effective than prompts in a single representation. The researcher randomly assigned 83 middle school students into four conditions: gameplay without reflection support, gameplay with textual support only, gameplay with pictorial support only, and gameplay with textual and pictorial support. All students first took a demographic survey and physics knowledge pretest, then played the game individually for 15 min, followed by a posttest and engagement survey. Findings showed that students received both textual and pictorial reflection prompts scored highest in the scientific knowledge posttest among all participant, accounting for their pretest score.

Although students play educational games with in-game reflection prompts might outperform those who play the game without such prompts in knowledge tests, Huang [16] and Nelson [18] contended that some students tended to pay inadequate attention to these prompts, especially when they were not required to respond to the prompts spoken or written. For example, when in-game prompts were designed to freeze on the screen for specific seconds to trigger students' reflection, Huang [16] found that some students thought the prompts distracting and tried to skip them. Similarly, Nelson [18] reported that a quarter of the students with access to the reflection prompts did not view any prompts at all. The average number of views of reflection messages was quite low. Student interviews and classroom observations revealed the reasons for low access to prompts: (1) Students did not know the purpose of the prompts, and (2) they exclusively focused on solving the game missions and purposely ignored the prompts [18].

Instructor Guidance

Instructor-guided reflection referred to the instructor providing post-gameplay collective or within-gameplay individual guidance with or without predefined prompts to help students reflect on their game experience. Unlike in-game reflection prompts, most instructor guidance was conducted after gameplay (see [10, 15, 17, 19]). Moreover, since instructor guidance involved human interaction, this type of reflection support tended to require students' responses (see [10, 13, 15, 17, 19]).

Three research [10, 15, 19] focused on instructor-guided reflection as post-gameplay collective debriefing. For example, Anderson and Barnett [10] conducted design-based research to investigate how to integrate a 3D action/racing game called Supercharged! in science lessons to help middle school students grasp the basic electromagnetic concepts. Class observation showed that some students were confused about how they were supposed to learn from gameplay, and few students critically reflected on their gameplay. Therefore, the teacher developed log sheets for students to record their game actions to detect patterns in their gameplay. And the teacher displayed some students' solutions and corresponding feedback to the class and guide students to interpret the feedback and predict results if using another solution in the debriefing. Nilsson and Jakobsson [19] also conducted design-based research on collective instructor guidance, but the instructor in their study guided students' reflection by posting several predefined questions. In this empirical qualitative study, 42 students (ages 14–15) from four Swedish schools reflected on their game experience of an urban simulation computer game called SimCity 4. These subjects were randomly selected from all participants of the Future City competition, where participants applied sustainability-related science concepts (e.g., photosynthesis, the greenhouse effect, the carbon cycle) to create a sustainable city proposal via the game. Teachers guided students to reflect on their proposals in a small group for 20–30 min. During the reflection, students discussed with their peers freely regarding six predefined reflection questions (e.g., "How was the design work conducted? What determined your design choices? Did you learn anything from playing the game?").

In addition to collective instructor reflection guidance, researchers also focused on instructors providing individual guidance [13, 17]. Two types of individual instructor-guided reflection were discussed: in-class reflection prompts and reflection journal.

Koops and Hoevenaar [13] asked a teacher to provide in-class reflection prompts when students sought help when playing a 2D physics game called SPACE CHALLENGE. The researchers argued that students experienced two states during gameplay: game state and learning state. Students intuitively acted on the feedback from the game environments in the game state and generated spontaneous conceptual knowledge, which could only be used in the specific game situation. However, in the learning state, students rationally reflected on the gaming experience and generated formal conceptual knowledge, which could be transferred to other real-life situations. In their study, researchers investigated if suddenly increasing the complexity of the game between consecutive levels and providing teachers' individual guidance would transit students from gaming state to learning state, thus helping students gain better conceptual understanding. They designed SPACE CHALLENGE, where players maneuvered a spaceship to collect diamonds. Three high school classes were randomly assigned into three groups, switch group—students played the game whose level difficultly increased substantially once a new physics concept was introduced, game group—students played the game whose levels were all consistent in difficulty, and control group—students received lecture-based instruction without gameplay. Both the switch group and the game group played the game in class for around 50 min with a teacher's facilitation. The teacher in the switch group would ask students reflection questions (e.g., "Did you notice what happened when you did not apply any force?" or "How do you effectively go through a corner?") when students failed the game levels and asked for help. The teacher in Koops and Hoevenaar's [13] study failed to implement the intervention as designed. It was hard for the teacher to provide individual guidance synchronously to the whole class. Students in the switch group frequently asked for help due to the complexity of game levels—most of their questions related to technical issues or game mechanisms. The teacher was unable to provide the predefined reflective prompts and offer assistance in time for everyone.

Compared to providing synchronous guidance, asking students to write self-reflective journals after their gameplay was more practical. Namgyel and Bharaphan [17] investigated if integrating simulation and game with teaching would improve students' understanding of the photoelectric effect. The teacher asked 31 12th grade students in Bhutan to write self-reflective journals after the intervention to reflect on their learning experience. Rather than facilitating learning, such reflection served as a measurement of students' attitudes towards the game-based learning experience.

Among all five research on instructor-guided reflection, two reported positive effects on students' learning [15, 19], one reported non-significant result [13], and two did not discuss it [10, 17].

Nilsson and Jakobsson [19] and Herrero et al. [15] conducted qualitative research and draw their conclusion concerning instructor-guided reflection's effects by thematically analyzing observation data. Researchers asserted that instructor-guided reflection helped students enhance their understanding of the underlying science knowledge by connecting the content knowledge with their game experience [15, 19]. Herrero et al. [15] provided an example of how the teacher heuristically guided students to think deeply and recall exact prior knowledge to explain their game actions. A student explained a certain game level using a Darwinian strategy. The teacher asked why the student said that. The student replied that natural selection happened. The teacher re-asked the why question. Finally, the student linked their game experience with exact content concepts and knowledge from Darwin's Theory of Evolution. Furthermore, Nilsson and Jakobsson [19] argued that collective reflection could lead to generative discussion, that is, students inspired by each other and generate ideas based on their own game experience. And the reflection on constraints of gameplay (e.g., the gap between game environments and real-world) helped students develop critical thinking towards the application of targeted science concepts.

However, Koops and Hoevenaar [13] reported non-significant effects of instructor-guided reflection. The researchers randomly assigned three high school classes into three groups, switch group—students played a game in hard mode and received instructor's reflection prompts when they sought help, game group—students played the same game in easy mode, and control group—students received lecture-based instruction instead of gameplay. The pre-and post-test results showed that students from the switch and game groups outperformed those in the control group in conceptual understanding. However, there was no significant difference between the switch group and the game group in the posttest score after controlling for their pretest scores. The non-significant results may be because the teacher failed to provide the reflection prompts for everyone as planned.

The teacher was busy with answering students' questions related to technical issues or game mechanisms. Researchers recommended the teacher or game designers to embed answers to commonly asked technical questions in the games in advance to improve the implementation of instructor-guided reflection.

4 Discussion

Students' reflection is important for them to make sense of their gameplay experience and connect gameplay with learning when playing educational games [5–8]. This study selected and reviewed 14 articles regarding the design and effects of students' reflection support in game-based science learning. Results showed that both in-game prompts and instructor guidance designed to scaffold reflection could prompt students' game-based science learning outcome. And such effects varied based on the design of reflection support.

In-game reflection prompts were predefined questions designed to help students reflect on their previous game experience (e.g., collected clues, game strategies, solutions) after completing milestone game events (e.g., completing a level). Findings revealed that students receiving in-game reflection prompts gained better game-based science learning outcome than those without such prompts. And such effects varied based on the content, number, and formats of the prompts. The findings align with the results of a systematic analysis conducted by Taub et al. [8], who asserted a positive effect of in-game reflection support on students' learning.

In-game prompts were triggered during gameplay, so some researchers did not require students' spoken or written responses to avoid distracting them from gameplay. However, it turned out that some students might ignore these prompts and did not exert reflection. Therefore, efforts are needed to direct students' attention to such prompts and ensure students' reflection.

Moreover, most research on in-game prompts employed the experimental method. Therefore, it is hard to generalize the findings to other populations and other science games of studies with participants from one school and one type of game. Further, some studies' population was not clearly defined, and their selection methods were either not reported or the convenient sampling (e.g., [16, 18]).

Unlike in-game prompts, instructor-guided reflection was mainly conducted collectively after gameplay. Teachers guided students to discuss shared issues in their gameplay or reflect on exampled students' game experience. Teacher-guided reflection tended to be longer (e.g., 20-min debriefing), deeper (e.g., asking follow-up questions), and more flexible (e.g., without predefined prompts) than reflection supported by in-game prompts.

Some research (e.g., [10, 17]) discussed the design of instructor-guided reflection but did not analyze its effects on students' learning outcome. Results from other research revealed that instructor guidance on students' reflection could help students enhance their understanding of the underlying science knowledge by connecting the content knowledge with their game experience. The findings were consistent with Kori et al. [6], who asserted that students significantly learn better by playing educational games with instructor-guided reflection than those without such supports. Moreover, results indicated that collective instructor guidance (i.e., class-wide debriefing) was more feasible than individual one (i.e., providing individual guidance to each student in class).

The effects of such support depend heavily on teachers' guiding skills. For examples, teachers should know how to organize academically productive discourse in game-based science lessons [20]. Moreover, answers to commonly asked technical questions should be prepared in advance to avoid taking up the time for productive discourse [13]. Most research on instructor guidance adopted the qualitative method and their evidence for the support's effect was researchers' observation. Therefore, it is hard to draw casual conclusions on the relationships between instructor-guided reflection and students' learning outcome.

5 Conclusion

This study analyzed the design and effects of reflection support in game-based science learning. Overall, both in-game reflection prompts and instructor guided-reflection are promising in facilitating students' science learning. This study sheds light on the design of reflection support from the game designers' and instructors' perspectives.

Regarding research on in-game reflection prompts, qualitative studies are needed to analyze how the in-game prompt works on students, how students respond to these prompts, and how the reflection facilitates students' learning. Compared to instructor guidance, in-game support is more likely to facilitate reflection tailored to students' game experience and personal characteristics. Future researchers should examine the design of customized or adaptive in-game reflection support. Regarding research on instructor-guided reflection, rigorous experimental studies are needed to verify the effects of such support on students' learning.

References

1. NGSS Lead States: Next generation science standards: for states, by states. The National Academies Press, Washington D.C. (2013)
2. Young, M.F., et al.: Our princess is in another castle: a review of trends in serious gaming for education. Rev. Educ. Res. **82**(1), 61–89 (2012). https://doi.org/10.3102/0034654312436980
3. Barab, S.A., et al.: Transformational play as a curricular scaffold: using videogames to support science education. J. Sci. Educ. Technol. **18**(4), 305–320 (2009). https://doi.org/10.1007/s10956-009-9171-5
4. Squire, K.D., Jan, M.: Mad city mystery: developing scientific argumentation skills with a place-based augmented reality game on handheld computers. J. Sci. Educ. Technol. **16**(1), 5–29 (2007). https://doi.org/10.1007/s10956-006-9037-z
5. Kiili, K.: Digital game-based learning: towards an experiential gaming model. Internet High. Educ. **8**(1), 13–24 (2005). https://doi.org/10.1016/j.iheduc.2004.12.001
6. Kori, K., Pedaste, M., Leijen, Ä., Mäeots, M.: Supporting reflection in technology-enhanced learning. Educ. Res. Rev. **11**, 45–55 (2014). https://doi.org/10.1016/j.edurev.2013.11.003
7. Moreno, R., Mayer, R.E.: Role of guidance, reflection, and interactivity in an agent-based multimedia game. J. Educ. Psychol. **97**(1), 117–128 (2005). https://doi.org/10.1037/0022-0663.97.1.117
8. Taub, M., Azevedo, R., Bradbury, A.E., Mudrick, N.V.: Self-regulation and reflection during game-based learning. In: Plass, J.L., Mayer, R.E., Homer, B.D. (eds.) Handbook of Game-Based Learning, pp. 239–262. MIT Press, Cambridge (2019)

9. Wouters, P., Van Oostendorp, H.: A meta-analytic review of the role of instructional support in game-based learning. Comput. Educ. **60**(1), 412–425 (2013). https://doi.org/10.1016/j.compedu.2012.07.018
10. Anderson, J.L., Barnett, M.: Learning physics with digital game simulations in middle school science. J. Sci. Educ. Technol. **22**(6), 914–926 (2013). https://doi.org/10.1007/s10956-013-9438-8
11. Ke, F.: A case study of computer gaming for math: engaged learning from gameplay? Comput. Educ. **51**(4), 1609–1620 (2008). https://doi.org/10.1016/j.compedu.2008.03.003
12. Lim, C.P., Nonis, D., Hedberg, J.: Gaming in a 3D multiuser virtual environment: engaging students in Science lessons. Br. J. Edu. Technol. **37**(2), 211–231 (2006). https://doi.org/10.1111/j.1467-8535.2006.00531.x
13. Koops, M., Hoevenaar, M.: Conceptual change during a serious game: using a lemniscate model to compare strategies in a physics game. Simul. Gaming **44**(4), 544–561 (2013). https://doi.org/10.1177/1046878112459261
14. Geden, M., Emerson, A., Carpenter, D., Rowe, J., Azevedo, R., Lester, J.: Predictive student modeling in game-based learning environments with word embedding representations of reflection. Int. J. Artif. Intell. Educ. **31**(1), 1–23 (2020). https://doi.org/10.1007/s40593-020-00220-4
15. Herrero, D., Del Castillo, H., Monjelat, N., García-Varela, A.B., Checa, M., Gomez, P.: Evolution and natural selection: learning by playing and reflecting. J. New Approaches Educ. Res. **3**(1), 26–33 (2014). https://doi.org/10.7821/naer.3.1.26-33
16. Huang, T.-T.: The effects of types of reflective scaffolding and language proficiency on the acquisition of physics knowledge in a game-based learning environment (Publication No. 10006486) [Doctoral dissertation, New York University]. ProQuest Dissertations and Theses Global (2016)
17. Namgyel, T., Bharaphan, K.: The development of simulation and game in 5E learning cycle to teach photoelectric effect for grade 12 students. Asia-Pacific Forum Sci. Learn. Teach. **18**(2), 1–31 (2017)
18. Nelson, B.C.: Exploring the use of individualized, reflective guidance in an educational multi-user virtual environment. J. Sci. Educ. Technol. **16**(1), 83–97 (2007). https://doi.org/10.1007/s10956-006-9039-x
19. Nilsson, E.M., Jakobsson, A.: Simulated sustainable societies: students' reflections on creating future cities in computer games. J. Sci. Educ. Technol. **20**(1), 33–50 (2011). https://doi.org/10.1007/s10956-010-9232-9
20. Michaels, S., O'Connor, C., Resnick, L.B.: Deliberative discourse idealized and realized: accountable talk in the classroom and in civic life. Stud. Philos. Educ. **27**(4), 283–297 (2008)

Peer-Assessment Enhanced Collaborative Learning in a Virtual Learning Environment

Di Zou[1], Haoran Xie[2](✉), and Fu Lee Wang[3]

[1] Department of English Language Education, The Education University of Hong Kong, New Territories, Tai Po, Hong Kong SAR, China

[2] Department of Computing and Decision Sciences, Lingnan University, Tuen Mun, Hong Kong SAR, China

[3] School of Science and Technology, The Open University of Hong Kong, Kowloon, Hong Kong SAR, China

Abstract. This research investigated the perceptions of a group of students in a university in Hong Kong concerning peer assessment enhanced collaborative learning in a virtual learning environment. A total of 31 Chinese learners of English participated in the project and conducted online collaborative learning and peer assessment in Moodle, ZOOM, and Flipgrid. They were interviewed afterwards and reported their perceptions of the learning process, the challenges that they encountered, and the strategies that they applied to overcome the challenges. The results showed that the students' perceptions of this approach to teaching and learning were overall positive. Concerning the main challenges, the students indicated that when they received massive amounts of feedback, they felt overwhelmed and did not know where to start for further improvement. They also found that peer suggestions were inconsistent sometimes, and when they received similar critical feedback repeatedly, they felt frustrated. To overcome these challenges, the students reported that they managed to prioritize the areas that they need to improve and started with the most important ones. They also asked follow-up questions concerning the controversial suggestions to figure out why their peers' suggestions were different and discussed within groups to decide which suggestions to follow. Moreover, they attempted to focus more on providing constructive feedback, rather than critical feedback. These results suggested that peer assessment enhanced collaborative online learning was an effective approach to active learning.

Keywords: Online collaborative learning · Peer assessment · Learner perception · Higher education

1 Introduction

1.1 Background of the Research

Covid-19 has expedited the process of cultivating a blended learning environment where students benefit from both online and face-to-face learning in Hong Kong [1]. It has also

R. Li et al. (Eds.): ICBL 2021, LNCS 12830, pp. 132–141, 2021.
https://doi.org/10.1007/978-3-030-80504-3_11

to some extent reformed the way of education in Hong Kong, as schools, colleges, and universities can now swiftly switch among synchronous and asynchronous online teaching and learning, as well as face-to-face teaching and learning [2]. Moreover, aligned with the Hong Kong Education Bureau's flexible and caring approach to education, many schools, colleges, and universities not only apply online mode of teaching and learning but also online examination for the sake of public health and safety. Both students and teachers are imposed to become familiar with various online learning and teaching tools (Padlet, Edpuzzle, Nearpod, Flip grid, etc.), platforms (e.g., ZOOM, Microsoft whiteboard, etc.), methods, and strategies [3–5].

This sudden change of teaching approach is challenging and places additional load on many teachers [6, 7]. In addition to designing and shooting videos and developing associated online learning exercises, they also need to grade students' work online and provide appropriate scaffolding when necessary [8]. All these are time-consuming and demanding.

1.2 Significance of the Research

Peer assessment is a process whereby students grade each other's work based on assessment criteria given by teachers [9]. In this process, students play the role of teachers to actively evaluate others' work from the perspective of experts. In addition to giving grades and scores, an important part of peer assessment is to provide constructive suggestions and comments that aim to help students to reflect on their work and further improve it [10]. Thus, it seems to be an effective alternative for teacher assessment and feedback. Moreover, through evaluating others' work on the basis of the assessment criteria and critically reviewing their strengths and weaknesses, students can enhance their knowledge of the target content and learn from their peers [11].

This is important for teaching in higher education, as teachers at the tertiary level normally need to deal with a large group of students, and it is not easy for them to read and comment on every student's every piece of work-in-progress. Moreover, students at the higher education level are normally mature and knowledgeable enough to conduct peer assessment. Many studies have found satisfactory learning outcomes concerning peer assessment enhanced teaching and learning in higher education [12].

However, most studies were conducted in the face-to-face mode of teaching and learning or blended mode of both online and face-to-face teaching and learning, while little research has been conducted to examine peer assessment assisted teaching and learning in the purely online mode. Therefore, in this research, we investigated the effects of peer assessment on collaborative learning in a completely virtual learning environment from the perspectives of learner perceptions, the challenges that they may encounter during the process, and the strategies that they might apply to overcome the challenges.

1.3 Research Questions

Our research questions are listed as follows.

(1) How did students perceive peer-assessment enhanced collaborative learning?

(2) What may be challenging for students when they conducted peer-assessment enhanced collaborative learning?
(3) What strategies did students apply to overcome the potential challenges?

2 Literature Review

2.1 Collaborative Online Learning

Collaborative online learning has become increasingly popular in recent years as it is an effective approach to engaging students in learning and encouraging them to support each other in fulfilling learning task requirements [6]. Collaborators can also support each other in this process to solve problems and overcome challenges together [12]. Compared to individual learning, collaborative learning is widely considered as advantageous in terms of improving students' learning performance, increasing their learning motivation, and developing their problem-solving abilities [9]. Research on collaborative online learning has found generally positive results.

2.2 Peer Assessment

Peer assessment is a process whereby students grade each other's work based on assessment criteria. When students are engaged in peer assessment, they are both raters and ratees, and they need to fully understand what the assignment requirements are [12]. This process is conducive to students' understanding of the instructional materials and can assist them in achieving the intended learning outcomes [6]. During this process, students can learn from each other and reflect on their own work.

Teachers and researchers have applied peer assessment in the teaching and learning of various subjects, including arts, sciences, and information technology. Many studies on the effects of peer assessment found that it can enhance students' learning of target knowledge and skills, increase their motivation and engagement, and develop their metacognitive abilities and critical thinking abilities [6].

3 Method

3.1 Research Design

This research involved three main stages. As shown in Fig. 1, in the first stage, the researchers introduced the project and the learning system to the participants and asked them to complete a pre-test. In the second stage, the participants were asked to conduct peer assessment enhanced collaborative learning and complete a group project. In the third stage, the participants were post-tested and interviewed.

The first stage lasted for around 30 min. All participants volunteered to join the project and agreed that their data can be used for research purposes. The whole project was conducted following relevant ethical guidelines and regulations.

The second stage lasted for around two months. Three online platforms (i.e., ZOOM, Moodle, and Flipgrid) were applied to implement the online teaching and learning. The participants were guided by the teacher to conduct peer assessment online based on the given assessment criteria. The teacher has over ten years of experience in teaching the course.

The third stage lasted for 40 min. The posttest was the same as the pretest. All participants were asked to complete a speaking exercise, and the same grading criteria were applied. After the posttest, the students were asked to participate in a group interview to reflect on their learning experience and report their perceptions of the learning processes. Similar research methods have been applied by many studies on technology enhanced language learning [13].

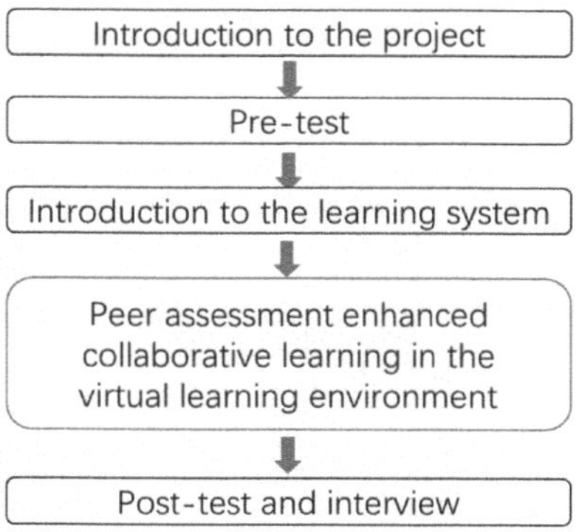

Fig. 1. The research design

3.2 Participants

A total of 31 Chinese learners of English participated in this research. They were all students at a local university in Hong Kong. Due to the covid-19, the university adopted a mode of 100% online teaching and learning for this group of students. Before participating in this project, they had been learning online for a semester, so they were able to participate in this project without any technical challenges.

These participants' first languages were Cantonese or Putonghua, and they all learned English as a foreign language. Their ages ranged from 22 to 25. They also shared similar educational backgrounds, and their English proficiency levels were similar. Moreover, their scores of the International English Language Testing System (IELTS) were around 6.5 and 7.0, indicating that they were advanced intermediate English learners.

3.3 The Online Learning Environment

Three online platforms were applied in this research. The first one is ZOOM, which was used to give lectures and conduct synchronous online communication. This platform was selected because of its stability and mature videoconferencing technology. As shown in Fig. 2, students could record the lectures conducted in ZOOM, unmute themselves and talk to the whole class verbally, and chat with others through sending text messages. These features were important for effective videoconferencing and synchronous online lecturing.

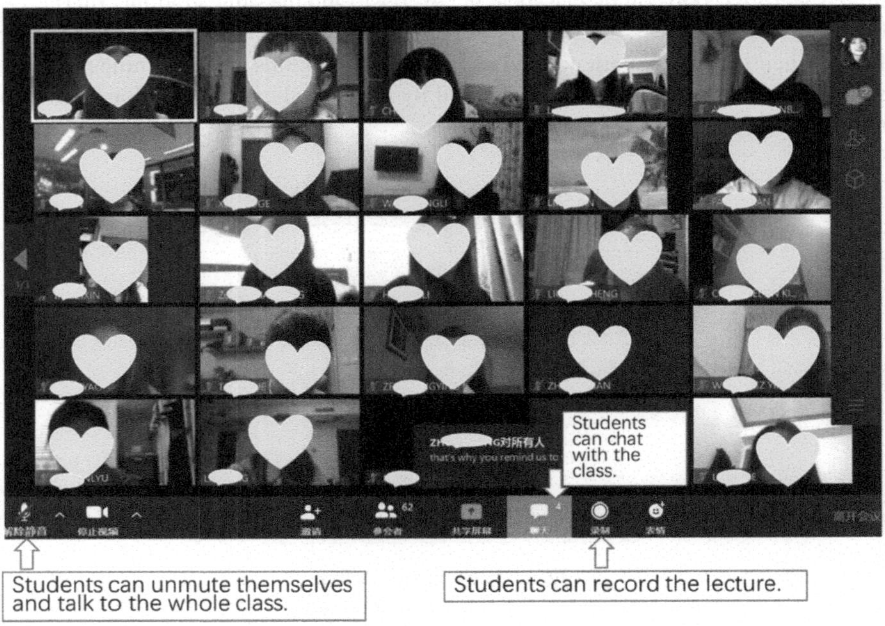

Fig. 2. The interface of ZOOM

The second online platform is Moodle. The teacher used it to share instructional materials, and the students submitted their assignments in it. This platform was selected as it was easy to use, and its interface was user friendly.

The third online platform is Flipgrid. The participants were asked to share their speaking practices in it and provide others with feedback based on the rubrics given by the teacher. Figure 3 demonstrates the interface of Flipgrid. Teachers can create topics, write explicit instructions and requirements for the topics, and ask students to respond to the topics by recoding short videos. The students could also watch their peers' videos and comment on them. They were asked to provide constructive feedback that could help their classmates to further improve their speaking and enhance their learning. Figure 4 shows the interface where students could click any videos they wanted to watch and provided feedback through adding text comments or recording short videos.

3.4 Assessment Rubrics

The assessment rubrics were provided by the teacher to guide students' peer assessment. The students were asked to evaluate the videos from four dimensions, content, language, delivery, and pronunciation.

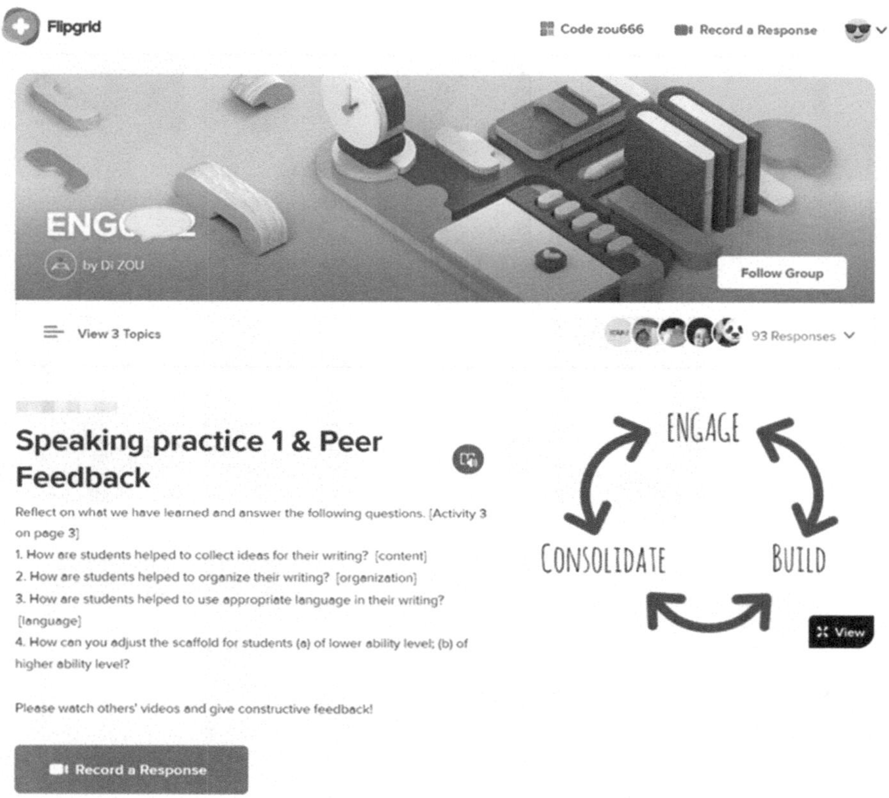

Fig. 3. The interface of Flipgrid

Specifically, the videos were evaluated to check whether they covered all the required contents. The language was examined from the perspectives of grammar and vocabulary. The delivery included body language, facial expressions, and use of presentation techniques. Additionally, the videos were graded in terms of the pronunciation and fluency.

3.5 Interview Questions

The interview aimed to collect students' perceptions of the learning processes and experiences. The interview was audio-recorded. Students could answer the guided interview questions in either Chinese or English, and they were encouraged to freely express what they thought and felt. Similar methods have been applied in many studies previously, positive outcomes of which have been reported as well [14, 15].

Sample interview questions include "do you like this peer assessment enhanced collaborative learning approach?" "what do you like and dislike?" "have you encountered any challenges during this learning process?" "if yes, what are they?" "have you

Fig. 4. The learning performance

applied any strategies to overcome these challenges?" and "if yes, what are they?" These questions were adapted from previous studies [16, 17].

4 Results

4.1 Learner Perceptions of Peer-Assessment Enhanced Collaborative Learning

The results showed that the participants had overall positive perceptions of peer-assessment enhanced collaborative learning online. The majority of the participants believed that this approach to teaching and learning was interesting and effective. They enjoyed learning in groups and felt that peer feedback could help them learn from others and reflect on their own learning performance.

When they conducted peer assessment and provide feedback and suggestions, they evaluated the work from a teacher's perspective. This could help them better understand and achieve the intended learning outcomes.

4.2 Challenges of Peer-Assessment Enhanced Collaborative Learning

The interview results showed three main challenges of peer-assessment enhanced collaborative learning online. Firstly, the students felt that they were overwhelmed by the massive amounts of suggestions and comments. Compared to teacher assessment and feedback, the amounts of peer assessment and feedback were much larger and seemed overwhelming. This is likely because the number of peers was 30 times greater than the teacher. After receiving huge amounts of feedback, students may feel at lost and did not know where to start for further improvement.

The second main challenge is that peer suggestions may sometimes conflict with each other, as different students may hold different opinions about the same issue and consequently provided controversial feedback and suggestions. This then confused the students who received inconsistent comments and assessment results. Many students reported that they did not which suggestions they should follow and how to further improve their performance in the following activities.

Additionally, many students found that as it was not easy for them to immediately improve their performance, especially their pronunciation and presentation delivery skills, in a short period of time, they received similar critical feedback concerning these problems repeatedly. This made them frustrated. Some students felt that their peers focused too much on their problems while did not notice their improvements compared to the previous practices.

4.3 Strategies for Peer-Assessment Enhanced Collaborative Learning

Nevertheless, the students applied effective strategies to deal with the challenges during the learning processes. Thus, despite the confusion and frustration, the students felt confident that they could solve the problems and overcome the challenges well. They therefore felt this peer-assessment enhanced collaborative learning approach effective for online teaching and learning.

Specifically, as demonstrated in Table 1, the students managed to prioritize the areas that they need to improve by reading all assessment results, grouping similar ones together, and focusing on the ones that were repeatedly pointed out by different peers. After identifying the most important ones, the students could start with them and make follow-up plans for the subsequent practices.

To overcome the second challenge, the students asked their peers follow-up questions to figure out why their suggestions were different. This process of understanding why different peers offered controversial suggestions concerning the same issue could help the students deepen their comprehension of the intended learning outcomes and consolidate their relevant knowledge. Moreover, the students managed to discuss within groups to decide which suggestions to follow, and this process was conducive to their improvement as well.

Additionally, the students shared in the class their frustrated feelings about being criticized repeatedly concerning similar problems, and then they agreed that peer assessment and feedback should aim to be constructive. They decided to focus on peer feedback that was helpful for their classmates to improve and provide more concrete suggestions and comments, instead of repeating similar criticism. In this way, students felt less challenging and considered the learning environment more supportive.

Table 1. Main challenges and strategies of peer-assessment enhanced collaborative learning.

Challenges	Solutions
When students received massive amounts of feedback, they felt overwhelmed and did not know where to start for further improvement	The students managed to prioritize the areas that they need to improve and started with the most important ones
Peer suggestions were inconsistent sometimes. Different peers may provide controversial suggestions for the same issue	The students asked follow-up questions concerning the controversial suggestions to figure out why their peers' suggestions were different and discussed within groups to decide which suggestions to follow
Students may receive similar critical feedback repeatedly and felt frustrated	The students shared their feelings and decided to focus more on providing constructive feedback, rather than critical feedback

5 Conclusion

5.1 Research Findings and Implications

In this research, we investigated a groups of Hong Kong university students' perceptions of peer-assessment enhanced collaborative learning online. After learning through this approach for two months, the students were interviewed and asked to reflect on their learning experiences, focusing on what challenges they encountered, and how they overcome them.

The results showed overall positive perceptions of this approach to online teaching and learning, indicating that peer assessment could be an effective alternative for teacher assessment. In this way, teachers' workload could be lightened, and students could be engaged in active learning in groups.

However, students might encounter challenges such as being overwhelmed by massive amounts of feedback, receiving inconsistent peer suggestions, and receiving similar critical feedback repeatedly. Nevertheless, these challenges could be overcome by prioritizing the important areas that need to be improved, asking follow-up questions to figure out why some peer suggestions were controversial, and working as a group to focusing on providing constructive feedback. Teachers and students are suggested to pay attention to these challenges and apply these strategies when they adopt the peer assessment enhanced collaborative learning approach to online teaching and learning.

5.2 Limitations and Future Research Directions

This research is limited in that the number of participants was limited, so future research may consider increasing the sample size. Another limitation is that the data concerning students' perceptions were only collected through interviews, and future research may conduct questionnaire surveys to collect more data in this respect. Moreover, this research only examined learner perceptions, and future research may consider investigating the students' learning outcomes, motivation, and development of 21 century skills.

References

1. Kohnke, L., Moorhouse, B.L.: Facilitating synchronous online language learning through Zoom. RELC J. (2020). https://doi.org/10.1177/0033688220937235
2. Moorhouse, B.L., Kohnke, L.: Using mentimeter to elicit student responses in the EAP/ESP classroom. RELC J. **51**(1), 198–204 (2020)
3. Zhang, R., Zou, D.: Types, purposes, and effectiveness of state-of-the-art technologies for second and foreign language learning. Comput. Assist. Lang. Learn. (2020). https://doi.org/10.1080/09588221.2020.1744666
4. Zhang, R., Zou, D.: Types, features, and effectiveness of technologies in collaborative writing for second language learning. Comput. Assist. Lang. Learn. (2020). https://doi.org/10.1080/09588221.2021.1880441
5. Zou, D., Luo, S., Xie, H., Hwang, G.J.: A systematic review of research on flipped language classrooms: theoretical foundations, learning activities, tools and research topics and findings. Comput. Assist. Lang. Learn. (2020). https://doi.org/10.1080/09588221.2020.1839502
6. Su, F., Zou, D.: Technology-enhanced collaborative language learning: theoretical foundations, technologies, and implications. Comput. Assist. Lang. Learn. (2020). https://doi.org/10.1080/09588221.2020.1831545
7. Zou, D., Xie, H., Wang, F.: Future trends and research issues of technology-enhanced language learning: a technological perspective. Knowl. Manag. E-Learn. Int. J. **10**(4), 426–440 (2018)
8. Zou, D.: Gamified flipped EFL classroom for primary education student and teacher perceptions. J. Comput. Educ. **7**, 213–228 (2020)
9. Zou, D., Xie, H.R.: Flipping an English writing class with technology-enhanced just-in-time teaching and peer instruction. Interact. Learn. Environ. **27**(8), 1127–1142 (2019)
10. Zou, D., Xie, H., Wang, F., Kwan, R.: Flipped learning with Wikipedia in higher education. Stud. High. Educ. **45**(5), 1026–1045 (2020)
11. Zou, D., Huang, Y., Xie, H.: Digital game-based vocabulary learning: where are we and where are we going. Comput. Assist. Lang. Learn. (2019). https://doi.org/10.1080/09588221.2019.1640745
12. Hsia, L., Huang, I., Hwang, G.: A web-based peer-assessment approach to improving junior high school students performance, self-efficacy and motivation in performing arts courses. Br. J. Edu. Technol. **47**(4), 618–632 (2016)
13. Zhang, R.F., Zou, D., Wang, F.L., Au, T.S., Xie, H.R.: A systematic review of research on e-book-based language learning. Knowl. Manag. E-Learn. Int. J. **12**(1), 106–128 (2020)
14. Zou, D.: Comparing dictionary-induced vocabulary learning and inferencing in the context of reading. Lexikos **26**(1), 372–390 (2016)
15. Zou, D.: Vocabulary acquisition through cloze exercises, sentence-writing and composition writing: extending the evaluation component of the involvement load hypothesis. Lang. Teach. Res. **27**(1), 54–75 (2017)
16. Zou, D., Lambert, J.: Feedback methods for student voice in the digital age. Br. J. Edu. Technol. **48**(5), 1081–1091 (2017)
17. Kohnke, L., Zou, D., Zhang, R.: Exploring discipline-specific vocabulary retention in L2 through app design: implications for higher education students. RELC J. (2020). https://doi.org/10.1177/0033688219899740

Personalised Learning in STE(A)M Education: A Literature Review

Kam Cheong Li and Billy Tak-Ming Wong(✉)

The Open University of Hong Kong, Hong Kong, China
{kcli,tamiwong}@ouhk.edu.hk

Abstract. This paper presents a review study on the characteristics and patterns of personalised learning in the context of STEM and STEAM (or STE(A)M) education, which involves the disciplinary integration of Science, Technology, Engineering, Mathematics, as well as Arts. It covered a total of 63 papers published in 2011–2020 collected from Scopus and Google Scholar. The results show the widespread practice of personalised learning, and the United States was the country with most studies carried out. In terms of the level of education, secondary education was a major focus. Mathematics accounted for the largest proportion of subject discipline in the studies, followed by Science and Engineering. Blended environment was the most popular mode of education, followed by the face-to-face classroom. The most frequent objective of personalised learning was to cater for students' learning styles. The popular means to achieve personalised learning included the use of blended learning, learning analytics, and adaptive e-learning systems. Regarding the research issue, above half of the studies evaluated the impact or effectiveness of a technology, system or device for personalised learning. Based on the results, potential areas of future work are suggested, such as the contextualised practice of STE(A)M education in various countries, and the personalisation in interdisciplinary STE(A)M education.

Keywords: Personalised learning · Personalisation · STEAM education · STEM education

1 Introduction

Personalisation has become an emerging trend in education delivery across the globe. Personalised learning refers to "instruction in which the pace of learning and the instructional approach are optimised for the needs of each learner" [1]. It involves the adaptation of learning objectives, materials, activities and instructional approaches to learners' needs and individual characteristics such as learning style, preference, skill level and knowledge [2]. Through personalisation, it is believed that learning would become "meaningful and relevant to learners, driven by their interests, and often self-initiated" [1].

STEM and STEAM (or STE(A)M) education—involving the disciplinary integration of Science, Technology, Engineering, Mathematics, as well as Arts in some practices—is an area where personalised learning has been increasingly adopted. It focuses on the development of students' problem-solving skills and creativity to tackle real-life problems with the knowledge of the STE(A)M disciplines [3]. Previous work on personalised

R. Li et al. (Eds.): ICBL 2021, LNCS 12830, pp. 142–151, 2021.
https://doi.org/10.1007/978-3-030-80504-3_12

learning in STE(A)M has addressed a broad range of aspects, such as the development of technologies to support personalised learning, the evaluation of the impact and effectiveness of personalised learning, and the comparison of personalised instruction with traditional approaches.

Despite the plenty of related work, there has yet to be a systematic review of the literature on personalised learning in STE(A)M education. Previous reviews have only provided an overview of the STE(A)M publications [4], or addressed specific areas such as teachers' perceptions [5], and regional development [6].

To address the literature gap, this paper presents a review of the studies on personalised learning in STE(A)M education. It covers a total of 63 articles published from 2011 to 2020. The findings reveal the characteristics and patterns of relevant work such as the levels of education and subject disciplines involved, the objectives of and means to achieve personalised learning in STE(A)M, as well as the research issues addressed in the studies.

2 Related Studies

Personalised learning emphasises learners' choice and ownership in driving their learning [7]. Taken into consideration learners' needs and characteristics, personalised learning is believed to more effectively support the satisfaction of learners' psychological needs, and promote a greater level of learning motivation and engagement [8]. As reviewed by Li and Wong [9], personalised learning has been frequently achieved by the use of educational technologies such as intelligent learning or tutoring systems, mobile devices, learning analytics, as well as the adoption of flexible curriculum and customisation of learning materials and learning support.

STE(A)M education has been widely advocated and promoted across the globe for the past two decades. A major focus of it lies in the inter- or trans-disciplinary integration of subject knowledge and exposure in learning activities to develop learners' capabilities to solve real-world problems [10]. Personalised learning has been proposed as a way to enrich STE(A)M education through leveraging relevant technological advances [11] and address the potential challenges in STE(A)M education [12]. Reviews on personalised learning [9, 13] and STE(A)M education [14, 15] also show common objectives in their respective educational practices, such as the enhancement of learning motivation, engagement, and effectiveness.

However, there has not been a review on the implementation of personalised learning in STE(A)M education. Related reviews have only covered either personalised learning [9, 16] or STE(A)M education [4, 15], and specific aspects in each of the two areas such as teachers' perceptions [5] and use of learning analytics [13, 14]. There is thus a literature gap in the characteristics and patterns of personalised learning in STE(A)M education, which has been addressed in the current study.

3 Research Method

This study aims to review the literature on personalised learning in STE(A)M education and identify the characteristics of its research and practice. Relevant literature was collected from Scopus and Google Scholar. Two sets of keywords were used for the search:

- ("personalised learning" OR "personalized learning") AND ("STEM" OR "STEAM") AND ("education" OR "teaching")
- ("personalisation" OR "personalization") AND ("STEM" OR "STEAM") AND ("education" OR "teaching")

Both journal and conference papers were collected for review from the two publication databases. The period of publications was 2011–2020. Only the papers published in English with full papers accessible were collected. Each of the collected paper was checked to ensure that it reported a case of personalised learning in STE(A)M education. Finally, a total of 63 papers were selected for the review.

The features of the selected papers were identified and categorised into: (1) countries/territories, (2) levels of education, (3) subject disciplines, (4) modes of education, (5) objectives of personalising learning, (6) means to achieve personalised learning, and (7) research issues. These categories were adopted from Li and Wong [9] and Kwan and Wong [15].

4 Results

4.1 Countries/Territories

Figure 1 shows the countries/territories where studies on personalised learning in STE(A)M education were conducted and the percentage of studies for each country/territory. The United States is the country with the largest number of relevant research work, while accounts for 39% of the literature reviewed. About 7%–9% of the studies were conducted in Ireland, Taiwan or Mainland China. Overall, there have been a total of 19 countries/territories with relevant studies, covering various continents in the world. The result suggests that this topic has attracted global attention.

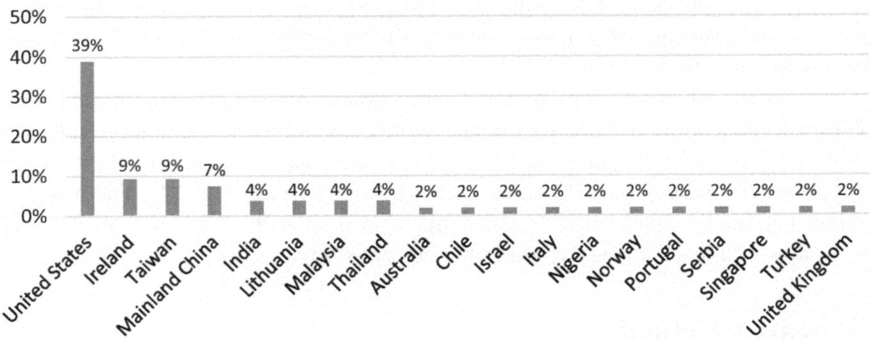

Fig. 1. Percentages of studies conducted in various countries/territories

4.2 Levels of Education

Figure 2 indicates the levels of education for the studies reviewed. Secondary education has been a major focus, in which 40% of the studies were carried out. This is followed by tertiary education (29%) and primary education (27%). Studies in kindergartens only contributed 4% of the literature. The distribution on levels of education is close to that for STE(A)M education in general as shown in Kwan and Wong [15].

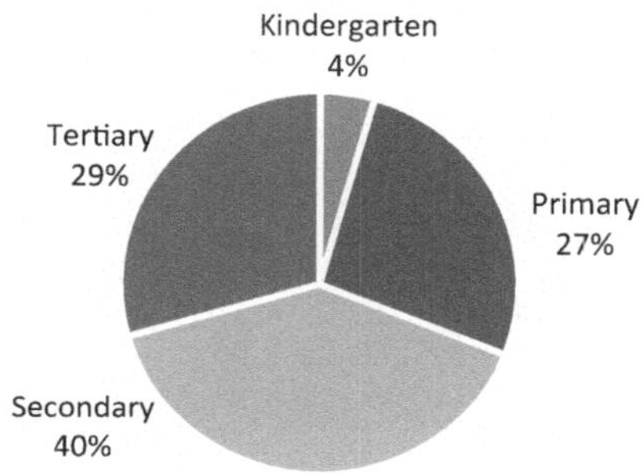

Fig. 2. Percentages of studies conducted at various levels of education

4.3 Subject Disciplines

Figure 3 shows the STE(A)M subject disciplines involved in the studies. A study may involve more than one discipline. Among the five STE(A)M disciplines, Mathematics accounts for the largest proportion (62%) of the studies, followed by Science (41%) and Engineering (40%). Arts has been involved only in a small proportion of studies (6%). It is worth-noting that 73% of the studies only involved one STE(A)M discipline.

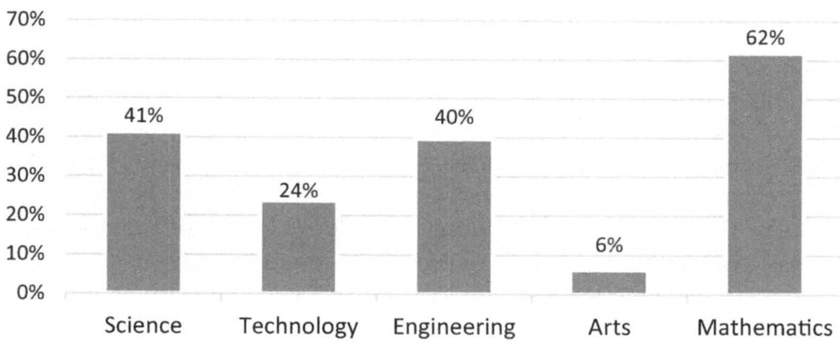

Fig. 3. Percentages of studies covering various subject disciplines in STE(A)M

4.4 Mode of Education

Figure 4 indicates the modes of education involved in the studies. Blended environment is the most popular mode which involves 35% of the studies. The education modes covered in a blended environment may cover face-to-face, web-based, mobile, etc. The face-to-face classroom is the second most popular mode of education, accounting for 30% of the studies. This is followed by the online environment (18%). Other than the above-mentioned ones which were adopted in studies as formal education, 11% of the studies were conducted in an informal self-study mode which allowed learners flexibility in the ways to learn. In addition, 6% of the studies were conducted in other modes of education, such as an outdoor environment.

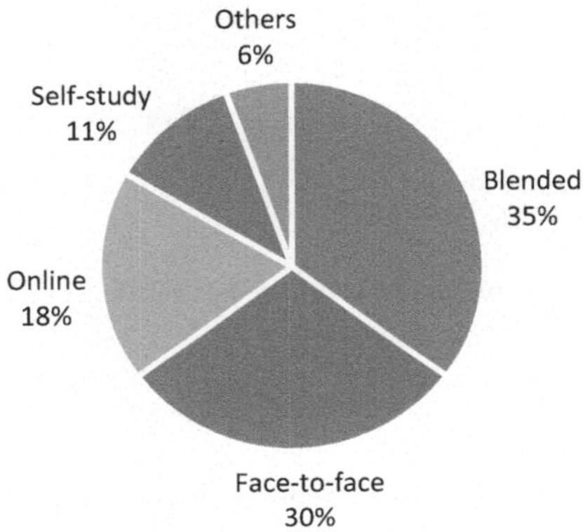

Fig. 4. Percentages of studies covering various modes of education

4.5 Objectives of Personalising Learning

Figure 5 indicates the objectives of personalising learning in the studies. A study may involve more than one objective. The largest proportion of studies focused on catering for learning styles (41%) as the way to personalise students' learning experience. About 25% of the studies focused on "enhancing learning motivation", "improving learning achievements" or "coping with learners' interest". This is followed by "improving learning engagement" (21%), "enriching learning experience" (17%), "improving learners' skills" (13%), "improving learning attitude" (11%), and "improving learning effectiveness" (8%). A few studies (3%) addressed other objectives such as enhancing self-efficacy and alleviating learners' anxiousness in STE(A)M learning.

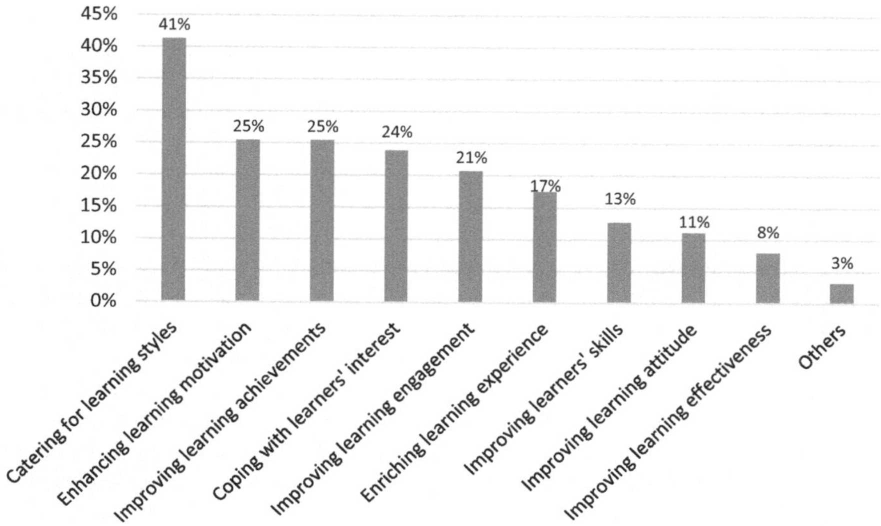

Fig. 5. Percentages of studies with various objectives of personalised learning

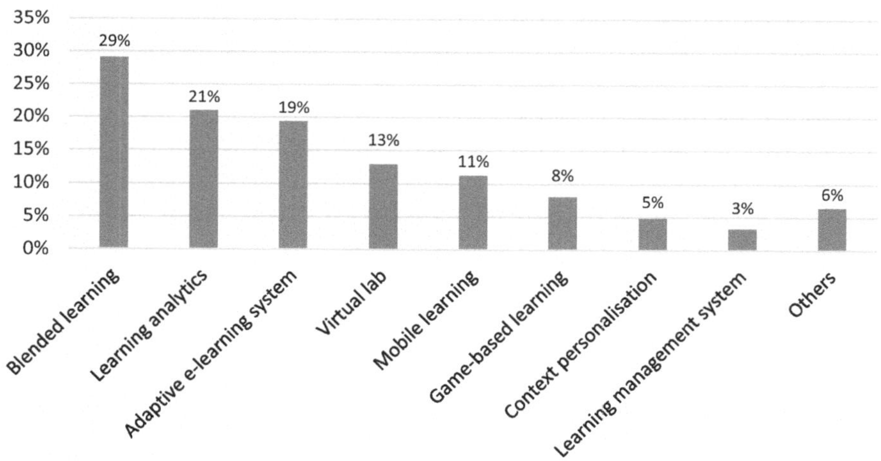

Fig. 6. Percentages of studies involving various means to achieve personalised learning

4.6 Means to Achieve Personalised Learning

Figure 6 indicates the means to achieve personalised learning in the studies. A study may involve the use of more than one means. The use of blended learning to address learners' preferences and needs through various channels is the most popular means, which involved 29% of the studies. This is followed by learning analytics (21%) and adaptive e-learning system (19%), both of which involve the utilisation of data to find out learners' patterns and ways to cope with their learning needs. Some studies addressed the personalisation of learning environments through the use of virtual lab (13%), mobile learning (11%) and game-based learning (8%). There were also small percentages of studies which adopted personalisation of the instructional contexts (5%) or with other means (6%) (e.g. simulators in computer network education and course recommendation systems).

4.7 Research Issues

Figure 7 shows the research issues explored in the studies. A study may address more than one issue. Among five categories of research issues summarised from the studies, the evaluation of the impact or effectiveness of a technology, system or device for personalised learning is the most popular one, which accounted for more than half (54%) of the studies. About one-fourth (24%) of the studies were explorative in nature, which aimed to find out suitable technologies, systems or devices for personalised learning. This is followed by the investigation of how these can be utilised (16%). The comparison between personalised and traditional instructional approaches contributed 14% of the studies. There were also 13% which examined learners' perception on personalised learning.

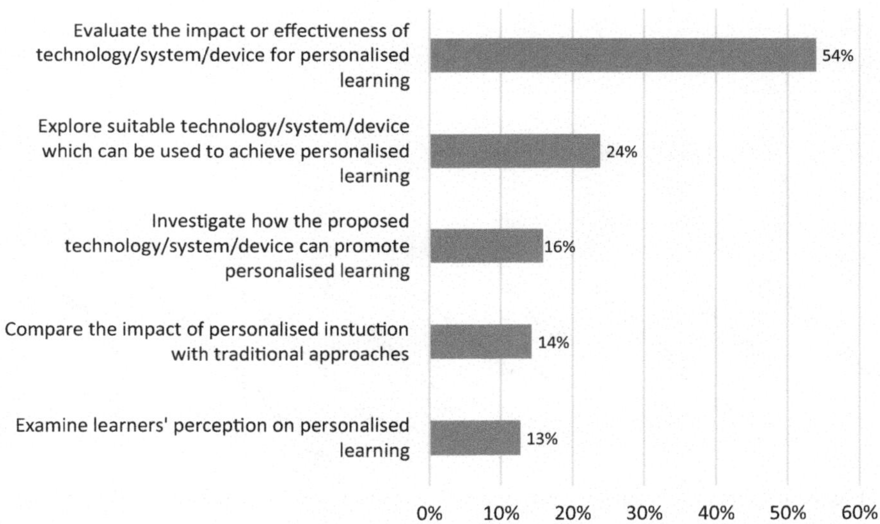

Fig. 7. Percentages of studies which addressed various research issues

5 Discussion

The findings of this study have revealed the characteristics and patterns of personalised learning in STE(A)M education. The various countries/territories where the studies were conducted show the widespread practice of personalisation. Comparing with the related reviews on STEAM education [15] and STEM education [17], there have been some consistent patterns, such as the United States and secondary education being the country and the level of education with the largest proportion of relevant studies, respectively. However these patterns are different from the review of Li and Wong [9], where in general personalised learning has been more commonly studied in higher education. The discordant findings of related reviews suggest that there have been special features of personalised learning in STE(A)M education.

There has been uneven coverage of subject disciplines in the studies. Mathematics has been the most popular discipline while Arts has been the least one. This may be due to the fact that the development of STEAM education was later than that of STEM education. It is also worth noting that interdisciplinary practice was not a majority in the studies reviewed, which is different from the related STEM and STEAM reviews [15, 17] where most studies involved more than one STE(A)M-related discipline.

Most of the studies were carried out in a blended learning environment or a conventional face-to-face classroom. This may be related to the finding that 67% of the studies were conducted in primary or secondary education, which usually involved physical contact with teachers and peers. Also, there has been a trend in recent years that more studies have been carried out in the tertiary education level with personalised learning practiced in online or self-study environments. Kintsakis and Rangoussi [18] pointed out that STE(A)M learning in such environments requires learners to be self-motivated and self-disciplined, which is challenging for younger learners.

The objectives in the studies revealed a common learner-centric feature which has been recognised as a key element of personalising learning. The learner-centric feature involves students' active participation in their learning—students own and co-design their learning while teachers are their guide [19, 20]. This feature also aligns with the emphasis of STE(A)M education on developing students' interest in and understanding of STE(A)M-related disciplines by linking them together to solve real-life problems [21]. In this sense, the introduction of personalised learning would be beneficial for students by promoting their involvement in the STE(A)M learning process.

Most of the means to achieve personalisation in STE(A)M learning involved the use of technology, e.g. online and mobile channels, data analytics, virtual environments, and computer games. The high level of technology adoption in personalised learning implies the need to have relevant technologies available for teachers and the readiness of the teachers to make effective use of them. However, Lee et al. [22] found that many schools in the United States—despite being the country with the largest proportion of relevant studies carried out—did not yet have a technology system which provides all the major functions for personalised learning. While the advantages of personalised learning has been widely shown in the studies, the development and provision of relevant technologies for educational institutions should also be addressed in future work for promoting the actual practice of personalised learning.

Regarding the research issues of the studies, the evaluation of effectiveness has been a majority. Most of studies proposed tools or systems for personalised STE(A)M learning, which usually involved an evaluation to assess their effectiveness. This pattern has been consistent with other related review findings [9, 15]. However, only 13% of the studies examined users' perceptions on personalised learning, which is comparatively lower than the overall proportion of personalised learning studies addressing this issue as reported in Li and Wong [9]. In this regard, future studies should examine more aspects of users' perception, such as acceptance and satisfaction.

6 Conclusion

This study has contributed to revealing the features and patterns of personalised learning in STE(A)M education. The findings show the diversity of personalisation in this context in terms of the countries/territories and levels of education in which relevant studies were carried out, the subject disciplines and modes of education involved, the objectives of and means to achieve personalised learning, and the research issues addressed. They provide an overview of the latest development in this area for STE(A)M teachers to enhance education delivery by introducing personalisation elements.

The findings also suggest potential areas of future work. More studies should be conducted for examining the specific contexts of STE(A)M education in different countries/territories and the practice of personalised learning which is effective to address the contexts. The personalisation in interdisciplinary STE(A)M education is another area which should receive more attention. Investigations should be done for the current status of technology adoption in personalised learning in STE(A)M education and the challenges involved. Also, in addition to the effectiveness issues, users' perceptions on new technologies and approaches for personalised learning, such as acceptance and satisfaction, should be studied.

Acknowledgments. The work described in this paper was partially supported by a grant from the Open University of Hong Kong (2021/011).

References

1. Xie, H., Chu, H.C., Hwang, G.J., Wang, C.C.: Trends and development in technology-enhanced adaptive/personalized learning: a systematic review of journal publications from 2007 to 2017. Comput. Educ. **140**, (2019)
2. Deng, Y., Lu, D., Chung, C.J., Huang, D., Zeng, Z.: Personalized learning in a virtual hands-on lab platform for computer science education. In: Proceedings of 2018 IEEE Frontiers in Education Conference, pp. 1–8. IEEE (2018)
3. Ozkan, G., Umdu Topsakal, U.: Exploring the effectiveness of STEAM design processes on middle school students' creativity. Int. J. Technol. Des. Educ. (2019). https://doi.org/10.1007/s10798-019-09547-z
4. Bozkurt, A., Ucar, H., Durak, G., Idin, S.: The current state of the art in STEM research: a systematic review study. Cypriot J. Educ. Sci. **14**(3), 374–383 (2019)
5. Margot, K.C., Kettler, T.: Teachers' perception of STEM integration and education: a systematic literature review. Int. J. STEM Educ. **6**(2) (2019). https://doi.org/10.1186/s40594-018-0151-2
6. Jayarajah, K., Saat, R.M., Rauf, R.A.A.: A review of science, technology, engineering & mathematics (STEM) education research from 1999–2013: a Malaysian perspective. Eurasia J. Math. Sci. Technol. Educ. **10**(3), 155–163 (2014)
7. Groff, J.: Personalized learning: the state of the field & future directions. Center for Curriculum Redesign (2017). https://www.media.mit.edu/publications/personalized-learning/

8. Alamri, H., Lowell, V., Watson, W., Watson, S.L.: Using personalized learning as an instructional approach to motivate learners in online higher education: learner self-determination and intrinsic motivation. J. Res. Technol. Educ. **52**(3), 322–352 (2020)
9. Li, K.C., Wong, B.T.M.: Features and trends of personalised learning: a review of journal publications from 2001 to 2018. Interact. Learn. Environ. (2020). https://doi.org/10.1080/10494820.2020.1811735
10. Liao, C.: From interdisciplinary to transdisciplinary: an arts-integrated approach to STEAM education. Art Educ. **69**(6), 44–49 (2016)
11. Hurson, A.R., Sedigh, S., Miller, L., Shirazi, B.: Enriching STEM education through personalization and teaching collaboration. In: 2011 IEEE International Conference on Pervasive Computing and Communications Workshops, Seattle, pp. 543–549 (2011)
12. Gillet, D., de Jong, T., Sotirou, S., Salzmann, C.: Personalised learning spaces and federated online labs for STEM Education at School. In: 2013 IEEE Global Engineering Education Conference, Berlin, pp. 769–773 (2013)
13. Li, K.C., Wong, B.T.-M.: Personalising learning with learning analytics: a review of the literature. In: Cheung, S.K.S., Li, R., Phusavat, K., Paoprasert, N., Kwok, L. (eds.) ICBL 2020. LNCS, vol. 12218, pp. 39–48. Springer, Cham (2020). https://doi.org/10.1007/978-3-030-51968-1_4
14. Li, K.C., Wong, B.T.M.: Trends of learning analytics in STE(A)M education: a review of case studies. Interact. Technol. Smart Educ. **17**(3), 323–335 (2020)
15. Kwan, R., Wong, B.T.M.: Latest advances in STEAM education research and practice: a review of the literature. Int. J. Innov. Learn. (forthcoming)
16. Li, K.C., Wong, B.T.-M.: How learning has been personalised: a review of literature from 2009 to 2018. In: Cheung, S.K.S., Lee, L.-K., Simonova, I., Kozel, T., Kwok, L.-F. (eds.) ICBL 2019. LNCS, vol. 11546, pp. 72–81. Springer, Cham (2019). https://doi.org/10.1007/978-3-030-21562-0_6
17. Li, Y., Wang, K., Xiao, Y., Froyd, J.E.: Research and trends in STEM education: a systematic review of journal publications. Int. J. STEM Educ. **7**, 11 (2020). https://doi.org/10.1186/s40594-020-00207-6
18. Kintsakis, D., Rangoussi, M.: An early introduction to STEM education: teaching computer programming principles to 5th graders through an e-learning platform: A game-based approach. In: 2017 IEEE Global Engineering Education Conference, Athens, Greece, pp. 17–23 (2017)
19. Bray, B., McClaskey, K.: Make Learning Personal: The What, Who, WOW, Where, and Why. Corwin, Thousand Oaks (2015)
20. DeMink-Carthew, J., Olofson, M.W., LeGeros, L., Netcoh, S., Hennessey, S.: An analysis of approaches to goal setting in middle grades personalized learning environments. RMLE Online **40**(10), 1–11 (2017)
21. Perignat, E., Katz-Buonincontro, J.: STEAM in practice and research: an integrative literature review. Think. Skills Creativity **31**, 31–43 (2019)
22. Lee, D., Huh, Y., Lin, C.Y., Reigeluth, C.M.: Technology functions for personalized learning in learner-centered schools. Educ. Technol. Res. Dev. **66**(5), 1269–1302 (2018)

Applying an Intelligent Learning Partner in Teacher Education for Improving CT-Related TPACK

Zhenzhen He[1(✉)], Changqin Huang[1,2], Tao He[1], and Kai Bo[1]

[1] South China Normal University, Guangzhou 510000, China
{zzhe,2019020740}@m.scnu.edu.cn
[2] Zhejiang Normal University, Jinhua 321004, China
cqhuang@zju.edu.cn

Abstract. Developing effective learning strategies and tools to improve teachers' computational thinking-related teaching ability is becoming an increasingly important issue in the digital age. In this study, an intelligent learning partner was designed and developed under the guidance of the framework of technological pedagogical content knowledge and peer-assisted learning strategy. Moreover, a quasi-experiment has been conducted in a blended learning community to evaluate the effect of the intelligent learning partner on improving teachers' computational thinking-related technological pedagogical content knowledge. The participants were 32 pre-service teachers, comprising an experimental group (n = 16) and a control group (n = 16). The experimental results showed that the intelligent learning partner enabled the teachers to apply more knowledge of computational thinking-related technological pedagogical content knowledge into their lesson plans. Besides, it was found that the intelligent learning partner not only facilitated the teachers to think about students' learning process, but also helped the teachers recognize the advantages of specific technology and pedagogy. Besides, participants' feedback on improving the design of intelligent learning partners indicated that emotional interaction and explanations were needed.

Keywords: CT-related TPACK · Intelligent learning partner · Lesson plan · Formative assessment · Peer-assisted learning

1 Introduction

Recently, computational thinking (CT) has been incorporating into national education systems globally [1]. However, few teachers have adequate knowledge about what CT is and how to teach CT [2, 3]. In the past years, many efforts have been made to help teachers acquire CT-related content knowledge [4–6]. Meanwhile, scholars have argued the importance of developing effective instructional supports to enhance teachers' CT-related technological pedagogical content knowledge (TPACK), because acquiring knowledge in subject matter is not enough to teach CT [7–9].

Consequently, several attempts have been made to develop effective methods for improving teachers' CT-related TPACK, such as introducing teachers with fundamental

R. Li et al. (Eds.): ICBL 2021, LNCS 12830, pp. 152–163, 2021.
https://doi.org/10.1007/978-3-030-80504-3_13

theories, resources, and teaching cases [3, 10–12]. In particular, research has proved that designing lesson plans is an effective way of promoting and evaluating teachers' TPACK [11, 13].

Nevertheless, designing pedagogy and technology-integrated CT-related lesson plans remains a challenge for many teachers [3, 14].

To solve this problem, researchers and educators have developed many methods to provide teachers with learning supports. For instance, lesson design rubrics and heuristics have been provided as contextualizing scaffolds to develop teachers' TPACK [10]. Furthermore, peer-assisted learning strategy has been widely used to enhance teachers' TPACK by providing them with opportunities to get suggestions from peers through a mutually beneficial process [5, 15, 16]. Peers' feedback could enhance teachers' TPACK and confidence [17–19].

Meanwhile, it is found that peers sometimes make problematic suggestions and assessments [20, 21]. Moreover, time constraints are severe and common obstacles to engaging teachers in these training activities [2, 22, 23].

Therefore, it is vital to further explore effective scaffoldings or convenient tools to help teachers develop their CT-related TPACK.

Recently, intelligent learning partners have gradually been known as convenient and effective tools for promoting learning outcomes [24, 25]. Based on artificial intelligence technology, intelligent learning partners provide individuals with timely and objective feedback, which could assist learners in organizing and integrating various learning contents [26].

Thus, in this study, an intelligent learning partner was developed to improve teachers' CT-related TPACK. Moreover, a quasi-experiment was conducted to evaluate the effect of the intelligent learning partner by answering the following research questions:

Research question 1: What are the discernible improvements in the teachers' CT-related TPACK?

Research question 2: What are the teachers' perceptions of learning with the intelligent learning partner?

2 Conceptual Framework

2.1 CT-Related TPACK

Recently, many countries have incorporated CT into their national education systems [1]. Meanwhile, considerable efforts have been made to advance teachers' understanding of CT concepts and enhance teachers' confidence in teaching CT [4–6]. However, acquiring knowledge in subject matter is not enough to teach CT [8, 9]. Integrating CT into the curriculum remains a big challenge for lots of teachers [2, 3].

To deal with this problem, TPACK has been adopted to develop teachers' CT-related teaching ability. TPACK emphasizes the nuanced interactions among technological knowledge (TK) about common instructional aids, pedagogical knowledge (PK) about teaching methods, and content knowledge (CK) about the subject matter. Moreover, the four kinds of synthesized knowledge are technological pedagogical knowledge (TPK), technological content knowledge (TCK), pedagogical content knowledge (PCK), and technological pedagogical content knowledge (TPACK) [7].

Accordingly, CT-related TPACK refers to the teaching ability of using technological knowledge, pedagogical knowledge, and content knowledge about CT.

In recent years, TPACK has been frequently employed to promote teachers' professional development in many CT-related domains. For example, a study indicated that the pre-service teachers could gain a better understanding of learning content by observing examples and generating ideas of CT teaching [3]. In particular, designing lesson plans has been proved to be a valid method of developing and measuring teachers' TPACK, as it requires and conveys teachers' knowledge of what, when, how and why pedagogy, content and technology should be integrated [11, 13, 14].

Yet, designing pedagogy and technology-integrated CT-related lesson plans remains a challenge for individual teachers [3, 14]. In addition, time constraints are serious obstacles to engaging teachers in teacher training courses [1, 2, 22].

2.2 Peer-assisted Learning

Peer-assisted learning is a form of learning in which learners with similar educational backgrounds get feedback from each other through a mutually beneficial process [27].

Peer-assisted learning has been frequently adopted in teacher education. For instance, peer-assisted learning has been used to enhance teachers' TPACK [15]. Moreover, peer-assisted learning has been applied in education courses to improve future K-12 teachers' understanding of CT-related concepts [5]. Peer-assisted learning has also been suggested as a way of improving teachers' online learning performance [16].

Many studies have reported the effectiveness of peer-assisted learning on promoting learning performance. For instance, peer-assisted learning could provide learners with a sense of partner knowledge awareness which enables them to develop shared understanding [17, 18]. Besides, it is often showed that peer-assisted learning allows learners to work autonomously, effectively and confidently [19, 27].

On the other hand, challenges arise when partners feel compared, dominated or in conflict with each other [20]. It is also mentioned that peers can bring up problematic and unfair suggestions and assessments [21]. Furthermore, there is the issue of time mismatch between peers, which causes undesirable learning experiences [23].

2.3 Intelligent Learning Partner

Intelligent learning partners are artificial intelligence technology-based learning tools that provide individuals with timely and objective feedback [25].

Intelligent learning partners have been accepted in many educational contexts, such as automatic essay assessment [24] and sentiment analysis of students' comments [26].

Researchers have discussed the potential effect of intelligent learning partners on promoting learning outcomes. For instance, it is often mentioned that intelligent learning partners can alleviate teachers' workload and allow learners to learn more autonomously and confidently [24, 28]. Besides, it is recommended that large-scale deployment of intelligent learning partners can bring benefits to research and business [25]. Meanwhile, there is growing concern about the negative effect of integrating intelligent learning partners into educational contexts. For example, automatic feedback is unable to provide sufficient insight into students' works [29]. Moreover, the feedback from some intelligent learning partners is hard to understand [28].

However, as far as we know, there are still no intelligent learning partners developed for improving teachers' CT-related TPACK.

3 Development of the Intelligent Learning Partner

3.1 The System Structure of the Intelligent Learning Partner

Researchers have claimed that designing lesson plans is an effective way of improving teachers' TPACK [11, 13, 14]. Moreover, learning support is a critical factor for teachers to complete their lesson plans and other training activities [5, 10, 15, 21].

In view of these findings, an intelligent learning partner was developed in this study. Under the guidance of the framework of TPACK and peer-assisted learning strategy, the intelligent learning partner was designed to act as a capable peer who could provide comprehensive and professional feedback on helping teachers integrate the knowledge of CT-related TPACK in their lesson plans.

The system structure of the intelligent learning partner is shown in Fig. 1. Once a lesson plan has been uploaded, its context will be analyzed by the CT-related TPACK information-analyzing module. Then, the analysis results will be presented in a structured format in the formative assessment-displaying module. Meanwhile, the lesson plan and analysis results are recorded by the behavior-recording module. Moreover, the note-saving module allows users to edit and download the analysis results.

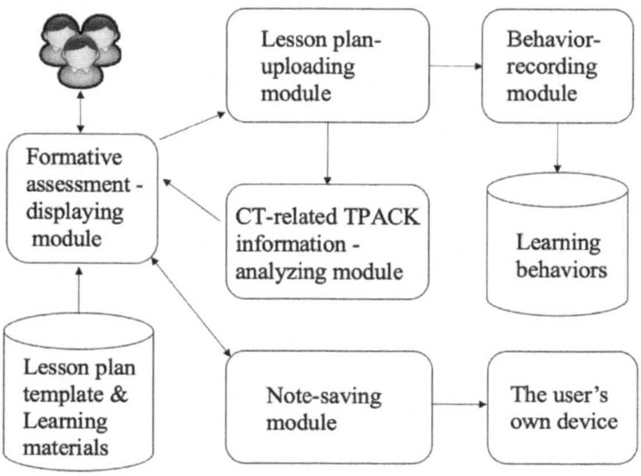

Fig. 1. The system structure of the intelligent learning partner

3.2 The CT-Related TPACK Information-Analyzing Module

In this study, the analysis process of an uploaded lesson plan in the CT-related TPACK information-analyzing module is shown in Fig. 2.

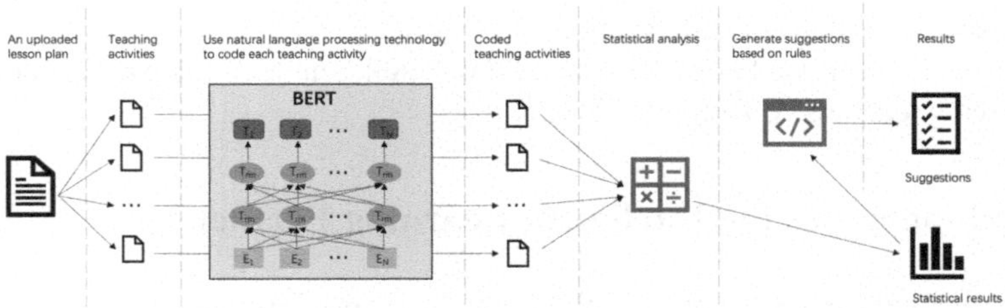

Fig. 2. The analysis process of an uploaded lesson plan

As suggested by Janssen, Knoef, and Lazonder [11], an uploaded lesson plan is first divided into a set of teaching activities. Within the framework of TPACK, each teaching activity is then classified into one of the eight codes (i.e. Pedagogy, Content, Technology, PCK, TPK, TCK, TPACK, and None). In this study, the classification process is performed by a set of classification models. More specially, Bidirectional Encoder Representations from Transformers (BERT), a popular natural language processing technology suitable for text classification, is used to train these classification models [26]. These classification models can identify whether an activity contains specific pedagogical knowledge, technical knowledge and CT-related content knowledge.

Based on the classification results, this module further generates statistical results. That is, the number of teaching activities and the proportion of each type of teaching activities. Finally, this module provides the user with feedback based on the statistical results and assessment rules. The assessment rules were developed through the Delphi method [30] and then integrated into this module.

3.3 The Usage of the Intelligent Learning Partner

When users access to the intelligent learning partner, a list of teaching methods, a list of CT-related concepts, and a list of CT-related teaching tools are presented to them. They select the specific knowledge that they want to be investigated from the three sets.

In addition, a lesson plan template is provided to users. Users are also allowed to send suggestions and questions to the developers of the intelligent learning partner. Figure 3 shows a screenshot of the intelligent learning partner.

After selecting the knowledge to be investigated, users upload their formatted lesson plan. The uploaded lesson plan will then be analyzed by the CT-related TPACK information-analyzing module and recorded on the cloud server for future research.

The CT-related TPACK information-analyzing module then returns the analysis results to the formative assessment-displaying module. As shown in Fig. 4, the intelligent learning partner can not only provide statistical results and suggestions, but also present the classification results of each teaching activity in a table. Moreover, users can take notes in the table before saving and downloading the results.

Fig. 3. A screenshot of the intelligent learning partner

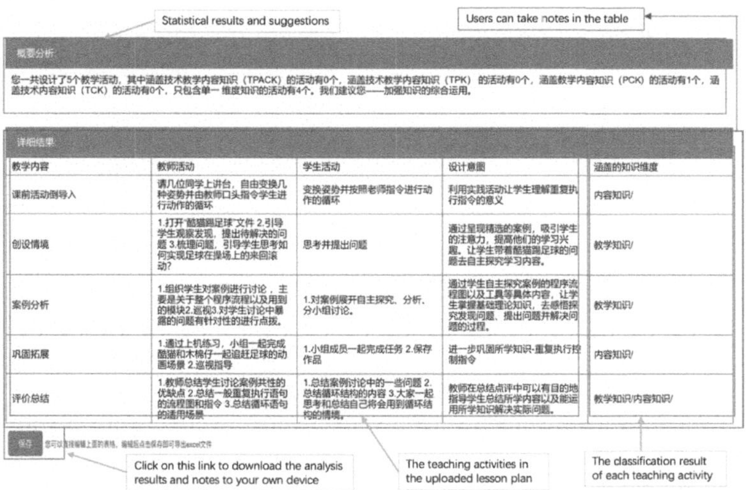

Fig. 4. A screenshot of the analysis results

4 Experimental Design

To evaluate the effect of the intelligent learning partner on improving teachers' CT-related TPACK, a quasi-experiment was conducted in a blended learning community.

4.1 Participants

In this study, the participants were 32 pre-service teachers majoring in educational technology. They were randomly assigned to an experimental group and a control group.

The experimental group with 16 teachers adopted the intelligent learning partner as learning assistance, while the control group with 16 teachers learned with peer-assisted learning strategy.

4.2 Instruments

The background questionnaire: It includes 11 items aiming to collect the participants' demographic characteristics, CT-related learning experience, and teaching experience.

The lesson plan template: The template is a form in which the teachers are instructed to specify basic organizational information (lesson title, teaching objectives, target students, etc.) and describe the teaching activities in a lesson. It also asks teachers to justify the decisions they made when designing lesson plans.

4.3 Procedure

Figure 5 shows the procedure of this quasi-experiment. First, the instruction of this study was presented. Then, the participants completed the background questionnaire individually.

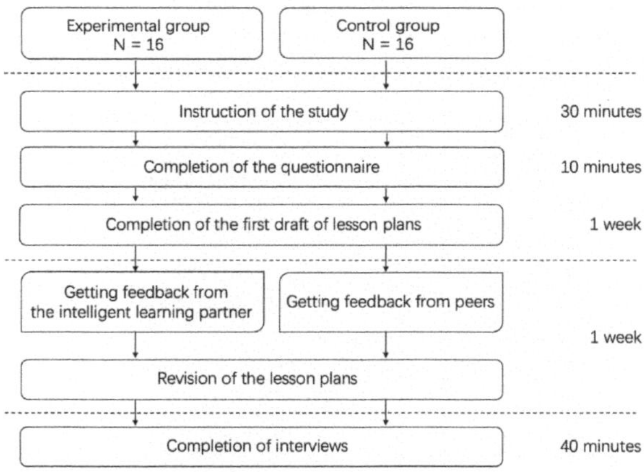

Fig. 5. Experimental procedure of the experiment

During the learning activities, each participant needed to complete a first draft of lesson plan according to the specific requirements.

The difference between the two groups was the learning assistance used to revise their lesson plans. The teachers in the control group got feedback from peers, while the teachers in the experimental group got feedback from the intelligent learning partner.

After a revised lesson plan was completed, we interviewed its owner.

5 Experimental Results

5.1 Discernible Improvements in the Participants' CT-Related TPACK

The questionnaire survey results showed that there was no significant difference in the participants' prior CT-related knowledge and experience between the two groups.

Inspired by the technology-integration quality assessment method [11], each lesson plan was scored. Further then, the quality of each lesson plan was quantified by the Formula 1, which was developed by using the Delphi method [30]:

$$Score_{quality} = Score_{tpack} * 40\% + Score_{tck} * 20\% + Score_{tpk} * 20\% + Score_{pck} * 20\% \quad (1)$$

The Independent sample t-test results showed that there was no significant difference in the CT-related TPACK of the two groups before this experiment. There was no significant difference in the quantity of teaching activities ($t = 0.66$, $p > 0.05$), nor in the quality of the first draft of lesson plans ($t = 0.15$, $p > 0.05$).

As shown in Table 1, there were differences between the two groups after the experiment. For the experimental group, there was significant improvement in the quality of the lesson plans ($t = -3.40$, $p < 0.01$), but not in quantity of teaching activities ($t = -1.00$, $p > 0.05$). On the contrary, the control group only had significant improvement in quantity of teaching activities ($t = -3.10$, $p < 0.01$).

Table 1. Paired t-test results of the lesson plans

Groups	Statistical items	The first draft of lesson plans		The revised lesson plans		*t*	*df*	*p*
		M	SD	M	SD			
Experimental group	The quantity of teaching activities	7.69	3.40	7.81	3.29	−1.00	15	0.333
	The quality of the lesson plans	1.11	0.67	1.56	0.63	−3.40	15	0.004
Control group	The quantity of teaching activities	7.06	1.65	7.69	1.70	−3.10	15	0.007
	The quality of the lesson plans	1.15	0.71	1.15	0.66	0.00	15	1.000

Figure 6 shows that the experimental group had more lesson plans containing teaching activities coded as TPACK. In particular, many of these teaching activities scored three points. That is, these activities presented a consideration of the students' learning process and a clear description of the advantage of technology and pedagogy for the teaching content. These results indicated that the teachers in the experimental group were more likely to think about their students' learning process and the advantage of technology and pedagogy for the specific CT-related teaching content.

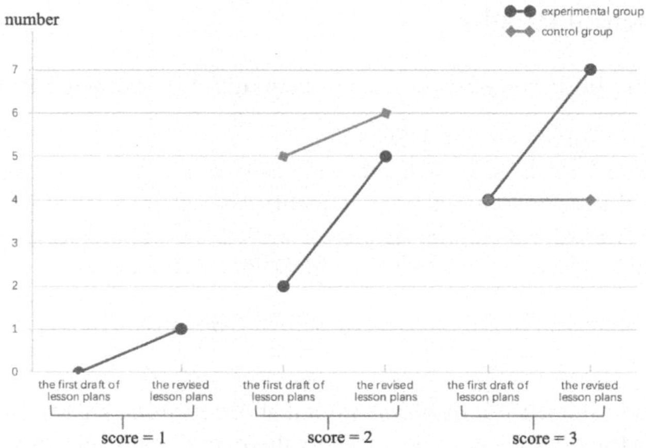

Fig. 6. The number of lesson plans containing teaching activities coded as TPACK

5.2 Participants' Perceptions of the Intelligent Learning Partner

The interview data was analyzed according to the three-layer coding procedure [31].

The experimental group highlighted the effectiveness of the intelligent learning partner. In particular, the most mentioned benefits were timeliness, availability, and objectivity of feedback.

On the other hand, the experimental group complained that the need to use a fixed lesson plan template and upload lesson plans was their dissatisfaction with the intelligent learning partner.

In addition, the teachers had some suggestions for improving the design of intelligent learning partners. First, they hoped intelligent learning partners could not only point out their problems, but also present reasons. Following that, it would be better if intelligent learning partners could recommend some excellent lesson plans and learning materials to them. Finally, some teachers expected intelligent learning partners to give them emotional interaction, especially encouragement and praise.

6 Discussion and Implications

In this study, an intelligent learning partner was developed and used to provide effective scaffolding to help teachers improve their CT-related TPACK. The experimental results showed that the intelligent learning partner could improve the teachers' CT-related TPACK. The interview results provided implications for the design and application of intelligent learning partners.

First, we found that the two groups improved in different aspects. The experimental group had significant improvement in the quality of the lesson plans, while the control group made progress in the quantity of teaching activities.

Such findings complement previous research that revising lesson plans is a valid method of developing teachers' TPACK [11, 13, 14]. More specially, these findings indicate the satisfactory power of the intelligent learning partner developed in this study.

Second, the interview results showed that the experimental group highlighted the effectiveness of the intelligent learning partner on improving their CT-related TPACK. The most mentioned benefits were timeliness, availability, and objectivity of feedback. In this study, it was convenient to interact with the intelligent learning partner. The experimental group could access to it at any time and get feedback from it as many times as they want.

The interview results confirmed the view that intelligent learning partners could provide effective and convenient learning assistance [24, 28]. Thus, intelligent learning partners are proposed for large-scale use in schools and homes [25].

In the meantime, there were some suggestions. First, the teachers hoped the intelligent learning partner could not only point out their problems, but also present reasons. Following that, excellent lesson plans and learning materials were also desired. In addition, some teachers expected the intelligent learning partner to give them emotional interaction, such as encouragement and praise.

Some researchers have pointed out that the feedback from intelligent learning partners should be easy to understand [28, 29]. Adding to this, this study offers two implications for improving the design of intelligent learning partners. First, intelligent learning partners should give the reasons for their judgments. Second, emotional interaction is desired.

7 Conclusion and Limitation

To sum up, an intelligent learning partner was designed and developed to help teachers enhance their CT-related TPACK. Furthermore, a quasi-experiment was conducted to explore the effectiveness and limitations of the intelligent learning partner. The results showed that the intelligent learning partner could provide timely, effective and objective feedback which helped the teachers improve the quality of their lesson plans. The intelligent learning partner not only facilitated the teachers to think about students' learning process, but also helped the teachers recognize the advantages of specific technology and pedagogy for the CT-related teaching content. Besides, suggestions on improving the design of intelligent learning partners were provided.

Despite the valuable findings, there are some limitations in this study. First, the participants in this study were pre-service teachers majoring in educational technology. Thus, the generalization of these findings might be limited to learners with similar educational backgrounds. Second, it would be better to conduct long-term experiments to evaluate the effect of the intelligent learning partner.

Statements on Ethics

This study was conducted in line with the ethical guidelines. The participants in this study were voluntary. They were also protected by hiding their personally identifiable information. The data collected for the quasi-experiment was stored in a password-protected computer database.

Acknowledgment. This work was supported by the Humanities and Social Sciences Planning Fund of the Ministry of Education (No. 18YJA880027).

References

1. Bower, M., et al.: Improving the computational thinking pedagogical capabilities of school teachers. Aust. J. Teach. Educ. **42**(3), 53–72 (2017)
2. Adler, R.F., Kim, H.: Enhancing future K-8 teachers' computational thinking skills through modeling and simulations. Educ. Inf. Technol. **23**, 1501–1514 (2018)
3. Mouza, C., Yang, H., Pan, Y.C., Ozden, S.Y.: Resetting educational technology coursework for pre-service teachers: a computational thinking approach to the development of technological pedagogical content knowledge. Aust. J. Educ. Technol. **33**(3) (2017)
4. Bean, N., Weese, J., Feldhausen, R., Bell, R.S.: Starting from scratch developing a pre-service teacher training program in computational thinking. In: Proceedings of the 2015 IEEE Frontiers in Education Conference 2015, pp. 1–8 (2015)
5. Yadav, A., Zhou, N., Mayfield, C., Hambrusch, S., Korb, J.T.: Introducing computational thinking in education courses. In: Proceedings of the 42nd ACM Technical Symposium on Computer Science Education, pp. 465–470 (2011)
6. Jaipal-Jamani, K., Angeli, C.: Effect of robotics on elementary preservice teachers' self-efficacy, science learning, and computational thinking. J. Sci. Educ. Technol. **26**, 175–192 (2017)
7. Mishra, P., Koehler, M.J.: Technological pedagogical content knowledge: a framework for teacher knowledge. Teach. Coll. Rec. **108**(6), 1017–1054 (2006)
8. Leonard, J., Mitchell, M., Barnes-Johnson, J., Unertl, A., Outka-Hill, J., Robinson, R., Hester-Croff, C.: Preparing teachers to engage rural students in computational thinking through robotics, game design, and culturally responsive teaching. J. Teach. Educ. **69**(4), 386–407 (2018)
9. Akyuz, D.: Measuring TPACK through performance assessment. Comput. Educ. **125**, 212–225 (2018)
10. Koh. J.: TPACK design scaffolds for supporting teacher pedagogical change. Educ. Technol. Res. Dev. **67**, 577–595 (2019)
11. Janssen, N., Knoef, M., Lazonder, A.W.: Technological and pedagogical support for pre-service teachers' lesson planning. Technolo. Pedag. Educ. **28**(1), 115–128 (2019)
12. Yadav, A., Stephenson, C., Hong, H.: Computational thinking for teacher education. Commun. ACM **60**(4), 55–62 (2017)
13. Tsouccas, L., Meletiou-Mavrotheris, M.: Enhancing the technological, pedagogical and content knowledge (TPACK) of in-service primary teachers in the use of tablet technologies. In: Proceedings of 16th World Conference on Mobile and Contextual Learning (2017)
14. Zha, S., Jin, Y., Moore. P., Gaston, J.: A cross-institutional investigation of a flipped module on preservice teachers' interest in teaching computational thinking. J. Digit. Learn. Teach. Educ. **36**(1), 32–45 (2020)
15. Bueno-Alastuey, M.C., Villarreal, I., Esteban, S.G.: Can telecollaboration contribute to the TPACK development of pre-service teachers? Technol. Pedag. Educ., 1–14 (2018)
16. Judele, R., Tsovaltzi, D., Puhl, T., Weinberger, A.: Collaborative learning in facebook: adverse effects of individual preparation. In: 47th Hawaii International Conference on System Science (2014)
17. Neugebauer, J., Ray, D.G., Sassenberg, K.: When being worse helps: the influence of upward social comparisons and knowledge awareness on learner engagement and learning in peer-to-peer knowledge exchange. Learn. Instr. **44**, 41–52 (2016)
18. Zufferey, J.D., Bodemer, D., Buder, J., Hesse, F.W.: Partner knowledge awareness in knowledge communication: learning by adapting to the partner. J. Exp. Educ. **79**, 102–125 (2011)

19. Millwood, R., Strong, G., Bresnihan, N., Cowan, P.: CTWINS-improving computational thinking confidence in educators through paired activities. In: WiPSCE 2016 (2016)
20. Bone, K., Bone, J., Grieshaber, S.: A peer assisted learning approach to pre-service teacher professional experiences in Australia: organisational friendships. Asia Pac. J. Teach. Educ. **47**(4), 347–360 (2019)
21. Sekendiz, B.: Utilisation of formative peer-assessment in distance online education: a case study of a multi-model sport management unit. Interact. Learn. Environ. **26**(5), 682–694 (2017). https://doi.org/10.1080/10494820.2017.1396229
22. Kale, U., et al.: Computational what? Relating computational thinking to teaching. TechTrends **62**, 574–584(2018)
23. Lillejord, S., Børte, K.: Partnership in teacher education-a research mapping. Eur. J. Teach. Edu. **39**(5), 550–563 (2016)
24. Lu, M., Deng, Q., Yang, M.: EFL writing assessment: peer assessment vs. automated essay scoring. In: SETE 2019, pp. 21–29 (2019)
25. Lu, Y., Chen, C., Chen, P., Chen, X., Zhuang, Z.: Smart learning partner: an interactive robot for education. In: International Conference on Artificial Intelligence in Education, pp. 447–451 (2018)
26. Zheng, J., Wang, J., Ren, Y., Yang, Z.: Chinese sentiment analysis of online education and internet buzzwords based on BERT. In: 2nd International Conference on Artificial Intelligence and Computer (2020)
27. Bain, P., Wareing, A., Henderson, I.: A review of peer-assisted learning to deliver interprofessional supplementary image interpretation skills. Radiography **23**, S64–S69 (2017)
28. Fangohr, H., et al.: Automatic feedback frovision in teaching computational science. In: ICCS 2020, pp. 608–621 (2020)
29. Mirmotahari, O., Berg, Y., Gjessing, S., Fremstad, E., Damsa, C.: A case-study of automated feedback assessment. In: 2019 IEEE Global Engineering Education Conference (2019)
30. Brady, S.R.: Utilizing and adapting the Delphi method for use in qualitative research. Int. J. Qual. Methods **14**(5), 1–6 (2015). https://doi.org/10.1177/1609406915621381
31. Strauss, A.L., Corbin, J.M.: Basics of Qualitative Research: Techniques and Procedures for Developing Grounded Theory, 2nd edn. Thousand Oaks, Sage (1998)

Using Chatbots in Flipped Learning Online Sessions: Perceived Usefulness and Ease of Use

Khe Foon Hew(✉), Weijiao Huang, Jiahui Du, and Chengyuan Jia

The University of Hong Kong, Pokfulam Road, Hong Kong SAR, China
kfhew@hku.hk

Abstract. Many educators in higher education are using blended learning as an important component of their academic programs. Of the many forms of blended learning, the flipped learning approach, has attracted much attention from many universities, where students learn course materials typically through online video lectures before class so that they can do more active learning in the classroom. Its actual implementation, however, is often beset with challenges, with student disengagement in pre-class online activities being one major problem reported in many previous flipped learning studies. Students who fail to complete the pre-class tasks often have difficulty in performing the follow-up in-class discussions with the instructors and peers. This study, which is part of a larger research project on engaging student in flipped learning, explored the use of two types of chatbots in flipped learning online sessions: Quiz Chatbot, and Self-Regulated Learning Chatbot. We described in detail the implementations of the two chatbots, and evaluated the chatbots in terms of its perceived usefulness, and perceived ease of use. We also examined the extent of student behavioral engagement with the chatbots. Suggestions to improve the chatbots were discussed, along with recommendations for future research.

Keywords: Flipped learning · Online learning · Chatbot · Blended learning

1 Introduction

1.1 Background

Flipped learning refers to a pedagogical approach that combines pre-class online learning with face-to-face (F2F) learning. Pre-class preparations may take various forms including watching video lectures, taking short quizzes, and having discussions with fellow students (Lo et al. 2017). During the face-to-face sessions, students are expected to utilize their time to apply the knowledge learned through problem-based discussions and presentations (Bishop and Verleger 2013).

Although the flipped learning approach is not a panacea for all education ills, it appears to promote significantly higher student achievement compared to the traditional instructor lecture approach (Strelan et al. 2020; van Alten et al. 2019). However, it is important to note that the positive learning outcome afforded by flipped learning is *only possible* if all students come prepared to the face-to-face class sessions. If students fail

R. Li et al. (Eds.): ICBL 2021, LNCS 12830, pp. 164–175, 2021.
https://doi.org/10.1007/978-3-030-80504-3_14

to complete the pre-class learning activities, the instructor will have no choice but to re-teach the materials in class. This would render the entire flipped learning approach no different than a traditional lecture.

Many previous flipped learning studies have found that a lack of student engagement in the pre-class activities to be a persistent and widespread problem. Diwanji et al. (2018), for instance, reported that only 27.7% of students often prepared for a class. In other studies, 39% of students reported that they did not do any preparation at all for the face-to-face classes (Sahin et al. 2015), and more than 70% students skipped the pre-class learning activities (Palmer 2015). Some of the main reasons for not preparing for classes included a lack of motivation for doing the pre-class activities (Lo et al. 2017), and failing to understand the pre-class course content because students have difficulty communicating with the instructor when watching videos at home (Scott et al. 2016).

To engage students in the pre-class activities, most studies linked the completion of pre-class tasks to a portion of students' final course grade (Diwanji et al. 2018; Elliott and Rob 2014). Students who complete the pre-class tasks (e.g., watch videos, answer quizzes) will be awarded some marks, while those who ignored the tasks will not receive any. Yet, using "marks-for-task-completion" may not necessary promote student in-depth thinking. Students may simply "play the game" of assessment by arbitrarily clicking on the quiz answers, or letting the videos play to completion without anyone actually watching them.

The purpose of the present study is to explore the use of chatbots in flipped learning online sessions. More specifically, this study is part of a larger research project that examines whether chatbots can be used as an innovative strategy to promote flipped learning student engagement in the online pre-class activities. In this article, we focus on providing a thick description of the development of two chatbots: Quiz bot, and Goal-setting bot, using a visual development tool – Dialogflow. We then evaluated the chatbots in terms of its perceived usefulness, and perceived ease of use from the students' perspectives. We also examined the extent of student engagement with the chatbots.

1.2 Chatbot

A chatbot is a computer programmed conversational tool bot that interacts with users on a certain topic using natural language (Diwanji et al. 2018). A chatbot can be either a text-based or audio-based dialog system that facilitates human-computer interaction by asking or answering questions (Fryer et al. 2017), and prompt students to complete their assignments (McNeal 2017).

Chatbots have the potential to reduce the transactional distance that frequently happens between learners and instructors in an online learning space. According to Moore's (1997) theory of transactional distance, there is a psychological and communication gap between the instructor and the learner in online learning space which creates room for potential misunderstanding. If transactional distance is reduced, learners are more likely to feel satisfied with their learning environment. Chatbots can help reduce the transactional distance by providing a dialogue for the learner to interact with the course content. There is preliminary evidence that chatbots can motivate students for learning and keep them engaged in the learning process (Diwanji et al. 2018), and decrease students' sense of isolation during online learning (Huang et al. 2019).

Despite the growing interest in chatbots, extant research is still in its infancy. Previous research has focused mainly on the use of chatbots in second or foreign language learning (Smutny and Schreiberova 2020) such as using chatbot to practice vocabulary knowledge with learners (Kim 2018). The use of chatbots outside the domain of second or foreign language learning is limited. We do not know much about the use of chatbots to support other forms of online course activities such as providing hints to quiz questions, or providing goal-setting recommendations to learners.

Chatbot-Building Tool

In this study, Dialogflow from Google was employed to develop our chatbots activities. We decided to use Dialogflow due to the following reasons: first, it is free and enables users to add chatbots into webpages. The Moodle learning management system was utilized by the university in the present study and it allows users to add embedded code related to Dialogflow for our online activities. Second, the visual development dashboard of Dialogflow requires no computer coding knowledge, which allows non-programming users to design chatbots easily.

The chatbots in our study were rule-based, rather than AI-based. Rule-based bots answer user questions based on a pre-determined set of rules that are embedded into them, while AI bots are self-learning bots that are programmed with Natural Language Processing and Machine Learning (Joshi 2020). We chose to use a rule-based bot (rather than an AI bot) because a rule-based bot is much simpler to build especially for people who do not have an IT background, and is much faster to train (Joshi 2020). Although AI bots can self-learn from data, it usually takes a long time to train them. More importantly, the self-learning ability of AI bots is not always perfect – for example, AI bots can learn something they are not supposed to, and start to post offensive messages (Joshi 2020).

A chatbot taking the role of a learning partner, named *Learning Buddy*, was integrated into university students' flipped online learning activities in two case studies. We developed two types of chatbot online activities in *Learning Buddy* – Quiz Chatbot and Self-Regulated Learning (SRL) Chatbot. The Quiz Chatbot offered students short quizzes and reinforce their understanding of the learning contents. The SRL Chatbot was designed to assist students to set their own personal goals when attending a course. Both chatbots provided information in the form of conversations with students.

2 Case I: Quiz Chatbot

2.1 The Development of the Quiz Chatbot

We integrated the Quiz Chatbot into Moodle where students received the online learning materials before they came to class. Students were required to interact with the Quiz Chatbot to assess the main learning contents before attending a tutorial session. The learning topic was social media. The training utterances, including questions, intents, entities, and appropriate responses, were designed based on the learning topic and manually added to the Dialogflow system. Intents refer to the goals or motive the user has in mind when conversing with a Chatbot (McGrath 2017). For example, if a user types "show me yesterday's weather temperature", the user's goal or motive is to retrieve information concerning the previous day's weather. An entity modifies an intent

(McGrath 2017). For example, if a user types "show me yesterday's weather temperature", the entities would be "yesterday", "weather", and "temperature". The Dialogflow system was able to learn from the training utterances and capture students' inputs during the conversation.

The Quiz Chatbot greeted students on the Moodle webpage via a live chat bubble (see Fig. 1). Next, three quizzes were asked by the Quiz Chatbot one after another. After students typed the answers, Quiz Chatbot would determine students' inputs and provide relevant feedback. We employed chit-chats between quizzes to create a friendly learning climate and engage students to complete the quiz task. For example, the Quiz Chatbot asked students "is this quiz helpful in comprehending the definition of social media?" to show its concern for students' learning process. If students appreciated the use of chatbot on knowledge understanding, Quiz Chatbot would respond "Thanks, happy to know that!"; otherwise, the chatbot would explain "I'm still being developed, and your response can help me become better. Hope you can find the next quiz helpful". Figure 2 showed the conversation flow between students and the Quiz Chatbot.

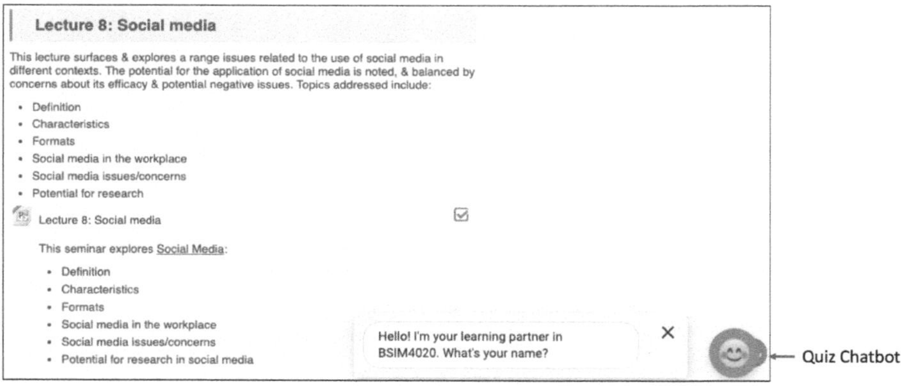

Fig. 1. Quiz Chatbot greeted students on Moodle

2.2 Data Collection and Analysis

Participants were students who enrolled in an undergraduate course at a public university in Hong Kong. We obtained the ethical approval of this study from the university Institutional Review Board. The researcher introduced the chatbot activity and informed students of the study before the course. To evaluate students' behavioral engagement, we collected conversation records between students and the Quiz Chatbot in the pre-class learning session. To investigate students' perceived usefulness and ease of use of the Quiz Chatbot, a five-point scale questionnaire was used (adapted from Davis 1989, p. 340). Davis (1989) defined perceived ease of use is defined as "the degree to which a person believes that using a particular system would be free of effort" (p. 320), whereas perceived usefulness refers to "the degree to which a person believes that using a particular system would enhance his or her job performance" (p. 320). The scale ranged from 1 (i.e., strongly disagree) to 5 (i.e., strong agree). The questionnaire was administrated to students in their pre-class learning. Students' perceived usefulness consisted of five items, for example, "*The Learning Buddy chatbot addressed my needs of the tutorial activity preparation*". Students' perceived ease of use was measure by another five items, such as "*I found it easy to use the chatbot to communicate*" and "*I found it easy to recover from errors encountered while using the chatbot*".

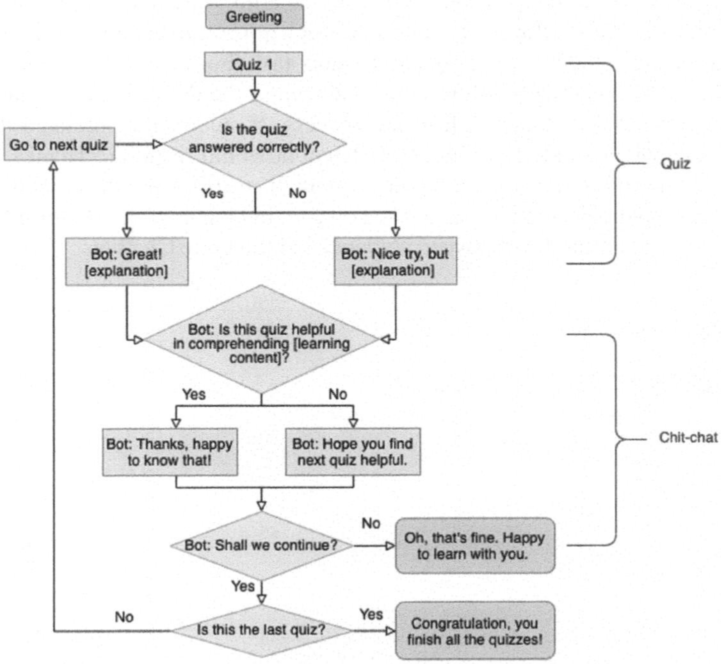

Fig. 2. The flowchart of the Quiz Chatbot design

There were 56 students enrolled in this course, and 17 students voluntarily participated in our study and interacted with the Quiz Chatbot during their pre-class learning. Within the 17 students, 15 of them finished all quizzes through the chatbot. Therefore, we collected these 15 students' chatbot conversation records and analyzed student-chatbot utterance turn, session length, and goal completion rate. Utterance turn or conversation step refers to the number of back-and-forth exchange between a chatbot and a user (Yao 2016). For example, if a chatbot says "hello" and the user replies "hello", this is one utterance turn. Session length, also known as session duration or handle time, can be defined as the amount of time that elapses between the moment a user starts to converse with a chatbot and the moment they end the conversation (Mead 2019). Goal completion rate refers to the number of times the chatbot succeeds in achieving its purpose, which is to help learners complete the quizzes in this case. Table 1 shows the descriptive statistics of students' behavioral engagement. The average utterance turns between students and chatbot was 14.6 times with a standard deviation of 3.48. Students spend an average of

4.73 min conversing with the Quiz Chatbot with a standard deviation of 1.62. The goal completion rate was 88%.

Table 1. Descriptive statistics for utterance turn and duration.

	N	Minimum	Maximum	Mean	Std. deviation
Utterance turn	15	11.00	23.00	14.60	3.48
Session length	15	2.00	8.00	4.73	1.63

A total of 7 students in this course completed the questionnaire. Table 2 shows the descriptive statistics of students' perceived usefulness and ease of use of the Quiz Chatbot. Students interacting with the Quiz Chatbot perceived a relatively high usefulness (*Mean* = 4, *SD* = .82) indicated by the item 5, which was "*Overall, I found the chatbot was useful in my learning*". Students have a strong perceived ease of use of the Quiz Chatbot (*Mean* = 4, *SD* = .58) by the item "*Overall, I found the chatbot easy to use*".

Table 2. Descriptive statistics for students' questionnaire

	Item	N	Mean (SD)
Usefulness	1. Using the chatbot enabled me to reflect on my pre-class learning	7	3.57 (1.27)
	2. Using the chatbot made it easier to comprehend the online learning contents	7	3.57 (.79)
	3. My comprehension of the learning contents would be easy to obtain with the use of the chatbot	7	2.86 (1.35)
	4. The chatbot enhanced my effectiveness in preparing my tutorial activity	7	3.00 (1.41)
	5. Overall, I found the chatbot was useful in my learning	7	4.00 (.82)
Ease of use	1. I found it easy to use the chatbot to communicate	7	3.71 (1.11)
	2. I didn't feel confused when I use chatbot	7	3.43 (1.13)
	3. The chatbot often behaves in expected ways	7	3.57 (.98)
	4. I found it easy to recover from errors encountered while using the chatbot	7	3.14 (1.35)
	5. Overall, I found the chatbot easy to use	7	4.00 (.58)

3 Case II: Self-regulated Learning Chatbot

3.1 The Development of Self-regulated Learning Chatbot

The Self-Regulated Learning (SRL) Chatbot helped students to set personal learning goals with regard to the course they attended. Students were required to interact with the SRL Chatbot on Moodle webpage before coming to the first class. The SRL Chatbot engaged students with five goal-setting questions. For each of the questions, potential options were offered to inspire the directions of students' self-regulated learning goals and expectations of the course. For example, before students attended the first lesson, the chatbot asked students "could you tell me what you want to gain most from this course?" followed by three options (Fig. 3). All students were given the opportunity to express their expectations. Based on the student's answer to each question, the SRL Chatbot would provide relevant recommendations that suit each student's preference. Students with low self-regulation skills would not feel lost and overwhelmed when they were required to set a goal. Together with the recommendations after each choice, students can have a better idea of achieving the particular goals they set for the course.

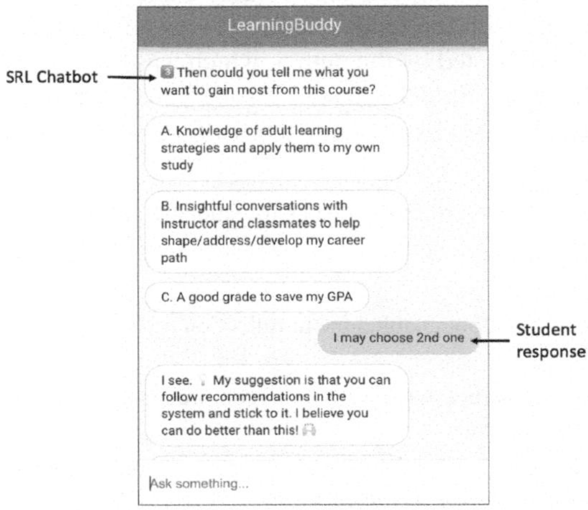

Fig. 3. The dialogue between SRL Chatbot and students

The instructor of this course participated in the SRL Chatbot design and development. Aligned with the course learning outcomes, the instructor worked out the goal-setting questions and relevant self-regulated learning recommendations. Then the chatbot developer categorized the data into *intents*, *entities*, and *responses* according to the Dialogflow system. The *intents* were pre-defined keywords of students' inputs. The *entities* were the synonyms and misspellings of keywords for different intents. Recommendations for self-regulated learning strategies were fed into *responses* data. To minimise students' off-topic replies, we labeled three potential options (A, B, or C) for each question posed. Figure 4 shows the flowchart for designing the SRL Chatbot. The SRL Chatbot was tested by the instructor and the developer before it was launched on Moodle.

3.2 Data Collection and Analysis

The participants were enrolled in another course in a public university in Hong Kong. The participants in Case II were different from the participants in Case I. Similar with

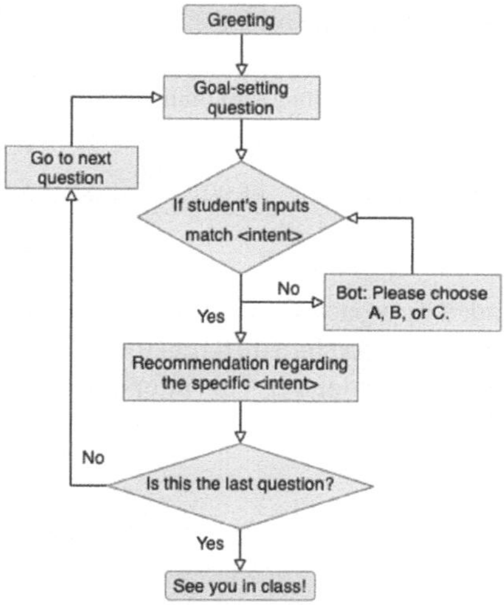

Fig. 4. The flowchart of the SRL Chatbot design

Case I, we evaluated students' behavioral engagement by measuring their conversation records with the SRL Chatbot (utterance turn, session length, goal completion rate). The goal completion rate in this case would be the number of times the SRL Chatbot was successful in helping students set their personal goals. Students' perceived usefulness and ease of use were examined by the same 5-point scale questionnaire used in Case I. The usefulness scale showed a high level of internal consistency with a Cronbach's alpha of 0.859. The Cronbach's alpha for perceived ease of use items was 0.742. We obtained the ethical approval of this study from the university Institutional Review Board. An open-ended survey was conducted to obtain students' opinions about the chatbot activity design. The open-ended survey mainly focused on (1) students' perceived engagement factors, and (2) students' suggestions to improve the chatbot.

Students ($n = 29$) set their learning goals with the assistance of the SRL Chatbot before coming to the first class. The results of students' behavioral engagement with the chatbot activity were shown in Table 3. Students interacted with the chatbot within an average of 7.97 turns, with a standard deviation of 1.36. The duration of student-chatbot conversation was average 4 min ($SD = 2.65$). The conversation records revealed that almost half of the students ($n = 14$) completed the goal-setting activity within 7 turns, followed by 8 students talking to the chatbot within 8 utterance turns. There were 3 students achieved 10 turns ($n = 2$) and 13 turns ($n = 1$). After finishing the goal-setting task, students continued to talk with the chatbot to ask for other topics. For example, students asked chatbot "Can you speak more words?" and "When is the assignment due?" The goal completion rate was 100%.

Sixteen students completed the questionnaire (Table 4). The average mean of students' perceived ease of use ($M = 4.25$, $SD = .68$) was slightly higher than that of the perceived usefulness of the SRL Chatbot ($M = 3.94$, $SD = .68$). Students reported that SRL Chatbot was easy to communicate. During the interaction, the SRL Chatbot performed in expected ways to help students to set personal goals.

Table 3. Utterance turns and duration for the Self-Regulated Learning Chatbot.

	N	Minimum	Maximum	Mean	Std. deviation
Utterance turn	29	7.00	13.00	7.97	1.35
Session length	29	1.00	11.00	4.00	2.65

We employed a grounded approach to analyze the open-ended survey, from which students' responses will be categorized into different themes inductively. Two researchers coded students' responses independently. The inter-coder agreement was 90%. The disagreement was resolved by a discussion between the two researchers.

Table 4. Descriptive statistics of students' questionnaire for the SRL Chatbot

	Item	N	Mean *(SD)*
Usefulness	1. Using the chatbot enabled me to reflect on my pre-class learning	16	3.94 (.77)
	2. Using the chatbot made it easier to comprehend the online learning contents	16	4.00 (.73)
	3. My comprehension of the learning contents would be easy to obtain with the use of the chatbot	16	2.75 (.68)
	4. The chatbot enhanced my effectiveness in preparing my tutorial activity	16	3.69 (.87)
	5. Overall, I found the chatbot was useful in my learning	16	3.94 (.68)
Ease of use	1. I found it easy to use the chatbot to communicate	16	4.19 (.54)
	2. I didn't feel confused when I use chatbot	16	4.19 (.54)
	3. The chatbot often behaves in expected ways	16	4.00 (.89)
	4. I found it easy to recover from errors encountered while using the chatbot	16	3.19 (.66)
	5. Overall, I found the chatbot easy to use	16	4.25 (.68)

The first open-ended question explored the various beneficial factors that students found related to the SRL Chatbot. The responses from 16 students indicated five factors: guidance, interaction, timely feedback, engagement, and personalization (see Fig. 5).

First, the interaction was remarked by 4 students who were engaged by the SRL Chatbot in a way of step-by-step conversation. Student B mentioned "*I like chatbot because it directs me step by step in goal-setting*". Second, students found the SRL Chatbot could help them to understand how and when to set goals for a course. For example, Student H mentioned "*I think the chatbot-assisted goal-setting activity can help me clarify my expectation for this course*". Third, conversing with the chatbot improved students' motivation to set learning goals. Student N acknowledged "*The chatbot is*

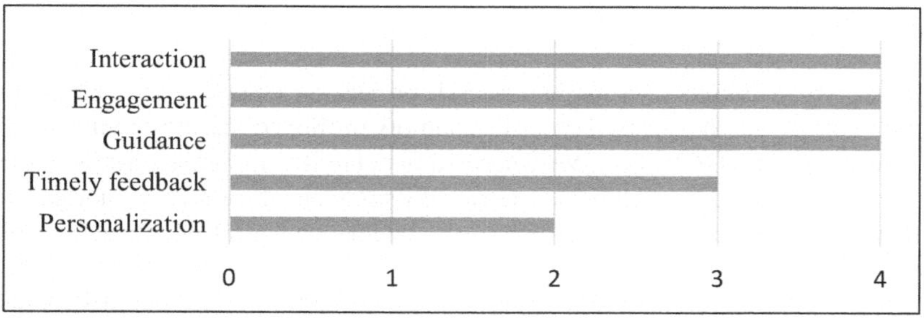

Fig. 5. Factors that engaged students in the SRL Chatbot

innovative". Fourth, the SRL chatbot provided prompt feedbacks during students' goal-setting process, which "*solved students' problems in time* (Student D)". Lastly, few students believed the SRL Chatbot "*cater to diversity* (Student O)" for individual's goal setting, in which the chatbot provided personalized recommendation to students based on their answers.

The second open-ended question focused on students' suggestions about the future improvements of the current SRL Chatbot. We categorized four directions to revise the chatbot activity: (a) richer recommendation, (b) more intelligence, (c) more interactive function, and (d) long-term use (see Fig. 6). First, in total of 7 students suggested the chatbot could provide more "*customized recommendation* (Student O)". For each goal-setting question, we pre-defined three options (i.e., A, B, and C) to assist students to label their inputs. However, "*more options* (Student A and Student B)" were expected to be offered. Second, students mentioned the SRL Chatbot could be more intelligent by "*answering faster* (Student J)" and "*chatting like Siri* (Student C)". Third, more interactive functions could be added during the conversation. Student K mentioned using "*emojis in the sentences*" could help enhance the interaction between students and the chatbot. Lastly, 2 students expressed their willingness to continue using the SRL Chatbot for more sessions. Student E expected the chatbot "*can help students setting a timetable and remind students about each assignment they should do in Moodle*".

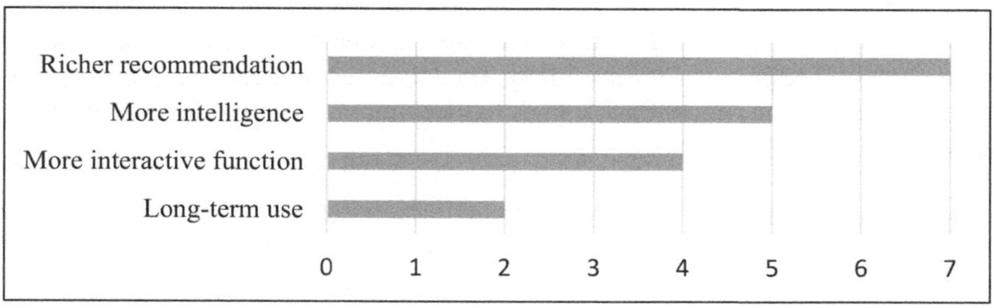

Fig. 6. Students' suggestions for improving the SRL Chatbot

4 Conclusion

This study, which is part of a larger research project on engaging student in flipped learning, explored the use of two types of chatbots in flipped learning online sessions: Quiz Chatbot, and SRL Chatbot. We described in detail the implementations of the two chatbots, and evaluated the chatbots in terms of its perceived usefulness, and perceived ease of use. We also examined the extent of student behavioral engagement with the chatbots.

Overall, we found positive user experiences with both the Quiz and SRL Chatbots with regard to the chatbots' perceived usefulness and perceived ease of use. Perceived usefulness and perceived ease of use have a direct impact on people's intentions to use an information tool or system (He et al. 2018). In other words, if a user feels that the chatbot enhances his or her learning, and that using the chatbot is be free of effort, the user will be willing to use the tool. Analyses of the users' conversation records with the Quiz and SRL Chatbots reveal that the average session length for both chatbots was 4 min. Although the ideal average session length will differ based on the context of the conversation, the longer the session length, the better a chatbot is at creating an engaging conversation experience for the user (Phillips 2018). At this moment, we are unable to state what the optimal average session length should be. However, from the Case II instructor's perspective, an average session length of 4 min is indicative of an engaging chatbot experience for the learners.

The average number of utterance turn was 14 for the Quiz Chatbot and 7 for the SRL Chatbot. The average number of utterance turn for the Quiz Chatbot was higher than that for the SRL Chatbot probably because learners tend to engage in more interactions when answering quiz questions (e.g., by asking the chatbot questions and the chatbot replies) than setting their own personal goals with a chatbot. Both chatbots registered high goal completion rates (88% for the Quiz Chatbot, and 100% for the SRL Chatbot) which suggest that the two chatbots were successful in fulfilling the purposes they were created for.

For future research, we plan to implement the two chatbots with larger samples of participants involving other courses. Using larger sample sizes and other courses can help us generalize the findings to other contexts. We also plan to measure the performance of the chatbots using other metrics such as chatbot fallback rate. Chatbot fallback rate refers to the number of times a chatbot is not able to understand a user's message and provide a relevant response (Phillips 2018). The lower the fallback rate, the higher will be the user satisfaction. In contrast, a high fallback rate means that more effort should be spent on training the chatbots.

Acknowledgement. The research was supported by a Teaching Development Grant 2019 awarded to the first author at the University of Hong Kong.

References

Lo, C.K., Hew, K.F., Chen, G.: Toward a set of design principles for mathematics flipped classrooms: a synthesis of research in mathematics education. Educ. Res. Rev. **22**, 50–73 (2017)

Bishop, J., Verleger, M.A.: The flipped classroom: A survey of the research. Paper presented at 2013 ASEE Annual Conference & Exposition, Atlanta, Georgia (2013). https://peer.asee.org/22585

Strelan, P., Osborn, A., Palmer, E.: The flipped classroom: a meta-analysis of effects on student performance across disciplines and educational levels. Educ. Res. Rev. 30 (2020). https://doi.org/10.1016/j.edurev.2020.100314

van Alten, D.C.D., Phielix, C., Janssen, J., Kester, L.: Effects of flipping the classroom on learning outcomes and satisfaction: a meta-analysis. Educ. Res. Rev. 28. https://doi.org/10.1016/j.edurev.2019.05.003

Diwanji, P., Hinkelmann, K., & Witschel, H. F. (2018). Enhance classroom preparation for flipped classroom using AI and analytics. *Proceedings of the 20thInternational Conference on Enterprise Information Systems,* 1, 477–483.

Sahin, A., Cavlazoglu, B., Zeytuncu, Y.E.: Flipping a college calculus course: a case study. Educ. Technol. Soc. **18**(3), 142–152 (2015)

Palmer, K.: Flipping a calculus class: one instructor's experience. Primus **25**(9–10), 886–891 (2015)

Scott, C.E., Green, L.E., Etheridge, D.L.: A comparison between flipped and lecture-based instruction in the calculus classroom. J. Appl. Res. Higher Educ. **8**(2), 252–264 (2016)

Elliott, R., Rob, Do students like the flipped classroom? An investigation of student reaction to a flipped undergraduate IT course. In: Proceedings of 2014 IEEE Frontiers in Education Conference (FIE), pp. 1–7 (2014)

Joshi, N.: Choosing between rule-based bots and AI bots. Forbes (2020). https://www.forbes.com/sites/cognitiveworld/2020/02/23/choosing-between-rule-based-bots-and-ai-bots/?sh=53a9ccb1353d

Fryer, L.K., Ainley, M., Thompson, A., Gibson, A., Sherlock, Z.: Stimulating and sustaining interest in a language course: an experimental comparison of chatbot and human task partners. Comput. Hum. Behav. **75**, 461–468 (2017)

McNeal, M.:. A Siri for higher ed aims to boost student engagement. EdSurge News (2016). https://www.edsurge.com/news/2016-12-07-a-siri-for-higher-ed-aims-to-boost-student-engagement

Moore, M.G.: Theory of transactional distance. In: Keegan, D. (ed.) Theoretical Principles of Distance Education, pp. 22–38. Routledge, New York (1997)

Huang, W., Hew, K.F., Gonda, D.E.: Designing and evaluating three chatbot-enhanced activities for a flipped graduate course. Int. J. Mech. Eng. Robot. Res. **8**(5), 813–818 (2019)

Smutny, P., Schreiberova, P.: Chatbots for learning: a review of educational chatbots for the Facebook Messenger. Comput. Educ. 151. https://doi.org/10.1016/j.compedu.2020.103862

Kim, N.-Y.: A study on chatbots for developing Korean college students' English listening and reading Skills. J. Digit. Converg. **16**(8), 19–26 (2018)

McGrath, C.: Chatbot vocabulary: 10 Chatbot terms you need to know. Chatbots Magazine (2017). https://chatbotsmagazine.com/chatbot-vocabulary-10-chatbot-terms-you-need-to-know-3911b1ef31b4

Davis, F.D.: Perceived usefulness, perceived ease of use, and user acceptance of information technology. MIS Q. **13**(3), 318–339 (1989)

Yao, M.: 5 metrics every chatbot developer needs to track. VentureBeat, The Machine (2016). https://venturebeat.com/2016/10/04/5-metrics-every-chatbot-developer-needs-to-track/

Mead, J.: What session length can tell you about your chatbot performance. Inf. Commun. (2019). https://inform-comms.com/session-length-chatbot-performance/

He, Y., Chen, Q., Kitkuakul, S.: Regulatory focus and technology acceptance: perceived ease of use and usefulness as efficacy. Cogent Bus. Manag. **5**, 1 (2018). https://doi.org/10.1080/23311975.2018.1459006

Phillips, C.: Chatbot analytics 101: the essential metrics you need to track. Chatbots Magazine. https://chatbotsmagazine.com/chatbot-analytics-101-e73ba7013f00

The Customized Mathematic Instruction Supported by an Intelligent Tutoring System and Its Effect During the COVID-19 Epidemic

Jiyou Jia[1(✉)] and Yanying Miao[2]

[1] Department of Educational Technology, School of Education, Peking University, Yiheyuanlu 5, Beijing 100871, China
jjy@pku.edu.cn
[2] No. 47 Middle School, Qingdao, Shandong, China

Abstract. To cope with the covid-19 epidemic challenge for school education, many researchers have conducted studies from different point of views. However, it is hard to find empirical study to examine the online learning's effect on school pupils' performance represented by regular exams. This study attempts to fill in this research gap. An intelligent tutoring system, Lexue 100 was utilized in mathematics online instruction during the COVID-19 epidemic outbreak time in a junior high school in Shandong Province China. Supported by this system, the teacher provided the students with differentiated assignments including class assignment, group assignment and individual assignment, as well as error sets. Those assignments could be completed before the class, in the class or after the class. A quasi-experiment was conducted to compare the effect of this online learning supported by the individualized assignment with that of uniform assignment to all students. The treatment group and control group had the statistically not significant difference in the regular school exams before the experiment as the pretest. At the end of the experiment, the treatment group performed better than the control group in the mid-term test as the posttest, reaching a statistically significant advantage 6.83% ($p < 0.01$) and an effect size 0.381. The individualized homework contributed to the performance improvement. Implications for online learning design and limitations are discussed.

Keywords: Online learning · Intelligent tutoring system · Epidemic · Mathematics instruction · Individual assignment

1 Introduction

During the outbreak of new covid-19 coronavirus worldwide, almost all educational institution had to close the classrooms and campus, and used online learning as the best way to maintain the teaching and learning schedule for all students. As reported by UNESCO (2020), about 138 countries and 1.37 billion students around the world

R. Li et al. (Eds.): ICBL 2021, LNCS 12830, pp. 176–187, 2021.
https://doi.org/10.1007/978-3-030-80504-3_15

were studying online at home. It was no exception for China. From Feb. 2020 to April 2020, all schools and universities in China used online learning instead of traditional classroom instruction. Different from in traditional and physical classroom instruction, online teaching and learning is challenging to the school teachers, pupils and parents. It was not allowed for the teachers to assign printed homework and to collect the students' answers in printed form. How to interest the students to the online learning sitting before the computer instead of sitting in the classroom? How to assign homework to the students and give them individual feedback? How to meet the different need of different students in online learning? All online instructors must face these common questions.

2 Related Work

To cope with the covid-19 epidemic challenge for school education, many researchers have conducted studies from different point of views. From Jan. First 2020 to March 13th 2021, more than one hundred (113) papers have been published in international journals and conference proceedings, and can be searched with the keyword combination "online learning" and "covid-19" and "school" through the previous ERIC or the current EBESCO (http://web.b.ebscohost.com/) online database. Most of the papers discussed the consequence and impact of this epidemic on educational stakeholders, suggested the technologies that could support online learning, or investigated the readiness, usability, attitude, feeling and satisfaction of school managers, teachers, students and parents towards online learning. The most used research method was quantitative research with online survey results.

Tajik and Vahedi (2021) designed and administered online surveys to obtain information on the educational gateways, television channels, social media, and MOOCs, which were used during the school closures in Iran. 92 K-12 instructors and 593 K-12 students participated in the surveys. The results showed that the method most used was social media, and the indicated cause for concern in that every student cannot benefit from all types of distance learning.

Midcalf and Boatwright (2021) conducted an online survey with 40 K-12 teachers and 35 parents with at least 1 child participating in an online learning environment due to school closings in the USA, and found both teachers and parents were concerned about the outcomes from the online learning environment that was implemented so quickly when schools were closed. They suggested that a prominent feature of online environments is the ability to present content and instruction in multiple ways, including personalizing instruction for each student's unique learning needs.

Bhaumik and Priyadarshini (2020) administered a survey with 100 students from senior secondary level of different schools of Delhi, India who might be equipped with better smartphone penetration and internet access than those from other states in India, and found access to online learning and online load on learners to be high. This study concluded that online pedagogy and digital skills of teachers and learners need to be strengthened for a possible roadmap ahead.

Poláková et al. (2021) conducted a survey at the Secondary Vocational School of Tourism and Gastronomy in Slovakia, and found that the majority of students were ready for distance online learning, and a great percentage of students had Internet access and technological devices to be used for educational purposes. This research shows that online learning is possible if both teachers and students are familiarized with this learning environment and are ready to cooperate.

Shamir-Inbal and Blau (2021) conducted an online survey including 133 elementary and secondary school teachers from Hebrew-speaking and Arabic-speaking schools in Israel, and revealed teachers' perceptions of pedagogical, technological, and organizational challenges and benefits of ERT (Emergency Remote Teaching), as well as a variety of pedagogical distance learning strategies used by teachers. The study raises the need to turn a curse into a blessing by incorporating the experience of remote technology-enhanced learning and online activities into the school agenda on a regular basis.

Wang et al. (2021) interviewed 26 Chinese primary school teachers who provided photos to represent their typical online teaching experience, and identified four themes including unpreparedness, concerns for at-risk students, constant change and diversity, and suggested technological innovation and advancement to meet the online learning need like developing suitable devices and software for children, designing simple plug-in gadgets, integration of pedagogical agents or robots, and inventing movable smart desks.

Notwithstanding, to our knowledge up to date, none of the above papers conducted empirical study to examine the online learning's effect on school pupils' performance represented by regular exams. This study attempts to fill in this research gap. An intelligent tutoring system was applied to school mathematics instruction during the COVID-19 epidemic outbreak time, and the students could be provided with differentiated assignments. A quasi-experiment was conducted to compare the effect of this online learning supported by the individualized assignment with that of uniform assignment to all students.

3 The Intelligent Tutoring System "Lexue 100"

"Lexue 100" (https://www.lexue100.com), with the Chinese meaning Happy Learning for 100 Percent, is a web-based intelligent tutoring system for school mathematics, developed by Beijing Lexue 100 Online Education Co. Ltd., and equipped with the OLAI (Online Learning Activity Index) model proposed by the authors' team (Jia and Yu 2017; Zhang and Jia 2017, Jia and Zhang, 2019) and the multimodal human-computer interaction designed by the authors' team (Jia et al. 2020).

Quiz-writing is the main learning activity in this online learning system. The system helps the teacher customize class teaching with rich and clearly ordered instructional resources including micro videos, lecture slides and all kinds of questions. The teacher can fast search and find the most appropriate resources to organize the online teaching.

4 The Mathematics Curriculum Design

During the epidemic outbreak from Feb. to April 2021, one junior middle school located in Shandong Province China participated in this research. Two classes in Grade One used the Lexue 100 system as online learning platform and belonged to the treatment group. The other four classes in Grade One had the same textbook and instructional content, but did not use the Lexue 100 system, thus belonged to the control group.

The teacher in the treatment group adopted flipped classroom strategy. The Lexue system was used before the class, during the class and after the class. To prepare the students for the new class, the teacher assigned some questions from the Lexue 100 system for the students to complete before the class. Of course some questions were too difficult for the students to correctly answer.

During the class, for the difficult questions with which most students made errors, the teacher specially introduced the solution to the questions and drilled key points hidden in the questions. Following the detailed explanation, the teacher usually assigned new questions for the students to answer immediately in a given time, for example in 10 min. As soon as the students submitted their answers, the teacher could view the students' answers, scores and the completion time.

After the class, the teacher assigned students' homework via the Lexue system. In traditional school teaching, all the students in a class always have the same homework. The advanced students become tired of the simple but tedious repetitive exercises, while the disadvantaged students have difficulty in completing the homework on time. On the contrary to the monotone assignment in traditional school classes, the teacher could provide three kinds of assignment: common assignment, group assignment and individualized assignment.

The first was the common assignment to all students. The fundamental requirements for every unit should be drilled in the common assignment. The assignment was normally composed of multiple choice questions and blank-filling questions with predefined answers. After the students wrote and submitted their answers, they could receive instant scoring and feedback, and the teacher could receive statistical report about the collective performance in the whole class. Figure 1 is the screenshot of the assignments report from the teacher's account view until April 22, 2020. For each assignment, the following information is shown: how many students have fully completed it, how many have partly completed it, and how many have not begun to write, and the mean score of the completed assignment with different colors: blue for excellent, green for good, orange for qualified, and red for weak. The teacher can get to know the students' mastery level and design the curriculum based on the statistical report, for example to pay special attention to the weak parts in the assignment.

The second kind of assignment was the group assignment. Three stratified groups were set up with differentiated students based on their performance in the common assignments, and are named as "excellent", "good" and "basic". So each group would be given different assignments corresponding to their knowledge level. The members in three groups were dynamically adjusted. If one student in the lower group improved his or her performance in the recent assignments, this student could be moved to an upper group, and vice versa. Figure 2 is a screenshot of the three groups and their members.

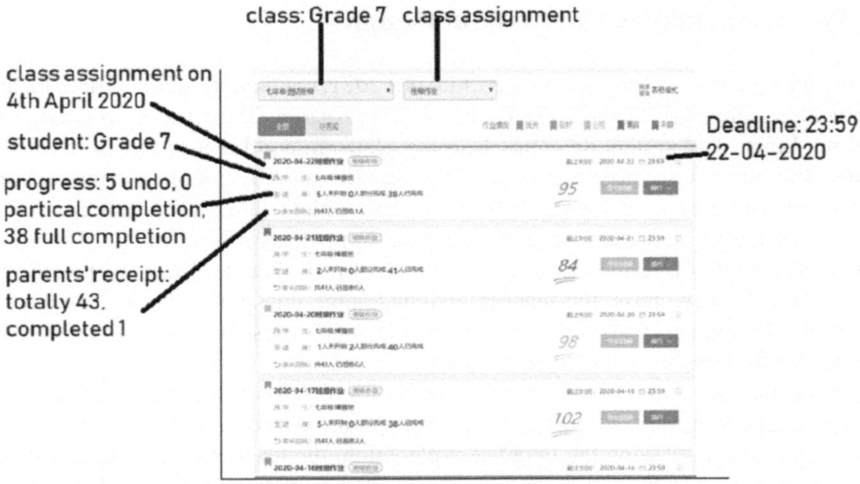

Fig. 1. One screenshot of the assignments' report from the teacher's account view until April 22, 2020

Fig. 2. Three groups and their members

The third kind of assignment was personalized assignment. For the excellent students who could complete all the assignment very well, the teacher assigned them extra challenging homework. For the students with learning difficulties, the teacher assigned them extra homework which is helpful for them to complete the regular assignments.

The students often wrote the assignment for the second or the third time in order to achieve a better grade. The color change from red to green indicated the mean grade's improvement and implied the students' great effort, as shown in Fig. 3.

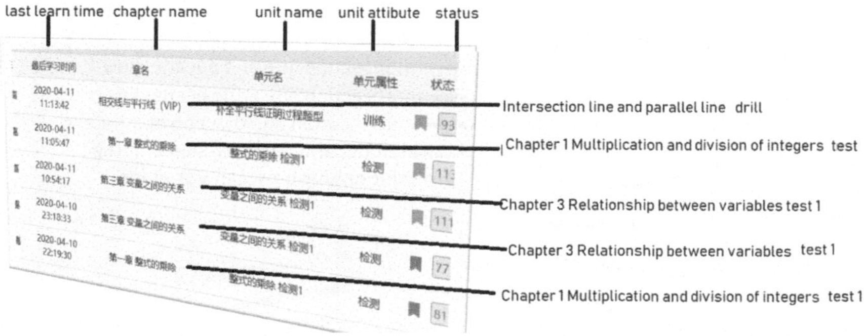

Fig. 3. The screenshot of the assignments' multiple completion indicated by the color change from red to green (Color figure online)

Besides the assignment, every student has his or her own error set. This error set was composed of the false answered questions by the student in the assignment. It was in fact totally individualized assignment for every student.

The knowledge key points analysis in the system provided the teacher with the students' performance grouping based on their grades in related assignments. Figure 4 shows one example of key points grouping for the instruction content in Chapter 3 "the relation between the variables". In this chapter, three key points are required including: the representation of variable relations with tables, the representation of variable relations with formulas, and the representation of variables with figures. For each of the key points, one equally long horizontal line is colored into five parts from the right to the left: blue for excellent, green for good, orange for qualified, red for weak, and grey for absent. The part length of every color represents the percentage of the students who are classified into that group.

If the teacher wanted to know the group members of one key point, he or she could click that key point, and viewed the member list of a group, as shown in Fig. 5. For each group the teacher could assign corresponding homework.

Because the weak students, or the students with learning difficulty, might be given too many supplementary assignment or had too many errors which should be corrected, the teacher would and could remove some challenging assignments from the students so that they could complete the appropriate assignments on time. Figure 6 shows that some new and individual assignment for one student was deleted by the teacher. The success in completing the new assignment could prevent the weak students from being frustrated once more, and strengthen their learning confidence.

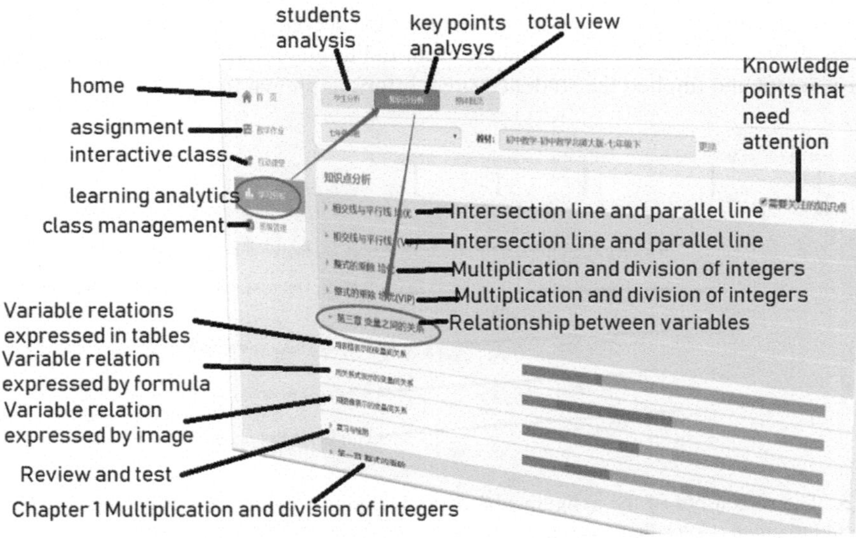

Fig. 4. The students' grouping for all key points in one chapter (Color figure online)

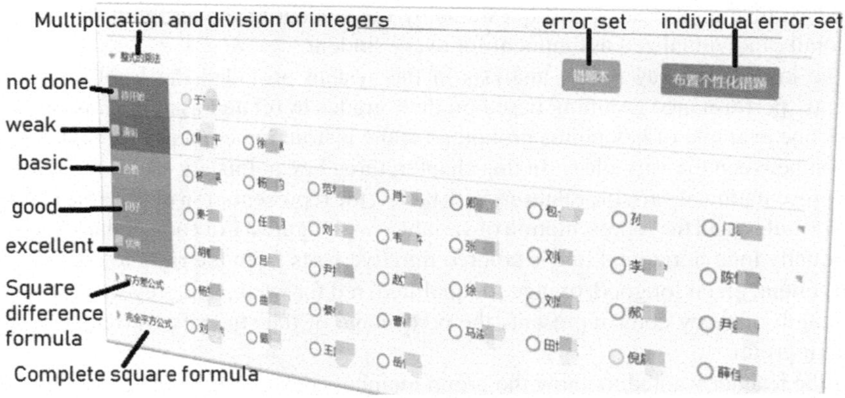

Fig. 5. The group member list

The totally customized and individualized assignments for all students relieve the student from the traditionally same and tedious assignment, and improve their learning efficiency.

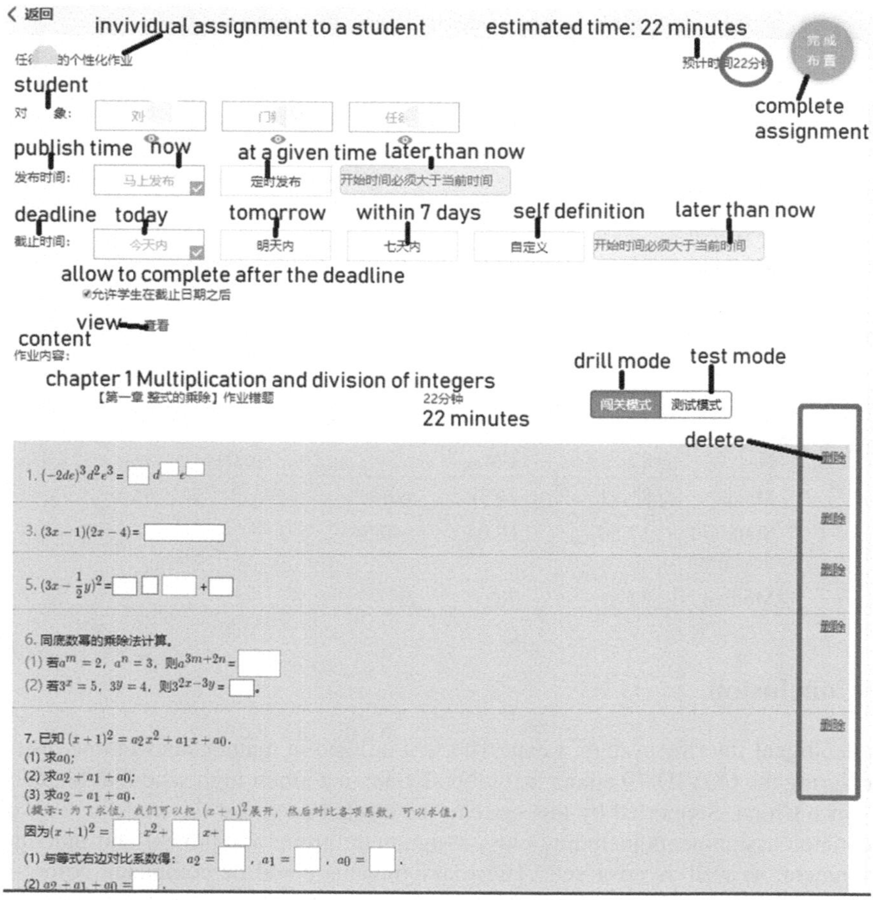

Fig. 6. One screen shot of the deletion function in specifying one student's individual assignment

5 Findings

To investigate the effect of the online learning with Lexue system during the epidemic, the students' grades from the final test in last term as the pretest and the students' grades from the mid-term test in April 2020 as the posttest were collected and analyzed.

In the pretest, the grade statistics is list in Table 1. The mean difference between the treatment group and control group is 2.33, and is statistically not significant level ($p = 0.46 > 0.05$ in independent sample t-test).

In the posttest, the grade statistics is list in Table 2. The mean difference between the treatment group and control group is 6.83, and is statistically significant level ($p < 0.01$ in independent sample t-test). The effect size based on Cohen's d is 0.381, a small to medium effect size. The treatment group statistically significantly improved its grade throughout the experiment.

Table 1. The grade statistics in the pretest

	Treatment	Control	Difference	p value in t-test
N	87	174		
Mean	81.60	79.28	2.33	0.46
Standard deviation	18.30	16.09	2.21	
Median	84	82	2	

Table 2. The grade statistics in the posttest

	Treatment	Control	Difference	p value in t-test
N	87	174		<0.01
Mean	81.21	74.38	6.83	
Standard deviation	17.50	18.04	−0.54	
Median	87	78	9	

6 Conclusion

An intelligent tutoring system, Lexue 100 was utilized in mathematics online instruction during the COVID-19 epidemic outbreak time in a junior high school in Shandong Province China. Supported by this system, the teacher provided the students with differentiated assignments including class assignment, group assignment and individual assignment, as well as error sets. Those assignments could be completed before the class, in the class or after the class. A quasi-experiment was conducted to compare the effect of this online learning supported by the individualized assignment with that of uniform assignment to all students. The treatment group and control group had the statistically not significant difference in the regular school exams before the experiment as the pretest. At the end of the experiment, the treatment group performed better than the control group in the mid-term test as the posttest with a statistically significant advantage 6.83% ($p < 0.01$) and an effect size 0.381.

7 Discussion and Implication

The positive effect of the online learning supported by an intelligent tutoring system was verified by the quasi-experiment in the mathematics subject of a junior high school during the COVID-19 outbreak time. The teacher's flipped-class design and the individualized homework to all students contributed to the performance improvement.

Unlike university students and workplace trainees, normally the K-12 children lack stronger self-regulation skills and thus are more prone to distractions in the online learning environment. The teachers' authority and guidance can strengthen the distant pupils' concentration on the learning content even without the parents' accompanying on site. In the empirical experiment, the math teacher utilized flipped-class design so that the students should prepare before the class, participate in the class and review the content after the class. The students were actively engaged in the math learning activities. More importantly, the learning activities were also implemented online through the intelligent tutoring system Lexue 100, which could give the students instant feedback and help without any more waiting time. The instant and one (virtual tutor) to one (student) interaction is more adaptive and more personalized, thus more helpful than the traditional one (teacher) to more (students) communication in the physical classroom or in the virtual online chatroom.

Besides the instant and adaptive human-computer interaction, the individualized homework assignment from the teacher and supported by the intelligent tutoring system Lexue 100 is both more interesting and more challenging to the students. Every student should complete his or her own specific homework assignment which was targeted at the problems the student had, and would feel difficult to copy others' answers because of the different homework.

The positive effect and reasons can be reflected in reviewed literatures that surveyed students, teachers and parents about their attitude and feeling toward online learning. Tajik and Vahedi (2021) concerned that every student cannot benefit from all types of distance learning. So in current study the teachers just used the intelligent tutoring system as the main platform. Midcalf and Boatwright (2021) suggested that a prominent feature of online environments is the ability to present content and instruction in multiple ways, including personalizing instruction for each student's unique learning needs. In the current research the teacher provided the students personalized assignment and instruction. Bhaumik and Priyadarshini (2020) argued for online pedagogy and digital skills of teachers and learners. In this research the teacher adopted flipped class pedagogy and equipped the students with a personalized tutoring system. Poláková et al. (2021) found that online learning is possible if both teachers and students are familiarized with this learning environment and are ready to cooperate. In this research the teacher and the students were easy to use the online learning system, and the students completed the teachers' assignment with strong engagement and self-regulation. Wang et al. (2021) suggested technological innovation and advancement to meet the online learning need like developing suitable devices and software for children, designing simple plug-in gadgets, integration of pedagogical agents or robots, and inventing movable smart desks. This empirical study just provides such a case that technological innovation and advancement with the example of an intelligent tutoring system can meet the online learning need.

The study has implication for both pure online learning in K-12 education in extreme situation like the school lockdown during epidemic outbreak period and blended learning in normal K-12 education. The teacher should utilize the mature emerging technology like intelligent tutoring systems to support the students with adaptive and individualized teaching and learning.

8 Limitation and Further Study

In the quantitative research, only the school exam scores were collected to assess the effect of the customized mathematic instruction supported by an intelligent tutoring system. If a survey for all students and an interview with some students could be conducted to collect the students' attitude and feeling toward the specific online learning which they hardly experienced in the learning process, the effect could be more demonstrated and the reasons leading to the positive effect could be revealed more in details.

Shamir-Inbal and Blau (2021) raises the need to turn a curse into a blessing by incorporating the experience of remote technology-enhanced learning and online activities into the school agenda on a regular basis. The pure online teaching and learning ended after the students in the experiment school returned to the school and the classroom at the end of April, 2020. But the online learning system was still used by the teacher to assign homework for the students. The teacher and principles were aware of the intelligence and importance of the online tutoring system, and began the practice of blended learning, or hybrid learning, which integrated the traditional classroom teaching with the online learning, and made full use the advantages of both teaching. It should be further investigated how this blended learning was conducted and what was its effect on the students and the teachers.

Acknowledgement. The paper is one product of the national educational technology research key project of Central Educational Technology Center China, "Personalized instruction research based on artificial intelligence and big data technology" (No.: 176220009) and Educational Big Data research project of Peking University "The adaptive and intelligent tutoring system research based on the data mining of large-scale students' online learning activities" (No.: 2020YBC07). The research is supported by the project "Lexue 100, Smart Education" of Beijing Lexue 100 Online Education Co., Ltd. The authors thank all the teachers and students who have participated in the program.

References

Bhaumik, R., Priyadarshini, A.: E-readiness of senior secondary school learners to online learning transition amid COVID-19 lockdown. Asian J. Distance Educ. **15**(1), 244–256 (2020)

Jia, J., Yu, Y.: Online learning activity index (OLAI) and its application for adaptive learning. In: Cheung, S.K.S., Kwok, L.-F., Ma, W.W.K., Lee, L.-K., Yang, H. (eds.) ICBL 2017. LNCS, vol. 10309, pp. 213–224. Springer, Cham (2017). https://doi.org/10.1007/978-3-319-59360-9_19

Jia, J., He, Y., Le, H.: A multimodal human-computer interaction system and its application in smart learning environments. In: Cheung, S.K.S., Li, R., Phusavat, K., Paoprasert, N., Kwok, L. (eds.) ICBL 2020. LNCS, vol. 12218, pp. 3–14. Springer, Cham (2020). https://doi.org/10.1007/978-3-030-51968-1_1

Jia, J., Zhang, J.: The analysis of online learning behavior of the students with poor academic performance in mathematics and individual help strategies. In: Cheung, S.K.S., Lee, L.-K., Simonova, I., Kozel, T., Kwok, L.-F. (eds.) ICBL 2019. LNCS, vol. 11546, pp. 205–215. Springer, Cham (2019). https://doi.org/10.1007/978-3-030-21562-0_17

Midcalf, L., Boatwright, P.: Teacher and parent perspectives of the online learning environment due to COVID-19. Delta Kappa Gamma Bull. Int. J. Prof. Educ. **87**(1), 24–34 (2021)

Poláková, P., Klímová, B., Dommett, E., Edirisingha, P.: The perception of slovak students on distance online learning in the time of coronavirus - a preliminary study. Educ. Sci. **11**(2), 81–88 (2021)

Shamir-Inbal, T., Blau, I.: Facilitating emergency remote K-12 teaching in computing-enhanced virtual learning environments during COVID-19 pandemic - blessing or curse? J. Educ. Comput. Res. (2021). https://doi.org/10.1177/0735633121992781

Tajik, F., Vahedi, M.: Quarantine and education: an assessment of Iranian formal education during the COVID-19 outbreak and school closures. Int. J. Educ. Dev. Inf. Commun. Technol. **17**(1), 159–175 (2021)

UNESCO. 1.37 billion students now home as COVID-19 school closures expand, ministers scale up multimedia approaches to ensure learning continuity (2020). https://en.unesco.org/news/137-billion-students-now-home-covid-19-school-closures-expand-ministers-scale-multimedia. Accessed 15 Jan 2021

Wang, Z., Pang, H., Zhou, J., Ma, Y., Wang, Z.: "What if…it never ends?": examining challenges in primary teachers' experience during the wholly online teaching. J. Educ. Res. (2021). https://doi.org/10.1080/00220671.2021.1884823

Zhang, B., Jia, J.: Evaluating an intelligent tutoring system for personalized math teaching. In: Proceedings of International Symposium on Educational Technology 2017, pp. 126–130 (2017)

Experience in Blended Learning

Roles Interaction During Mobile-Blended Collaborative Learning: The Impact of External Scripts

Cixiao Wang(✉)

School of Educational Technology, Faculty of Education, Beijing Normal University, No.19, Xinjiekouwai St, Haidian District, Beijing 100875, China
wangcixiao@bnu.edu.cn

Abstract. Roles played by group members is an important topic within the collaborative learning field. External scripts (ES) providing collaboration skills are one of the prominent scaffolding technology in CSCL (Computer-Supported Collaborative Learning). This study designed a mobile-blended collaborative learning environment to explore how ES affect collaborative roles. A three-round inquiry experiment was conduct to investigate the role emergence and coordination over time. Reflection questionnaires and group worksheets were collected from the experiment class (31 students) with ES and control class (33 students) without ES. Qualitative thematic analysis and quantitative statistical analysis were adopted. Five role categories (coordinator, integrator, inquirer, facilitator, and marginal) and a role transition formula were proposed in this study. Results indicate that ES affects task awareness of group members and the rotation of social status in mobile-blended collaboration with a 1:1 tablet-to-student ratio.

Keywords: Computer-Supported Collaborative Learning · Blended learning · Mobile learning · External scripts · Inquiry learning

1 Introduction

Virtual manipulative (VM) refers to the interactive representation of physical counterparts (tables, figures, and instructions) displayed on digital devices [1]. VM could enable students to learn scientific concepts and phenomena by conducting hands-on experiments in blended environments [2]. With the increasing interest of the world in the application of mobile technology in science education, a new method of applying VM in mobile blended learning environments arises at the historic moment [3]. Meanwhile, when adopting VM in scientific inquiry activities, instructor guidance, which is also one of the main instructional technologies supporting the learning process [4], should be considered in the instructional design.

In computer-supported collaborative learning (CSCL), the prominent scaffolding technology is the collaboration script [5]. External scripts (ES), a type of learning technology providing collaboration skills during CSCL, are designed by instructors and explicitly imposed on groups [6]. Dillenbourg and Evans [1] pointed out that the factors

R. Li et al. (Eds.): ICBL 2021, LNCS 12830, pp. 191–202, 2021.
https://doi.org/10.1007/978-3-030-80504-3_16

of social interactions in CSCL include multiple users, display orientation, territoriality, and roles. As scaffolds for group work, ES could facilitate collaboration by regulating group actions and role distributions among group members [7].

Previous studies have focused on learning performance when using VM in blended collaborative inquiry activities [8, 9] and the effect of scripts on group outcomes [10, 11]. However, how group members interact with each other under different ES conditions and corresponding group interaction has received less attention. In terms of group interaction, roles are considered important factors in revealing types of interaction during group work [12]. To better understand how role interaction varies under the impact of ES, we conducted three rounds of scientific inquiry experiments in two classes (provided with ES or not) of participating primary schools. Further, we examined how ES impacts mobile-blended collaborative learning from the perspective of role interaction. Two research questions are addressed as follows.

(1) What kinds of roles emerged during students' mobile-blended collaboration in the two classes?
(2) How did these roles distribute and transit during the three-round inquiry learning in the two classes?

2 Literature Review

2.1 External Scripts in CSCL

In the science classroom, inquiry tools and teacher guidance are the main teaching techniques to support science learning activities in each inquiry stage [4]. In CSCL, apart from digital devices, the script is the specific technology that supports the group process [5]. Collaboration scripts are scaffolds that aim to facilitate collaboration by structuring interactive processes [13]. Scripts facilitate collaboration by sequencing the activities, structuring the interaction, and guiding the discussion [14]. Specifically, interaction scripts involved in the collaboration are designed so that the roles of participants, the actions engaged in, and the sequence of events could prompt collaborative processes, thus making sure the intended learning takes place [6]. Moreover, previous studies have found that CSCL with external scripts significantly influenced students' learning performance compared to those without external scripts [11, 14].

There are two kinds of collaboration scripts: internal scripts and external scripts. Internal scripts are developed from long-term teamwork, including roles and division of labor, and interaction mode relating to collaboration skills and members' experience [15]. By contrast, external scripts are designed externally by teachers or other learning promoters and explicitly imposed on learners as a guidance structure to prompt them how to act [6]. Instructed scripts and prompted scripts are often used for group query tasks [16]. Specifically, instructed scripts convey designers' expectations concerning the way students conduct tasks, while prompted scripts display cues that encourage learners to play roles such as "critic" or "analyzer" [16]. Besides, the effect of external script on the collaboration is related to students' prior knowledge and experience with the script [10, 17]. Therefore, external scripts, working as instructional technologies provided by instructors, may influence group interaction over time.

2.2 Roles Emerged During Collaboration

During collaborative learning, scripts are related to the collaboration skills and roles of group members. The role of group members has become an important topic of discussion within the CSCL field [18]. When it comes to roles in this particular field, there are typically two perspectives. One is an emerging roles perspective which focuses on spontaneously emerging roles during collaboration, the other perspective is scripted roles which refers to roles guided by the instructor or designers to support group interactions and enhance inquiry performance [19]. Since the scripted role enables students to perform the specified tasks and perform the expected behavior in the process of collaboration, script role is a more concerning issue for teachers and researchers [18].

The roles students play in the collaborative learning context can reflect the coordination rules of a group. To investigate the effects of specific roles on group interaction and academic performance, several researchers classify roles from two perspectives into various types. Belbin [20] pointed out that there are nine types of roles in a team: shaper, implementer, completer, coordinator, resource investigator, team worker, plant, monitor, and specialist. However, this classification emphasizes more personal characteristics than role functions, such as defining group tasks. By contrast, the classification of Johnson and Johnson [21] seems to be more suitable to describe roles in science classrooms. Johnson and Johnson [21] divided the functions of roles in teamwork into four categories: formative, functional, summative, and promotive. However, in collaborative inquiry learning-related literature, scant attention has been paid to role description, especially the changes of role-taking among group members.

3 Methods

3.1 Participants

In this study, 64 fifth-grade students (with 33 females, 31 males; aged 11 on average) from two classes of a public primary school located in Beijing, China, participated the experiments voluntarily. The experiment class (with ES during collaboration) has 31 students and the control class (without ES during collaboration) has 33 students. The two classes were taught by the same science teacher. All students from the two classes were randomly assigned to 6 groups, with 5–6 students in each group. These groups were long-term collaborative learning groups. The group leader of each group was assigned by the science teacher and fixed. Also, the science final examination results of the last academic year indicated no significant difference between the two classes ($t = 1.689$, $p = .114 > .05$), which meant that students in the experiment and control classes had a similar academic level in the science curriculum.

3.2 External Scripts

The external scripts in this study were designed to provide guidance and suggestions on collaborative inquiry learning activities. There were two forms of the external scripts. First, before the learning activities, the science teacher adopted a slide to represent instructions on the group inquiry (e.g., turn-taking, be friendly, etc.). Second, during the learning activities, a paper card was provided to each group by the science teacher, which gave cues that encouraged students to take a specific role, "inspector". The role of inspector was assigned to a particular student based on the discussion of the group leader and other members, which worked to regulate collaborative inquiry and encourage group members to continue participation.

3.3 Inquiry Tools

VMs of this study were three teaching simulation tools selected from the PhET learning platform (phet.colorado.edu). The learning content of the three VMs were organized into three inquiry themes: Refraction of Light (Lig.), Electrical Circuits (Ele.), and Electromagnetic Induction (Mag.). These themes were all based on the fifth-grade science curriculum and corresponding textbook. The science textbook was published by Beijing Press and it belonged to the Beijing Compulsory Education Curriculum Reform of 'Primary Science'.

Each student was provided a tablet that could run the selected VMs, showing a 1:1 tablet-to-student ratio. Tablets in the school were the same type of device as the Android system. The screen size of the tablets is 8 inches with a screen ratio of 5:8. All the involved students had a prior learning experience with these tablets. Group members sit around a table to take inquiry learning activities in their science classroom.

3.4 Procedure

In the Spring semester of 2019, three rounds of scientific inquiry experiments were conducted. The data used in this study were collected from these experiments. During each round of the scientific inquiry experiment, inquiry activities were conducted in line with the procedure shown in Fig. 1.

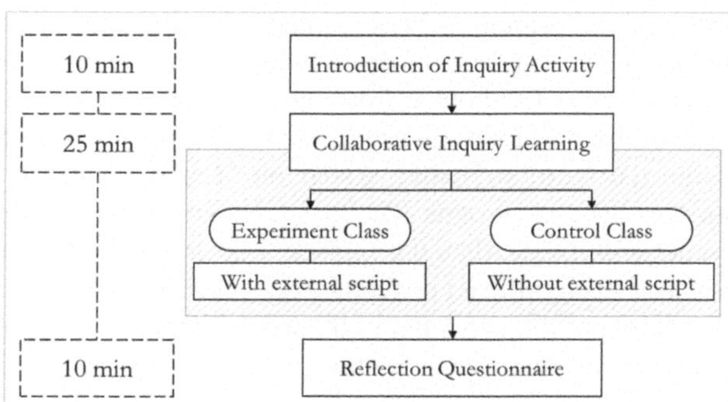

Fig. 1. Diagram of the experiment procedure

All three inquiry experiments included three parts: a 10 min introduction of inquiry activity, a 25 min collaborative inquiry activity, and a 10 min reflection session. The collaboration process (25 min) was guided by a group worksheet, providing inquiry tasks and procedures for students to work with. In order to make sure that all rounds of inquiry activities have the same intervention condition, the science teacher and the researcher were jointly designed and conducted all the inquiry activities.

3.5 Instruments

Group Worksheet

Group worksheets were developed by the researcher and the science teacher according to science curriculum standards. Each group worksheet included two inquiry tasks aiming to measure different aspects of inquiry effectiveness. The first task focused on examining groups' concept interpretation, while the second concentrated on examining groups' problem-solving performance. The total score of the worksheet was 100 points, with 50 points each for two tasks. Group worksheets also help to collect the inquiry score of each group.

Reflection Questionnaire

To investigate students' role interaction, two primary science teachers and one primary Chinese teacher designed a reflection questionnaire. The reflection questionnaire contains questions including "What role did you play in the group inquiry? What did you do?", which were used to explore the roles students played in the group inquiry. This questionnaire was offered to students at the end of each inquiry experiment. The data collected from the questions facilitated the analysis of students' role interaction.

3.6 Data Analysis

This study used three methods to examine the role interaction of participating students in collaborative inquiry learning activities: thematic analysis, descriptive analysis, and statistical analysis.

With participants' answer text in the reflection questionnaire, a qualitative thematic approach [22] was utilized to label the roles students played during collaboration. In the open coding process, the roles that students reported in the Lig. reflection questionnaires were firstly labeled according to similarities of work students reported. Then, the same coding procedure was applied in analyzing data collected from the other two themes. Considering the validity of labeled roles, the open coding process was conducted by two researchers separately. This thematic analysis process facilitated the clarification of emerging roles students played as well as the classification of the roles.

In the descriptive analysis, Radar map and Sankey diagram, as two visualization tools were utilized to illustrate students' role distribution and transition through the three-round of the experiment. In addition, we proposed a formula to calculate the value of the role transition of each class. In statistical analysis, a t-test was used to analyze the impact of ES on inquiry performance.

4 Results

4.1 Role Emergence

Role Label
In the open coding processes, 11 role labels were summarized via qualitative thematic analysis: leader, inspector, recorder, integrator, investigator, experimenter, proposer, facilitator, observer, spectator, and null (see Table 1). It was found that expect group leader, other roles students played often changed in the process of inquiry learning.

Table 1. Role labels and descriptions.

Role label	Role description	Examples
Leader	Leading group members to conduct and work out inquiry tasks	"manage the group inquiry discipline and the division of tasks"
Inspector	The role provided in external scripts	"supervise the group discussion and prevent it from deviation"
Recorder	Recording inquiry processes and results with the guidance of a group worksheet	"I wrote down the results of the discussion on the worksheet."
Integrator	Incorporating ideas and suggestions generated from group discussions	"My main task was to conclude, the role I played was 'glue'."
Investigator	Proposing suggestions on solving problems and drawing conclusions	"I focused on investigating and answering questions, I was the king of inquiry."
Experimenter	Experimenting with tablet(s)	"experimenter, testing the brightness of the bulb again and again"
Proposer	Making recommendations on conducting the inquiry experiment for group members	"As an advisor, I worked out the second problem with my group partners."
Facilitator	Facilitating group members to complete group tasks	"Assistant, help others when they faced with problems."
Observer	Observing the inquiry and collaboration of group members	"Observer, I watched the discussion of my group."
Spectator	A role that student regarded oneself as the spectator	"I did not do anything, only stared." "I was the disregarded one."
Spectator	A role that student regarded oneself as the spectator	"I did not do anything, only stared." "I was the disregarded one."
(null)	Students did not report the role they played in reflection questionnaires	

Role Category
During the analysis course, it was found that some students usually play two or more roles at the same time; for example, group leaders usually took the role of inspector (marked as "leader & inspector"). According to the similarity of actual functions of role labels, role labels are divided into five categories: coordinator (R1), integrator (R2), inquirer (R3), facilitator (R4), and marginal (R5). The categories description is shown in Table 2. The coordinator (R1) focused on the division of tasks, collaboration, and coordination, including the group leader, inspector, group leader, and inspector. Integrator (R2) was responsible for incorporating and recording the inquiry process, including recorder, integrator, group leader & recorder, inspector & recorder, leader & inspector & recorder. Inquirer (R3) contained roles focusing on conducting experiments and drawing conclusions. The facilitator (R4) included roles that provided suggestions and assistance during group discussion. Finally, marginal (R5) referred to roles located at the margins and made fewer contributions to the group inquiry.

Table 2. Role labels and descriptions.

Role category	Category description	Role labels
Coordinator (R1)	Responsible for the division of tasks, collaboration and coordination, and supervision of discussion processes	group leader, inspector, group leader & inspector
Integrator (R2)	Incorporating group members' perspectives, recording inquiry processes, and filling out the worksheet	recorder, integrator, group leader & recorder, inspector & recorder, group leader & inspector & recorder
Inquirer (R3)	Conducting inquiry experiments and drawing conclusions	investigator, experimenter
Facilitator (R4)	Making recommendations and undertaking assistant tasks	facilitator, proposer
Marginal (R5)	Marginal roles during collaboration	observer, spectator, and null

4.2 Role Coordination

Role Distribution
The role distribution of the two classes in the three-round experiment was shown in Table 3. Radar map and Sankey diagram were applied to visualize the distribution and transition of emergent role categories, respectively. The radar map facilitated the demonstration of the role distribution in participating classes (Fig. 2).

As shown in Fig. 2, the role distribution of experiment class in the three-round experiment was found: inquirer (R3) accounted for the most, followed by the integrator (R2) and facilitator (R4), while the roles of coordinator (R1) and marginal (R5) accounted for the least. In the control class, the proportion of facilitator (R4) was the lowest, while inquirer (R3) accounted for the highest proportion (43.16%). Compared with

Table 3. Role labels and descriptions.

	Experiment class		Control class	
Role category	*N*	%	*N*	%
Coordinator (R1)	18	19.35%	13	15.79%
Integrator (R2)	21	22.58%	18	21.05%
Inquirer (R3)	26	27.96%	31	43.16%
Facilitator (R4)	20	21.51%	22	10.53%
Marginal (R5)	8	8.60%	10	9.47%
Total	93	100.00%	95	100.00%

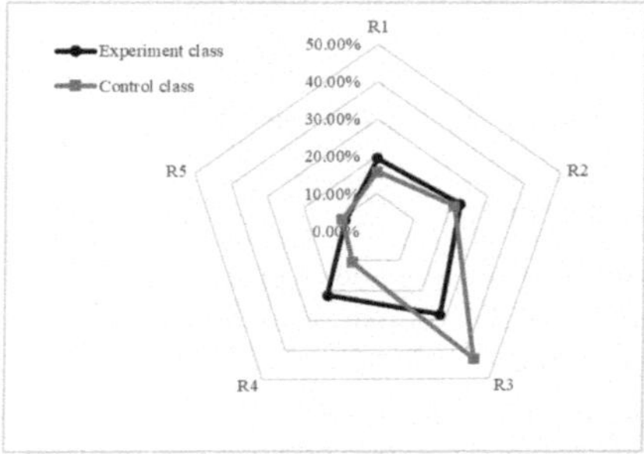

Fig. 2. The radar map of role distribution

the experiment class, the control class without ES had more inquirers (R3) and fewer facilitators (R4).

Role Transition

Sankey diagram was used to visualize the role transition of participating classes; that is, the flow of roles that occurred during inquiry processes (Fig. 3). The symbol '#' represents students who were absent from this round of experiments.

Since one student might take two or more roles at the same time, especially those students who took the roles of the group leader and inspector, it was necessary to clarify the role transition from the coordinator (R1) to other role categories and from other categories to the coordinator (R1).

R1 → other categories. When there were no ES, this role transition represented the work shift of the group leader. When participating groups were provided with ES, this role transition indicated the work shift of the group leader as well as the role transition from inspector to other roles.

Other categories → R1. When there were no ES, this role transition also represented the work shift of the group leader. When ES was provided, role transitions included the work shift of the group leader and the role transition from other roles to the inspector.

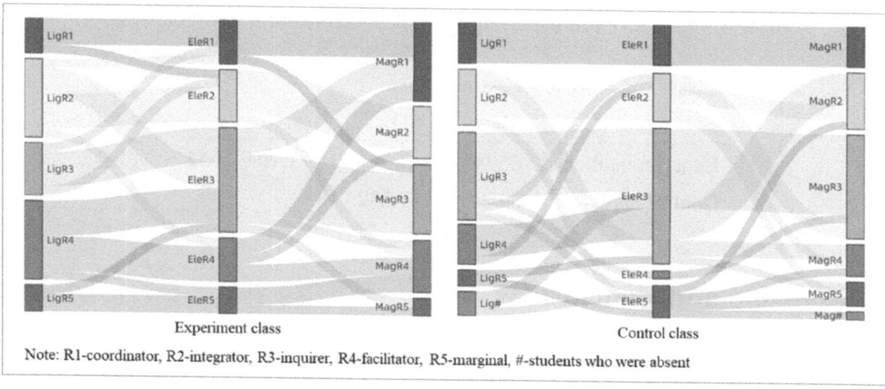

Fig. 3. The Sankey diagram of role transition

From Fig. 3, we could find that the proportion of inquirer (R3) roles in the control class was larger than the experiment class. This comparison described that when group members were not provided with ES, they tended to treat themselves as those who took inquiry roles in the group inquiry and fewer members take other responsibilities.

Besides, in this study, we assumed that each role category refers to different social status. Thus, we set the values of R5 to R1 to 1 to 5, a reverse score. Then, we created a formula to calculate the value of role transition (RT) of each class.

$$\text{RT}=\sum(r_{bi} - r_{ai})n_i/\sum n_i \tag{1}$$

In the formula (1), wherein $r_a \neq 0$. r_a means the level of the role category a student played in the previous round experiment, r_b means the level of the role category a student played in the latter round experiment. n_i refers to the number of students that has the same transition of r_a to r_b; $r_a \neq 0$ means that if a student was absent in the previous round experiment, the role transition of his/her was not included in the calculation. According to this formula, we calculate that the RT value of the two classes. RT values of the experiment class and control class are −0.194 and −0.086, respectively. This indicates that the absolute role transition degree of the experiment class was larger than that of the control class. Besides, from Fig. 3, we could see that there are more group members from lower social status changed to higher lower social status in experiment class, vice versa.

4.3 Inquiry Learning Performance

After the three-round experiment, we collected 36 group worksheets. As shown in Table Tab4, according to the t-test result ($t = 1.104, p = .652 > .05$), there was no significant difference between the two classes. Also, although the mean difference is large (5.56), the variance also leads to an insignificant result. This result may be affected by the composition of groups (i.e., roles interaction itself), the inquiry themes, and other factors.

Table 4. t-test result of the group worksheets scores of the two classes.

Class	Post-test				
	Mean	SD	*N*	*t*	*p*
Experimental class	65.00	14.951	18	1.104	.652
Control class	59.44	15.232	18		

5 Discussion and Conclusions

5.1 Various Roles in Mobile-Blended Collaboration

In this study, to examine the dynamics of collaborative roles, both emerging roles, and scripted roles were discussed and explored in a three-round experiment. The mobile-blended learning environment preserves the advantages of face-to-face interaction, which are used to support rich communication [23]. Thus, various role labels emerged during collaborative inquiry learning: leader, inspector, recorder, integrator, investigator, experimenter, proposer, facilitator, observer, spectator, and null. Further, according to the situation of concurrent roles, five categories were summarized: coordinator, integrator, inquirer, facilitator, and marginal.

5.2 ES Affects Task Awareness of Group Members

In the 1:1 tablet-to-student ratio, each student had a tablet to operate on, so that all the group members have the assess to virtual manipulatives [24]. Thus, inquirers account for the largest proportion in the two classes. When digital learning resources are sufficient, students could build a sense of ownership of VMs [25]. With the sense of ownership, students would tend to think they are the inquirers who are in charge of inquiry experiments. Meanwhile, the control class without ES had more inquirers and fewer facilitators than the experiment class. This indicates that if provided with ES, group members would pay more attention to the group task and play other roles (e.g., coordinator and facilitator,) to facilitate collaboration.

5.3 Rotation of Social Status Mediated by ES

Although scores of group worksheets didn't show a significant difference, we could draw that the absolute role transition degree of groups with ES was larger than those of groups without ES. Moreover, students in experiment class had more role mobility across social status, indicating that ES might promote more coordination-related actions in groups. Besides, the social status level of roles in this study may be not available for other learning situations, such as 1:m tablet-to-student ratios [24]. When there is only one tablet in a group, the inquirer role may have a higher social status level, as the operation of the limited virtual manipulative is important for the promotion of group tasks.

5.4 Highlights and Limitations

By addressing role interaction under different conditions, this study clarified the role transition of participating students from the time dimension. The design of roles in ES could be a potential way to facilitate collaboration and the rotation of social status in a group. Findings from our research also have practical implications for designing external scripts for collaborative inquiry learning activities and giving role-related instructional intervention.

Besides, there are also several limitations in this study. First, we didn't involve individual learning performance in the data analysis, which may lead to the lack of a more comprehensive link between role interaction and inquiry performance. Second, the ES is not designed to provide specific guidance according to the 1:1 tablet-to-student ratio condition. Adaptive ES might affect the role interaction and then affect the inquiry performance. In future work, to find the effect of role interaction on learning inquiry performance, we intend to propose specific ES to different tablet-to-student ratio conditions.

Acknowledgment. This research is supported by the project "Research on the management of education reform and innovation in the era of 'Internet plus'" supported by The National Natural Science Foundation of China (NSFC) [Grant No. 71834002].

References

1. Evans, M.A., Feenstra, E., Ryon, E., McNeill D.: A multimodal approach to coding discourse: Collaboration, distributed cognition, and geometric reasoning. Int. J. Comput. Supported Collab. Learn. **6,** 253 (2011)
2. Olympiou, G., Zacharia, Z.C.: Blending physical and virtual manipulatives: an effort to improve students' conceptual understanding through science laboratory experimentation. Sci. Educ. **96,** 21 (2012)
3. Crompton, H., Burke, D., Gregory, K.H., Gräbe, C.: The use of mobile learning in science: a systematic review. J. Sci. Educ. Technol. **25**(2), 149–160 (2016). https://doi.org/10.1007/s10956-015-9597-x
4. Lazonder, A.W., Harmsen, R.: Meta-analysis of inquiry-based learning: effects of guidance. Rev. Educ. Res. **86**, 681 (2016)
5. Tchounikine, P.: Learners' agency and CSCL technologies: towards an emancipatory perspective. Int. J. Comput.-Support. Collab. Learn. **14**(2), 237–250 (2019). https://doi.org/10.1007/s11412-019-09302-5
6. King, A.: Scripting collaborative learning processes: a cognitive perspective. In: Fischer, F., Kollar, I., Mandl, H., Haake, J.M. (eds.) Scripting computer-supported collaborative learning. CULS, vol. 6, pp. 13–37. Springer, Boston (2007). https://doi.org/10.1007/978-0-387-36949-5_2
7. Kollar, I., Fischer, F., Slotta, J.: Internal and external collaboration scripts in web-based science learning at schools. In: Koschmann, T., Suthers, D., Chan, T.W. (eds.) International Conference on Computer Supported Collaborative 2005: The next 10 years!, vol. 331, Lawrence Erlbaum, Mahwah (2005)
8. Yuan, Y., Lee, C.Y., Wang, C.H.: A comparison study of polyominoes explorations in a physical and virtual manipulative environment. J. Comput. Assisted Learn. **26**, 307 (2010)

9. Zacharia, Z.C., Olympiou, G.: Physical versus virtual manipulative experimentation in physics learning. Learn. Instruct. **21**, 317 (2011)
10. Wang, X., Kollar, I., Stegmann, K.: Adaptable scripting to foster regulation processes and skills in computer-supported collaborative learning. Int. J. Comput. Support. Collab. Learn. **12**(2), 153–172 (2017). https://doi.org/10.1007/s11412-017-9254-x
11. Ramirez, H.J.M., Monterola, S.L.C.: Co-creating scripts in computer-supported collaborative learning and its effects on students' logical thinking in earth science. Interact. Learn. Environ. 1 (2019)
12. Simpson, A., Bannister, N., Matthews, G.: Cracking her codes: understanding shared technology resources as positioning artifacts for power and status in CSCL environments. Int. J. Comput. Support. Collab. Learn. **12**(3), 221–249 (2017). https://doi.org/10.1007/s11412-017-9261-y
13. Kollar, I., Fischer, F., Hesse, F.W.: Collaboration scripts – a conceptual analysis. Educ. Psychol. Rev. **18**, 159 (2006)
14. Vogel, F., Wecker, C., Kollar, I., Fischer, F.: Socio-cognitive scaffolding with computer-supported collaboration scripts: a meta-analysis. Educ. Psychol. Rev. **29**(3), 477–511 (2016). https://doi.org/10.1007/s10648-016-9361-7
15. Kollar, I., Fischer, F., Slotta, J.D.: Internal and external scripts in computer-supported collaborative inquiry learning. Learn. Instruct. **17**, 708 (2007)
16. Dillenbourg, P., Jermann, P. Designing Integrative Scripts. Scripting computer-supported collaborative learning: cognitive, computational and educational perspectives, p. 275. Springer, New York (2007). https://doi.org/10.1007/978-0-387-36949-5
17. Mende, S., Proske, A., Körndle, H., Narciss, S.: Who benefits from a low versus high guidance CSCL script and why? Instr. Sci. **45**(4), 439–468 (2017). https://doi.org/10.1007/s11251-017-9411-7
18. Cesareni, D., Cacciamani, S., Fujita, N.: Role taking and knowledge building in a blended university course. Int. J. Comput. Support. Collab. Learn. **11**(1), 9–39 (2015). https://doi.org/10.1007/s11412-015-9224-0
19. Strijbos, J., Weinberger, A.: Emerging and scripted roles in computer-supported collaborative learning. Comput. Hum. Behav. **26**, 491 (2010)
20. Belbin, R.: Management Teams. Wiley, New York (1997)
21. Johnson, D.W., Johnson, R.T.: Learning Together and Alone: Cooperative, competitive, and Individualistic Learning 2 edn. Prentice-Hall Inc, Hoboken (1987)
22. Braun, V., Clarke, V.: Using thematic analysis in psychology. Qual. Res. Psychol. **3**, 77 (2006)
23. Reychav, I., Wu, D.: Mobile collaborative learning: the role of individual learning in groups through text and video content delivery in tablets. Comput. Hum. Behav. **50**, 520 (2015)
24. Wang, C., Ma, Y., Wu, F.: Comparative learning performance and mental involvement in collaborative inquiry learning: three modalities of using virtual lever manipulative. J. Sci. Educ. Technol. **29**(5), 587–596 (2020). https://doi.org/10.1007/s10956-020-09838-4
25. Antle A.N.: Scratching the surface: opportunities and challenges from designing interactive tabletops for learning. In: Lee, V.R. (ed.) Learning Technologies and the Body: Integration and Implementation in Formal and Informal Learning Environments, p. 55 Routledge, New York (2014)

Students' Evaluation of Performance-Centred Blended Learning Assessment in Japan: Can-Do and Cannot-Do Notions

Terumi Miyazoe(✉)

Tokyo University of Science, Shinjyuku 162-8601, Tokyo, Japan
t.miyazoe@rs.tus.ac.jp

Abstract. Tests can make students feel insufficiently capable. A 100% performance-centred assessment (PA) instructional design is therefore considered a better option. This study examines a PA design wherein no tests are included, and its effects and benefits are investigated from the perspective of students. The two-semester course based on this instructional design was held for one academic year in an undergraduate English programme at a Tokyo university. A survey administered after the course experience obtained 67 valid responses revealing a high level of positivity towards the PA course design. Additionally, the course succeeded in building students' self-efficacy and language use in a more strategic manner. Students also acknowledged the differences in the functionality between the test and PA methods, signifying a higher level of learning attained. Therefore, it can be concluded that a PA-centred course design has significant potential to deepen learning with skill-based education at the higher education level, providing a viable solution when conducting tests in person is not feasible, as during the ongoing COVID-19 pandemic.

Keywords: Performance-based assessment · Blended learning · Can-Do · AI text mining · Emergency · Language education

1 Introduction

Japanese society strongly emphasises winning competitive, high-stakes examinations [1, 2], a social norm historically linked to the traditional imperial examination system conducted to select high ranking civil servants, which is common in its neighbouring Asian countries as well [3, 4]. This study explores a potentially improved instruction design that shows higher efficiency and effectiveness in teaching and learning than the test-centred teaching approach, by using performance-based assessment (PA) in higher education skill-based blended courses.

PA refers to a concept in which grading is decided by the accumulation of performance and products as an alternative to the periodic traditional paper-and-pen written examinations that rely more on rote memory. In a chapter devoted to PA, Cantu and Warren [5] review and list commonly accepted definitions of PA, among which the definition most closely matching the aim of the current research is as follows:

R. Li et al. (Eds.): ICBL 2021, LNCS 12830, pp. 203–213, 2021.
https://doi.org/10.1007/978-3-030-80504-3_17

> Performance assessment, also known as alternative or authentic assessment, is a form of testing that requires students to perform a task rather than select an answer from a readymade list. For example, a student may be asked to explain historical events, generate scientific hypotheses, solve math problems, converse in a foreign language, or conduct research on an assigned topic [6].

In language education, there is abundant research on PA and criterion-reference tests. An in-depth literature review to plan the current research concludes that the arguments between PA and objective testing seem to have reached the stage of acknowledging that both methods have pros and cons and now focus more on specific issues regarding the inner mechanisms of scales/raters and the conditions under which these methods are used and interpreted. Apparently, no research design has explicitly investigated students'—'evaluatees'—evaluation of assessment implementation design and the learning outcomes from it. Cizek [7] suggests that 'a potentially fruitful line of research lies in combining the needs of standard setters with the knowledge base in instructional design' (p. 28). The present research was conducted in this vein, wherein PA was fully embedded in the instructional design of a blended format to examine its potential effectiveness.

2 Methods

2.1 Research Tools

Two relatively new research tools/concepts—the use of an online survey with a slider bar question format and AI text mining—were employed in the present study. The online survey system Survey Monkey (https://www.surveymonkey.com/) was used as it provides sophisticated survey making, delivery, and analysis functions. An online survey also has several other merits in that it offers anonymity, accessibility, and cost and time savings [8]. In the survey, the slider bar question format asked respondents to mark their agreement level in integers from 0–100. Despite its popularity and wide use, there have been arguments about the validity of Likert-type scale questions [9, 10]; statistically, the slider bar offers a more precise and granular representation than categorical rating. Online surveys and slider bar responses have been tested in previous research by the author, confirming that their functionality would offset the weaknesses of the paper-based survey method [11].

To analyse the text comments to the survey's open-ended questions, AI text mining was used. A beta-version of the AI-based text mining system (User Local: AI text mining: https://textmining.userlocal.jp/) that also processes Japanese language text is available. The system provides the results ranging from a basic word cloud, word frequency, and concurrent keywords, to an advanced negative/positive emotional analysis, hierarchical clustering, digest, and highlighting. Text analysis for qualitative data dates to its theorisation as grounded theory by Glaser [12]: the author of this paper practised the manual coding technique using computer-based analytics such as ATLASti and SPSS Text Analytics [13]. AI text mining has been drawing much attention in Japan recently; however, its use remains limited to corporations and laboratory research that necessitate extensive funds and/or skills such as Visualisation Engine (https://www.pa-consul.co.jp/) and KIBT (https://www.scsk.jp). The present study also tests its usefulness in small-scale research by individual researchers.

2.2 PA-Centred Blended Instructional Design

In this study, students of seven classes followed the same course design of a blended format. Table 1 summarises the characteristics of potential students in this study for registration in these courses.

Table 1. Registration profile of students in the study

	Target students	Majors
A2	Freshmen	Mathematics/Physics/Chemistry
B1	Sophomores	Mathematics/Chemistry
B2	Sophomores	Mathematics/Applied Chemistry

All the courses used the same core course textbooks (Unlock Reading and Writing Series 2–4 from Cambridge University Press, 2014) but differed in target English proficiency levels, including A2, B1, and B2 in the CEFR Common European Framework of Reference for Languages scales [14]. All students were part of the Faculty of Science of a Tokyo university, majoring in Physics, Chemistry, or Mathematics.

The courses were a blend of 30 in-class meetings over one year, with homework assignments comprising three to five essay compositions (writing) on paper and Cambridge LMS (https://www.cambridgelms.org/), course references, and oral audio file submissions (speaking) via the learning management system Moodle (https://moodle.org/), as per the new design. Moodle also served as a repository for the students' portfolios during the course.

The final course evaluation was held solely based on PA, with no test components included. All the writing submitted by the students was edited by the instructor and returned with numerical feedback: six points from the three-aspect evaluation method (syntax, content, and the goal of each unit) were used to attenuate subjectivity and add analytical features into the PA. A three-point feedback scale was used for speaking assignments graded roughly as satisfactory, neutral, and unsatisfactory; listening to each other's submission was recommended to the students for self-learning but was not compulsory. Additionally, although regular deadlines for assignment submission were set, late submission was accepted with a one-point deduction as a minor penalty for encouraging regular completion of tasks. The grading policy was explained clearly at the course orientation in all classes: the students could choose to take the current class or switch to another that was usually assessed via a high-stakes final examination as an alternative.

2.3 Data Collection

To evaluate the PA-centred course design in this research, an author-designed survey was used to collect information from the students. The survey was administered during the last session before the final day of returning the course grades, thereby minimising the possibility of the course grade influencing evaluation of the course experience. To obtain a good response rate, students were allowed to respond to the survey via online or on paper [15]—the online survey system was identical to a PDF version of the questionnaire from the paper version. The survey contained 28 questions and the system estimated that answering the survey online would require approximately six minutes. The survey asked for students' perceptions on specific aspects of 1) assignments (difficulty, content, frequency, and method of completion), 2) self-evaluation based on 'can-do' notions regarding the changes in specific language areas, 3) evaluation on the appropriateness of PA in the course, 4) demographic features (age and gender), and 5) open-ended questions regarding the instructional design and management. An English translation of the survey can be obtained by contacting the author of this paper.

The course employed in this research excluded 'tests'. However, one among the seven classes was in a different division of the same faculty (in Table 1, the Applied Chemistry major class). In this particular class, other than the present study's course scheme, the students were required to pass the TOEIC English proficiency test (https://www.ets.org/toeic) at the end of each semester. After the survey, the researcher obtained each student's signed written permission allowing for the use of their TOEIC scores as a reference in calculating the class average to triangulate the survey results.

3 Results

3.1 Respondents' Profiles

Among the 67 valid responses the male: female: no-wish-to-give (NG) student ratio was 64.2%:31.3%:4.5%, respectively, which approximates the students' gender profile similar to that published by the Faculty (73%:27%) [16]. Ages varied from 18 to 29 years; 83% were 19–21 years old. The students were taking English courses at different stages: according to the survey, they were divided evenly, with the CEFR Level A2 group slightly outnumbering the other groups. The 67 responses were all acceptable, that is, no entry seemed careless or illogical (e.g., simultaneously checking the like and dislike boxes), and no missing responses were found throughout the questionnaire.

3.2 Evaluation of Performance-Based Assessment

Question 1 asked about their overall course experience and generated a mean score of 83.67, that is, their perception of the value of this particular learning experience was highly positive and welcomed. Table 2 summarises the results of Qs. 21–22 that asked them to assess the validity of the evaluation methods for the audio and writing assignments: students revealed a high level of support for these methods as well.

The two students who chose the 'other' option left similar comments suggesting they wished to make the 'three-point-rating scale' a 'five-point-rating' one, which does not specifically indicate that they regarded the rating itself as 'negative'. In summary, the feedback was positive regarding the PA-centred course design and the level of acceptance of the semi-analytical PA assessment was also high.

Table 2. Students' overall course evaluations

Q 21 Audio assignment evaluation	Frequency	Percent	Q 22 Writing assignment evaluation	Frequency	Percent
Good	60	89.6	Good	64	95.5
Bad	5	7.5	Bad	3	4.5
Other	2	3.0	Other	0	0

3.3 Change in 'Can-Do' Notions

Figure 1 presents the results of Questions 13–18, which, using the slider bar format, asked students whether their proficiencies in each skill had improved. The zero at the leftmost corner of the slider indicates no improvement as per students while 100 at the rightmost corner corresponded to a high level of improvement. Different students have different notions of improvement; nonetheless, an average of 62.22 points towards the positive would indicate that students perceived an improvement in their overall skills, which cannot be ascertained in standard classrooms in Japanese culture. Among the four skills, the relatively low evaluation of speaking skill improvement may be attributed to the weakness in the simulative feature of the oral assignments in the course; conversely, students believed that their writing ability had largely improved.

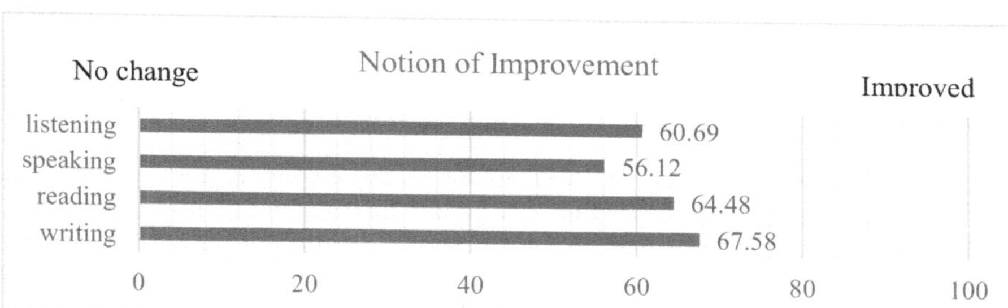

Fig. 1. Students' notions of improvement in the four skills.

Table 3 summarises Question 19 about students' perceptions regarding their own change in specific areas of English use after the course experience. The left collects all the items selected from multiple responses showing a positive perception, whereas the right notes the negative perceptions. Although several other factors need to be considered, the graphs reveal the students highly positive attitude towards different areas of English use; however, a small number of students suffered from a negative attitude.

Table 4 summarises the TOEIC results coincidentally available (in Table 1, the Applied Chemistry major class), corresponding to approximately 30% of the total respondents. Among them, 16 students consented to the use of the data for co-analysis and triangulation of the survey data. The TOEIC tests were held twice towards the end of spring and fall semesters; incidentally, they formed pre-/post-tests for the B2 class before and after the fall course of the present research. The total average scores increased by approximately 33 points in the total from summer to winter. The improvement measured via the outer objective test medium supports the students' perceptions about their improvement from the survey: the students not only felt that they had improved, they actually had.

Table 3. Students' 'can-/cannot-do' notions after the course experience

'Can-dos'			'Cannot-dos'		
	Frequency	Percent		Frequency	Percent
wants to speak English	35	52.2	does not want to speak English	2	3
wants to write English	20	29.9	does not want to write English	4	6
wants to read English	35	52.2	does not want to read English	3	4.5
wants to listen to English	33	49.3	does not want to listen to English	1	1.5
can use English	15	22.4	cannot use English	0	0
have confidence in using English	16	23.9	lose confidence in using English	3	4.5
learn to like English	25	37.3	learn to dislike English	1	1.5

Table 4. Change in the TOEIC scores of one B2 class

	2018 July			2018 December		
	Listening	Reading	Total	Listening	Reading	Total
Class average scores	248.8	233.1	481.9	257.5	257.5	515.0

3.4 Relation Between Group Features and Assessments

A one-way ANOVA was executed to compare the means among the three groups (A2, B1, and B2) to determine whether they had a significant correlation to any specific question item. Regarding Questions 13–16 (Table 5) on notions of improvement in the four skills (0: no progress, 100: improved), the test for homogeneity of variances as well as ANOVA significant values showed that the three groups were sufficiently homogenous for comparison, and the means were not considered to present a statistically significant difference. In other words, the factors of initial English proficiencies in the study were unlikely to affect the outcomes on the PA instructional design, that is, the design would likely function at any level of English proficiency.

Table 5. Notions of improvement in the four skills by group

	Q 13 Writing	Q 14 Reading	Q 15 Speaking	Q 16 Listening
A2	64.63	65.30	65.22	64.78
B1	72.24	63.33	54.43	62.95
B2	66.63	64.58	45.05	52.37

The same process was executed for Questions 1 and 17–18 (Table 6), which covered the students' overall evaluation of the learning experience using PA, as well as their preference ratios between exams and performance (0: test only, 100: performance only) if the students were to design their education, both in general and for the current course. All the group sets were considered statistically homogenous to enable mean comparison. Most importantly, the ANOVA showed that the mean scores among three groups for only Question 1 were statistically significant; that is, B1 found the learning experience most meaningful, followed by A2 and then B2. Interestingly, all three groups considered the appropriateness of mixing approximately 15% of the test elements for the current instructional design. Contrarily, all groups considered that mixing 20% to 25% of the test elements may be adequate for courses in general.

Table 6. Preference of instructional design by group

	Q 1 Overall	Q 17 General	Q 18 Current
A2	82.41	77.15	84.48
B1	90.62	72.95	84.00
B2	77.79	80.58	87.58

Figure 2 presents a by-group analysis of Question 20, which asked, 'If you became a teacher in the future, which evaluation method would you use?' Interestingly, an examination-only assessment policy was not considered the most effective by any of the three groups. It is noteworthy that no student in the B1 group wished to maintain the traditional 100% exam-only design that they would have been so much accustomed to; this tendency was more or less the same with the A1 and B2 groups.

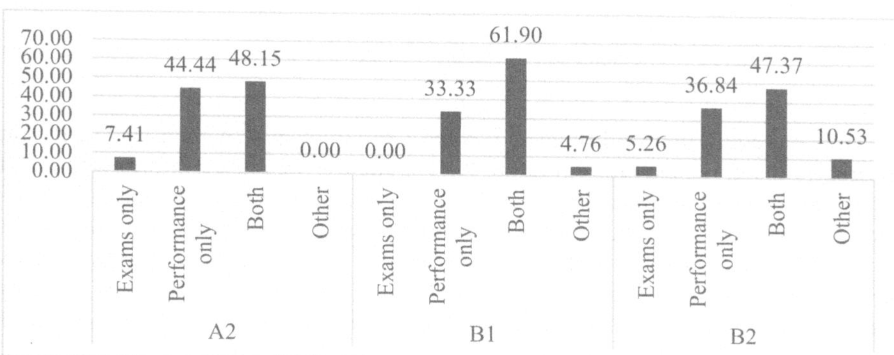

Fig. 2. Preference of assessment pattern as instructional design by group.

3.5 Open-Ended Comments

Questions 25–28 were open-ended. Q 25 referred to the issue of subjectivity within educational measurements: 'Performance-based assessment is different from mid-term and final exams, but similar in that the teacher evaluates what students have produced.

Please write any comments you may have on this point'. The question was phrased in this manner to avoid leading the students to favour one of the assessments as much as possible. Q 26 asked students the most useful thing they learnt from the course, Q 27 asked about any improvements that needed to be made in the future instructional design, and Q 28 requested any further comments. Numerous comments were given, which made the application of AI text mining possible for Questions 25–46 (student comments), Questions 26–52, Questions 27–35, and Questions 28–39, excluding those who left a note such as 'nothing special'.

Figure 3 illustrates the word cloud and hierarchical clustering representations for Question 25. The four key concepts expressed in the largest characters were 'performance', 'evaluation', 'strengthen', and 'accumulation'; thereafter, the hierarchical clustering explained how these concepts are related in the comments. With a 10-line digest auto-generated by the AI, the PA seemed to positively reflect the day-to-day accumulation of efforts, although it could only vaguely clarify what point was scored. These findings seemed a fair and reasonable summative interpretation of the comments from Question 25.

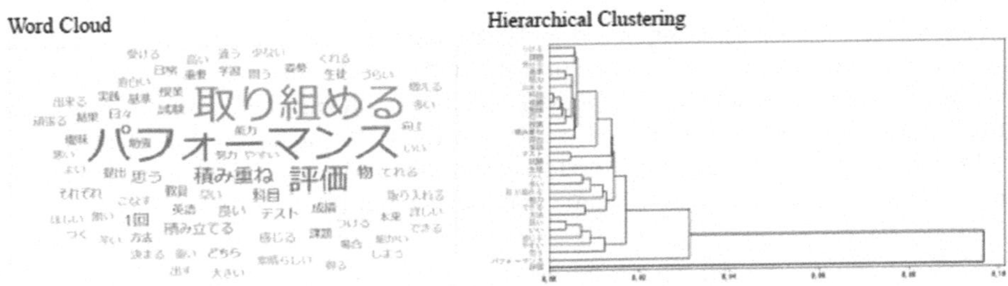

Fig. 3. Word cloud and hierarchical clustering for Question 25.

Figure 4 presents the word cloud and scored-word frequency of nouns and verbs that appeared in the comments for Question 26. The highest frequency in the word cloud was the use of the terms 'can use', 'TOEIC', 'research paper', and 'speaking'. Scored-word frequency suggests the words of importance using the term frequency–inverse document frequency (tf–idf) statistical arrangement that characterises the documents over the simple frequency of appearance [17]. From the 10-line digest, the students seemed to think that the course can be used to speak in English with foreigners, read and write research papers in English, and prepare for TOEIC tests.

In response to Question 27, 12 out of 35 comments stated, 'It is fine like this', whereas the rest noted different points, particularly regarding class management. The AI included five lines out of ten that said 'It's fine as it is' with slightly different phrasing, proportional to the 12 out of 35 comments. It also listed three specific points:

- An average class size of 20 is preferable.
- Some course exam evaluations should be added.
- Some additional assignments are fine.

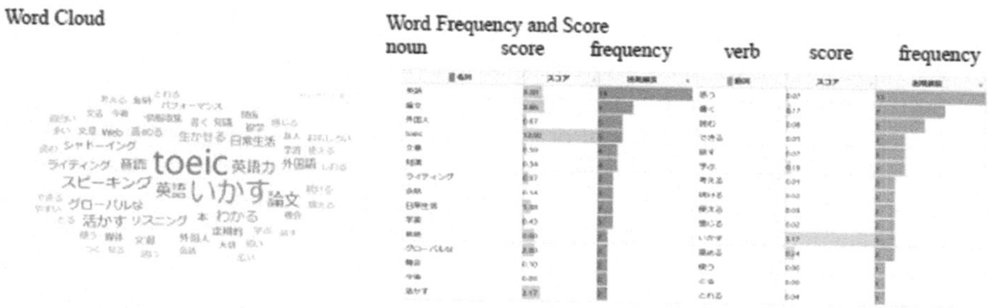

Fig. 4. Word cloud and scored-word frequency for Question 26.

These points for improvement were noted by single comments from three of the students; the AI seemed to consider these points significant and listed them in that manner. In the additional comments for Question 28, many students made polite remarks of thanks besides adding that the course was 'fun'.

4 Summary and Discussion

This research examined the perceived effectiveness of PA in blended learning via student evaluations. The course was designed with a 100% PA policy, and its learning outcomes were assessed via a survey. Specifically, the research found 1) a high level of positivity towards the PA-centred course design (Table 2), 2) high notions of improvement covering all the four skills and specific areas in use (Fig. 1), 3) applicability of the design regardless of the students' initial English levels (Table 5), and 4) only a small number of students who wished the courses (both the current course and in general) to be 100% test-based (Fig. 2). The positive attitude of the students towards the design of the course was further confirmed by the English proficiency test results (Table 4) drawn from outside the current research scheme for triangulation.

Based on these findings, three points are selectively discussed, as follows. The first point concerns students' self-confidence or 'can-do' notions. Students in Japan tend to underestimate their real abilities, perhaps as part of a culturally estimated virtue [18]. Their uncertainty about their own abilities cause them to interpret low scores as even lower: the can-do notion, that is, directing their attention to comparing their past status to the current to see the progress they have made, as was investigated via the survey questions, may actually be beneficial for students as they begin to think, 'I can now handle it better than before', which is easier than if presented a digital number from pen-paper tests that would make them think, 'I am going to do worse on the next test'. Placing PA as a core to check their progress may be a better option in Japanese culture, particularly in subject areas such as language education in which self-confidence is critical for production.

The second point relates to the potential use of PA-centred instructional design of blended type in the wider context of situations like the pandemic that we currently face. Education the world over is now facing an unprecedented challenge, namely, the near-impossibility of sharing the same physical space for teaching and learning in a classroom. Consequently, numerous test events such as term-examinations and some on-site English proficiency tests have had to be postponed or cancelled. PA-centred instructional design can be a viable alternative in these circumstances as it allows teachers to evaluate without the constraints of time and the challenges of physical space sharing. For a long time, identifying students and their digital products has been a hurdle in online learning: the asynchronous voice recording type of homework as was applied in the current study could be a feasible solution, more effective if combined with synchronous online sessions in which spontaneous vocal response from attendees can be realised. If automated in an LMS, voice-based authentication of students' digital products [19] would be a simple but practical solution to numerous problems involved in online teaching and testing.

The last point concerns our coexistence with an AI-powered society. In the current research, AI played a key role in the database search and text mining. The 3–5–10 line digests of the AI text mining produced a slight number of odd statements or selected particular sentences that were unexpectedly highlighted. For instance, in the word cluster in Fig. 4, the two expressions 'English' and 'English ability' used by the students could be interpreted as a sign that the students had begun to distinguish 'studying English' from 'acquiring the language'; however, the AI did not seem to differentiate between them. Nevertheless, all these processes would necessitate a lengthy period for collection and analysis without the aid of AI, requiring co-coders and co-researchers to verify and balance any human errors/bias that would naturally be involved. If used appropriately, AI can certainly be a useful tool to offset these issues with larger data sets and when researcher time is limited.

5 Conclusion

The PA course design is effective in helping students' learning process, regardless of their learning stage. Moreover, the combinatory design of mostly performance-based with some test-based assessments will make the course more authentic, acceptable, and more relevant to students. This course design could potentially be applicable to several other courses in fields where performance as outcomes is involved. The fact that students in this study gained confidence in their language ability and showed their willingness in acquiring these new skills is encouraging; this information would be difficult to obtain through a conventional course design with a one-time final exam. Assessment should preferably be embedded in the instructional process in such a way that it encourages and produces progress in students' learning. With a combination of online teaching and learning, the performance-centred approach could also provide a viable solution in emergency situations, such as the COVID-19 pandemic, when meeting for tests is not easily realised worldwide.

References

1. Doyon, P.: A review of higher education reform in modern Japan. High. Educ. **41**(4), 443–470 (2001)
2. Tomoda, A., Mori, K., Kimura, M., Takahashi, T., Kitamura, T.: One-year prevalence and incidence of depression among first-year university students in Japan: a preliminary study. Psychiat. Clin. Neuros. **54**(5), 583–588 (2000)

3. Lee, M., Larson, R.: The Korean 'examination hell': long hours of studying, distress, and depression. J. Youth Adolesc. **29**(2), 249–271 (2000)
4. Yu, L., Suen, H.K.: Historical and contemporary exam-driven education fever in China. KEDI J. Edul. Pol. **2**(1), 17–33 (2005)
5. Cantu, D.A., Warren, W.J.: Teaching History in the Digital Classroom. Routledge (2015)
6. Sweet, D.: Performance assessment. Education: Consumer Guide, September 1993. https://www2.ed.gov/pubs/OR/ConsumerGuides/perfasse.html
7. Cizek, G.J.: An NCME instructional module on: setting passing scores. Educ. Meas. **15**(2), 20–31 (1996)
8. Wright, K.B.: Researching Internet-based populations: advantages and disadvantages of online survey research, online questionnaire authoring software packages, and web survey services. J. Comput. Mediat. **10**(3), (2005). https://onlinelibrary.wiley.com/doi/full/10.1111/j.1083-6101.2005.tb00259.x
9. Norman, G.: Likert scales, levels of measurement and the 'laws' of statistics. Adv. Health. Sci. Educ. **15**(5), 625–632 (2010)
10. Jamieson, S.: Likert scales: how to (ab)use them. Med. Educ. **38**(12), 1217–1218 (2004)
11. Miyazoe, T.: A study on OERs, MOOCs, and LMOOCs for university students: how do they perceive and use them? Educ. Stud. **60**, 1–7 (2018)
12. Glaser, B.G.S., Strauss, A.L.: The discovery of grounded theory: strategies for qualitative research. Aldine Transaction (1967)
13. Miyazoe, T., Anderson, T.: Learning outcomes and students' perceptions of online writing: Simultaneous implementation of a forum, blog, and wiki in an EFL blended learning setting. System **38**(2), 185–199 (2010)
14. Council of Europe: The CEFR levels (2019). https://www.coe.int/en/web/common-european-framework-reference-languages/level-descriptions
15. Christensson, P.: QR code definition. Tech Terms, 5 March 2015. https://techterms.com/definition/qr_code
16. Tokyo University of Science (TUS): Undergraduate students' profile, 1 May 2019. https://www.tus.ac.jp/info/foundation/gakubu.html
17. Leskovec, J., Rajaraman, A., Ullman, J.D.: Data mining. In: Leskovec, J., Rajaraman, A., Ullman, J.D. (eds.) Mining of Massive Datasets, pp. 1–19. Cambridge University Press (2014)
18. Matsuno, S.: Self-, peer-, and teacher-assessments in Japanese university EFL writing classrooms. Lang. Test. **26**(1), 75–100 (2009)
19. Miyazoe, T., Anderson, T.: Advancement in online education. In: Lin, Q. (ed.) Voice interaction online, pp. 39–67. Nova Science Publishers, Inc. (2012)

Examining Beginners' Continuance Intention in Blended Learning in Higher Education

He Yang[1,2], Jin Cai[1], Harrison Hao Yang[3(✉)], and Xiaochen Wang[4]

[1] School of Computer, Hubei University of Education, Wuhan 430205, China
[2] Wuhan Huada National E-Learning Technologies Co., Ltd., Central China Normal University, Wuhan 430070, China
[3] School of Education, State University of New York at Oswego, Oswego, NY 13126-3599, USA
harrison.yang@oswego.edu
[4] College of Teacher Education, Capital Normal University, Beijing, China

Abstract. Blended learning became unprecedentedly widespread due to the pandemic of COVID-19, especially in higher education. As a result, a lot of college students were beginners with this new technology-based learning method. The purpose of this study was to find out the key factors that impact beginners' continuance intention in blended learning. The structural equation modeling was used to verify a model that integrates intrinsic goal orientation and academic self-efficacy into the Expectation-Confirmation Model of IS Continuance. A total of 342 college students who were the first time experiencing blended learning responded to the survey as beginners. The results showed that performance expectancy, intrinsic goal orientation, and satisfaction significantly impacted beginners' continuance intention in blended learning. Meanwhile, performance expectancy, intrinsic goal orientation, and confirmation significant impacts on their continuance learning intention through mediating variable satisfaction. Academic self-efficacy didn't directly impact college students' continuance learning intention significantly, but it can indirectly impact continuance intention through intrinsic goal orientation. In the end, this study put forward several guidelines for educators of improving beginners' blended learning experience to increase their continuance intention.

Keywords: Blended learning · Continuance intention · Expectation-confirmation model · Intrinsic goal orientation · Academic self-efficacy

1 Introduction

Blended learning is a learning method that combines face-to-face classroom teaching with online learning [1]. It has been accepted by many higher education institutions and there has been a lot of research proving that blended learning has the potential to improve both the effectiveness and efficiency of the learning experience [2]. As such, blended learning has received considerable attention in higher education. There are a lot of studies about blended learning, from various models [3] to instructional design

R. Li et al. (Eds.): ICBL 2021, LNCS 12830, pp. 214–225, 2021.
https://doi.org/10.1007/978-3-030-80504-3_18

strategies, as well as the relationship between online learning and blended learning [4, 5], the challenge in blended learning [6], and blended learning case studies [7, 8]. Previous research confirmed that blended learning was an efficient way to give effect to student-centered learning. The teaching and learning environment in blended learning was found to be more flexible. It provided greater time flexibility for students, improved learning outcomes, and increased teacher-student interaction. As well, it was also proved to increased student engagement in learning [9]. Although blended learning has been considered a trend in higher education learning models, it has only been implemented in limited courses for certain students.

However, the unexpected worldwide pandemic of COVID-19 made online learning popular in an unprecedented way [10]. Along with the diffusion of online learning, blended learning changed from optional to require after the pandemic. Instead of a crisis-response migration method of universities in the first few months, a large number of universities began to revisit blended learning as a sustainable conventional learning method in their daily teaching [11]. A nationwide survey of over 600 million instructors and students in universities implemented from 7 to 14 April 2020 showed that more than 80 percent of the instructors were going to take online learning or blended learning after the pandemic [12]. In such an unprecedented scale-up revolutionary for learning model, many instructors and students from different regions, major and technology capabilities in higher education became new blended learning practitioners. For these beginners, their initial experience of blended learning was extremely important for them to decide whether they were willing to continue with this kind of new learning model in subsequent courses. Moreover, compared with acceptance, the continuance intention can reflect the learner's direct attitude, rather than the indirect willingness impacted by others. Finding out the key factors that impact beginners' continuance intention is important to help them do well in the continuance blended learning courses. At the same time, it's valuable for instructors to implement blended learning well. However, few studies have investigated beginners' intention after they experienced blended learning. This paper tried to find out the key factors that impact beginners' continuance intention in blended learning. We just hope the results of our study will help instructors and administrators to design, develop, implement, and evaluate the large-scale blended learning initiative.

2 Research Framework

2.1 Expectation-Confirmation Model of Information System Continuance

The Expectation-Confirmation Model of Information System Continuance (ECM-ISC) is combined with Davis' technology acceptance model (TAM) [13] and Richard L. Oliver's expectation-confirmation theory (ECT) [14]. ECM-ISC had been commonly used to evaluate IS users' continuance intentions [15, 16]. According to Fig. 1, there are four core variables in ECM-ISC model. Among them, perceived usefulness came from TAM. It indicates the extent to which a person believed that using a specific system can enhance his or her performance at work. IS continuance intention refers to whether a user was willing to continue using such an information system. Confirmation was especially designed for ECM-ISC and refers to users' feeling of the consistency between their expectation and the information system's actual performance [17].

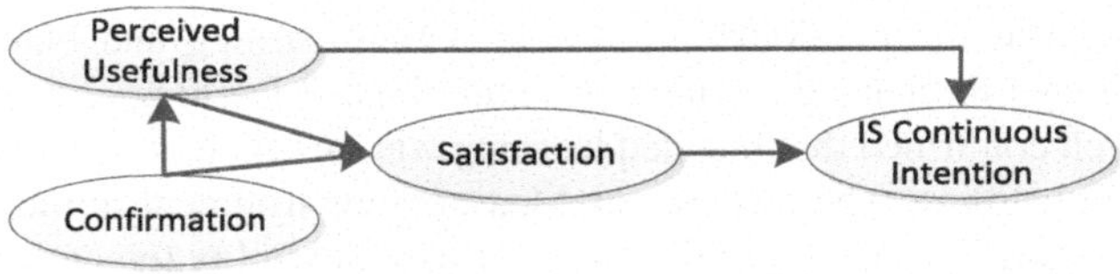

Fig. 1. Expectation-confirmation model of information system continuance

Blended learning is a kind of information system, so it is suitable for ECM-ISC. Various previous studies proved that the variables above were able to affect continuance intention in e-learning [16], MOOC [18], mobile learning [19], and blended learning [20, 21].

2.2 Performance Expectancy

Unified Theory of Acceptance and Use of Technology (UTAUT) is a technology acceptance model formulated by Venkatesh [22]. Performance expectancy (PE) is a construct used to describe the level to which a person perceived that technology would help him or her to achieve better results. Compared to the term perceived usefulness (PU) in TAM, PE was more suitable in this paper in order to describe the academic achievement blended learning would help the user to get. So, we replaced PU with PE [23, 24].

2.3 Intrinsic Goal Orientation

Self-determination theory emphasizes the satisfaction of fundamental needs and the development of true intrinsic motives [25]. Roca and Gagne's research showed that it was a complement to IS continuation theory in terms of explaining the intention to continue learning [16]. Intrinsic motivation refers to people's spontaneous cognition of the activities they are engaged in [26]. Previous studies had shown that intrinsic motivation was useful in predicting e-learning continuance intention. Moreover, studies supported the notion that intrinsic motivation has a positive impact on satisfaction [25]. Intrinsic goal orientation was a component of the MSLQ questionnaire—it concerned the degree to which students perceived themselves to be participating in a task for reasons of intrinsic motivation (e.g. challenge, curiosity, mastery, etc.) [27]. In this study, intrinsic goal orientation was employed to test intrinsic motivation.

2.4 Academic Self-efficacy

According to Bandura's definition, self-efficacy is an individual's subjective evaluation of his or her ability to complete a certain aspect of work [28]. Bhattacherjee connected self-efficacy with IT continuance, and IT self-efficacy was taken as a new construct. It was confirmed by empirical research that continuance intention is significantly affected by IT self-efficacy [29]. Other previous studies also confirmed that self-efficacy is an effective measurement for continuance intention [30]. In general, people with high self-efficacy are more likely to try to complete a task and stick with it longer than those with low self-efficacy [31]. In this study, we discussed the continuance intention of blended learning, it was not only an IT system but a learning model mixed with information technology. Specially, we took academic self-efficacy instead of IT self-efficacy.

3 Research Questions, Proposed Model and Hypotheses

3.1 Research Questions

This study proposed a research model which extended the ECM-ISC model with two constructs (see Fig. 2), in order to find out key factors that enhanced a beginner's intention to continue with blended learning. First, intrinsic motivation was featured as core constructs to test whether it would impact continuance intention. Second, academic self-efficacy was added to find out whether beginners with higher academic self-efficacy would show stronger continuance intention in blended learning. The research questions were:

RQ1: Are there any relationships between performance expectancy, confirmation, satisfaction, intrinsic motivation, academic self-efficacy, and continuance intention in blended learning for beginners?

RQ2: What are the most important key factors that will impact beginners' continuance intention with blended learning?

3.2 Research Model and Hypotheses

Based on the literature study above, the research model is shown as Fig. 2 and the hypotheses are reproduced below.

Hypothesis 1 (H1): Performance expectancy is positively related to the degree of blended learning continuance intention.
Hypothesis 2 (H2): Students' satisfaction with blended learning is positively related to the degree of continuance intention.
Hypothesis 3 (H3): Students' intrinsic goal orientation is positively related to the degree of blended learning continuance intention.
Hypothesis 4 (H4): Students' academic self-efficacy is positively related to the degree of blended learning continuance intention.
Hypothesis 5 (H5): Performance expectancy is positively related to the degree of blended learning satisfaction.
Hypothesis 6 (H6): Students' confirmation of blended learning is positively related to satisfaction.
Hypothesis 7 (H7): Students' intrinsic goal orientation is positively related to satisfaction with blended learning.
Hypothesis 8 (H8): Students' confirmation of blended learning is positively related to performance expectancy.
Hypothesis 9 (H9): Students' academic self-efficacy is positively related to intrinsic goal orientation.

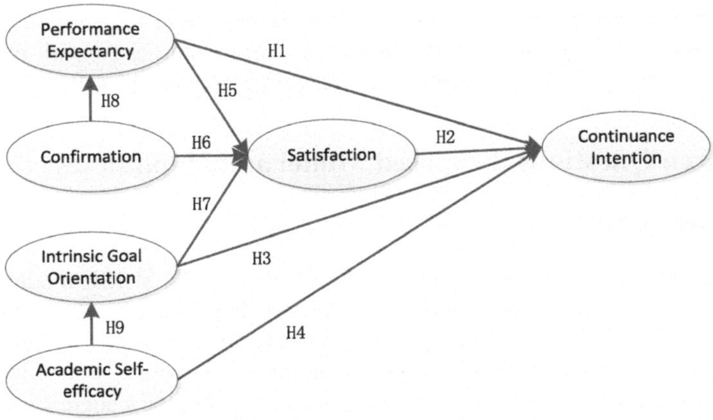

Fig. 2. Research model

4 Method

4.1 Participants

A survey was implemented in order to validate the hypotheses. The participants of this survey were beginners majoring in Psychology, Arts, Business, Mechanics, etc. which guaranteed the generalizability of this study. They were freshmen from a university in Wuhan in which blended learning was not prevalent before the pandemic of COVID-19. Since electronic products are strictly controlled in primary and secondary schools, blended learning is seldom implemented in K12 in China. So, these participants were regarded as beginners of blended learning. All participants took a blended learning course named "Fundamentals of Computer" in the fall semester. Since Fall 2020 was the first semester for these beginners, it was the first time they had tried blended learning. In addition, at the beginning of the survey, all the students were told the purpose of this study. As a result, a total of 403 from 471 beginners responded to the survey; the recovery rate is 85.6%. 342 valid questionnaires were collected (227 females and 115 males); the applicable rate is 84.9%.

4.2 Instrument

The survey was built on previous related literature. A Likert five-point scale was used in the questionnaire, involving 6 variables: Performance expectancy (4 items), confirmation (3 items), satisfaction (4 items), continuance intention (2 items), Intrinsic goal orientation (4 items), and academic self-efficacy (8 items). It was reviewed and validated several times by experts in this field. Confirmation, satisfaction, and continuance intention questions were adapted from Bhattacherjee's ECM-ISC scale [17], the reliability of the original scale was 0.82–0.88. Among the ECM-ISC scale, perceived usefulness questions were replaced by performance expectancy scaled from UTAUT which was more suitable for this study [22], reliability of PE was 0.91–0.92. Intrinsic Goal Orientation and academic self-efficacy questions were adapted from MSLQ Questionnaire

[27], the original reliability of them was 0.74 and 0.93. The questionnaire was released on an online survey platform and all the students were given enough time to complete and submit their answers.

4.3 Data Analysis

SPSS19.0 was employed to process data in this study. Smart PLS v.3.3.2 was used to build a research model and validate the mutual relationship between the key impact factors of students' continuance intention of blended learning.

5 Results

5.1 Overview of the Survey

The results showed that the response range was located between 3.91 and 3.94. Continuance intention ($M = 3.91$, $SD = .53$) turned out to have the lowest average response value examined. Intrinsic goal orientation ($M = 3.97$, $SD = .41$) turned out to have the highest average response values of the survey.

5.2 Reliability and Validity Analysis

The Standardized Root Mean Square Residual (SRMR) is a fitness measure of PLS-SEM that is used to avoid model misspecification [32]. A value less than 0.08 is considered to fit well [33]. The value of SRMR of this model was 0.04, so the proposed model was checked as acceptable.

Table 1. Reliability and validity of the survey

	Items	Reliability		Convergent validity	Discriminant validity					
		Alpha	CR	AVE	AS	C	CI	IM_	PE	S
AS	8	.95	.96	.73	**.86**					
C	3	.92	.95	.87	.69	**.93**				
CI	2	.90	.95	.91	.67	.80	**.95**			
IM	4	.92	.94	.80	.77	.75	.76	**.90**		
PE	4	.95	.97	.88	.70	.86	.80	.76	**.93**	
S	4	.94	.96	.85	.70	.86	.87	.77	.83	**.92**
Criteria		>0.70	>0.70	>0.50						

AS academic self-efficacy, *C* confirmation, *CI* continuance intention, *IM* intrinsic goal orientation, PE performance expectancy, S satisfaction

Cronbach's Alpha and Composite Reliability (CR) were used to measure the degrees of internal consistency of the results. Average Variance Extracted (AVE) was used to conduct validity [34]. As shown in Table 1, the parameters of Cronbach's alpha and CR exceeded 0.7 and all the parameters of AVE exceeded 0.5. The correlation among the square root of AVE and the latent variables were compared to evaluate the discriminant validity, [35]. The result showed that all latent correlations were below the corresponding AVE square roots. So, the constructs of the survey used in this study had good reliability and validity.

5.3 Hypotheses Testing

PLS algorithm was used to check the fitness of the structural model with available data. Within the PLS method, coefficient of determination (R^2) is a popular parameter [36]. R^2 was 0.788 for the CI endogenous latent variable, 0.594 for the IM, 0.744 for PE, 0.790 for S. Therefore, all the endogenous latent variables were well explained.

Table 2. Verification of research hypotheses

Hypothesis	Path	Path coefficient	T value	*p* value	Result	R^2
1	PE -> CI	.199	2.64**	.008	Supported	.788
2	S -> CI	.598	7.49***	.000	Supported	
3	IM -> CI	.136	1.98*	.048	Supported	
4	AS -> CI	.006	0.12	.902	Rejected	
5	PE -> S	.233	3.12**	.002	Supported	.790
6	C -> S	.485	6.57***	.000	Supported	
6	IM -> S	.231	4.48***	.000	Supported	
7	C -> PE	.863	43.24***	.000	Supported	.743
8	AS -> IM	.771	21.89***	.000	Supported	.593

R^2 coefficient of determinations; $*p < 0.05$; $**p < 0.01$; $***p < 0.001$

The bootstrapping method (5000 resamples) was used to calculate path coefficients (β value). Table 2 showed T-values and p-values of the path coefficients and R^2. As shown in Table 2 and Fig. 3, all other path coefficients were statistically significant except for AS -> CI. Only H4 was rejected, the others were supported.

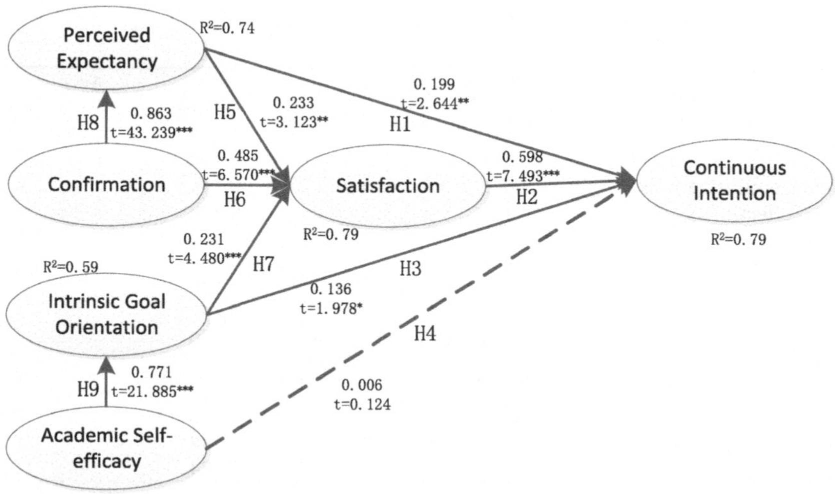

P<.05, **P<0.01, ***P<0.001

Fig. 3. Verification results of the structural model

PE (β = 0.199, p < 0.01), S (β = 0.598, p < 0.001) and IM (β = 0.136, p < 0.05) were positively related to CI, accounting for 78.8% of R^2. In addition, PE (β = 0.233, p < 0.01), C (β = 0.485, p < 0.001) and IM (β = 0.231, p < 0.001) positively impacted S, accounting for 79.0% of R^2. C (β = 0.863, p < 0.001) had a significant positive effect on PE, accounting for 74.3% of R^2. Furthermore, AS (β = 0.771, p < 0.001) had a significant positive effect on IM, accounting for 59.3% of R^2.

5.4 Analysis of Indirect and Total Effects Among Key Factors

Figure 3 and Table 3 shows the direct and indirect effects of each factor. PE and IM had both direct and indirect impacts on CI, S acted as the mediating variable. Although the direct path from AS to CI was rejected, two indirect paths were leading from AS to CI, IM and the combination of IM and S acted as partial mediators.

Besides, C had no direct impact on CI but had three indirect paths on CI through PE, S and the combination of PE and S. IM, PE and C had a direct impact on S. The results showed that IM played a mediating role between AS and S, while PE played a mediating role in the relationship between C and S.

Table 3. Analysis of indirect and total effects between key factors

	Path	Effect Value	Path coefficient	Account (indirect/total)
PE -> CI				41.3%
Direct effect	PE -> CI		0.199	
Indirect effect	PE -> S -> CI	0.233*0.598=0.140	0.140	
Total effect			0.339	
C -> CI				100%
Direct effect				
Indirect effect	C -> S -> CI	0.485*0.598=0.290	0.290	
	C -> PE -> CI	0.863*0.199=0.172	0.172	
	C -> PE -> S -> CI	0.863*0.233*0.598=0.120	0.120	
Total effect			0.582	
IM -> CI				50.4%
Direct effect	IM -> CI		0.136	
Indirect effect	IM -> S -> CI	0.231*0.598=0.138	0.138	
Total effect			0.274	
AS -> CI				100%
Direct effect				
Indirect effect	AS -> IM -> CI	0.771*0.136=0.178	0.178	
	AS -> IM -> S -> CI	0.771*0.231*0.598=0.107	0.107	
Total effect			0.285	
AS -> S				100%
Direct effect				
Indirect effect	AS -> IM -> S	0.771*0.231=0.105	0.105	
Total effect			0.105	
C -> S				29.3%
Direct effect			0.485	
Indirect effect	C -> PE -> S	0.863*0.233=0.201	0.201	
Total effect			0.686	

6 Discussion and Conclusion

To find out the impact of key factors on beginners' continuance intention in blended learning, this study took a survey on the first-year students in Hubei University of Education who used blended learning for the first time in the 2020–2021 fall semester. Smart PLS was used to find the relationship between key impact factors and continuance intention (CI). As a result, the three key factors, PE, S and IM directly impacted CI. In addition, C and AS indirectly impacted CI.

Students' satisfaction with blended learning had the strongest effect on their continuance intention which was consistent with the previous study [19]. As a subjective, comprehensive feeling of students and a common judgment element of teaching quality, there were a lot of studies on learning satisfaction and its impact factors, such as computer self-efficacy, system functionality, content feature, performance expectancy, interaction, and learning climate [37].

In this paper, PE, IM and C were the main factors that impacted S. It was interesting to find that PE and IM impacted CI both indirectly and directly, which agreed with the results of previous studies [18]. PE denotes students' beliefs regarding whether the use of blended learning will enhance their learning performance. Other studies indicated that students who thought blended learning was useful in their education would be more likely to adopt it [38]. Therefore, instructors should help students to build a positive belief in blended learning at the early stage of learning. For example, use lectures or social influences to help students understand the potential advantages of blended learning and show successful blended learning courses to students. IM referred to intrinsic motivation. It enabled students to engage more deeply in learning, gain better conceptual learning, and persist longer [39]. Instructors were required to design and implement effective strategies to improve students' intrinsic goal orientation. Such as poll students with thought-provoking questions to keep their attention, show how to use course information to solve real problems, make classroom expectations clear, give students ample time to practice new skills [40].

In our research model, although C and AS did not directly affect CI, they had indirect effects on CI. C referred to the confirmation of the benefits of blended learning that students felt personal after experiencing blended learning for a period. C positively impacted CI through PE, S and their combination, which were consistent with previous research results [17]. This indicated that the accomplishment of students' expectations on the performance of blended learning was positively connected to their satisfaction and would indirectly impact the continuance intention [19]. It's interesting to note that, AS was tested not to have a significant impact on CI directly. This finding didn't support the original hypnosis. However, it had an indirect relationship with CI. IM, the combination of IM and S played roles of partial mediators between AS and CI. Improving students' academic self-efficacy is helpful to enhance their intrinsic goal orientation to improve their intention to adopt blended learning. Research demonstrated that teaching methods and the type of learning environment were able to improve self-efficacy in the classroom. Designing suitable challenging tasks, using specific teaching and learning strategies, implementing peer learning, concentrating on student interest and choice, strengthening the efforts and use the right strategies, emphasizing recent successes and giving focused frequent and task-specific feedback, and stressing functional attribution statements were all proven ways to improve academic self-efficacy [41].

7 Limitation

It should be noted that the samples of this study were limited to one university, and thus may not necessarily represent the diversity of the group of beginners. The range and source of the sample need to be expanded in the next study Since COVID-19 is a huge promotion of online learning and blended learning thus not only students but also instructors were impacted. This study only focused on the group of students. It is suggested future studies focus on instructors especially those beginners.

Acknowledgement. This study is supported by the key project of Scientific Research Project of Education Department of Hubei Province (D20193002). It is also supported by China Postdoctoral Science Foundation funded project (2018M640738).

References

1. Graham, C.R.: Blended learning systems. In: The handbook of Blended Learning: Global Perspectives, Local Designs, vol. 1, pp. 3–21 (2006)
2. Garrison, D.R., Kanuka, H.: Blended learning: uncovering its transformative potential in higher education. Internet High. Educ. **7**(2), 95–105 (2004)
3. Yang, H.H., Zhu, S., MacLeod, J.: Collaborative teaching approaches: extending current blended learning models. In: Cheung, S.K.S., Kwok, L.-F., Shang, J., Wang, A., Kwan, R. (eds.) ICBL 2016. LNCS, vol. 9757, pp. 49–59. Springer, Cham (2016). https://doi.org/10.1007/978-3-319-41165-1_5
4. Tayebinik, M., Puteh, M.: Blended learning or e-learning? arXiv preprint arXiv:1306.4085 (2013)
5. Koohang, A.: A learner-centred model for blended learning design. Int. J. Innov. Learn. **6**(1), 76–91 (2009)
6. Oliver, M., Trigwell, K.: Can 'blended learning' be redeemed? E-learning Digital Media **2**(1), 17–26 (2005)
7. de Jong, N., Savin-Baden, M., Cunningham, A.M., Verstegen, D.M.L.: Blended learning in health education: three case studies. Perspect. Med. Educ. **3**(4), 278–288 (2014). https://doi.org/10.1007/s40037-014-0108-1
8. Jung, I., Suzuki, K.: Blended learning in Japan and its application in liberal arts education. In: The Handbook of Blended Learning-Global Perspectives, Local Designs, pp. 267–280 (2006)
9. Baepler, P., Walker, J., Driessen, M.: It's not about seat time: blending, flipping, and efficiency in active learning classrooms. Comput. Educ. **78**, 227–236 (2014)
10. Daniel, S.J.: Education and the COVID-19 pandemic. Prospects **49**(1–2), 91–96 (2020). https://doi.org/10.1007/s11125-020-09464-3
11. Johnson, N., Veletsianos, G., Seaman, J.: US Faculty and administrators' experiences and approaches in the early weeks of the COVID-19 pandemic. Online Learn. **24**(2), 6–21 (2020)
12. Yang, Z.: Promote the internationalization of higher education by informatization. In: China Education Daily, China (2020)
13. Davis, F.D.: Perceived usefulness, perceived ease of use, and user acceptance of information technology. MIS Q. **13**, 319–340 (1989)
14. Oliver, R.L.: A cognitive model of the antecedents and consequences of satisfaction decisions. J. Mark. Res. **17**(4), 460–469 (1980)
15. Chen, S.-C., Yen, D.C., Hwang, M.I.: Factors influencing the continuance intention to the usage of Web 2.0: an empirical study. Comput. Hum. Behav. **28**(3), 933–941 (2012)
16. Roca, J.C., Gagné, M.: Understanding e-learning continuance intention in the workplace: a self-determination theory perspective. Comput. Hum. Behav. **24**(4), 1585–1604 (2008)
17. Bhattacherjee, A.: Understanding information systems continuance: an expectation-confirmation model. MIS Q. **25**, 351–370 (2001)
18. Daneji, A.A., Ayub, A.F.M., Khambari, M.N.M.: The Effects of perceived usefulness, confirmation and satisfaction on continuance intention in using massive open online course (MOOC). Knowl. Manage. E-Learning **11**(2), 201–214 (2019)
19. Alshurideh, M., Al Kurdi, B., Salloum, S.A.: Examining the main mobile learning system drivers' effects: a mix empirical examination of both the Expectation-Confirmation Model (ECM) and the Technology Acceptance Model (TAM). In: Hassanien, A.E., Shaalan, K., Tolba, M.F. (eds.) AISI 2019. AISC, vol. 1058, pp. 406–417. Springer, Cham (2020). https://doi.org/10.1007/978-3-030-31129-2_37
20. Cheng, Y.-M.: What drives nurses' blended e-learning continuance intention? J. Educ. Technol. Soc. **17**(4), 203–215 (2014)

21. Sabah, N.M.: Motivation factors and barriers to the continuous use of blended learning approach using Moodle: students' perceptions and individual differences. Behav. Inf. Technol. **39**(8), 875–898 (2020)
22. Venkatesh, V., et al.: User acceptance of information technology: toward a unified view. MIS Q. **27**, 425–478 (2003)
23. Hamzat, S.A., Mabawonku, I.: Influence of performance expectancy and facilitating conditions on use of digital library by engineering lecturers in universities in south-west, Nigeria. Library Philosophy and Practice, pp. 1–16 (2018)
24. Khayati, S., Zouaoui, S.K.: Perceived usefulness and use of information technology: the moderating influences of the dependence of a subcontractor towards his contractor. J. Knowl. Manage. Econ. Inf. Technol. **3**(6), 68–77 (2013)
25. Sørebø, Ø., et al.: The role of self-determination theory in explaining teachers' motivation to continue to use e-learning technology. Comput. Educ. **53**(4), 1177–1187 (2009)
26. Teo, T.S., Lim, V.K., Lai, R.Y.: Intrinsic and extrinsic motivation in Internet usage. Omega **27**(1), 25–37 (1999)
27. Pintrich, P.R., et al.: Reliability and predictive validity of the Motivated Strategies for Learning Questionnaire (MSLQ). Educ. Psychol. Measur. **53**(3), 801–813 (1993)
28. Bandura, A.: Social Foundations of Thought and Action. Englewood Cliffs, NJ, pp. 23–28 (1986)
29. Bhattacherjee, A., Perols, J., Sanford, C.: Information technology continuance: a theoretic extension and empirical test. J. Comput. Inf. Syst. **49**(1), 17–26 (2008)
30. Mathieson, K.: Predicting user intentions: comparing the technology acceptance model with the theory of planned behavior. Inf. Syst. Res. **2**(3), 173–191 (1991)
31. Schunk, D.H.: Goal setting and self-efficacy during self-regulated learning. Educ. Psychol. **25**(1), 71–86 (1990)
32. Hair, J.F., et al.: Common beliefs and reality about partial least squares: comments on Rönkkö and Evermann (2014)
33. Hu, L.-T., Bentler, P.M.: Fit indices in covariance structure modeling: sensitivity to underparameterized model misspecification. Psychol. Methods **3**(4), 424 (1998)
34. Wong, K.K.-K.: Partial least squares structural equation modeling (PLS-SEM) techniques using SmartPLS. Mark. Bull. **24**(1), 1–32 (2013)
35. Fornell, C., Larcker, D.F.: Evaluating structural equation models with unobservable variables and measurement error. J. Mark. Res. **18**(1), 39–50 (1981)
36. Tompson, R., Barclay, D., Higgins, C.: The partial least squares approach to causal modeling: personal computer adoption and uses as an illustration. Technol. Stud. Spec. Issue Res. Methodol. **2**(2), 284–324 (1995)
37. Wu, J.-H., Tennyson, R.D., Hsia, T.-L.: A study of student satisfaction in a blended e-learning system environment. Comput. Educ. **55**(1), 155–164 (2010)
38. Tselios, N., Daskalakis, S., Papadopoulou, M.: Assessing the acceptance of a blended learning university course. J. Educ. Technol. Soc. **14**(2), 224–235 (2011)
39. Vansteenkiste, M., Lens, W., Deci, E.L.: Intrinsic versus extrinsic goal contents in self-determination theory: another look at the quality of academic motivation. Educ. Psychol. **41**(1), 19–31 (2006)
40. Carman, J.M.: Blended learning design: five key ingredients. https://www.it.iitb.ac.in/~s1000brains/rswork/dokuwiki/media/5_ingredientsofblended_learning_design.pdf
41. Margolis, H., McCabe, P.P.: Improving Self-Efficacy and Motivation: What to Do, What to Say (2006)

Content Development for Blended Learning in Pharmaceutical Preparations

Narinee Phosri[1(✉)] and Verayuth Lertnattee[2]

[1] Sirindhon College of Public Health, Suphanburi 72000, Thailand
narinee.pho@phcsuphan.ac.th

[2] Faculty of Pharmacy, Silpakorn University, Nakhon Pathom, Thailand

Abstract. The purpose of this research was to improve the pharmacy technician students' comprehensive knowledge and practice in pharmaceutical preparations by using blended learning with PharTech E-learning. The e-learning program was developed for the students to submit their pharmaceutical preparation assignments during their hospital internship. In this tool, users are able to create keywords related to assignment contents, upload electronic data files to share with friends, search and download peers' assignments. The results found that the number of students with blended learning intervention achieved the learning outcomes more than that of the traditional learning group, not only theoretical but also practical education. Most students gave positive feedback on the PharTech E-learning program satisfaction, blended learning activity satisfaction and evaluation process satisfaction. The e-learning is effective in enhancing students' knowledge and skill. Internship experience in pharmaceutical preparation can transfer among the learners through online learning.

Keywords: Blended learning · E-learning · Content development · Pharmaceutical preparation · Pharmacy technician

1 Introduction

In teaching a basic pharmaceutical preparation class for pharmacy technician students, the instructors usually face difficult contents. The number of staff was limited for monitoring students in a laboratory class. In addition, when the students went on an internship program, they are unable to be practise to cover all the recipes. These might cause ineffective learning for the students, which can be seen from the currently registered data. The result showed that this performance had the lowest number of students passing the comprehensive examination at the end of the graduate. Education with traditional learning, only face-to-face learning between learners and teachers inside a classroom, may lead to low students' learning achievement, whereas blended learning, which combines online learning and traditional face-to-face learning, can be more beneficial [1–5]. Therefore, we created a blended learning model with our e-learning designed program (PharTech E-learning) to improve knowledge and skill for pharmacy technician students in the performance of the pharmaceutical preparation and be a pattern to applying for teaching in other subjects.

R. Li et al. (Eds.): ICBL 2021, LNCS 12830, pp. 226–236, 2021.
https://doi.org/10.1007/978-3-030-80504-3_19

In the rest of this paper, Sect. 2 provides the background of pharmacy technician and pharmaceutical preparations, blended learning, and the PharTech E-learning program. Section 3 focuses on a method. Section 4 presents the result of the research, and the discussion is described in Sect. 5. A conclusion and future work are given in Sect. 6.

2 Background

2.1 Pharmacy Technician and Pharmaceutical Preparations

A pharmacy technician is a health care provider who assists in the pharmaceutical department and works under pharmacists' supervisions. In Thailand, a pharmacy technician education program that offers a diploma degree aims at providing students with fundamental knowledge and skills in pharmacy services. A basic pharmaceutical compounding performance is a required skill of pharmacy technician students who study a basic pharmaceutical preparation subject. In addition, this ability is to be evaluated by the time the students graduate.

2.2 Blended Learning

Blended learning, a combination of face-to-face learning and electronic learning (e-learning), is capable of increasing the efficiency of education and students' learning achievement [1, 6, 7]. Therefore, it is appropriate for generation Z students and 21st century learners. In contrast, traditional learning, only face-to-face learning between learners and teachers inside a classroom may lead to low students' learning achievement. Blended learning can develop students in many skills, including thinking and analytical skills, communication skills, and information and technology skills [2, 4, 8]. The effectiveness of blended learning has been largely studied. The previous studies commented on that it had a positive effect on health professions [4, 7–13].

2.3 Content Development on the PharTech E-learning Program

PharTech E-learning program was designed to encourage learning outside the classroom and transfer knowledge and practice from students to the others. In this online program, a username and a password were used to login into the program. The users are able to enter their personal data, learn with self-directed, create keywords related to assignment contents, upload electronic data files to share with friends, search and download peers' projects and manage learning by themselves anywhere on their own timetables. In this platform, three types of information could be applied, i.e., text, document file and multimedia file. The text was used to define the title, keyword, and summary content. Document file was presented in the information of master formula that consists of a pharmaceutical recipe, ingredient and functions, equipment, calculation, manufacturing process, container and storage, and drug labelling. For multimedia file, students were required to create a video of the important process from the beginning to the end of the product.

We attached a searching box into the program so that the students are able to use their keywords, title and summary content to look up the uploaded contents from the program. On the other hand, the students assigned to upload the contents have to create keywords in Thai and/or English, and the instructors will review the keywords. Then the instructors give feedbacks and suggest the appropriate keywords to the students. The benefit of assigning keywords to the contents is that the instructors can classify the uploaded materials.

Due to the limitations of the course, the students are unable to practise entire pharmaceutical preparations, which are expected to perform in a real-world situation. In general, students will about 2–3 recipes in an internship course. Moreover, multimedia materials concerning pharmaceutical productions such as extemporaneous formulas are insufficient for the students to study independently. Therefore, the PharTech E-learning was designed to gather and archive information on the various pharmaceutical preparations from the different hospitals during students' internships. Also, such information could be used as learning materials for the upcoming students. They can know internship hospital. This platform helps the new students prepare their knowledge and skills before going to an internship and support the learners to understand the pharmacy technician roles in a real situation. The benefit of using this e-learning before their internship, the students have an opportunity to choose the formulas of interest that they have never practised in college. Moreover, even if it is the uploaded same recipe but may be practising with different hospitals or trainer, the students can achieve the learning in various methods. Importantly, both the learners and instructors can obtain updated pharmaceutical knowledge and skill.

3 Methods

3.1 Participants

The participants were the second-year pharmacy technician students of Sirindhorn College of Public Health Suphanburi. In the academic year 2017, the students were educated with a traditional learning method as the control group ($n = 37$). The students in the academic year 2018 that used blended learning education with the PharTech E-learning were the experimental group ($n = 33$). The latter group was divided into 15 subgroups which the numbers of students per group were two or three.

3.2 Blended Learning

The Blended learning design with implementation in the experimental group was divided into three phases. The first phase was the step before using a blended learning course. The instructor conducted a meeting for student orientation, informing learning objectives, the activity schedule, e-learning program and tasks to be completed as the group assignment. For the group assignment, the students went on an internship program at the hospitals. Each group was assigned to make a video presentation on a pharmaceutical preparation and a pharmaceutical formulation document report, one formulation per group. At the end of the internship course, the assignment was submitted by uploading on the PharTech E-learning program. At the beginning of the blended learning activity, the participants took the pre-test examination of both theory and practice. The second phase, the blended learning activity, consists of face-to-face lecture teaching, laboratory practice, and e-learning as an adjunct learning activity. The participants were post-tested examination to assess the increase in the knowledge and skills in the last phase. The diagram of the process is shown in Fig. 1.

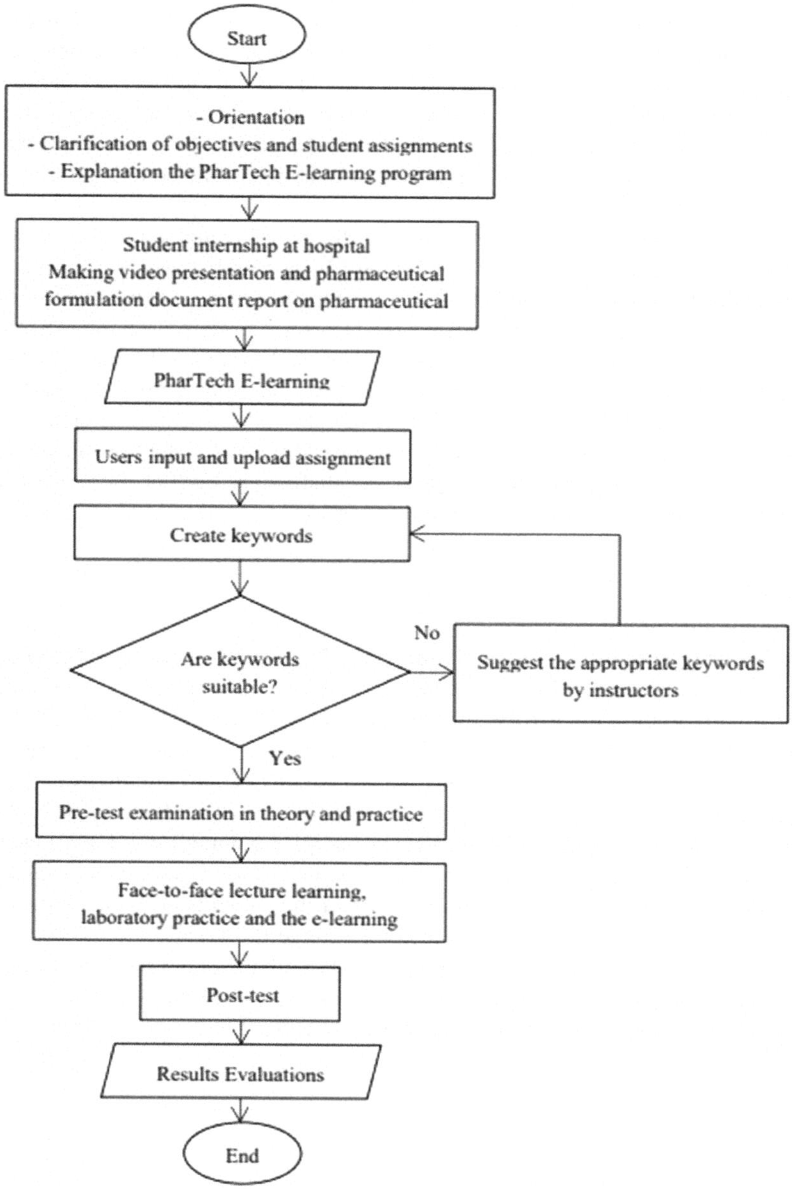

Fig. 1. The process of using blended learning with the PharTech E-learning.

3.3 Data Analysis

The first analysis, the pre-test and the post-test were developed to test the students' abilities to measure blended learning effectiveness with the PharTech E-learning program. The examination has been criticized and quality checked by three experts regarding content and conforming to study objectives. There were two sections of the tests, including a theoretical section and a practical section. The theoretical section was a set of 20-multiple-choice questions, while the practical section was a basic pharmaceutical preparation skill test. The criteria to pass these examinations were obtaining 65% and 75% in theoretical and practical parts, respectively. We calculated the differences between the percentage of the number of students who passed the pre-test and the post-test in individual groups. Then we compared those figures of the control group with the experimental group.

In the second analysis, we only focused on the experimental subgroups. The other pre-test and the post-test were designed with the 15-open-ended questions related to the assignment that the students uploaded on the e-learning program were used to evaluate the students' learning achievement after using blend learning activity. The mean differences between pre-test and post-test were analyzed using the Wilcoxson Signed-Rank test.

Moreover, a questionnaire assessing the students' acceptance of blended learning activity with a 5-point Likert scale was used to evaluate learners' satisfaction that focused on three domains, including the PharTech E-learning program satisfaction, blended learning activity satisfaction and evaluation process satisfaction. Further-more, open-ended comments were used as free text additional feedback.

4 Results

This study focused on using blended learning with PharTech E-learning in the pharmacy technician in pharmaceutical preparations. Participants' demographics were collected in Table 1. Almost all of the participants were female. The mean cumulative grade point average of the participants in the control group and experimental group were 3.14 + 0.42 and 3.15 + 0.34, respectively. Basic Pharmaceutical Compounding I and II were the courses that related to pharmaceutical preparations. In Basic Pharmaceutical Compounding I, the students study and practise the principles and methods of pharmaceutical manufacturing. Then, they study and practise drug preparation in various dosage forms in Basic Pharmaceutical Compounding II. Most of the students both the control group and the experimental group received grade in the range B+ to C+ .

In the evaluation of the blended learning activity with the PharTech E-learning in the pharmaceutical preparation topic, the students' learning comprehensive achievement in the theoretical and practical sections was shown in Table 2.

Table 1. Demographics of participants

Demographics	Control group (N = 37)	Experimental group (N = 33)
Male	4 (10.81%)	5 (15.15%)
Female	33 (89.19%)	28 (84.85%)
CUM-GPA	3.14 ± 0.42	3.15 + 0.34
Basic pharmaceutical compounding I grade		
A	3 (8.11%)	2 (6.06%)
B+	7 (18.92%)	9 (27.27%)
B	14 (37.84%)	10 (30.30%)
C+	8 (21.62%)	7 (21.21%)
C	5 (13.51%)	5 (15.15%)
Basic pharmaceutical compounding II grade		
A	4 (10.81%)	5 (15.15%)
B +	11 (29.73%)	8 (24.24%)
B	11 (29.73%)	9 (27.27%)
C +	7 (18.92%)	8 (24.24%)
C	4 (10.81%)	3 (9.09%)

CUM-GPA = Cumulative Grade Point Average

Table 2. The number and percentage of passed the examination students.

The examination	Control group (N = 37)	Experimental group (N = 33)
Theoretical section		
Pre-test	31/37 = 83.78%	16/33 = 48.48%
Post-test	29/37 = 78.38%	26/33 = 78.79%
Differences	−5.40%	30.31%
Practical section		
Pre-test	29/37 = 78.38%	17/33 = 51.52%
Post-test	30/37 = 81.08%	33/33 = 100.00%
Differences	2.70%	48.48%

In the theoretical section, the number of students in the control group who passed the post-test decreased by 5.40% compared with those who passed the pre-test. In contrast, the number of students who passed the post-test in the experimental group considerably increased by 30.31%. In a practical section, compared with the pre-test, the number of the control group students who had qualified pharmaceutical preparation skill were 2.70%

higher in the post-test. In the experimental group, entire students passed the post-test, which increased by 48.48%.

In the PharTech E-learning assignment upload, display screen within the program was shown in Fig. 2 and examples of video presentations on pharmaceutical preparation were presented in Fig. 3. The number of preparations in each category was reported in Table 3 and Table 4. There were 14 general preparations and 1 extemporaneous preparation in classification on pharmaceutical manufacturing processes and 7 liquid preparations and 8 semi-solid preparations in classification on dosage forms.

Table 3. The number of pharmaceutical formulas classification by pharmaceutical manufacturing processes.

Pharmaceutical manufacturing process	Number
General preparations	14
Extemporaneous preparations	1
Total	15

Table 4. The number of pharmaceutical formulas classification by dosage forms.

Dosage forms	Number
Liquid	7
Semi-solid	8
Total	15

After being applied with the blended learning activity in the pharmaceutical preparation topic, the mean of the post-test score considerably increased compared with the mean of the pre-test score in the 15 open-ended questions summarized in Table 5. The results indicated that the subjects had statistically significant learning achievement post-test higher than pre-test scores ($p = 0.000$).

Table 5. The results of assignment test in the experimental group.

Scores	Min	Max	Mean + SD
Pre-test	4.50	11.50	8.30 ± 1.36
Post-test	11.00	15.00	13.52 ± 1.12

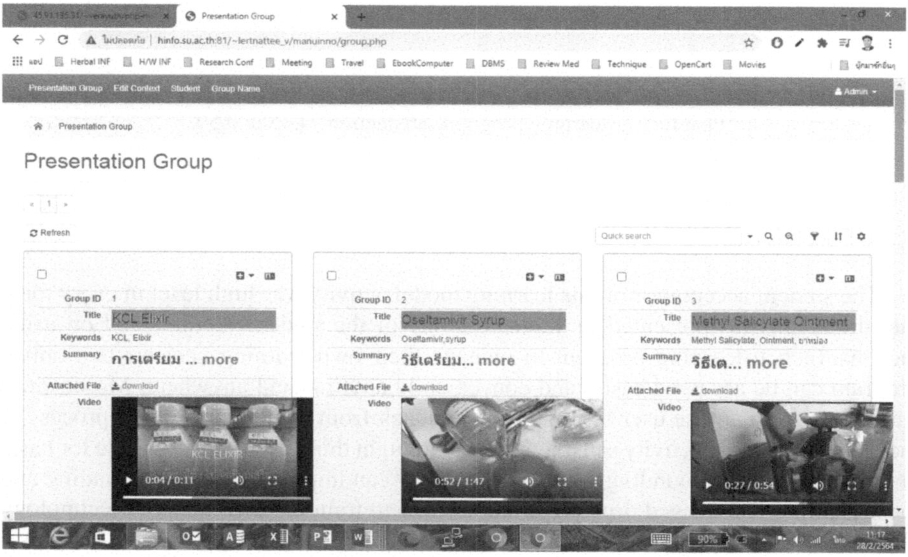

Fig. 2. Images of the PharTech E-learning display screen.

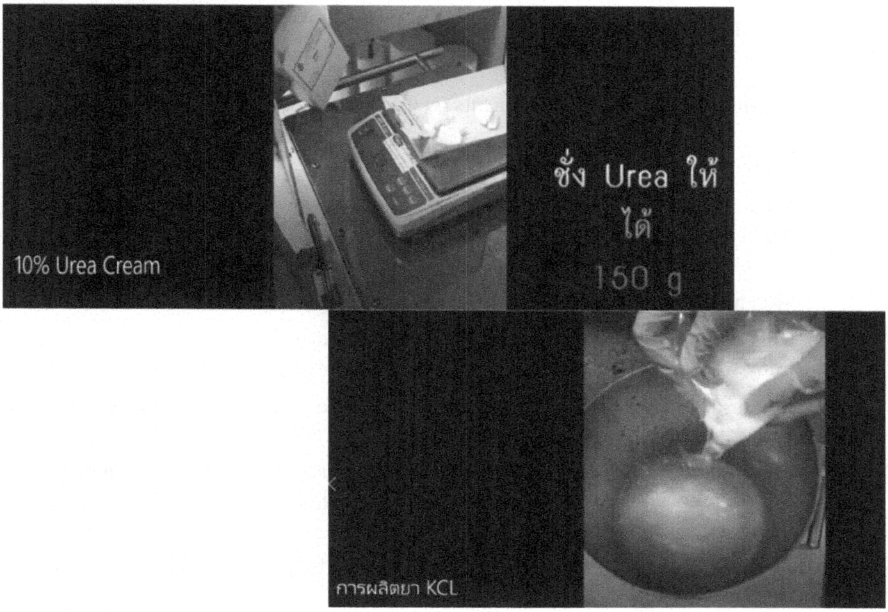

Fig. 3. Images of video presentations on pharmaceutical preparation.

Table 6. Student satisfaction on the blended learning with the PharTech E-learning.

Student satisfaction	Mean + SD
PharTech E-learning program satisfaction	4.45 ± 0.50
Blended learning activity satisfaction	4.35 ± 0.53
Evaluation process satisfaction	4.45 ± 0.50

The student acceptance of this learning model activity was high level in every topic that the result was presented in Table 6. Many of the students commented on using the PharTech E-learning program to manage their own learning because this online program can be accessed easily and conveniently anytime and anywhere. Moreover, it was designed to arouse user interest. The feedback from the students in the process of the blended learning activity satisfaction, they thought this activity was suitable for basic pharmaceutical compounding performance. They can improve their understanding and the e-learning encouraged drug preparation skills to train in laboratory and technology skill. The students felt that the pre-test not only help assess themselves and their level of knowledge and skill but also stimulate them additional learning.

We implemented the e-learning program for the second-year students in this academic year. The example comments from students on using the PharTech E-learning in pharmaceutical preparation were showed in Table 7.

Table 7. The example comments on using the PharTech E-learning.

Example	Comment
No. 1	It may be a benefit during the internship. In my opinion, when I was practising drug preparation in the laboratory class because of group learning. I was unable to complete the whole process
No. 2	Watching VDO helps me to provide the knowledge and skills
No. 3	This program is appropriate for basic pharmaceutical compounding performance. I think that it helps me to preparing for the comprehensive examination
No. 4	It helps me get back on the content if I don't understand in preparation process and watch it again
No. 5	This assignment in the e-learning program can encourage students' technology skill. Moreover, I like the searching box designed, which there are not in the traditional e-learning classroom
No. 6	I hope there will be other subjects using blended learning with this program, it is very good

5 Discussion

In this analysis, the main findings are the effectiveness of using blending learning with the PharTech E-learning platform. This activity significantly improved pharmacy technician students' knowledge and skills in basic pharmaceutical compounding performance. The participants responded well to this activity of instruction. The findings of our research align with previous studies which support the use of blended learning model [8–10, 12].

There are several advantages of our blended learning with the PharTech E-learning program. Frist, the instructors could prioritize materials and activities incorporating various learning activities and teaching models. Second, this model encouraged active learning because our blend learning was designed to report pre-test results immediately which students can do their self-assessments and fulfill their knowledge. Third, the utility of submitting group assignments with multimedia file and document file where other students can review content and practice processes, even if they did not act in a real situation. Besides, they can consult other friends when in doubts. Lastly, this model is flexible in learning time and place.

Compared with the control group, the experimental group had a far more improve in learning achievement in both theoretical and practical sections. Especially in the practical section, this could be the result from group assessment with video provided the students to visualize in a real situation. Using video enables linking theory to practice, repeat viewing, which promotes autonomous learning [9].

It should be noted that the learners consider highly acceptable on e-learning program satisfaction. Although our online learning program was a new platform for the students, they are not familiar, but the program is easy to access and use.

There are several limitations to this work. First, the study was a single institution, and our participants were small in size. Second, the focus of instruction was on basic pharmaceutical compounding performance only. The results may not be generalizable to other sample or other performances since blended learning effectiveness depends on many factors, such as student characteristics, knowledge background, learner's computer literacy and time management [6]. Another limitation was the duration of the learning activity was limited as a short course period because there was only 2 weeks after the internship, whereupon the students were tested with the national comprehensive examination for pharmacy technician. Finally, we evaluated effectiveness by measuring knowledge and skill immediately. Additional learning period or long term follow up are required.

6 Conclusion and Future Work

Blended learning was useful for pharmacy technician students in basic pharmaceutical compounding performance as stimulating and supporting learning. The student can improve in knowledge and skill after learning in blended learning with the PharTech E-learning. Online learning which collected the student assignments from hospital internship. In this program, the users can upload document and video files. In addition, they can create keywords for searching the content within the program. However, the PharTech

E-learning program still needs to improve in collaborative learning and learner interaction, such as chat function. As a further development, we plane this model to continue and implement in other subjects or courses.

Acknowledgements. The authors thank Sirindhon College of Public Health Suphanburi for providing funding for this study and we very grateful to our students for participating in the activities and providing useful feedback.

References

1. Boelens, R., De Wever, B., Voet, M.: Four key challenges to the design of blended learning: a systematic literature review. Educ. Res. Rev. **22**, 1–18 (2017)
2. Dziuban, C., Graham, C.R., Moskal, P.D., Norberg, A., Sicilia, N.: Blended learning: the new normal and emerging technologies. Int. J. Educ. Technol. High. Educ. **15**(1), 1–16 (2018). https://doi.org/10.1186/s41239-017-0087-5
3. Hrastinski, S.: What do we mean by blended learning? TechTrends **63**, 564–569 (2019)
4. Huynh, R.: The role of E-learning in medical education. Acad. Med. **92**, 430 (2017)
5. Rasheed, R.A., Kamsin, A., Abdullah, N.A.: Challenges in the online component of blended learning: a systematic review. Comput. Educ. **144**, 103701 (2020)
6. Kintu, M.J., Zhu, C., Kagambe, E.: Blended learning effectiveness: the relationship between student characteristics, design features and outcomes. Int. J. Educ. Technol. High. Educ. **14**(1), 1–20 (2017). https://doi.org/10.1186/s41239-017-0043-4
7. Liu, Q., Peng, W., Zhang, F., Hu, R., Li, Y., Yan, W.: The effectiveness of blended learning in health professions: systematic review and meta-analysis. J. Med. Internet Res. **18**, e2 (2016)
8. Farahani, I., Laeer, S., Farahani, S., Schwender, H., Laven, A.: Blended learning: improving the diabetes mellitus counseling skills of German pharmacy students. Curr. Pharm. Teach. Learn. **12**, 963–974 (2020)
9. Coyne, E., Rands, H., Frommolt, V., Kain, V., Plugge, M., Mitchell, M.: Investigation of blended learning video resources to teach health students clinical skills: an integrative review. Nurse Educ. Today **63**, 101–107 (2018)
10. Lee, C.Y.: How to improve the effectiveness of blended learning of pharmacology and pharmacotherapy? A case study in pharmacy program. Technol. Knowl. Learn. **25**(4), 977–988 (2020). https://doi.org/10.1007/s10758-020-09447-5
11. Li, C., He, J., Yuan, C., Chen, B., Sun, Z.: The effects of blended learning on knowledge, skills, and satisfaction in nursing students: a meta-analysis. Nurse Educ. Today **82**, 51–57 (2019)
12. Tripathi, R.K., Kurle, D.G., Jalgaonkar, S.V., Sarkate, P.V., Rege, N.N.: Implementation of supplemental E-learning models for blended learning in pharmacology. Natl. J. Physiol. Pharm. Pharmacol. **7**, 1084–1090 (2017)
13. Turk, B., Ertl, S., Wong, G., Wadowski, P.P., Löffler-Stastka, H.: Does case-based blended-learning expedite the transfer of declarative knowledge to procedural knowledge in practice? BMC Med. Educ. **19**, 1–10 (2019)

Activity Design for Cultivating Students' Journalistic Skills and Inquiry-Mind in a Blended Learning Environment

Xiaohong Zhang[1](✉), Kaoru Matsubayashi[2], and Kenichi Kubota[3]

[1] Kumamoto University, Kumamoto City, Kumamoto, Japan
[2] The Graduate School of Information and Communication, Tokyo, Japan
[3] Kansai University, Takatsuki City, Osaka, Japan

Abstract. Developing students' journalistic skills online is a big challenge in the field of journalism education. In addition, inquiry-mind is an important critical thinking disposition to write better news reports. The purpose of this study was to examine how to design a course to cultivate students' journalistic skills and inquiry-mind in a blended learning environment based on a case study. This research was conducted in a Japanese university course, called "Internet Journalism in Practice". The authors conducted Participant Observation to identify the interactions between the lecturer and students and administered questionnaires to clarify whether the course fostered students' inquiry-mind. The authors identified that the following five design elements were important in the blended learning environments. These elements were: (1) visualization of scaffolding of news reports writing, (2) surprising game experience, (3) role-playing as journalists in a team, (4) situational support of critical thinking and writing techniques and (5) encouraging students' active participation on challenging assignments online after they reached a higher level of journalistic skills and critical thinking. In addition, the challenge of using the five design elements during the COVID-19 pandemic was discussed.

Keywords: Blended learning environment · News reports writing skills · Inquiry-mind · Journalism · Activity design

1 Introduction

With the development of the internet, online reporting has gained an important role in mass media [1]. Therefore, educators are making efforts to teach students how to write news reports for the internet. Students need to think critically and determine which news reports are newsworthy and how to report them [1–3]. Thus, designing a course to improve students' online journalistic skills based on their inquiry-mind for writing reports is crucial.

Online reporting required students to use technology quickly and efficiently. Blended learning, combining face-to-face and online learning [4], provides a favorable environment that encourages students to write news reports online. Since blended learning is not

R. Li et al. (Eds.): ICBL 2021, LNCS 12830, pp. 237–250, 2021.
https://doi.org/10.1007/978-3-030-80504-3_20

simply combining face-to-face learning with online learning [4], what occurred and how students learned in the designed course, is also important [5]. Valuable information can be obtained from case studies, based on thorough observation and quantitative analysis [5]. This research, based on a case study, proposes to clarify how to design a journalism course that develops students' journalistic skills and inquiry-mind, in a blended learning environment.

2 Online Journalistic Skills and Inquiry-Mind in Higher Education

2.1 Journalistic Skills for Online Report

Today's journalism graduates encounter a new field of online journalism that is constantly changing because of new technologies and the convergence of different media in higher education [1]. Despite the increasing importance of writing and computer skills, interviewing and editing remain essential journalistic skills [1, 3]. To improve students' news writing skills, realistic news writing environments help students to experience the pressures of working as journalists and improves their performance. Ma and Yuen administered an open-ended questionnaire to analyze whether the platform for journalistic writing at universities, motivated students to write news reports [6, 7]. They concluded that the platform was helpful for students to practice their writing skills. Evans identified that creating a safe environment that allows students to make and recognize their mistakes was important [8].

2.2 Critical Thinking and Inquiry-Mind When Writing News Report

Critical thinking is a reasonable and reflective thinking focused on deciding what to believe or do [9]. A vital part of journalistic writing is to judge facts, choose what to believe, and understand how to report the information. When writing hard news (news reports) or soft news (feature articles), journalists need to analyze the data, judge and choose important or valuable information, and use easily understood words to inform the public [2]. Thus, critical thinking is essential for journalists to write good news reports [1, 3].

Critical thinking has the two aspects of skills and disposition [9, 10]. Some studies identified that critical thinking skills could be taught through thinking procedures. However, critical thinking disposition was hard to foster through clear instructions [10, 11].

Based on a survey of a program specially designed to improve critical thinking skills of freshman undergraduate students in Japan, inquiry-mind, a critical disposition that involves thinking from new angles and aspects, was important, although difficult to foster in a term [12]. Interesting media analysis activities which respected students' opinions helped students examine more angles or perspectives in a free and critical learning environment [11]. However, these two studies did not clarify whether students' inquiry-mind improved in a news reporting course.

2.3 Cultivating Students' Journalistic Skills and Critical Thinking in Blended Learning Environment

Online reporting required students to use technology quickly and efficiently [13]. The blended learning environments that integrated advanced forms of communication technology tools provides a favorable environment to develop university students' journalistic skills and critical thinking [14–16]. Huang and Yeh developed a blended learning course which included online discussions in a gamified platform with classroom lecture and discussions to enhance students' critical thinking through experiential activities to improve news writing 2017 [15]. During the 18-week experiential instruction period, "clear goals, challenges and quests, feedback, competition and cooperation, actual grading and visible status, access/unlocking content, onboarding time restrictions, freedom of choice, and new identities and roles, as well as avoidance of over-justification" contributed to improving students critical thinking skills and dispositions [15]. Matsiola, Spiliopoulos, Kotsakis, Nicolaou and Podara identified that student' journalistic growth was enhanced by highly creative, concise assignments and clear goals throughout the course in 2019 [16].

2.4 Problem Statement

Students' journalistic skills and inquiry-mind need to improve based on their active learning experience [11, 13]. Although some studies indicated that both news writing skills and critical thinking disposition, such as inquiry-mind, are important, few studies identified how to design activity to cultivate them. Thus, attention needs to be paid to developing activity design to foster students' journalistic skills and inquiry-mind in university courses that focus on online journalism.

2.5 Activity Design Principles to Foster Journalistic Skills and Inquiry-Mind

Csikszentmihalyi identified that the balance between challenging students and providing necessary skills to meet the challenge needs careful attention [17]. Students are anxious if activity goals are extent too far beyond their existing skills. However, students may feel bored when they solve problems with their existing skills and little effort [17]. Thus, the assignment that create challenges that requires effort is crucial. Furthermore, instructional scaffoldings and making thinking visible are useful strategies to support students to think deeply and broadly [18]. In addition, emotional aspects, such as surprise, and feelings of success, have the benefit of encouraging students to improve their performance [17, 19].

The authors propose that clarifying the outcomes of the activity design, to cultivate students' journalistic skills and inquiry-mind based on the principles, is essential. This study identifies the effects of an activity design based on a case study.

3 Research Objective

Based on the above, the purpose of this study is to examine how to design a course to cultivate students' journalistic skills and inquiry-mind in blended learning environments.

To attain this research objective, the authors used a case study approach in a journalism course at a Japanese university. The research questions driving this study are:

1) How did students achieve the news writing goals?
2) Were students' inquiry-mind fostered? If so, how?
3) What roles did face-to-face and online learning activities play in the designed course?

By further clarifying the research questions, this design can be used by other university lecturers, who hope to improve students' online news writing skills and foster students' inquiry-mind in the media literacy lessons in the future. In addition, information related to rethinking blended learning courses can be beneficial during the COVID-19 pandemic.

4 Research Methods

4.1 Activity Design of "Internet Journalism in Practice"

This research examined a journalism course called "Internet Journalism in Practice" which was a training course, at K University in Japan, to develop skills for writing news to be a journalist. The goals of this course were (1) applying the four patterns of frame to write news reports online; (2) fostering students' inquiry-mind to trigger them to investigate in person, critically analyze and provide the facts to the readers. The students in the class were sophomores, juniors, and seniors. One lesson was 90 min. Thirty undergraduates participated in this course during the fall term in 2018.

Activities design for "Internet Journalism in Practice" included writing activities based on topics in a term and blended learning activities in one lesson (Fig. 1).

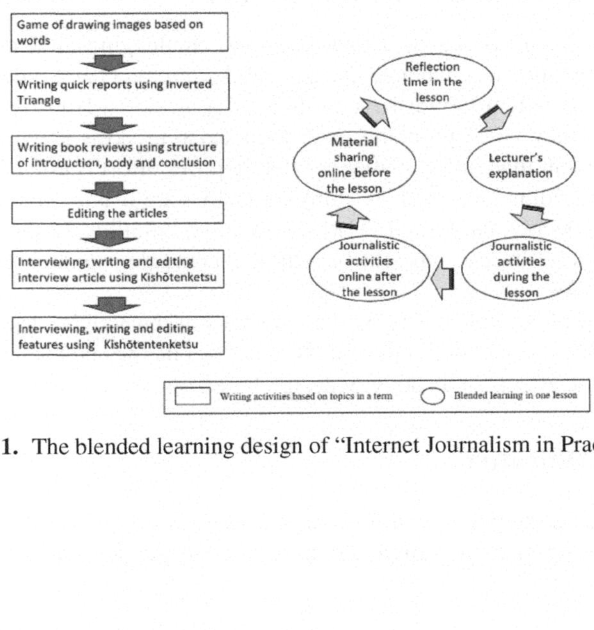

Fig. 1. The blended learning design of "Internet Journalism in Practice"

4.1.1 Writing Activities Based on Topics in a Term

This course was designed with 14 lessons that were divided into six components in a term. The components consisted of (1) a game of drawing images based on words, in the first lesson, (2) quick reports using an Inverted Pyramid, (3) writing a book review using the structure of introduction, body and conclusion, (4) editing reports, (5) interviewing, writing, and editing an interview article using *Kishōtenketsu* (introduction, development, turn and conclusion), (6) interviewing, writing, and editing a feature article using *Kishōtentenketsu* (Fig. 2).

Kishōtenketsu is a writing frame that organizes articles with introduction, development, turn and conclusion in the report. *Kishōtentenketsu* is a frame that organizes articles with introduction, development, evidence, turn and conclusion (Adding evidence to the structure of *Kishōtenketsu*). *Kishōtentenketsu* was a new frame based on the lecturer's long journalist experience [20].

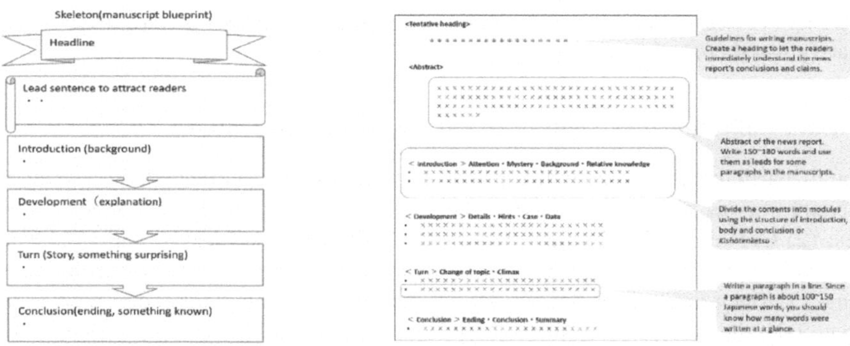

Fig. 2. Structure of Kishōtenketsu (the left) and Kishōtentenketsu writing (the right)

4.1.2 Blended Learning Activities in One Lesson

The blended learning was designed as follows:

Material Sharing Online Before the Lesson. Students received material from the lecturer through Office 365 and read relevant information that they found interesting.

Reflection Time in the Lesson. The lesson reflected on what was taught and the types of activities that students completed during reflection time.

Lecturer's Explanation. The lecturer explained basic journalistic principles, writing techniques and the four patterns of frame. The four patterns of frame were (1) Inverted Triangle which put important information in the beginning in the news, (2) the structure of introduction, body and conclusion, (3) *Kishōtenketsu*, and (4) *Kishōtentenketsu*.

Journalistic Activities in the Lesson. For more than 60 min of the lesson, students interviewed, wrote and edited news reports.

Journalistic Activities Online After the Lesson. Students participated in an interview activity, wrote, and edited news articles after the lesson.

4.2 Mixed Methods

In this study, the authors administered mixed methods to collect and analyze the data. To clarify how the interactions between the lecturer and students occurred, and the roles that face-to-face and online activities played in the course, the author conducted participant observation and wrote field notes to depict what occurred in the course. Participant observation is a qualitative method, that provides comprehensive and holistic descriptions of certain phenomena, to deeply understand some situations observed by researchers [21, 22]. In addition, the authors administered questionnaire investigations to clarify whether students' inquiry-mind was fostered.

4.3 Data Collection and Analysis in Participation Observation

Through participant observation, fourteen field notes were collected. The analyzing procedure was as follows: (1) Divide the data based on meaning and attach focused codes; (2) Create and label axial codes based on the focused codes; and (3) Identify theoretical codes [23]. From the analysis, forty axial codes were created from the focused coding. Fourteen theoretical codes were created based on the axial codes. The authors indicated the theoretical codes in bold type and cited the fieldnotes data with italic type (Table 1).

4.4 Data Collection and Analysis of Questionnaire Investigation

A questionnaire based on the inquiry-mind using the Scale of Critical Thinking developed by Hirayama and Kusumi was created [10]. The Scale of Inquiry-mind included ten items, such as "I learned many things through communication with different people", "I was interested in the opinions that differ from their's", and "I was interested in discussing topics with different people in the course". Students answered using a five-point scale (strongly agree, agree a little, neither agree nor disagree, disagree a little, strongly disagree). The scores were analyzed from five to one with five given to strongly agree and 1 to strongly disagree. Students received pre-test, mid-test, and post-test questionnaires during the first, seventh and final lesson, respectively. Of the questionnaires returned, 15 of 30 were valid. A T-test was used to statistically analyze the data.

Table 1. Theoretical codes and axial codes based on field notes.

No.	Theoretical Codes	No.	Axial Codes
1	Surprising game experience	①	Game of drawing images based on words in the first lesson
		②	Students' surprising experience in the first lesson
2	Lecturer's concise explanation about news reports writing technique based on four patterns of frames	③	Four types frames in news reporting
		④	Structures of news report, book review, interview reports and feature article when using four frames
		⑤	Concrete writing techniques
		⑥	Basic journalism knowledge and principles
		⑦	Visualizing the image of the report's structure to help students use the four types frames more deeply
3	Computer supported collaborative activities in the classroom	⑧	Concrete rules of activities
		⑨	Clear goal setting of activities
		⑩	Face-to-face interview activities in the classroom
		⑪	Computer supported writing activities using four types frames in the classroom
4	Lecturer's situational support in practice	⑫	Flexible guidance based on the situation in individual activities
		⑬	Flexible guidance based on the situation in group activities
5	Evaluations and suggestions about submitted news reports during reflection time	⑭	Reflection on jouralism principles
		⑮	Reflection on activities occurred in the last lesson
		⑯	Sharing evaluations and suggestions about the submitted news reports
6	Lecturer's concise explanation about inquiry-mind when writing news reports	⑰	Guidance to think from the reader's point of view
		⑱	Guidance about the attitude of doubting oneself
		⑲	Importance of fact confirmation
7	Situational support for critical thinking in activities	⑳	Guidance to think from the reader's point of view from the teacher who observed while students were writing
8	Advice about the thinking methods based on the submitted news reports	㉑	Advice about the thinking ways based on the submitted news reports
9	Rich material sharing online	㉒	Providing a wealth of materials about news reports writing
		㉓	Notice of prior preparation of the lesson
		㉔	Sharing of materials during class
10	Journalistic activities online after the lesson	㉕	Finishing a book review using the structure of introduction, body and conclusion
		㉖	Editing news reports and uploading to the private site
		㉗	Finishing an interview article using Kishōtenketsu and uploading to the private site
		㉘	Interviewing, writing and editing a feature article using *Kishōtentenketsu* and uploading to the private site
11	Teacher's support after the lesson	㉙	Task sharing and reminders after the lesson
		㉚	Providing related materials for tasks after the lesson
		㉛	Support for students after the lesson
12	Role play as journalist	㉜	Division of roles within the group
		㉝	Time restriction to meet the dealines for the reports
		㉞	An environment where students could act freely
		㉟	Publishing students' articles in private site on wordpress.com
13	Improvement of students' journalistic skills	㊱	Awareness originating from the experience of interviewing, writing articles and editing
		㊲	Improved news writing skills
14	Improvement of students' inquiry mind	㊳	Raising interests in article writing
		㊴	Changes of students' inquiry-mind
		㊵	Emergence of senses of accomplishment in article writing

5 Results and Discussion

Based on the analysis, the authors found that (1) students applied the four patterns of frame to news reports through an experiential process, (2) students' inquiry-mind was fostered in the course, and (3) face-to-face and online learning served different roles (Fig. 3).

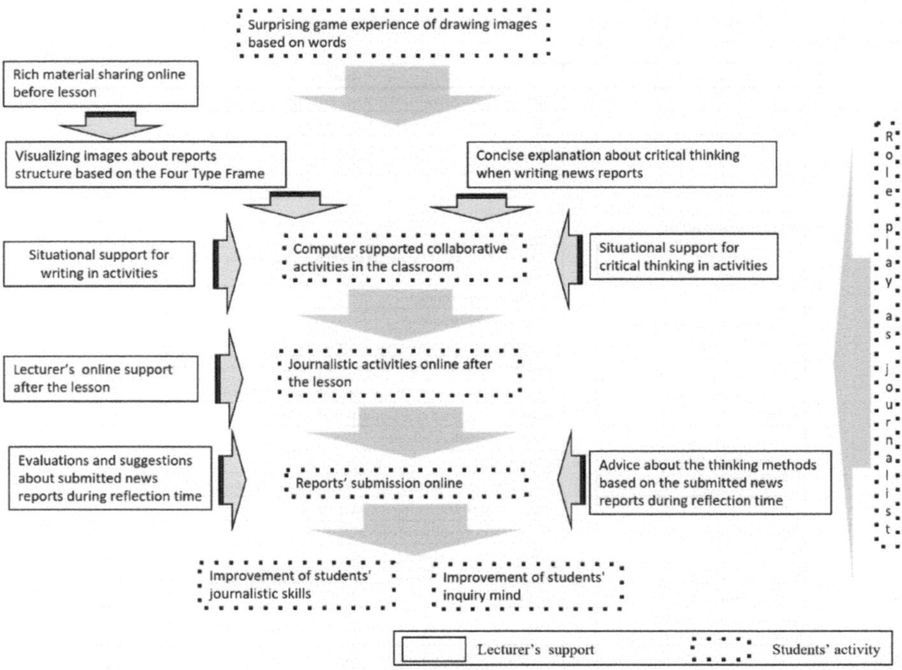

Fig. 3. Relationship of theoretical codes in "Internet Journalism in Practice"

5.1 Applying the Four Patterns of Frame to News Reports Through an Experiential Process

Before students accomplished their writing goals by applying the four patterns of frame, their learning process was as follows:

Students participated in a **surprising game experience** of drawing images based on words in the first lesson. The lecture showed a picture to some students and asked them to tell other students what they saw using words. The other students drew images based on what they heard. After students finished their drawing, the lecturer showed the original picture. Students observed that they felt extremely surprised when they saw that the images, which they drew were so different from the original picture. After this game, the lecturer explained that journalists need to help readers to create the same image about news events, although this was challenging work that requires journalists to inquire and write better, accurate, news reports.

From the second to the fourteenth lesson, students **played the role of a journalist** and wrote different styles of news reports using the four patterns of frame. The first frame was an Inverted Pyramid style which was used to write breaking news. The second frame was the structure of introduction, body, and conclusion that was easily used for a book review. Students wrote interview reports using *Kishōtenketsu*. *Kishōtenketsu* was the third frame which developed from a four-part organization of Chinese poetry. Finally, students worked in groups to write feature articles using *Kishōtentenketsu* from the tenth to fourteenth lessons.

Students received **rich material by using email to share online before each lesson.** These materials included the four patterns of frame and some writing techniques. When the lesson started, the lecturer **visualized images about report structures based on the four patterns of frame,** after he provided a concise explanation about the news reports. Then, students worked on news reports based on **computer-supported collaborative activities in the classroom.** While students were working, the lecturer provided **situational support for writing in activities.** Since writing news reports based on interviews, information collection and analysis needed much time, students continued their **journalistic activities online after the lesson.**

After the lesson, the lecture provided **online support,** such as reminding students of the deadline to submit assignments, providing problem-solving methods, and supporting students who could not finish the tasks. After students submitted their news reports, the lecturer **evaluated and provided suggestions on how to improve the submitted news reports during reflection time.** As a result, students **improved their journalistic skills** because they could use the four frames to effectively complete news reports on time and experienced success in practice.

The authors identified that students' journalistic skills improved through their active participation. At the same time, the lecturer's scaffolding, with concise explanation, situational support, goal setting, and evaluation for each report style writing, helped students to achieve their writing goals. These results were consistent with the findings of Huang and Yeh in 2017, and Matsiola, Spiliopoulos, Kotsakis, Nicolaou and Podara in 2019. However, the acceptance and quick adaptation, of the four patterns of frame to visualize images about the structure of their report, was a new finding [18]. This finding indicated that visualized images about report structures needed to be considered in journalistic skills course design.

5.2 Students' Inquiry-Mind Fostered in the Course

From the analysis of the T-test, significant differences were found between the pre-test and mid-test, the mid-test and post-test, and the pre-test and post-test in the students' inquiry-mind. The difference between the pretest and mid-test was significant ($t = 2.36$, $df = 14$, $p < .05$). The difference between the mid-test and post-test was significant ($t = 3.82$, $df = 14$, $p < .01$). The difference between pre-test and post-test was significant ($t = 4.40$, $df = 14$, $p < .01$). These results indicated that students' inquiry-mind was fostered in this course.

From the comparison of student behaviors drawn from field notes, students showed increasing passion for news writing. In particular, they made great efforts to write feature articles. This indicated that this course cultivated their inquiry-mind based on observation of student participation. This finding was the same with the analysis of the T-test. Samples of student observations and comments are listed below.

Group 2 during the breaking news writing activities, where they needed to write a breaking news in 25 minutes after watching a mayor's interview video. Student A worked hard to find 5W1H (who, when, where, what, why and how) in his memo. He had difficulty finding the necessary information in a short time and felt tired. (The 3rd lesson, 39th field note)

Group 2 in feature writing activities. A member played the Gachapon Game to decide the topic of the feature article. He recognized that the topic was about a wolf and job-hunting. After he went back to his group, they discussed and contemplated how to write about the wolf and job-hunting. B: *"Let's think about the features of the Wolf. I think wolves eat animals."* A: *"We need to think of something new…… (In the book review activity) I took a book that I knew well from home for book review writing. But the lecturer asked us to exchange books (Laugh). There is little meaning if we write something ordinary."* (The 10th lesson, the 42nd field note)

Group 2 in feature writing activities. Four group members (A, B, C, D) discussed how and when to hold editing meetings during the New Year holidays. B: *"I have a part-time job before ten o'clock PM. But after that time, I am OK."* A: *"We need to contact each other to exchange information as soon as possible. So, let's meet at ten o'clock PM every day during the New Year holidays."* (The 12th lesson, the 20th field note)

From the analysis of the field notes, three elements in the course were related to the students' inquiry-mind, as followed:

(1) Guidance of critical thinking from the lecturer. **The lecturer explained the importance and methods of critical thinking** when writing news reports before the activities. **Situational support for critical thinking in activities** helped students pay attention to their thinking process. The lecturer also **gave advice to students about the thinking methods based on the submitted news reports during reflection time**. Throughout the course, the lecturer encouraged students to think critically by having them consider the reader's point of view (axial code⑰), maintain an attitude of self- doubt (axial code⑱) and understanding the importance of fact confirmation (axial code⑲). Since critical thinking skills and dispositions influence each other [9], students thought more critically and their inquiry-mind was fostered in the course.

(2) **Role-playing as journalists in a team**. During the course, students completed their reports within a team. They had different roles, such as interviewer, editor, photo shooter, and editor-in-chief (axial code ㉜) with everyone playing a role. All assignments were completed within time restrictions (axial code ㉝). Students played their roles in an environment where they could act freely (axial code ㉞). Finally, they published various articles on a private site at wordpress.com (axial

code ㉟). In teams where students could realistically simulate journalistic activities, students changed their roles from students to journalists in a concrete situation.

(3) **Surprising game experience**. Game elements, such as drawing images and drawing lots, helped students relax, have fun and feel safe when trying to improve their articles. During these moments, students encountered surprising experiences that generated contradictions that furthered their reflection and created new perspectives [17, 24]. Unanticipated gaming activities results might influence students to consider more deeply how to create the same images with the readers whom they encountered as journalists.

5.3 The Roles that Face-to-Face and Online Learning Served in the Course

Based on the relationship of theoretical codes, the authors found that face-to-face support from the lecturer, computer-supported collaborative activities in lessons and online activities before and after lessons served different functions to improve students' journalistic skills and inquiry-mind.

Face-to-face support from the lecturer improved students' basic journalistic skills and thinking methods. The concise explanation of **visualizing image about reports structure based on the four patterns of frame** and situational support (**situational support for writing in activities** and **situational support for critical thinking in activities**) helped students to recognize and understand the basic principle of writing and thinking methods.

Through **computer-supported activities**, students learned to write, edit, and upload news reports to a private site. This type of activity encouraged student learning in a shorter time than traditional news articles printed on paper. Furthermore, computer-supported activities helped students understand the features of online journalism.

Online activities, before and after each lesson, were integral characteristics of this course, since in Japan most learning in practice often occurred in the classroom. **Rich material sharing online before lessons** helped students know what they would learn before the lesson started. **The journalistic activities online after the lesson** had a tendency of increasing students' active participation after they obtained basic interview, writing, editing and thinking skills and increased inquiry-mind. Providing continuous new activities to expand skills is also necessary after students obtained some skills [17]. This finding indicated that students could actively participate in challenging, online assignments that increase in difficulty and complexity, if they reached a certain level of journalistic skills and obtained the attitude of inquiry-mind.

6 Five Design Elements to Develop Students' Journalistic and Inquiry-Mind

Overall, students' journalistic skills and inquiry-mind developed from the following five design elements: (1) visualization of scaffolding of news reports writing, (2) surprising game experience, (3) role-playing as journalists in a team, (4) situational support of critical thinking and writing techniques, and (5) encouraging students' active participation on challenging assignments online after they reached a higher level of journalistic skills and critical thinking. Element (1) indicated that the four patterns of frames were effective instructional scaffoldings to support students who wrote new reports. Element (2) (3) (4) had positive impacts for both journalistic and inquiry-mind. Surprising game experience triggered students to rethink how to write news reports better [17]. Role-playing, as journalists in a team, created a gamified environment with a high level of anxiety about time limitation but was enjoyable and interesting to perform. Element (4) situational support of critical thinking and writing techniques not only solved the problems students encountered in concrete situations [18], but also increased students' confidence and sense of security [17, 19].

The COVID-19 pandemic forced most face-to-face classes to change to online classes in Japan. The question remains as to whether it is possible to apply this blended learning course design to a fully online learning course, which combines synchronous and asynchronous online learning [25, 26].

Since the face-to-face lessons were based on computer-supported activities, the design elements, (1), (2), and (3) can be implemented in synchronous online learning activities by using video conference technologies, such as Zoom, to replicate the traditional classroom online [26]. To help students' role-play as journalists in a team (3), group work online was necessary. The lecturer can create Zoom Breakout Rooms to support students' collaboration and communication [26]. Furthermore, element (5) can be easily implemented in asynchronous online learning activities after the synchronous online learning activities.

A challenge is how to provide (4) situational support to develop critical thinking and writing techniques in synchronous, online learning activities when students work in Breakout Rooms. The lecturer' situational support in synchronous online activities can overcome communication barriers between students and address students' reluctance to engage in challenging higher levels tasks [26]. Since the lecturer does not know what happened in Breakout Rooms, the lecturer can use the Chat function to send information to specific Breakout Rooms and ask students to use common files (such as Google Documents) to share their problems when they have difficulties [26]. In addition, creating a team of trained teaching assistants to support students is also beneficial to manage the synchronous online activities [25].

7 Conclusions and Future Perspective

This study examined the design of "Internet Journalism in Practice" a course developed to cultivate students' news report writing and inquiry-mind of critical thinking disposition. Based on a case study that used mixed methods analysis, the authors identified five crucial design elements: (1) visualization of scaffolding of news reports writing, (2) surprising game experience, (3) role-playing as journalists in a team, (4) situational support of critical thinking and writing techniques, and (5) encouraging students' active participation on challenging assignments online after they reached a higher level of journalistic skills and critical thinking.

This study did not examine the articles students wrote and dialogue between teacher and students in situated support. Future studies could conduct a content analysis of the students' articles and a dialogue analysis of what occurred between the teacher and students. Perhaps, further research of this activity design can be examined at an online course that was introduced in a university in Tokyo. It is crucial to analyze how the full online activity design helped students to improve their journalistic skills and inquiry-mind.

References

1. Pierce, T., Miller, T.: Basic journalism skills remain important in hiring. Newsp. Res. J. **28**(4), 51–61 (2017)
2. Mencher, M.: Melvin Mencher's News Reporting and Writing, 11th edn. McGraw-Hill Education, New York (2008)
3. Huang, E., Davison, K., Shreve, S., Davis, T., Bettendorf, E., Nair, A.: Bridging newsrooms and classrooms: preparing the next generation of journalists for converged media. Assoc. Educ. J. Mass Commun. **8**(3), 221–262 (2006)
4. Thorne, K.: Blended Learning: How to Integrate Online and Traditional Learning. London and Sterling, Kogan Page, London (2003)
5. Dziuban, D.C., Picciano, G.A., Graham, R.C.: Conducting Research in Online and Blended Learning Environments: New Pedagogical Frontiers. Routledge, London (2015)
6. Ma, W.W.K., Yuen, A.H.K.: A qualitative analysis on collaborative learning experience of student journalists using Wiki. In: Fong, J., Kwan, R., Wang, F.L. (eds.) ICHL 2008. LNCS, vol. 5169, pp. 103–114. Springer, Heidelberg (2008). https://doi.org/10.1007/978-3-540-85170-7_9
7. Ma, W.K.W., Yuen, H.K.A.: News writing using wiki: impacts on learning experience of student journalists. Educ. Media Int. **45**(4), 295–309 (2008)
8. Evans, M.: Storytelling in the newsroom: an investigation into practice-based learning methods in the training and employment of tomorrow's journalists. J. Educ. **5**(2), 37–45 (2016)
9. Ennis, R.H.: A taxonomy of critical thinking dispositions and abilities. In: Baron., J.B., Sternberg, R.J. (eds.) Teaching Thinking Skills: Theory and Practice. W. H. Freeman and Company. pp. 9–26. W. H. Freeman & Co. New York (1987)
10. Hirayama, R., Kusumi, T.: Effect of critical thinking disposition on interpretation of controversial issues: evaluating evidence and drawing conclusions. Jpn. J. Educ. Psychol. **52**, 186–198 (2004)
11. Zhang, X., Kubota, K., Kubota, M.: Activity design for cultivating students' critical thinking dispositions in a blended learning environment through a case study of media literacy course. In: Cheung, S.K.S., Li, R., Phusavat, K., Paoprasert, N., Kwok, L. (eds.) ICBL 2020. LNCS, vol. 12218, pp. 210–223. Springer, Cham (2020). https://doi.org/10.1007/978-3-030-51968-1_18
12. Kusumi, T., Tanaka, Y., Hirayama, R.: Teaching critical thinking in the first-year experience of higher education. Cogn. Stud. **19**(1), 69–82 (2012)
13. Hall, J.: Online Journalism: A Critical Primer. Pluto Press, London (2001)
14. Lu, K., Yang, H, H., Shi, Y., Wang, X.: Examining the key influencing factors on college students' higher-order thinking skills in the smart classroom environment. Int. J. Educ. Technol. High. Edu. **18**(1), 1–13 (2021)
15. Yeh, Y., Huang, L., Yeh, Y.: Knowledge management in blended learning: effects on professional development in creativity instruction. Comput. Educ. **56**(1), 146–156 (2011)
16. Matsiola, M., Spiliopoulos, P., Kotsakis, R., Nicolaou, C., Podara, A.: Technology-enhanced learning in audiovisual education: the case of radio journalism course design. Educ. Sci. **9**(62), 1–16 (2019)

17. Csikszentmihalyi, M.: Flow and education. In: Csikszentmihalyi, M. (ed.) Applications of Flow in Human Development and Education: The Collected Works of Mihaly Csikszentmihalyi, pp. 129–151. Springer, Dordrecht (2014). https://doi.org/10.1007/978-94-017-9094-9
18. Richhart, R., Church, M., Morrson, K.: Making Thinking Visible: How to Promote Engagement, Understanding, and Independence for All Learners. Jossey-Bass, San Francisco (2011)
19. Holzman, L.: The Overweight Brain: How our Obsession with Knowing Keeps us from Getting Smart Enough to Make a Better World. East Side Institute Press, New York (2018)
20. Matsubayashi, H.: Writing Strategies as Journalist without Hesitation: Four Patterns of Frame Based on Practice from Professional. Keio University Press, Tokyo (2018)
21. Jorgensen, L.D.: Participant Observation: A Methodology for Human Studies. SAGE Publications, London (1989)
22. Jorgensen, L.D.: Principles, Approaches and Issues in Participant Observation. Routledge, New York (2020)
23. Charmaz, K.: Constructing Grounded Theory. SAGE Publications, Inc., California (2014)
24. Piaget, J.: The Equilibration of Cognitive Structures: The Central Problem of Intellectual Development. University of Chicago Press, Chicago (1985)
25. Jong, N., Verstegen, D., Tan, F., O'Connor, S.: A comparison of classroom and online asynchronous problem-based learning for students undertaking statistics training as part of a Public Health Masters degree. Heath Sci Educ. **18**, 245–264 (2013)
26. Henriksen, D., Creely, E., Henderson, M.: Folk pedagogies for teacher educator transitions: approaches to synchronous online learning in the wake of COVID-19. J. Technol. Teach. Educ. **28**(2), 201–209 (2020)

Institutional Policies and Strategies

Using Design Thinking in Educational Game Design: A Case Study of Pre-service Teacher Experience

Yuling Zhang and Juanjuan Chen(✉)

Zhejiang University, Hangzhou 310058, Zhejiang, China
{zhangyuling22,juanjuanchen}@zju.edu.cn

Abstract. Despite the growing interest in game-based learning (GBL), teachers often have difficulties in its classroom implementation. Teachers' perceptions about games and their abilities to integrate techniques are barriers to the use of digital games in their teaching. This study aimed to promote teachers' technical competence and improve their perceptions of GBL by engaging them in a game design course. Twelve pre-service science teachers participated in this course, which incorporated design thinking and teaching-related techniques. Qualitative data including the final products of the game design task, open-ended surveys, and semi-structured interviews were collected. The results indicated that the experience of designing educational games improved pre-service teachers' perceptions of GBL. Secondly, although the design thinking model contributed to the learning process and the final products, more learning scaffolds and visualization techniques were needed.

Keywords: Game-based learning · Design thinking · Game design · Teacher education

1 Introduction

Game-based learning (GBL) has been gaining researchers' attention in recent years because of its educational potential. Compared with conventional instructions, learning through gameplay complies with the contemporary habits, interests, and needs of learners in the digital age. Teachers need to incorporate GBL into informal learning settings. While a majority of teachers would consider using games, there are certain factors that prevent them from using GBL as instructional tools, including limited teaching time, lack of appropriate games, and their own limited capacities to use GBL [1, 2]. Specifically, teachers often lack the skills and experience to design appropriate games for their students. Some researchers believe that involving teachers in the design process of educational games is beneficial for the classroom implementation of GBL. Games that are developed by teachers to meet specific curriculum objectives are believed to be more suitable and effective for integration into a classroom [2]. Meanwhile, as teaching is perceived as a design science, designing games helps teachers to acquire the knowledge and technical skills needed in their professional development [3].

R. Li et al. (Eds.): ICBL 2021, LNCS 12830, pp. 253–263, 2021.
https://doi.org/10.1007/978-3-030-80504-3_21

Teachers' perceptions and experiences play an important role in their actual use of digital games in the teaching and learning process [4]. Therefore, it is important to offer teachers the opportunity to participate in GBL and the game design process. Although there are a number of studies on teachers' perceptions of GBL and game design, there are very few studies on teachers' involvement in game design, and even fewer on the impact of such involvement on their attitudes and abilities.

This study therefore aimed to support teachers in designing educational games by offering them a course that incorporated design thinking. More specifically, our research questions were as follows:

RQ1: What are the learning outcomes for pre-service teachers from a game design course?
RQ2: How do they view the usefulness of design thinking in the course?
RQ3: How does the experience of participating in the design of games affect their perceptions of game-based learning?

2 Literature Reviews

2.1 Teachers as Game Designers

Despite the benefits of GBL, teachers often find it difficult to implement GBL in their teaching. The difficulty may result, in particular, from teachers' negative perceptions of games [2]. Rather than as a tool for activating classroom learning, games are considered by some teachers as mere entertainment without any benefits for learning. Moreover, teachers' lack of ability to integrate ICT into their teaching may be another barrier [5]. To implement game-based teaching better, teachers need to update their knowledge of GBL and enhance their ICT literacy.

Some researchers have suggested enhancing teachers' ICT literacy through engaging them in designing games [2]. Designing games involves following a process to solve an ill-structured problem. During this process, designers can improve their higher-order thinking, such as problem-solving, self-directed learning, and collaboration. Consistent with the notion of constructionism and learning by design, designing educational games helps designers to develop more learning and teaching skills, which is beneficial for their ICT literacy and professional development [3]. More importantly, teachers who are involved in designing games to meet students' needs are more likely to form a belief in learner-centered teaching [6, 7].

The few studies on teachers' participation in game design have acknowledged the advantages of this approach, while also indicating some problems. For example, teachers may lack the technical skills necessary to complete the game design tasks or achieve the desired game efficacy [1], they may need to collaborate to improve the learning experience and the final products, as creativity may constrain their designs [8], and, even with access to simple tools, some teachers are still reluctant to use games in teaching [9]. Therefore, there is a great need to support teachers in the game design process and eliminate the gaps between games and classroom implementation.

2.2 Scaffolding for Teachers When Designing Games

Conventional teacher education has been focused on developing teachers' basic teaching knowledge and skills, but it has paid little attention to teaching them how to design meaningful learning, and, in particular, how to apply new concepts and technologies according to students' needs [10]. Integrating GBL into teacher education may further develop teachers' professional knowledge and skill repertories, as GBL involves competencies like teaching, technology, collaboration, and creativity [11]. To design and implement GBL, teachers should be able to recognize the value of games, apply games in their classrooms, and design games for instructional purposes [12].

Given teachers' lack of ability in game design, several platforms have been developed specifically for teaching purposes. These platforms, including Aris (developed by Wisconsin [13]) and Kodu (developed by Microsoft [14]), require limited coding skills for designing educational games. However, designing educational games does not necessarily require any professional tools or skills. Klemke et al. [1] explored the use of the Wiki platform to allow teachers to design games with various themes. Melero and Hernández-Leo [15] utilized the puzzle board metaphor as a design strategy and provided scaffolding for teachers with game templates.

As pointed out by Li [8], since teachers prefer working in groups, collaboration should be encouraged. Collaboration has been shown to contribute greatly to both the process and the final products of the design when the teamwork is well structured [3]. With a shared vision, teachers can inspire and learn from each other.

In addition, both technical support and process support are crucial for design success. Rather than specialized game design platforms, we prefer the use of tools related to teaching, as the use of teaching-related tools to design a game would be more conducive to its implementation.

Finally, in response to the need for process support, design thinking was incorporated into our course as teachers are usually unfamiliar with the game design process. Design thinking is a powerful problem-solving tool for ill-structured problems such as designing educational games. It emphasizes the user-centered design of innovative products, which exactly matches the goal of designing learner-centered educational games. Additionally, instructional design is a continuous iterative cycle of design and redesign [10]. In design thinking, designers also need to analyze customers' needs constantly, and then iterate and optimize their products [16]. A well-known model of design thinking is the Stanford model [17], which consists of five modes: empathize, define, ideate, prototype, and test. It emphasizes the accurate analysis of needs, the creation of solutions using teamwork, the visualization of the solutions, and continuous iteration and optimization. Design thinking can not only provide scaffolding for teachers in the design process but also further develop their competencies in areas like empathy, teamwork, and communication [18].

3 Method

3.1 Study Participants and Context

This study was part of a course delivered to postgraduates in the college of education of a Chinese university. The course focuses on the application of information technology in education and popular science, with GBL as a key component. The voluntary participants (N = 12) were all first-year postgraduates (4 males and 8 females), with ages ranging from 21 to 25 years, majoring in Science and Technology Education. These pre-service teachers had never taken a design course. While half of them played games regularly, just one had experience of designing games for instructional purposes.

In this study, we developed the curriculum with design thinking: the pre-service teachers were required to design mobile games. The course was held at the end of 2020 and lasted for four weeks.

3.2 Overview of the Game Design Curriculum

The purpose of the course was to enable pre-service teachers to learn how to design games. In addition to engaging in lecture-based learning in class, they were required to complete several design tasks, to align the learning theories with learning design practice.

To optimize the learning process, we brought in a design thinking process model modified from the Stanford model [17]. To address the need for evaluation and feedback in GBL, the design thinking model was reorganized into six phases: empathize, define, ideate, prototype, iterate, and present (see Fig. 1). In particular, the model was not simply streamlined, but was iterative and nonlinear. Based on this model, the course was designed as shown in Table 1. This model served as a scaffold in the teaching process, and the learners were self-directed to complete the learning tasks, and the learners were self-directed to complete the learning tasks.

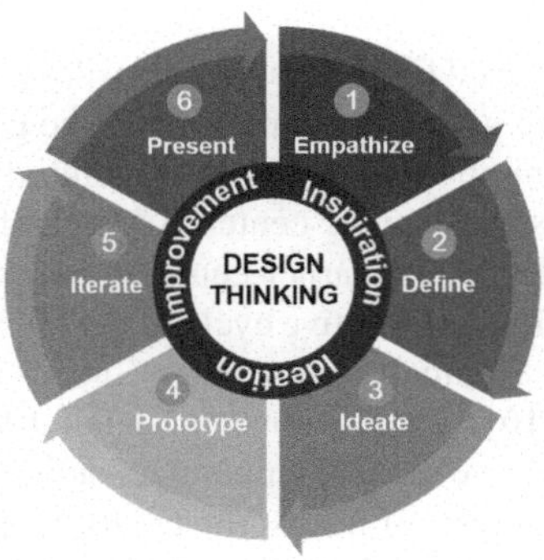

Fig. 1. The design thinking process model adapted from the Stanford model

3.3 Tools and Learning Environment

The Moodle platform was harnessed as a bridge between learning and game design. Moodle is an open-source learning management system (LMS), and is one of the most widely used LMSs in higher education. Leveraging its open-source property, many researchers have developed plug-ins according to specific teaching and research needs. Treasure

Table 1. The game design course based on design thinking

Schedule	Week 1	Week 2		Week 3	Week 4	
Design phase	Empathize	Define	Ideate	Prototype	Iterate	Present
Description of the phases	**Empathize**: Investigate the learning environment and the characteristics of learners, and collect the learners' needs in this environment **Define**: Analyze the collected needs to distill the problem to be solved **Ideate**: On the basis of the defined problem, put forward creative solutions to the problem, negotiate and choose valuable solutions **Prototype**: Visualize the solutions in a prototype **Iterate**: Test the prototype, constantly refine and optimize the solutions **Present**: Present the solutions, and gain possible feedback from users					
Activities	**Week 1**: Select museums to conduct field research, identify learning topics, collect design material. **Week 2**: Define learning activities (e.g. learners, learning goals, content), design games (including game content and mechanisms) **Week 3**: Create prototypes of the games in paper-based and digital forms **Week 4:** Test and iterate the prototypes, present the final products, evaluate the products with teacher and among peers					

Hunt is one of Moodle plug-ins developed for location-based learning. This plug-in includes both content editing and map editing modes, providing a template for designing games. Teachers can master this plug-in quickly without requiring programming skills. Also, games created with the Treasure Hunt plug-in can be easily integrated with other learning content on the Moodle platform.

To enrich the interactions of the games, we also used H5P. H5P is open-source interactive content based on the HTML5 protocol. Using its editing plug-in, which is integrated on the Moodle platform, learners can quickly create, modify and share web content with rich interactive forms such as photo hotspots, sorting, interactive videos, etc. Additionally, this reusable interactive content can be applied on multiple platforms and can be integrated into the games made with Treasure Hunt.

Moreover, a blended learning environment was developed for the curriculum implementation. We constructed an online course on Moodle with documents, videos, and H5P interactive games. The pre-service teachers were given full access so that they could create and modify content freely on the platform. In the classroom, we provided the teachers with a free learning environment, including Wi-Fi, an independent discussion space, drawing paper, and the other necessary tools.

3.4 Measures and Instruments

Different sets of data were collected to keep track of the pre-service teachers' game-based learning experiences and perceptions. The data included the observation of their design processes, pre- and post-surveys, the games they created, and semi-structured interviews.

We administered an open-ended survey to learn about the pre-service teachers' learning experiences and their perceptions of GBL. The questions were adopted from Li [19], for example, "How do you see students learning from designing games? What are the pros and cons?" and "If you were to design educational games for your students, what challenges do you think you might encounter?".

3.5 Procedure

At the beginning of the study, the participating students were informed of the experiment procedure, and signed a consent form. During the first week of the course, the participants were randomly divided into four groups. After a brief introduction to the design tasks, the four groups set out to investigate their selected museums in the field. They explored the learning environments and collected the materials needed to design their games. The following week, the design methods and technical tools were introduced to them. The pre-service teachers brainstormed and all drew mind maps of their designs for a game. During the third week, the participants received detailed instructions on how to use the platform and tools, and attempted to make prototypes in both paper-based and digital form. In the last week, after being tested and iterated, their final products were presented and assessed by both their peers and the teacher of the course.

4 Results and Discussion

4.1 The Learning Outcomes

With respect to the learning outcomes, the pre-service teachers selected four museums to investigate, and ultimately managed to collaboratively design four games and corresponding learning activities with gaming. The specific products are shown in Table 2.

From an analysis of the products shown in the table, all the teams were able to complete a basic game design in the limited time schedule. From the perspective of education, these game-based activities are relatively clear about the targeted learners. The pre-service teachers considered the learners' competence and interest in arranging the content and difficulty of the game. As for the game genres, two categories of games can be identified: treasure hunts and role-playing games [20]. In treasure hunts, players are required to find objects in specific areas following given hints. Designing role-playing games is generally more difficult than designing treasure hunts, as role-playing games have a stronger narrative nature. When designing role-playing games, designers need to consider the graduation mechanism and the links between different levels. In addition to the most commonly used mechanisms (such as points, ranks, and leaderboards), more complicated mechanisms (such as narrative, collection, and feedback) are needed. The

Table 2. Summary of the games designed by the pre-service teachers

	Archaeological ruins of Liangzhu City	*Metropolitan life in Chang'an*	*The Grand Canal*	*Umbrella*
Theme	The civilization of Liangzhu City	The lifestyle of ancient Chang'an	The culture of water transport	The art and history of umbrellas
Target learners	Secondary students	Secondary students	Primary students	Senior students in primary school
Number of levels	5	4	6	4
Game genre	Treasure hunt	Treasure hunt	Role-playing game	Role-playing game
Game mechanisms	Points, feedback	Points, ranks, bonuses, feedback	Narrative, points, feedback	Narrative, collecting, points, feedback, leaderboard
Presentation	H5P interactive content and prototype based on Treasurehunt	H5P interactive content and prototype based on Axure	H5P interactive content and prototype based on Treasurehunt	H5P interactive content and prototype based on Axure
Game images	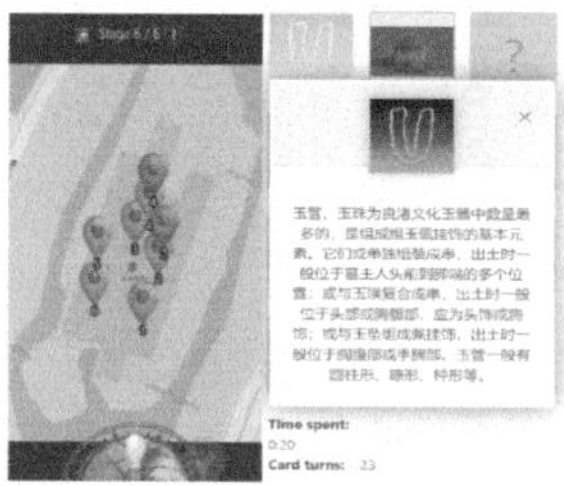	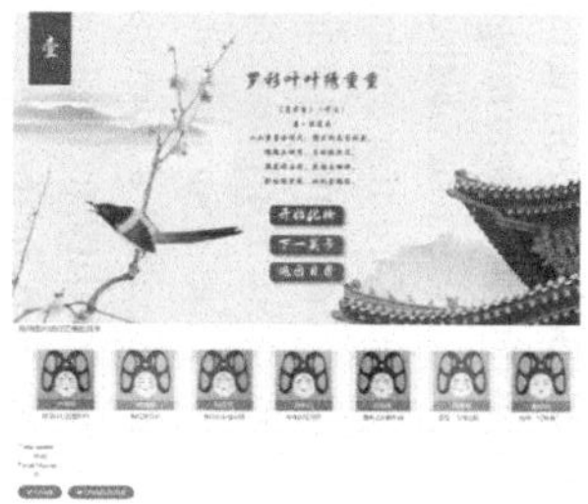		
Scores	89.96	91.42	87.40	89.89

adoption of varieties of mechanisms may contribute to better playability and immersion. In addition, all the groups adopted a feedback mechanism. This meant that they were all aware of the educational nature of the game, as expected. In the prototyping process, the participants were provided with Treasure Hunt and H5P as prototyping tools. To our surprise, some groups were dissatisfied with the mechanisms and visual features of these two tools. Instead, they turned to the professional prototyping tool Axure to create a more aesthetically pleasing interface.

However, with respect to their design content, we found that none of the groups was able to display their ideas fully in paper-based or digital prototypes. First, part of the problem came from the limited time available, which meant they had to abandon some of their detailed designs for the game content. Second, the problem also reflected their lack of ability to visualize. More than half of the pre-service teachers claimed that they did not know what a prototype was. As a consequence, these pre-service teachers were capable of designing elaborate game content and mechanisms but had difficulty in visualizing their ideas. This would be a major constraints in their efforts to become more proficient game designers.

Evidence also showed that preservice teachers gained technical skills through the game design curriculum. Most of the pre-service teachers had no prior expertise in designing or computer programming, but their final products indicated that they were capable of designing and implementing educational games with the proper support. It is not difficult for teachers to learn the techniques associated with game-based instruction, such as the Moodle platform and H5P interactive content. Moreover, the pre-service teachers self-regulated their learning according to the specific design needs. For instance, they actively learned the use of the professional prototyping software Axure for better visual features. Before the course, most (58%) of them mentioned that the biggest problem they might encounter in designing educational games was with the technical aspects; the mean score for pre-service teachers' self-reported ability to design games was 4.83/10. When the course ended, the majority (66%) of the pre-service teachers believed that their greatest achievement in the course was in the skill of game design. Their self-reported ability to design games improved to an average of 7.25. Involving the pre-service teachers in the design of educational games had empowered their ability and confidence in the application of technology.

4.2 The Perception of Design Thinking

Most (75%) of the participants explicitly said in the interviews that design thinking contributed to their final product. One of the pre-service teachers even mentioned that "Design thinking provides a clear process flow for design tasks". However, the majority of the participants (66%) felt that their group did not completely follow the design model. Some of the pre-service teachers felt they were more focused on the ideating and prototyping parts of the model, while other aspects, such as empathizing and definition, were less visible.

An analysis of the interviews indicated that a greater consideration of the learning environment and content made the pre-service teachers' design pattern different from design thinking. While the feedback showed the potential of design thinking to provide powerful support in solving complex problems, adjustments to the model were needed due to the different design targets. Another interesting finding was that, although clarifying the learning objectives and the needs of the learners was crucial, the pre-service teachers did not pay sufficient attention to this in designing the informal learning.

The ideation and prototyping phases were considered the most useful parts of the design thinking. An implication of this is that the pre-service teachers may have found tangible design processes more useful, as they were required to submit products during these phases. Empathy and definition in design thinking should play a greater role in allowing teachers to form a learner-centered teaching belief. In this respect, more tangible learning scaffolds should be provided during these two phases. For instance, templates that help teachers define their learners' needs and design goals could be provided.

4.3 The Perceptions of GBL

The questionnaires filled in by the pre-service teachers before and after the course reflect the change in their understanding of GBL. We examined their perceptions of learning through gameplay and game design. Before the course, most of the participants (75%) were neutral or negative about GBL. They believed that GBL could stimulate learners' interest, but it was inefficient and difficult to control. As for teaching with games, they thought it would be better suited to extracurricular activities, such as field trips, rather than ordinary classrooms. When it came to learning from designing games (such as learning through Scratch), 92% of the pre-service teachers said they would like to try it, but most (58%) of them could not ascribe an advantage to doing so. On the whole, before the learning activities their attitude towards GBL was conservative. They had almost never participated in GBL, and they were worried about designing educational games and about the teaching efficacy of GBL.

In the post-course questionnaire, pre-service teachers had a more positive view of GBL: 83% of them explicitly stated that they would use games in their future teaching. When it came to learning through game design, 92% of the teachers could name at least one advantage. Most of them (58%) saw it as a novel and interesting learning experience, as designing games enhanced their understanding of GBL and enabled them to learn techniques, design processes, and collaborative approaches. The relevant feedback is as follows:

> *I learned how to use H5P. I used to think that it must be very difficult, but when I made this little game, I felt that I could get good feedback and I was motivated to keep doing it!*
>
> *From the dashboard, I saw the game was constructed step-by-step. Maybe we are not professional, but it increased our experience, improved our communication skills among team members, and developed some creativity.*

5 Conclusion

In this study, we developed a game design curriculum for pre-service teachers to enhance their ability to teach based on games. Design thinking was used as the main scaffolding strategy. The motivation behind this approach was to provide these pre-service teachers with guidance in the design process and to shift their teaching beliefs into a learner-centered pedagogy. To address the teachers' lack of technical competence (reflected in the existing studies), tools that do not require programming skills were integrated into the curriculum. By combining the Moodle platform with the Treasure Hunt plug-in and H5P, the teachers were able to design location-based games in various forms and using different content. These tools are all associated with teaching, and thus teachers may apply them to other teaching situations once they have mastered their use. We conducted an exploratory study using the curriculum to investigate the pre-service teachers' experience in design-based learning and the changes in their abilities in and attitudes toward game-based teaching after the course. Based on our analysis of the questionnaires, interviews, and final products, our preliminary conclusion is that the game design course, based on design thinking, was helpful in improving the pre-service teachers' ability in game-based teaching. They experienced the process and acquired the method of designing educational games, improved their ability and confidence in the application of technology in teaching, and changed their attitude toward GBL.

However, this study received more than just positive reviews. From the analysis of the design patterns, it can be seen that only the ideation and prototyping phases played a full role in the six phases of design thinking. Not enough attention was paid to the most critical parts: problem definition and empathy. This finding implies that problem definition and empathy need to be emphasized to the learners when incorporating design thinking. In addition, when designing and implementing design-based learning, especially learning tasks that involve the use of technology, we need to provide learners with adequate learning time and appropriate scaffolding.

Moreover, this research has several limitations. First, the participants of this research were postgraduate students especially major in science and technology education. Therefore, the generalizability of the finding is somewhat limited for the sample size and the majors. Care should be taken when the curriculum is implemented in other contexts and for other participants. Second, the investigation of teachers' designing games is limited by the course duration. Thus, this case study focused on the design process and the final products. More investigation, such as the practical implementation of students' game playing in museums may give a better insight into pre-service teachers' learning efficacy.

References

1. Klemke, R., van Rosmalen, P., Ternier, S., Westera, W.: Keep it simple: lowering the barrier for authoring serious games. Simul. Gaming **46**, 40–67 (2015). https://doi.org/10.1177/1046878115591249
2. Osman, K., Bakar, N.A.: Teachers and students as game designers: designing games for classroom integration. In: de Freitas, S., Ott, M., Popescu, M.M., Stanescu, I. (eds.) New Pedagogical Approaches in Game Enhanced Learning: Curriculum Integration. IGI Global (2013). https://doi.org/10.4018/978-1-4666-3950-8
3. Kali, Y., McKenney, S., Sagy, O.: Teachers as designers of technology enhanced learning. Instr. Sci. **43**, 173–179 (2015). https://doi.org/10.1007/s11251-014-9343-4
4. Huizenga, J.C., ten Dam, G.T.M., Voogt, J.M., Admiraal, W.F.: Teacher perceptions of the value of game-based learning in secondary education. Comput. Educ. **110**, 105–115 (2017). https://doi.org/10.1016/j.compedu.2017.03.008

5. Hsu, C.-Y., Tsai, M.-J., Chang, Y.-H., Liang, J.-C.: Surveying in-service teachers' beliefs about game-based learning and perceptions of technological pedagogical and content knowledge of games. J. Educ. Technol. Soc. **20**, 134–143 (2017)
6. Akcaoglu, M., Kale, U.: Teaching to teach (with) game design: Game design and learning workshops for preservice teachers. Contemp. Issues Technol. Teach. Educ. **16**, 60–81 (2016)
7. Romero, M., Barma, S.: Teaching pre-service teachers to Integrate serious games in the primary education curriculum. Int. J. Serious Games **2** (2015). https://doi.org/10.17083/ijsg.v2i1.43
8. Li, Q.: Enactivism and teacher instructional game building: an inquiry of theory adoption and design consideration. Educ. Technol. Res. Dev. **66**, 1339–1358 (2018). https://doi.org/10.1007/s11423-018-9584-z
9. Uluay, G., Dogan, A.: Pre-service teachers' practices towards digital game design for technology integration into science classrooms. Univers. J. Educ. Res. **4**, 2483–2498 (2016)
10. Wu, B., Hu, Y., Wang, M.: Scaffolding design thinking in online STEM preservice teacher training. Br. J. Educ. Technol. **50**, 2271–2287 (2019). https://doi.org/10.1111/bjet.12873
11. Nousiainen, T., Kangas, M., Rikala, J., Vesisenaho, M.: Teacher competencies in game-based pedagogy. Teach. Teach. Educ. **74**, 85–97 (2018). https://doi.org/10.1016/j.tate.2018.04.012
12. Chen, S., Zhang, S., Qi, G.Y., Yang, J.: Games literacy for teacher education: towards the implementation of game-based learning. Educ. Technol. Soc. **23**, 77–92 (2020)
13. Field Day - ARIS. https://fielddaylab.org/make/aris/. Accessed 16 May 2020
14. Kodu - Visual Programming Language for creating Xbox games. https://www.microsoft.com/en-us/research/project/kodu/. Accessed 04 Feb 2021
15. Melero, J., HernÁndez-Leo, D.: Design and implementation of location-based learning games: four case studies with "QuesTInSitu: The Game". IEEE Trans. Emerg. Topics Comput. **5**, 84–94 (2017). https://doi.org/10.1109/TETC.2016.2615861
16. Razzouk, R., Shute, V.: What is design thinking and why is it important? Rev. Educ. Res. **82**, 330–348 (2012). https://doi.org/10.3102/0034654312457429
17. Köppen, E., Meinel, C.: Empathy via design thinking: creation of sense and knowledge. In: Plattner, H., Meinel, C., Leifer, L. (eds.) Design Thinking Research. UI, pp. 15–28. Springer, Cham (2015). https://doi.org/10.1007/978-3-319-06823-7_2
18. Henriksen, D., Richardson, C., Mehta, R.: Design thinking: a creative approach to educational problems of practice. Think. Skills Creativity **26**, 140–153 (2017). https://doi.org/10.1016/j.tsc.2017.10.001
19. Li, Q., Lemieux, C., Vandermeiden, E., Nathoo, S.: Are you ready to teach secondary mathematics in the 21st century? J. Res. Technol. Educ. **45**, 309–337 (2013). https://doi.org/10.1080/15391523.2013.10782608
20. Avouris, N., Yiannoutsou, N.: A review of mobile location-based games for learning across physical and virtual spaces. J. Univers. Comput. Sci. **18**, 2120–2142 (2012). https://doi.org/10.3217/jucs-018-15-2120

The Effects of Using Tablet PCs on Student Self-regulated Learning and Learning Achievement

Yinghui Shi[1], Qiuyu Pu[1], Ling Chen[1], Kexin Jia[1], and Harrison Hao Yang[1,2](✉)

[1] Central China Normal University, Wuhan 430079, China
harrison.yang@oswego.edu
[2] State University of New York at Oswego, Oswego 13126, USA

Abstract. This study aimed to investigate the effects of using tablet PCs on junior high school students' self-regulated learning and learning achievement in Chinese language courses. An experiment was conducted using a sample of 100 students from two classes of a junior high school in Northwest China. One class, as the experimental group, employed an instructional approach with tablet PCs. Other class, as the control group, used a traditional lecture-based approach without the tablet PCs. Students in the two classes studied Chinese language courses for two months. The results showed that the students with tablet PCs have significantly higher learning achievement and self-regulated learning abilities than those of students without tablet PCs.

Keywords: Junior high school student · Tablet PC · Self-regulated learning · Learning achievement

1 Introduction

With the rapid development of information and communication technologies (ICTs) and the popularity of mobile learning terminals, tablet PCs are increasingly widely used in classrooms [1, 2]. Tablet PCs have changed the ways of teaching and learning, more greatly emphasizing constructivist and collaborative learning approaches, as well as flexible and adaptive teaching approaches [3]. Studies have shown that tablet PCs do have promising potential in promoting the learning process for students of different ages and learning requirements [4, 5]. There are numerous advantages of using tablet PCs in classroom instruction, such as encouraging students to deeply study a certain issue, sharing ideas and learning materials, enabling students to actively participate in the classroom [6], and providing feedback to students in real time via the tablet PCs.

Due to the widely use of tablet PCs, students can receive more information, and meanwhile, they need to acquire more skills [7]. Among these, self-regulated learning (SRL) is a very important one. SRL refers to students consciously and systematically managing their learning process to achieve goals [8]. In past decades, many studies have shown that SRL has a great influence on student learning achievement [9]. Researchers have shown that students with strong SRL skills are more likely to succeed [10, 11].

R. Li et al. (Eds.): ICBL 2021, LNCS 12830, pp. 264–274, 2021.
https://doi.org/10.1007/978-3-030-80504-3_22

While more attention has been paid to explore SRL in the online learning environment (e.g., [12, 13]), few studies have been conducted on SRL in the classroom environment. Moreover, as far as we know, almost no study has been conducted on the effects of using tablet PCs on students' SRL. Besides, the effects of using tablet PCs on student learning achievement have been one of the hot research topics, while the results are often mixed in the educational context. Therefore, this study intends to explore the effects of using tablet PCs on students' SRL and learning achievement.

2 Literature Review

2.1 Tablet PCs and Self-regulated Learning

A tablet PC is a small, portable personal computer with an operating system and an integrated tactile screen that enables the users to access the Internet and interact with fingers or stylus pen. The tablet PCs have great potential as an educational resource due to their versatility, portability, and functionality [14]. Effective use of tablet PCs in the classroom can facilitate educational activities [15], enhance the interaction between teachers and students, promote students' active learning, express and present their ideas, and help teachers improve teaching methods and improve teaching efficiency [16]. Some studies regarding the employment of tablet PCs in the educational context have been carried out in recent years (e.g., [17]).

Self-regulated learning (SRL) is a comprehensive learning process that requires learners to actively participate in learning in terms of metacognition, motivation, and behavior [18]. Individuals with strong SRL abilities can be characterized by their ability to plan, manage, and control their learning process, and thus they can learn faster and obtain better learning achievement [19].

Using tablet PCs in the classroom enables students to obtain more and higher-level skills needed for the current transition from mass education to personalized learning, while SRL is one of the important skills [7]. The direct real-time feedback provided by the tablet PCs reduces students' distraction, because it allows students to continue with the next task instead of doing nothing in class while waiting for teacher's feedback [20]. Therefore, tablet PCs provide a lot of opportunities for SRL. Researchers have pointed out that tablet PCs can help students self-regulate, master the learning process, and collaborate with others [21]. In a pilot study of the FATIH project, a positive and meaningful relationship was found between the acceptance level of tablet PCs and the SRL level of students [22]. However, few studies have been investigated the effects of using tablet PCs on student SRL in the content course.

2.2 Tablet PCs and Learning Achievement

The effect of using tablet PCs in classrooms on student learning achievement has been widely studied. [23] pointed out that tablet PCs play an especially important role in improving the effectiveness and efficiency of the learning and teaching process. In a quasi-experimental study focusing on high school physics classes of pendulum movements, [24] found that the use of mobile devices, including tablet PCs, could improve students' learning achievement effectively. Similarly, a systematic review showed the use of tablet PCs in mathematics education can also enable students to achieve better results in mathematics [25]. However, some other studies indicated that tablet PCs did not improve student learning achievement. For example, the results of [26] indicated that there is no difference between the tablet PC (iPad) intervention classroom and the control classroom in a mathematics course. The mixed results suggested that the effects of classroom instruction with table PCs on student learning achievement are still unclear.

2.3 The Research Questions

To examine the effects of classroom instruction using tablet PCs on students' SRL and learning achievement, two research questions were proposed:

1. Do the students who learn with tablet PCs show better learning achievement than those who learn without tablet PCs?
2. Do the students who learn with tablet PCs show higher SRL than those who learn without tablet PCs?

3 Method

3.1 Participants

A total number of 100 seventh-graders from two classes of a junior high school in Northwest China participate in the present study. Two classes were randomly divided into two groups: the experimental group (E-group, n = 51) and the control group (C-group, n = 49); each group was composed of one class. Figure 1 showed the characteristics of the participants.

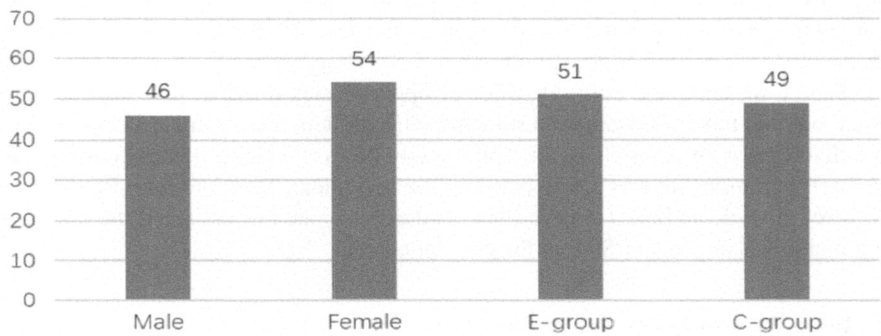

Fig. 1. Brief descriptions of the participants.

Two teachers were involved in this study. One teacher was responsible for the teaching of the E-group and the other for the C-group. Both teachers of similar age with more than five years' experience in teaching, and their classroom instruction followed the same lecture manuscripts, which were compiled by the school's academic affairs office. Before the experiment, the teacher in the E-group was trained to use the tablet PC proficiently, and had rich teaching experiences and corresponding instructional approaches with tablet PC. Students in the E-group also received relevant training and were able to use the tablet PCs for classroom learning proficiently.

3.2 Classroom Environment with Tablet PCs

The classroom mentioned in this study contains a touch-control integrated device (TID), a wireless local area network (WLAN), and a cloud-based learning platform (CLP). Using TID in the classroom instead of the traditional blackboard, provide more opportunities for interaction between teachers and students. The TID was used to show the learning contents, topics of discussion, tests, and assignments. With the coverage of WLAN in the whole classroom, students could use the tablet PCs to search for information and communicate with teachers and their peers. Teachers would publish various learning resources on the CLP, and students could access and download learning materials according to their learning needs.

In this study, the tablet PCs were mainly used for: 1) students' autonomous learning on the learning contents, including preview lessons and review lessons; 2) complete tests and submit the answers to teachers during the class; 3) interact with the teachers and peers, such as asking questions, receiving feedback; and 4) complete assignments after the class. Students used the tablet PCs to watch instructional videos, communicate with peers, and submit exercises assigned by the teacher. Teachers use the tablet PC to share resources, publish exercises and tasks, evaluate students' learning performances and give feedback in real-time.

3.3 Instructional Approaches

To examine the effects of using tablet PCs on student's learning achievement and SRL, a quasi-experimental study was carried out. The E-group used the instructional approach with tablet PCs, while the C-group used the same instructional approach without tablet PCs.

Instructional Approach with Tablet PCs. The instructional approach with tablet PCs refers to the use of tablet PC in the classroom to display learning contents and promote the interaction between teachers and students. A flipped learning model was employed in classroom instruction in this study.

In this instructional approach, the tablet PC was the main interactive tool for classroom instruction. It is not only used to show the learning content but also used for teachers' questions and feedback and students' answers. For example, teachers could send learning resources to students' tablet PCs in real-time for students to learn, or teachers could send practice questions to students' tablet PCs for students to quickly answer and submit. The teacher could also provide timely feedback to the students through the TID, to realize the real-time interaction between teachers and students.

In the classroom, teachers could use the TID and the CLP to provide students with a large number of learning tools, learning services, and course materials to meet students' varied learning needs. Besides, with the learning tools and services provided within the tablet PCs themselves, students could also interact with each other or with their teachers.

Instructional Approach Without Tablet PCs. In this instructional approach, students don't use tablet PCs in the classroom. Before and after the class, the teacher and students would use instant messenger (such as QQ and WeChat) to communicate and sharing learning materials. The TID was the main interactive tool in the learning process. It was usually used to display the learning contents. This instructional approach is usually considered to be teacher-centered, learning content-oriented, and promoted through practices and exercises, but there is less classroom interaction between the teacher and students [27]. A comparison of the two instructional approaches is shown in Table 1.

Table 1. A comparison of the two instructional approaches.

	Instruction with tablet PCs	Instruction without tablet PCs
Before Class	Teacher: Uploads learning materials to the CLP and sets learning tasks. Students: Log into the CLP to study with the learning materials, participate in online discussions and complete the tasks set by the teacher	Teacher: Uploads learning materials to the QQ group, sets learning tasks Students:Study with the learning materials in the QQ group, participate in online discussions, and complete learning tasks
In Class	Teacher: Uses the TID and CLP to provide learning tools, course materials, and learning services, interact with students, and give responses and feedback Students: Use TIDs and tablet PCs to participate in the learning activities, such as asking questions, independent exploration, cooperative learning, interact with peers, sharing, and get feedback from the teacher	Teacher: Uses the TID to display multimedia teaching resources, writing on the blackboard, and interact with students face to face Students: Listen to the teacher passively, answer questions passively, and complete the exercises
After Class	Teacher: Shares resources, arranges extended learning tasks, checks answers, and offers online help, etc. through the CLP Student:Use mobile terminals to browse the teaching resources (micro-classes, videos, pictures, text resources, etc.) on the teaching cloud platform, and obtain learning help, etc.	Teacher:Assigns homework, review students' homework Students: Complete homework and submit it to the QQ group

3.4 Learning Contents

The learning contents in this experiment were three units of Chinese language textbook, which was published by People's Education Press for seventh-grade students. Each unit includes two parts: reading and writing. In the reading part of the three units, different types of articles, such as fable, fairytale, novel, poem, and prose are presented as reading materials for students. In the writing parts of the three units, students are practiced to improve their thinking, imagination, and creativity of writing in the writing tasks.

3.5 Measuring Tools

To examine the effects of classroom instruction using tablet PCs on students' learning achievement, the pre- and post-tests were employed in this study. The pre-test was carried out to ensure that all students in the two groups had the same level of prior Chinese language knowledge. The post-test was the final examination of grade seven in this school. The full score for both the pre-test and post-test is 100.

To measure the effects of classroom instruction using tablet PCs on students' SRL, the Academic Self-Regulated Learning Scale (A-SRL-S) developed by [28] was adapted and employed in this study. The A-SRL-S is composed of seven factors, including 14 items for memory strategy (MS), 5 items for goal setting (GS), 12 items for self-evaluation (SV), 8 items for seeking assistance (SA), 5 items for environmental structuring (ES), 5 items for learning responsibility (LR), and 6 items for organizing (OG). Each item is responded with a five-point Likert scale (from 1 = Strongly disagree to 5 = strongly agree). The total Cronbach's alpha value of the questionnaire was 0.95, and the Cronbach's alpha values of the seven dimensions were 0.86, 0.89, 0.85, 0.78, 0.65, 0.77, and 0.76 respectively, which indicated that the A-SRL-S is of high credibility.

3.6 Procedure

At the beginning and end of the course, all the participants were asked to take pre- and post- tests and the A-SRL-S survey. Before the start of the experiment, the pre-test and pre-survey were conducted, which included an assessment of students' learning achievements and SRL. After a two-month-long teaching experiment, both the post-test and post-survey were conducted simultaneously in both groups. Data analysis was conducted by SPSS software.

4 Results

4.1 Students' Scores on Learning Achievement

To examine the level of students' prior knowledge of the Chinese language, a pre-test was conducted. An independent sample T-test was conducted on student scores of the pre-test. As shown in Table 2, the results demonstrated that there is no significant difference between the two groups in the pre-test scores ($t = -1.13$, $p > 0.05$), which indicated that students in the two groups have the same level of prior knowledge before the teaching experiment.

Table 2. T-test results for students' learning achievement scores in the pre-test.

Groups	N	Mean	SD	t	p
E-group	51	68.68	12.86	−1.13	0.26
C-group	49	72.01	16.39		

At the end of the teaching experiment, a one-way analysis of covariance (ANCOVA) was conducted to examine the difference between the two groups in the post-test for students' learning achievements. To decrease the interference of the pre-test scores on the experimental results, the pre-test scores were used as a covariate and the post-test scores as dependent variables. Table 3 showed that the ANCOVA results were significant ($F = 11.38$, $p < 0.001$), which suggested that the E-group had a significantly higher post-test score than that of the C-group.

Table 3. ANCOVA results for students' learning achievement scores in the post-test.

Groups	N	Mean	SD	Adjusted mean	SE	F
E-group	51	75.97	9.83	77.08	0.96	11.38^{***}
C-group	49	73.58	14.00	72.43	0.98	

$^{***}p < 0.001$.

4.2 Students' Scores on Self-regulated Learning

Students' SRL was examined with the A-SRL-S before and after the teaching experiment. An independent sample T-test was conducted on student pre-survey of the A-SRL-S before the learning experiment began. As shown in Table 4, the T-test results ($t = 1.02$, $p > 0.05$) indicated no significant difference in the two groups' pre-survey scores of SRL. In the sub-factors of SRL, there is no significant difference in most factors between the groups except the ES factor, which showed that the E-group has a significantly higher mean score than that of the C-group ($t = 2.60$, $p < 0.05$).

After the teaching experiment was ended, a post-survey on the A-SRL-S was carried out for assessing students' SRL. A one-way ANCOVA was carried out on student post-survey scores of SRL, to eliminate the interference effect of the pre-survey scores of SRL. As shown in Table 5, the ANCOVA results showed that the overall mean score of SRL of the E-group is significantly higher than that of the C-group ($F = 35.25$, $p < 0.001$). In the sub-factors of the SRL, there are significant differences in all the seven factors, which suggested that E-group students' SRL has been greatly promoted.

Table 4. T-test results for students' pre-survey scores of SRL.

Variables	E-group (N = 51)		C-group (N = 49)		t
	Mean	SD	Mean	SD	
SRL	4.10	0.60	3.98	0.57	1.02
MS	4.12	0.69	3.98	0.69	1.00
GS	3.69	1.26	3.40	1.24	1.19
SV	4.13	0.67	3.95	0.65	1.39
SA	4.12	0.88	4.13	0.60	−0.11
ES	4.18	0.54	3.82	0.81	2.60*
LR	4.24	0.82	4.39	0.59	−1.07
OG	4.16	0.62	4.22	0.77	−0.49

*$p < 0.05$.

Table 5. ANCOVA results for students' post-survey scores of SRL.

Variables	E-group (N = 51)		C-group (N = 49)		F
	Adjusted mean	SD	Adjusted mean	SD	
SRL	4.51	0.08	3.83	0.08	35.25***
MS	4.42	0.10	3.81	0.10	18.63***
GS	4.42	0.15	3.27	0.15	28.12***
SV	4.46	0.09	3.85	0.09	24.08***
SA	4.58	0.09	3.88	0.09	30.55***
ES	4.45	0.11	3.81	0.11	15.61***
LR	4.67	0.09	4.07	0.09	20.84***
OG	4.75	0.10	4.04	0.10	23.85***

***$p < 0.001$.

5 Discussion and Conclusion

This study aims to explore the effects of classroom instruction with tablet PCs on students' learning achievement and SRL. The results indicated that the E-group had significantly higher mean scores on learning achievement and SRL than those of the C-group, which suggested that using tablet PCs in the classroom can improve students learning achievement and SRL.

This study found that classroom instruction with tablet PCs can improve students' learning achievement effectively. The findings are partially consistent with the results of [29]. This may due to the fact that the E-group students have a more flexible and convenient learning environment, accompanied by a better learning experience with the help of tablet PCs and CLP. Without the tablet PCs, students in the C-group can only use

QQ group to learn materials before the class and submit homework after the class. In addition, students in the E-group had more chances to interact with their teachers, classmates and learning content via tablet PCs [30]. While students in the C-group learned in a passive way by following the teacher's instruction without the tablet PCs, learning with tablet PCs provides E-group students with a convenient and fast digital learning environment, which can support students' various activities to acquire knowledge, thus optimizing students' learning efficiency and improving their learning achievement.

The results of the study also found that classroom instruction with tablet PCs can effectively improve students' SRL. The results are partially consistent with the findings of [31], which stated that the good use of open educational resources and technologies, such as portable devices, can cultivate students' SRL. [32] found several key attributes that can support students' SRL, such as personalization, learner-control, scaffolding, interaction, and cues for reflection. [31] also pointed out that learning motivation, planning and management, and self-monitoring are key aspects in promoting students' SRL. Compared with classroom instruction without tablet PCs, students learning with tablet PCs have more opportunities to learn by themselves and monitor their learning process, interact with the teachers and peers through the tablet PCs, which can provide students with almost all these key attributes and aspects. This instructional approach is believed to have the potential to enhance student's abilities of SRL, cooperative learning, inquiry learning, independent thinking, and problem-solving, and thus to improve students' learning achievement. Therefore, it is not difficult to understand why students in the E-group showed significantly higher SRL than those in the C-group. Moreover, facts have proved that prompting SRL can effectively improve the learning outcomes of students [33], thus students with higher SRL lead to a higher score in their learning achievement, as proven in the present study.

It should be noted that the present study has certain limitations. Firstly, this study only examined the impacts of classroom instruction with tablet PCs on junior high school students' Chinese language courses, and the results of this study may not fully reflect the effect of classroom instruction with tablet PCs on other subject areas. Secondly, this study was limited to two classes of participants, and the duration lasts for only two months. Therefore, future studies are encouraged to involve more subjects and more students at different educational levels in a long-term experiment. Moreover, great attention should be paid to designing and implementing of classroom instruction with tablet PCs to improve students' learning achievement and SRL. Future studies should take full advantage of the potential of classroom instruction with tablet PCs in supporting classroom interaction, real-time feedback, and other aspects, to realize the effective integration of ICTs and classroom instruction.

Acknowledgment. This work was supported by the National Natural Science Foundation of China (Grant No. 61907019).

References

1. Pegrum, M., Oakley, G., Faulkner, R.: Schools going mobile: a study of the adoption of mobile handheld technologies in Western Australian independent schools. Australas. J. Educ. Technol. **29**, 66–81 (2013)

2. Nouri, J., Pargman, T.C.: When teaching practices meet tablets' affordances. Insights on the materiality of learning. In: 2016 European Conference on Technology Enhanced Learning, Lyon, France (2016)
3. Manuguerra, M., Petocz, P.: Promoting student engagement by integrating new technology into tertiary education: the role of the iPad. Asian Soc. Sci. **7**, 61–65 (2011)
4. Cerratto Pargman, T., Nouri, J., Milrad, M.: Taking an instrumental genesis lens: new insights into collaborative mobile learning. Br. J. Educ. Technol. **49**, 219–234 (2017)
5. Li, S.C., Pow, J.W., Wong, E.M., Fung, A.C.: Empowering student learning through tablet PCs: a case study. Educ. Inf. Technol. **15**, 171–180 (2010)
6. Godsk, M.: Tablets for learning in higher education: the top 10 affordances. In: Bastiaens, T., Marks, G. (eds.) Proceedings of e-Learn 2013–World Conference on e-Learning in Corporate, Government, Healthcare, and Higher Education, pp. 1892–1897. Association for the Advancement of Computing in Education (AACE), Las Vegas, NV, USA (2010)
7. Corlett, D., Sharples, M., Bull, S., Chan, T.: Evaluation of a mobile learning organizer for university students. J. Comput. Assist. Learn. **21**, 162–170 (2005)
8. Zimmerman, B.J., Schunk, D.H.: Handbook of Self-Regulation of Learning and Performance. Routledge, New York (2011)
9. Wang, C.-H., Shannon, D.M., Ross, M.E.: Students' characteristics, self-regulated learning, technology self-efficacy, and course outcomes in online learning. Distance Educ. **34**, 302–323 (2013)
10. Bellhäuser, H., Lösch, T., Winter, C., Schmitz, B.: Applying a web-based training to foster self-regulated learning: effects of an intervention for large numbers of participants. Internet High. Educ. **31**, 87–100 (2016)
11. Broadbent, J.: Comparing online and blended learner's self-regulated learning strategies and academic performance. Internet High. Educ. **33**, 24–32 (2017)
12. Jansen, R.S., van Leeuwen, A., Janssen, J., Kester, L.: Validation of the revised self-regulated online learning questionnaire. In: Pammer-Schindler, V., Pérez-Sanagustín, M., Drachsler, H., Elferink, R., Scheffel, M. (eds.) EC-TEL 2018. LNCS, vol. 11082, pp. 116–121. Springer, Cham (2018). https://doi.org/10.1007/978-3-319-98572-5_9
13. Broadbent, J., Poon, W.L.: Self-regulated learning strategies & academic achievement in online higher education learning environments: a systematic review. Internet High. Educ. **27**, 1–13 (2010)
14. Santamarta, J.C., Hernández-Gutiérrez, L.E., Tomás, R., Cano, M., Rodríguez-Martín, J., Arraiza, M.P.: Use of tablet pcs in higher education: a new strategy for training engineers in European bachelors and masters programmes. Procedia Soc. Behav. Sci. **191**, 2753–2757 (2010)
15. Şimşek, M., Doğru, İ.A.: Tablet PC based classroom. Procedia Soc. Behav. Sci. **116**, 4246–4249 (2014)
16. Casas, I., Ochoa, S.F., Puente, J.: Using tablet PCs and pen-based technologies to support engineering education. In: 13th International Conference on Human-Computer Interaction, San Diego, CA, USA (2019)
17. Dundar, H., Akcayir, M.: Tablet vs. paper: the effect on learners' reading performance. Inter. Electron. J. Elem. Educ. **4**, 441–450 (2014)
18. Jansen, R.S., van Leeuwen, A., Janssen, J., Conijn, R., Kester, L.: Supporting learners' self-regulated learning in massive open online courses. Comput. Educ. **146**, (2020)
19. Kizilcec, R.F., Pérez-Sanagustín, M., Maldonado, J.J.: Self-regulated learning strategies predict learner behavior and goal attainment in massive open online courses. Comput. Educ. **104**, 18–33 (2017)
20. Henderson, S., Yeow, J.: iPad in education: a case study of iPad adoption and use in a primary school. In: 2012 International Conference on System Science (HICSS), Maui, Hawaii, USA (2012)

21. Palaigeorgiou, G., Papadopoulou, A.: Promoting self-paced learning in the elementary classroom with interactive video, an online course platform and tablets. Educ. Inf. Technol. **24**, 805–823 (2019)
22. Gokcearslan, S.: Perspectives of students on acceptance of tablets and self-directed learning with technology. Contemp. Educ. Technol. **8**, 40–55 (2017)
23. Ergun, O.: A study of primary school teachers' and Turkish language teachers' anxiety about tablet pc assisted teaching. Int. Educ. Stud. **11**, 66 (2018)
24. Hochberg, K., Becker, S., Louis, M., Klein, P., Kuhn, J.: Using smartphones as experimental tools—a follow-up: cognitive effects by video analysis and reduction of cognitive load by multiple representations. J. Sci. Educ. Technol. **29**, 303–317 (2020)
25. Dubé, A.K., Alam, S.S., Xu, C., Wen, R., Kacmaz, G.: Tablets as elementary mathematics education tools: are they effective and why. In: Robinson, K.M., Osana, H.P., Kotsopoulos, D. (eds.) Mathematical Learning and Cognition in Early Childhood, pp. 223–248. Springer, Cham (2019). https://doi.org/10.1007/978-3-030-12895-1_13
26. Carr, J.M.: Does math achievement happen when ipads and game-based learning are incorporated into fifth-grade mathematics instruction? J. Inf. Technol. Educ. **11**, 269–286 (2012)
27. Shi, Y., Peng, C., Wang, S., Yang, H.H.: The effects of smart classroom-based instruction on college students' learning engagement and internet self-efficacy. In: Cheung, S.K.S., Kwok, L.F., Kubota, K., Lee, L.-K., Tokito, J. (eds.) ICBL 2018. LNCS, vol. 10949, pp. 263–274. Springer, Cham (2018). https://doi.org/10.1007/978-3-319-94505-7_21
28. Magno, C.: Assessing academic self-regulated learning among Filipino college students: the factor structure and item fit. Int. J. Educ. Psychol. Assess. **5**, 61–76 (2010)
29. Yamaç, A., Öztürk, E., Mutlu, N.: Effect of digital writing instruction with tablets on primary school students' writing performance and writing knowledge. Comput. Educ. **157**, (2020)
30. Enriquez, A.G.: Enhancing student performance using tablet computers. Coll. Teach. **58**, 77–84 (2010)
31. Wong, T.-L., Xie, H.R., Zou, D., Wang, F.L., Tang, J.K.T., Kong, A., Kwan, R.: How to facilitate self-regulated learning? A case study on open educational resources. J. Comput. Educ. **7**, 51–77 (2020)
32. Van Laer, S., Elen, J.: In search of attributes that support self-regulation in blended learning environments. Educ. Inf. Technol. **22**, 1395–1454 (2017)
33. Lai, C.-L., Hwang, G.-J.: A self-regulated flipped classroom approach to improving students' learning performance in a mathematics course. Comput. Educ. **100**, 126–140 (2016)

Students' Reflection on Online Distance Learning: Advantages, Disadvantages, Recommendations

Ivana Simonova(✉), Ludmila Faltynkova, and Katerina Kostolanyova

University of Ostrava, Ostrava, Czech Republic
{ivana.simonova,katerina.kostolanyova}@osu.cz,
faltynkova@epol.cz

Abstract. The paper presents the results of research dealing with online distance instruction in the Czech Republic. It particularly focuses on students' feedback, detecting advantages, disadvantages, and recommendations when teaching in this manner. The main research objective was to (1) discover how students assess their learning in online distance courses, (2) consider the collected experience and opinions, and (3) reflect them into recommendations for further teacher and learner training in how to exploit online distance instruction efficiently. First, the process of online distance instruction in the Czech Republic was described and requirements were set which should be applied when designing and conducting online distance courses. Then, feedback from 272 respondents, students of upper secondary and higher education institutions, was collected. Students reflected on 64 courses which received positive or negative assessment. Advantages, disadvantages, and recommendations detected in both groups of courses were thought. Respondents' experience and opinions were monitored via a questionnaire consisting of eight open-answer items. Finally, the process of online distance learning was considered from the view of the collected data. Results proved that, as expected, even deeper teacher training is required. Main problems were detected in (1) the low level of teacher competency in this field in general, (2) time management, and (3) lack of technical support to learners. However, the fact that the necessity of learners' competency in online distance learning must be also developed was mentioned by a few respondents.

Keywords: Covid-19 pandemic · Online distance learning · Upper secondary · Higher education · Advantage · Disadvantage · Recommendation

1 Introduction

The covid-19 pandemic is an immense challenge to education all over the world. Efforts to slow the spread of the pandemic resulted in the closure of schools of all levels, i.e. an immediate shift away from the face-to-face instruction to the distance manner, mostly enhanced by the latest information and communication technologies (ICT) and conducted in the online mode. Thus, the education is exposed to the biggest change running

R. Li et al. (Eds.): ICBL 2021, LNCS 12830, pp. 275–286, 2021.
https://doi.org/10.1007/978-3-030-80504-3_23

in the live manner. Facing the new situation, questions appear whether both teachers and learners have appropriate competencies to succeed in online distance instruction. Generally, whether the teachers are able to teach and pupils and students are able to learn in an online distance manner. The main objective of this paper is to present the results of the research which deals with students' assessment of instruction conducted through online distance courses at selected schools in the Czech Republic.

2 Theoretical Background

Online distance education has been developing for nearly two decades within the Czech higher education system. Starting from the first trials shortly after 2000, this approach has been expanded and improved mainly at faculties preparing IT specialists. The reason was these institutions had appropriate technical and technological equipment, and academic staff could be systematically trained in didactics, e.g. [1–3].

At the same moment, the didactic rules binding for this process were set so that this mode could be accredited for higher education. The rules reflect (1) Comenius' didactic principles and (2) TP(A)CK framework; later on, (3) SAMR model was also implemented. These three preconditions for efficient ICT-enhanced education were accepted several years before the covid-19 pandemic started; however, they are expected to be applied in the design of online distance instruction even these days.

Principles defined by the Czech scholar and humanist J.A Comenius (1592–1670) in the 17th century were originally designed for face-to-face instruction. Comenius belonged among the fifty recognized thinkers in the field of education since Confucius' time [4]. During the whole life, he was trying to fulfil his own didactic motto *Omnes, omnia, omneno* [Everything to everybody via all available ways], thus forming the basis of the Czech educational science [5]. He wanted children – pupils – to understand the world; therefore, he introduced the world to them in a way they were capable to understand. To reach the objective, he required e.g. open access to learning for all children, reflecting the learner's age and level of knowledge, beginning with concrete items and facts previously known to learners, building the structure of knowledge in a systematic, continuous, step-by-step manner, using clear examples to illustrate new learning content, and finishing with new, abstract knowledge acquired by learners. Most of the principles are still alive and valid and form the basis of Czech education system [6]. Comenius also took a psychological view into consideration, when putting the emphasis on didactic methods to be natural, nonviolent, and consistent with mental development. As stated by Capkova [7], *Omnia sponte fluant, absit violentia rebus* [Let everything flow freely, without violent disruption], he required. Later on, Piaget summarized his principles when proving that there exists an interrelation between cognitive functions and activity, the principle of positive and affective motivation, the principle of consecutive development, the aspects of facilitation/inhibition of the educational process, and the principle of teacher-learner cooperation [8].

When ICT came to be a firm part of education, new requirements for teachers' competencies arose. They were defined as the intersection of technological, pedagogical (and) content knowledge – TP(A)CK [9]. The conjunction *and* leads us to the fact that knowledge and skills in technology do not transfer automatically into efficient teaching, but teachers have to be trained in using them [10].

SAMR model [11] assists teachers in the implementation of the latest (smart) technologies into the process of instruction. The model consists of four successive steps (levels) which cover two areas (Enhancement, Transformation). Each area includes two steps (Substitution and Augmentation within Enhancement; Modification and Redefinition within Transformation). In steps 1 and 2, the learning content is enhanced (Substitution) and improved (Augmentation) by the technology, in steps 3 and 4, teacher exploits the technology to make changes in educational forms (Modification), or uses completely new forms which could not be enabled without the technology (Redefinition) [12]. In other words, at the Substitution level, identical tasks and activities are performed as can be conducted without technology, i.e. there is not any functional change in teaching and learning. At the Augmentation level, technology works as an effective tool enhancing the process of instruction; thus students may become more involved in the process. At the Modification level, the first step is made between enhancing the 'traditional' teaching/learning and accomplishing substantial changes within this process through the use of technology. This is a significant change; new methods and tools are used that enable e.g. listening activities, rewriting texts etc. Finally, the Redefinition level appears, providing a completely new approach and strategy that could not be allowed without technology – it is not the target but means enhancing students' learning.

3 Methodology

3.1 Process of Online Distance Instruction

The first period of online distance instruction in the Czech Republic started in March 2020 and covered approximately a period of three months (depending on the school level). The closure of schools was immediate and unprecedented. This fact was reflected in the quality of online distance instruction at that time – teachers did not have sufficient competencies in teaching online, schools did not have appropriate equipment (both hardware and software), all learners had neither own computers (notebooks, tablets), nor the skills to learn online. Immediately after the closure, public TV provided lessons to primary school pupils, step-by-step, various web pages started to offer texts, experiments, exercises, tests, and other didactic means to support learning from home. Generally, both parents and teachers expected it would be a single period of ICT-enhanced learning which would be finished by the end of the school year (June 2020). However, the covid-19 pandemic did not disappear during the summer holidays (July–August 2020), and showed up again. The school year started in September 2020, entirely providing teachers a short period to briefly prepare learners for online distance instruction. Meanwhile, teachers were briefly trained in developing the competency in teaching in this manner before lessons started (in August 2020). In the institutions which are under the focus of this research, teachers attended 10-hour-long course in which both theoretical knowledge and practical skills were included. Reflecting this fact, teachers were expected to design and conduct their lessons in compliance with Comenius' principles, exploiting TP(A)CK framework, and SAMR model. MS Teams was selected as a nation-wide platform by the Czech Ministry of Education. Whereas in the spring period (March–June 2020) learners' participation in online distance instruction was voluntary, in August 2020, a new act was introduced defining this way of instruction as compulsory for each learner [13]. Moreover, during the summer months, didactic recommendations for teachers were produced by the Ministry of Education providing principles and rules of successful distance education [14]. Unfortunately, they were rather general and schematic, neither distinguishing learners' age, nor other criteria, e.g. applying the Comenius' principles mentioned above. They rather reminded of promotional slogans: Join every learner, Communicate, Follow the rules, Support others, Monitor and appraise the process. Therefore, schools organized the training by themselves, being aware of all related negatives to the future quality of education which the lack of teacher's competency in this area can cause. In February 2021, another semester started with online distance instruction conducted in MS Teams.

3.2 Research Objectives and Expectations

Online distance instruction, which is under the focus of this research, was conducted from September 2020 to January 2021. Teachers were expected to teach their subjects in the form of courses in MS Teams; the courses were expected to be designed and conducted in accord with Comenius' principles, TP(A)CK framework, and SAMR model. As online distance instruction appears rather unexpectedly at all school levels and cannot be replaced by "traditional", time- and research-verified face-to-face instruction, it is highly required to have feedback on this process. In this research, students' reflection on this manner of instruction was under focus. The crucial questions are how the process is conducted, particularly if appropriate didactic principles are implemented, the latest technologies exploited, teachers sufficiently competent for conducting the process, and finally, whether learners can reach learning objectives. Arising from the questions, *the main objective of this research was to (1) discover how students assess their learning in online distance courses, (2) consider the collected experience and opinions, and (3) reflect them into recommendations for further teacher and learner training in how to exploit online distance instruction efficiently.*

Teachers' qualification and competency are crucial preconditions in the process. If the design of online distance courses follows didactic principles and the courses are conducted in compliance with them, we can expect learners can reach the planned learning outcomes which are defined in Framework Education Programme for Upper Secondary Education [15] and by the syllabi of particular courses within higher education.

3.3 Research Methods and Tools

A questionnaire method was exploited for data collecting. The questionnaire consisted of eight items. Respondents provided their opinions on learning in online distance courses and described their experience in the form of open answers: (1) What were the main advantages of learning in online distance courses?; (2) What were the main disadvantages?; (3) What would you recommend towards improving online distance learning?; (4) What are your other comments on this way of learning?

Respondents described learning in two courses taught in an online distance manner. First, in a course in which didactic principles were appropriately implemented, their learning was fluent, the use of study materials and teaching methods efficiently targeted towards reaching the expected learning objectives. Students enjoyed learning in these courses and were satisfied with the way how the courses were designed and conducted and considered learning through them efficient. These courses received positive assessment and are called P-courses further on. Second, students provided their experience and opinions from courses, learning in which they did not like and did not consider it helpful for learning. In their opinion, these courses did not bring them to acquire the new knowledge efficiently (if ever). These courses received negative assessment and are called N-courses further on.

3.4 Research Sample

Totally, data were collected from 272 respondents. More respondents were of female gender (M = 94; F = 178). They attended three institutions:

- upper secondary school for medical staff (N = 131; M = 22; F = 109),
- advanced studies for higher medical staff (N = 69; M = 30; F = 39),
- university, faculty of education, department of information technologies or English language and literature (N = 72; M = 42; F = 30).

Upper secondary students formed the sample group of secondary students; students of advanced studies and university students were included in the sample of higher education (HE).

Respondents provided their opinions on 64 online distance courses conducted by 72 teachers. All monitored courses were taught 2–3 times per week (90–135 min) by qualified teachers, i.e. the teachers had qualification in the field and in teaching. The institutions were intentionally selected for the following reasons: (1) The preparation of medical staff, of higher medical staff, of prospective teachers of IT subjects and English language belongs to the profile fields of graduation exams which have been under the focus of the system of education since 2008 [16]. (2) The institutions under research were authors' home institutions so that the conditions for conducting online distance courses were firmly set. Moreover, the authors also participated in teacher training in online distance instruction and continuous consultation as mentioned above. (3) All researched courses included both theory and practice (in hospitals, laboratories, and schools); however, only theoretical courses taught in the online distance manner were under the focus of research.

4 Results

Results are structured in five subchapters, dealing with advantages and disadvantages in online distance learning, both in courses reaching positive and negative assessment. Then, students' recommendations and additional comments are included in the reflection.

4.1 Advantages Detected in P-Courses

In courses with positive assessment (P-courses), the length of answers was from six to 289 characters including spaces, the average length was 43 characters including spaces. Answers were accepted both in bullets and full sentences.

The most appreciated advantages of online distance learning were detected in two areas: (a) the convenience of the home environment for learning, (b) time management. As a result of the convenience of the home environment for learning ($N = 139$), students mentioned the increase in motivation to learning (23), learning at an individual pace (14), no stress from learning, particularly that they did not understand the learning content (4), they did not have enough time for meeting the requirements: finishing online tests (16), preparation of presentations and fulfilling tasks (7), preparation for online exams (4). Numerous students appreciated the time flexibility of online distance learning (47) – some of them liked they had more leisure time (16), either for hobbies, or for themselves, others were happy, they did not have to commute to school (21), they did not have to get up early (17), even they could learn from bed (13). More time for learning in general was expressed by 61 students, 36 ones emphasized they learned more. Rather low occurrences were detected in the lack of teacher-student contacts (39) and student-student contact (22), other two students mentioned it was good for them not to meet those students they did not liked. The need for competency of autonomous learning was expressed; some students thought that they had the competency before the observed period (14) or they strengthened it (13), none of them felt a lack of competency. A few students appreciated that they developed IT competency (8) within online distance learning, saved money for not commuting (18), had more study materials available compared to the face-to-face lessons (16), some of them were presentations with sound records (22). One student emphasized how creative the teacher was, two students appreciated the teachers' openness and possibility to contact them any time. Seven students did not find any advantage when learning in an online distance manner, three students' response was I do not know. The majority of above-mentioned advantages was summarized by student #107 who stated that: *"The greatest advantage of this way of learning is that I did not waste time on commuting, scheduled learning to my preferences, was not exposed to stress, and could work from the comfort of my home, which was much better for learning"*.

We most appreciate the answer by student #121 who defined the advantage as follows: *"The best thing of online distance learning is we have time to help in hospital"*.

4.2 Advantages Detected in N-Courses

In courses with negative assessment (N-courses), the length of answers was from seven to 219 characters including spaces, the average length was 26 characters including spaces.

Despite the negative assessment of these courses, the most appreciated advantages of online distance learning related to time management, i.e. time flexibility (47), which included more leisure time (32), learning at an individual pace (12), sufficient time for learning (25), doing homework – tasks (22), online tests (28), presentations (14), no commuting to school (35), no getting up early (42), enough time to profile subjects (31), lessons were mostly held in the morning, i.e. in the time which is better for learning than late afternoon (21). The convenience of the home environment was mentioned by fewer students (19), as well as the availability of more study materials, exercises, and online tests (15). However, similarly to the advantages in P-courses, students were aware the autonomy in learning is necessary – in this case, they mentioned it as a missing feature (28). One student had repeated technical problems with the computer, three students declared they were not able to learn anything in N-courses, and other four students appreciated the teachers' efforts and good teacher-student communication. Seven students did not know what to answer, 33 ones did not find any advantage when learning in N-courses.

In spite of the fact that the conditions for learning through N-courses were poor or borderline, the truth is on the student #106'side, who summarized: *"It was my decision whether to learn or not. However, much effort was required ... "*.

4.3 Disadvantages Detected in P-Courses

In courses with positive assessment (P-courses), the length of answers was from eight to 642 characters including spaces, the average length was 52 characters including spaces. The most criticized disadvantages of online distance learning were detected in three areas: (a) technical problems, (b) students' motivation to learning, (c) teachers' competency and experience.

Within the general technical problems (42), which caused students' absence in lessons or not understanding the learning content, if the connection was not strong and fluent (34), the low quality of the Internet connection was the most frequently emphasized problem (39). In some students, teachers thought the problems were intentionally made to disturb the instruction or not to participate (13).

Insufficient motivation to learn was also frequently mentioned (47), as well as low concentration on learning (32). Contrary to the above-presented subchapters on advantages, when online distance learning from home was considered convenient by the students, here, some students state they were disturbed by siblings or family environment and consider learning from home to be a disadvantage. This finding can be connected to socially weak conditions of the family.

Despite all teachers were trained in general online distance instruction, particularly in using MS Teams, students consider some of them unexperienced, others did not meet the didactic requirements – learners described their instruction to be chaotic (14), not providing enough information on tasks and deadlines (34), conducting rare communication with students (42), providing little explanation but having high demands (9), showing little effort (23), displaying presentations only followed by online tests (4). Moreover, students' experience is that the teaching organization differs in each course a little, which results in a waste of time when finding study materials, tasks, exercises, tests, and deadlines (23). Students conceded their own procrastination (18), laziness (9), cheating in tests (15), but they longed for missing social contacts (32), even with teachers (16). They complain about the long time in front of the computer (17), monitoring their behaviour during lessons (9) and online distance exams (4) by camera. On the other hand, they understand it is difficult for teachers not to see students' responses when speaking. They sum up, it is difficult to acquire the learning content without direct contact with teachers (29), to learn autonomously (14), to understand problems without practical experience (23). Additionally to the above mentioned, student #73 states that *"It is more efficient and much comfortable for me to listen without being disturbed, concentrate, and then understand the problem. I also understand teachers who reject to exploit online tests for assessing students' knowledge (because of cheating)"*.

4.4 Disadvantages Detected in N-Courses

In courses with negative assessment (N-courses), the length of answers was from six to 647 characters including spaces, the average length was 47 characters including spaces. The most criticized disadvantages of online distance learning were detected in three areas: (a) T-S communication, (b) conducting of online distance instruction, (c) students' self-control.

Students complained about low frequency and late responses from teachers (44), which resulted in problems with understanding the learning content and/or missing deadlines for submitting tasks. Some teachers sent study material without explanation (32), they required much work on tasks and in worksheets, however, the work did not target towards building new knowledge (17), it was groundless and purposeless work. As a result, students were not able to acquire new learning content (28), they felt they did not know much (37), if no practical lessons were held (26), no aids were available (4). Moreover, some of them were aware that hard self-control is needed (18), autonomy in learning (28), high motivation (26), and concentration (12). Some students did not find the home environment convenient for their learning (22). Other students concluded that teachers were not competent enough for online distance instruction (18), they did not exploit the tools of MS Teams appropriately (36), in some cases, they proclaimed they did not like this way of teaching (27). On top of that, technical problems, including mainly low quality of Internet connection, were detected (25). Additionally, students state they hated online lessons (14), particularly cameras (3). A missing social contact was declared by one student only. Answer in 16 students was I do not know. All these factors cause stress in students (and teachers), and have a strong impact on the process of instruction; no wonder students gave a negative assessment to these courses. Moreover, some of them required lessons should be inspected by headmasters (6). As student #73 summarizes: *"Irregular lessons, too many study materials, hardly any communication with teachers, and low-quality Internet connection cannot result in efficient learning and good knowledge of students"*.

4.5 Recommendations for P-Courses and N-Courses

In courses with positive assessment (P-courses), the length of answers was from 17 to 348 characters including spaces, the average length was 44 characters including spaces. Thirty-four students' answers were Nothing to recommend, twenty-two students stated I do not know. In the context of recommendations, we think both answers can be considered identical, declaring the students do not have any recommendations on these courses. Additionally, 29 students expressed that online distance courses suited their learning. In courses with negative assessment (N-courses), the length of answers was from 16 to 1,030 characters including spaces, the average length was 42 characters including spaces. Sixteen students' answers were Nothing to recommend, eleven students stated I do not know.

In both types of courses, recommendations focused on the following areas: (a) time management, (b) providing feedback to students, (c) exploiting one tool for conducting online distance instruction. In brackets, first, occurrences in P-courses are presented, followed by occurrences in N-courses after the +sign.

The main recommendation dealt with scheduling the online distance lessons. Students required each online lesson was divided in two parts; in the first part, new learning content was explained and practiced, in the second part, students' questions were answered by teachers (23 + 28). Another requirement was the lessons had been firmly planned (28 + 31), not announced a few hours (in the evening or night) before. Identical recommendation was with online tests (15 + 20) because students are not continuously connected and may miss the test.

Most students would appreciate more time devoted to explanation (19 + 24), providing teachers' feedback whether they correctly acquired new learning content (29 + 41), in the form of online answers to questions (11 + 0), discussions during online lessons (26 + 28) or in the written form (16 + 0). Opposing proposals appeared: some students required more or longer online lessons in general, without specifying the main purpose (22 + 0), or fewer lessons and more autonomous work (16 + 0), less time in front of the computer to save the eyes (14 + 39), breaks between lessons to rest the eyes (17 + 0), more or fewer tasks for homework (6 + 0) etc.

Moreover, one tool (platform) should be exploited for online distance instruction (9 + 3); students and teachers should be trained in using it (34 + 11). Teachers' effort and engagement could be higher to motivate students towards better performance (13 + 27). And, technical support from the school administrator (if available) would be appreciated (6 + 24). In N-courses, students strongly required online distance lessons were held in all subjects, not only presentations sent via e-mail (0 + 26). Several students expressed their wish of having online distance learning no more (6 + 8), others proclaimed recognition and support when stating *Both sides do maximum* (student #43) or *It is difficult for both the students and teachers* (student #96). An appeal to follow was expressed by student #62: *"If you want to know anything, you have to learn it by yourself"*.

4.6 Additional Comments on P-Courses and N-Courses

In courses with positive assessment (P-courses), the length of answers was from 20 to 229 characters including spaces, the average length was 51 characters including spaces. In courses with negative assessment (N-courses), the length of answers was from seven to 138 characters including spaces, the average length was 40 characters including spaces. Both in P-courses and N-courses, comments were either identical to the recommendations presented above, or students provided various types of justifiable complaints on didactic problems which appeared in the courses, e.g. lack of study materials, tests, meaningful activities and exercises, mistakes in tests and their assessment, missing final assessment etc. As student #26 stated: *"We wish we had more competent and creative teachers."*, or *"In some lessons, we finished with singing a song."* (student #4).

5 Conclusion, Limits, and Further Research Activities

To sum up the collected data, from the view of the number of observed courses (64), even occurrences around ten responses are of rather strong value. Unfortunately, not in each course Comenius' principles were applied to a maximum extent; however, some features could be discovered. Methods, tools, and outcomes relating to SAMR model were not detected in students' reflections, the impact of TP(A)CK framework could be found with some teachers only. The finding shows that students' attention was mainly paid to the following features and areas in P-courses and N-courses:

1. home environment;
2. teachers' competency in online distance teaching, particularly time management, appropriate teaching methods, and communication;
3. technical support to the process.

Whereas the home environment was considered a comfortable and convenient advantage for learning in P-courses, some students considered it disturbing and lowering their concentration in N-courses. Thus, it suggests that the conditions differed substantially. If students had their own rooms and computers, the home environment was appreciated by them. In the opposite case, if students shared the room and/or computer with siblings, the learning conditions were not suitable for learning. Thus, the social aspect plays an important role in students' learning.

Teachers' competency in online distance teaching was considered the crucial skill for conducting the process in an efficient and pleasant manner in P-courses and N-courses. Both features contribute to the final result. If appropriate teaching methods are applied and enhanced by ICT, the process results in expected learning outcomes and students' satisfaction is supported, which consequently makes an impact on their motivation to further learning. And, if the environment is pleasant for learning, mainly stimulating and inspiring, not causing stress, the process of learning can run fluently. If students have enough study materials of various types, delivered to them in various ways and explained if teachers assess students' performance and provide feedback on their learning continuously so that students were able to make corrections before the final fixing of new knowledge. Whereas in P-courses teachers' effort in conduction online distance instruction was appreciated, in N-courses students complained that there hardly was any effort on the teachers' side, and the interest in student learning was missing.

Time management, which firmly plans the scheduling of lessons, consultations, tests, and exams on a regular basis, in "active" time (not late evenings, night), and which also provides enough space for T-S, S-T communication. This feature closely relates to the teachers' competency mentioned above.

Technical support was required mostly by students in N-courses, particularly from an alive person – administrator, not from an electronic document on the Internet, mainly if the quality of Internet connection was low. This resulted in the fact that they did not see and hear all what was said and done in online lessons, they were disconnected in key moments of the lessons, presentations, tests, exams, … (whether it happened intentionally or not was not investigated within this research). We can guess whether it related to the low quality of the hardware and software used (these students often learned through smartphones, they did not have computers, notebooks, or tablets available), and thus to the weak social conditions of the students, as it was with the convenience of the home environment for learning.

To sum up the above-mentioned findings, if Comenius' didactic principles were implemented in online distance instruction, they were appreciated by students and courses were included in P-courses. If only some of them were applied, or all were omitted (as can be deduced from some students' comments), the courses were ranked in N-group. Therefore, under current conditions, teachers' qualification should be widened and competency in online distance teaching should be strongly required, as several students also mentioned. We understand that teachers' work is even more demanding these days; however, the efficiency of teaching will not improve until teachers' skills in the field improve. Then, the requirements of TP(A)CK framework will be met, and SAMR model can be applied. Only at this level, the latest ICT will efficiently enhance the online distance learning. Unfortunately, we were not able to discover from students' feedback whether the SAMR model was implemented in the design of courses.

Unfortunately, when assessing online distance instruction during the whole semester, we must conclude that our expectations were not met. Much work must be done in building teachers' competency in online distance teaching. However, at the same time, students' competency in online distance learning must be improved. Not much time has been devoted to student training so far. Moreover, study materials are highly needed in the digital format, which can help in teaching in general, and in the SAMR model application as well. Finally, online distance communication must be part of the instruction; half of the time as a minimum should be devoted to speaking with students.

Of course, the findings of this research are limited by the sample, which included courses conducted at intentionally selected educational institutions in one country and assessed by their students in a total amount of 272. However, the results provide us with the insight in the state and give the basis for improvements in the future. For further research, we suggest attention should be paid to adaptive learning from the view of learning styles and motivation types. Methodologies for online distance instruction should be set for various subjects (at all levels of school education), didactics of online distance teaching and learning should be included in pre-service teacher preparation, and in-service teachers should be trained within life-long education courses.

Acknowledgement. The paper is supported by SGS02/PdF/2021 project Online distance education. Optimization reflecting students' and teachers' experience.

References

1. Poulova, P., Sokolova, M., Simonova, I.: ICT contribution to the process of e-learning implementation in the field of education. In: Kallel, A., Hassahiri, A., Bulucea, C.A., Mastorakis, M. (eds.) Advanced Educational Technologies-6th WSEAS/IASME International Conference on Educational Technology, Kantaoui, Sousse, Tunisia, pp. 157–161. WSEAS (2010)
2. Simonova, I., Poulova, P.: Changes in students' attitudes towards electronic education in 2003 – 2010. In: Dondon, P., Martin, O. (eds.) Latest Trends on Engineering Education, 7th WSEAS International Conference, Athens, pp. 343–348. WSEAS (2010)
3. Cerna, M., Poulova, P.: User testing of language educational portals. E+M. Ekonomie a Manage. **12**(3), 104–117 (2009)
4. Černá, M.: Johann amos comenius and his legacy at the information age. In: Cheung, S.K.S., Lee, L.-K., Simonova, I., Kozel, T., Kwok, L.-F. (eds.) ICBL 2019. LNCS, vol. 11546, pp. 46–56. Springer, Cham (2019). https://doi.org/10.1007/978-3-030-21562-0_4
5. Comenius, J.A.: Didaktika velka [The Great Didactics], 3rd edn. Komenium, Brno (1948)
6. Comenius, J.A.: Selections From His Works. SPN, Praha (1964)

7. Capkova, D.: Pojetí vzdělání jako celoživotního procesu v díle Komenského [The concept of education as a lifelong process in the work of Komensky]. Pedagogika **5**, 703–722 (1970). http://pages.pedf.cuni.cz/pedagogika/?attachment_id=8897&edmc=8897. Accessed 12 Mar 2021
8. Piaget, J.: Jan Amos Comenius, por Jean Piaget. https://www.ufrgs.br/psicoeduc/piaget/jan-amos-comenius-por-jean-piaget/. Accessed 11 Mar 2021
9. Herring, M., Koehler, M.J., Mishra, P.: Handbook of Technological Pedagogical Content Knowledge, 2nd edn. Routledge, Milton Park (2016)
10. Thompson, A.D., Mishra, P.: Breaking news: TPCK becomes TPACK! J. Comput. Teach. Educ. **24**(2), 38–64 (2007)
11. Puentedura, R.: SAMR model. SAMR Model - Technology Is Learning. google.com. Accessed 11 Mar 2021
12. Netolicka, J., Simonova, I.: SAMR model and Bloom's digital taxonomy applied in blended learning/teaching of general English and ESP. In: 2017 International Symposium on Educational Technology (ISET), Hong Kong, 2017, pp. 277–281. IEEE (2017). https://doi.org/10.1109/iset.2017.68
13. Act N. 349/2020 Coll., 349/2020 Sb. (psp.cz). Accessed 26 Feb 2021
14. Ministry of Education: Principy a zásady úspěšného vzdělávání na dálku_podrobný materiál_A3.pdf, MŠMT ČR (msmt.cz) [Principles and rules of successful distance education]. Accessed 26 Feb 2021
15. Eurydice: Teaching and Learning in Upper Secondary Education | Eurydice (europa.eu). Accessed 28 Feb 2021
16. Act N. 242/2008 Coll., §78–79 https://www.zakonyprolidi.cz/cs/2008-242#cl1. Accessed 24 Feb 2021

Cultural Factors in Urgent Transition to Online Learning During the COVID-19 Pandemic – Case Studies from Japan and China

Shudong Wang[1](✉) and Aipeng Chen[2]

[1] Shimane University, Nishikawatsu-cho 1060, Matsue, Shimane, Japan
wangsd@soc.shimane-u.ac.jp
[2] Shucheng No. 1 High School, 411 Meihe Road, Chenguan, Shucheng, China

Abstract. The Covid-19 Pandemic has greatly changed the world and world education. This paper reviews the forced urgent transition to complete online learning in two different scenarios during the Covid-19 Pandemic in 2020. The two different scenarios are a Japanese university and a Chinese senior high school. Rather than simply listing actions of how online learning was conducted in these two schools, this research focuses on what role the cultural factors played in the transition. The authors primarily investigated the cultural differences in terms of institutional decision making, teachers' online instructions, students' online learning behaviors, and the involvement of students' families between two schools in two different countries. Several interesting cultural differences reflected in the transition were found: as for decision and information delivery, email was the major communication tool in Japan, while social media group was most welcomed in China; as for online instructions, the Japanese university teachers were concessive, while the Chinese teachers were somewhat dominant; As for online learning recourses, Japanese students have less than their Chinese students; As for online learning behavior, Japanese students minded self-disclosure in virtual classes while Chinese students were open; As for family role, Chinese parents were much more heavily involved in their children's online learning… As the transformation to technology-driven education is still continuing with and will continue after the Covid-19 Pandemic, the findings from this research will leave us in no doubt that educators who need to take part in online teaching in local, regional, national, and international contexts need to seriously consider impact of cultural factors.

Keywords: Culture factors · Transition to online learning · The Covid-19 Pandemic

1 Introduction

In early 2020, the Covid-19 Pandemic began to spread throughout the world. During 2020, people became panicked by such a sudden and deadly so-called once-in-a-century crisis. In order to limit its spread via human transmission shops were closed, offices

R. Li et al. (Eds.): ICBL 2021, LNCS 12830, pp. 287–297, 2021.
https://doi.org/10.1007/978-3-030-80504-3_24

shut-down, students asked to stay at home. Chinese schools did not fully re-open until September, 2020. Up to May 14, 2020, 86% of Japanese kindergartens, elementary schools and high schools remained closed [1]. Some Japanese universities are still half-closed as at this time in March 2021, when this paper is written.

In 2020, when social distance started, schools were abruptly asked to shift to online instruction from in-person teaching. According to LINE Research [2], by April 24, 52 days on from school closure, only 1% of high schools in Japan had switched to online learning, while most of the others simply had students do paper homework at home or offered digital handout download via email or school websites.

The first author is based in Japan but had no way to obtain data from any of these high schools. We therefore had no choice but to compare a university in Japan at which the first author works and a senior school in China where the second author works. Undoubtedly, these two different types of schools vary in many aspects such as students' characteristics, school management, education content, and so on. However, this paper is not intended to compare these differences. We aim only to focus on cultural differences reflected in the urgent transition to online learning which have not been studied in other research [3–5].

This paper tries to delineate which cultural factors has what impact on the transition to online learning during the risk. The authors assume that although schools may feature very differently in academy, but cultures behind them are commonly shared nationally. The culture of high school online learning may be also applied to university level in the same country. When designing online learning models, one must be aware of the existence of such cultural factors and make full use of them, or avoid cultural conflicts and taboos so that online learning can achieve its greatest outcomes.

This research tries to answer the following questions:

1. How culture is reflected in school's policy making during the 2020 transition?
2. What are the differences between two countries in regard to teachers' online instruction style, and why?
3. Does culture impact students online learning behaviors?
4. To what extent were students' family involved in the urgent transition? And what role did the families play during the special time?

2 Research Method

As the research only investigated two single educational institutions, case study method is adopted. The first author is an associate professor working at Shimane National University, Japan (Hereinafter "The Japanese University A"). He has been researching on and practicing e-learning for many years. He taught five online classes in 2020 and was involved in designing online course syllabi for his department. The second author is a reputable senior teacher at Shucheng No. 1 High School (Hereinafter "Chinese Senior High School B"), Shuchneng, China. He has been incorporating ICT to his Chinese teaching and achieved excellent results over the past decade. The second author was also a vice-principal responsible for teaching affairs for his school. After the outbreak of the Covid-19 Pandemic, he acted not only as a decision maker but also as an active in-service teacher.

Some data used for this research comes from the authors' subjective observations, some other is first-hand and quantitative data. By analyzing such data this research can gain concrete, contextual and in-depth knowledge about the specific and detailed facts that occurred during the transition to online learning during the Covid-19 Pandemic in 2020. The case study will allow the authors to explore the key characteristics, meanings, and implications of the urgent, forced transition occurring within the two institutions [6, 7].

The Japanese University A is a typical middle-sized national university in the western area of Japan. Students are from different areas of the country and are representative of youngsters of the age. The Chinese Senior High School B is a typical senior high school in east China with a middle-sized student enrolment number, of an average academic level, and an average government investment.

The data we collected includes the minutes of meetings, entries to school websites, emails or messages to teachers and students, online lesson videos and screenshots, and results of exams used to verify online learning efficacy.

With the above data, we primarily investigated and compared cultural impact on school decision-making, teachers' preparation for the transition and their actual online teaching. We also look at students' online learning behaviors. As the transition was urgent and exigent at an unprecedented risk, we were also interested in the extent to which students' parents were involved.

3 Cultural Factors in Transition to Online Learning

3.1 Decision-Making and Delivery

In both schools, apart from PowerPoint, some teachers had never made use of any other digital tools for instructions prior to the pandemic, and were not familiar with any form of online learning. The Japanese University A has Moodle, a very powerful open-source learning management system, Office 365 for organization use, but utilization was very low. The Chinese Senior High School B did have ICT workshops for all teachers in the past few years, but only a minority had been actively using what they had learnt for actual teaching. Facing such a fierce situation, not only teachers, but also the schools' management went through a period of initial chaos. Students, parents, society - as well as the educational administrations - were all anxiously watching the school and were expecting swift decisions on transition to online learning.

The Japanese have a culture for setting up "countermeasures headquarters" ("Tay-isaku Honbu" in Japanese) to deal with emergencies or urgent tasks. Such a headquarter may include organization leaders, section leaders, experts and routine enforcers. The Japanese University A set up "Covid-19 Countermeasures Headquarter" in March, 2020. All decisions regarding Covid-19 matters were made by this headquarter and they were passed on to teachers and students via its executive office.

Similar to the Japanese University A, the Chinese Senior High School B formed a Leading Group to deal with the crisis. They did not specially set up a "countermeasures headquarter" by name as such. They made decisions as usual but more centrally at principal level, and decision were delivered to teachers via the principal's office. Different from the Japanese University A which directly contacted students and teaching staff, notifications in the Chinese Senior High School B were delivered mainly through grade headteachers and class headteachers.

From April 15, 2020 when the "countermeasure headquarter office" was set up, to March 5, 2021, 80 announcements were sent out to teachers and staff at the Japanese University A. From January 26, 2020 to April 20, 2020 the Leading Group at the Chinese Senior High School B sent 39 messages in total.

Email is the most used tool for decision delivery at the Japanese University A. Although the university has official accounts of Facebook, Line, YouTube and Twitter, and each account has more than one thousand followers or subscribers, these social medial tools have never been used as two-way communication tools - rather as a one-way bulletin board.

At the Chinese Senior High School B, most announcements were made through WeChat groups with a few through QQ groups and the school short message service. WeChat, similar to LINE but with more functions, is the most popular social media tool currently used in China. At Chinese Senior High School B, a class headteacher usually has every parent's WeChat account on his/her contact list. A student's parent, either father or mother, or both, must join the WeChat group formed by the class headteacher. A subject teacher must be in the group owned by the class headteacher. A class headteacher must be in the group owned by the grade headteacher and the grade headteachers must be in the group of which the principal is the owner. Instead of using emails, the majority of the class announcements were transmitted to students and their families through WeChat groups at the Chinese Senior High School B.

At both schools, the official website was a medium not only for decision delivery and information spread not only for stakeholders, but also as references, history records or memorandum for the general public for broader view.

Figure 1 shows that the Japanese University A carefully divided Covid-19 announcements and information into different categories so that certain group of people – students or staff or parents or communities around the university can quickly spot the information that they need. While the entries on the web site of the Chinese Senior High School B (See Fig. 2) were not classified.

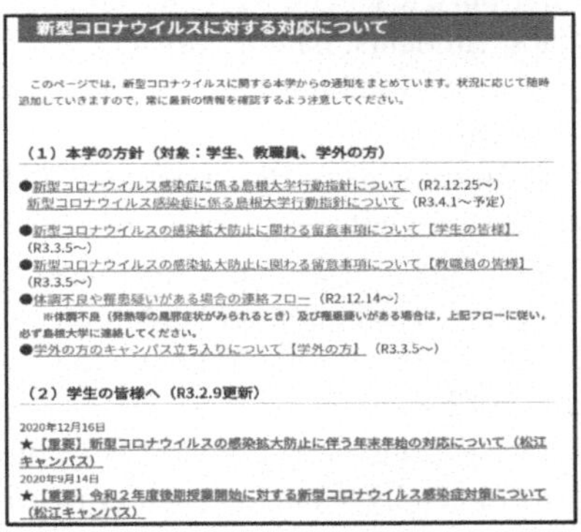

Fig. 1. Special Covid-18 site of the Japanese University A

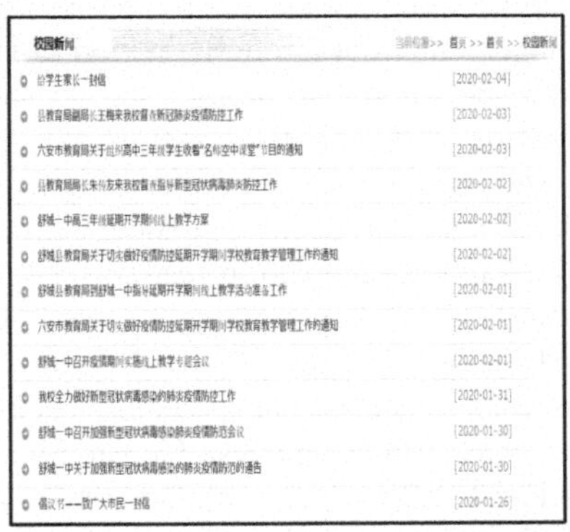

Fig. 2. Covid-19 related news in Senior High School B Website

By the middle of March, 2021, the Japanese University A had 48 Covid-19 related entries on its website, while the Chinese Senior School B had 54 in the first 3-month period. (See Table 1). As the Covid-19 spread was basically curbed in China and schools returned to normal - The Chinese Senior School B had very few Covid-19 related entries after May, 2020.

Table 1. Web site entries related to Covid-19

Web site entries related to Covid-19	University A (Japan) (April 12 , 2020 - March 5, 2021)	Senior High School B (China) (January 26 , 2020 - April 28, 2020)
General information for all	6	53
Announcements for students	19	
Announcements for staff	15	
Announcements for students' parents and families	3	
For the people in the community	3	
The other	2	
Total	**48**	**54**

3.2 Teachers' Online Instructions

At the Japanese University A, a guideline for online teaching was issued in April. Although the guideline suggested several platforms available at the university, it allowed teachers to freely choose which to use on their own volition. The Chinese Senior High School B issued an action plan for urgently switching to online learning at the beginning of February. Both schools organized seminars or workshops to teach staff online instruction techniques.

Note (See Table 2) that both schools used synchronous, asynchronous, video-on-demand instruction modes, however, the platforms and live tools are different. The Japanese University A used Moodle and Microsoft Office 365 as platforms, while the Chinese Senior School B used the WeChat group and the QQ group. Live instruction tools such as Zoom, Microsoft Teams, WebEx used by the Japanese University A were all US-made software, none was local from Japan. However, the Tencent Meeting ("Tengxun Huiyi" in Chinese,) WeChat and QQ used by the Chinese Senior High School B were all made-in-China tools.

Additional difference is that online resources available for Chinese high school students during the pandemic are huge. In Application Platform of Basic Education developed by Anhui Provincial Education Department, learning recourses range from video lessons for almost every unit, every chapter, every section of every subject, to numerous tests and drills. While, in Japan, Japanese MOOC has only 340 courses available [8]. "NHK for schools" [9] does have videos or audio lessons for every unit on every senior high subject, however, these recourse materials are only for the history records broadcasted by NHK, - Japan Broadcasting Corporation - in its educational channel in the past.

At the Japanese University A, teachers gave online lectures either synchronously or asynchronously and they required students to submit homework online after the lesson.

Table 2. Online instruction instruments

	Online Instruction Modes	Platforms	Live Tools	Resources
Japanese University A	Synchronous online instruction Asynchronous online instruction Lesson Videos on Demand	Moodle Microsoft Office 365	Zoom Microsoft Teams WebEx	
Chinese Senior High School B	Synchronous online instruction Asynchronous online instruction Lesson Videos on Demand	WeChat group QQ group	Tencent Meeting WeChat QQ	Anhui Application Platform of Basic Education Resources

Teachers may receive questions by email or via the platform, but were not responsible for watching and supervising students' extracurricular learning. While at the Chinese Senior High School B, teachers, especially, class headteachers had much higher "interference" with students' learning after the class. Some class headteachers even gave "morning-calls" in WeChat group every day, asking students to get up to "read aloud" English and Chinese. They also required students' parents to upload photos or videos to "prove" that their children were indeed learning at home.

The following is a typical beginning of a day for class headteachers, Mr. Xu and Mr. Cheng in their class WeChat group:

6:41 Class Headteacher Mr. Xu: @Zhu's mother, @Song's mother...... "Good morning!"
6:56 Class Headteacher Mr. Xu: @Ding's Mother, @Wang's mother, @Wang's mother..."Good morning!"
7:13 Class Headteacher Mr. Xu: "What happened to No. 23 student?"
7:18 Class Headteacher Mr. Cheng: @Wang's parent @ Zhou' mother @ Wang's mother. "Well done! God help those who help themselves!"
7:17: Wang's mother: "Thank you, Mr. Cheng."
7:21 Class Headteacher Mr. Cheng: @All. "Today's learning atmosphere is good! By 7:00 am, 30 students had been studying. Thank the parents for cooperation!"

Meanwhile, one after another in the WeChat groups, students' parents were uploading learning "proofs" - photos or videos taken when their sons or daughters were studying at home.

The second author of this paper, a Chinese teacher, kept diaries about his online instruction experiences during the school closure.

"February 22. I called Student Wu at 8:00 in the morning. It was his grandmother who picked up the phone saying he was still sleeping. Finally, Student Wu himself started to answer the phone. I asked him: "why were you absent from last two online lessons?" He replied, "I don't have a smart phone". I added, "then can you please spend at least 30 min a day on self-studying Chinese?" Wu replied "OK" ... Wu's class headteacher Tang told me later that Student Wu used to have a smartphone but was "confiscated" by his father because Wu was playing games on smartphone every day".

In Japan, neither high school teachers nor university professors can have such privacy "intrusion" to students' life. At the Japanese University A, some students claimed that they hated to show face during a live lesson. Some other students said synchronous class had them feel pressure. The university then compromised to these complaints in the end: students can attend online classes without turning on their web camera; one department of the university finally decided to adopt asynchronous mode to deliver all courses during the whole semester.

3.3 Students Online Learning Behaviors

Wang, Iwata & Douglas [10] explored Japanese students online learning habits and styles. When given a mandatory e-learning task, Japanese university students usually intensively study right before the deadline. This style did not change when the students self-isolated during the Covid-19 Pandemic.

In Table 3, the assignment allowed submission from June 16 to 18:00, June 22, 2020 in a mandatory English course taught by the first author at the Japanese University A. The submission time recorded by Moodle shows that nobody turned in homework on June 16. The earliest submission was June 18, two days after the submission was enabled. Of all 23 students, 17 submitted in the last three days and 9 submitted within the 10 h before the deadline.

Table 3. Students rushed to submit homework right before deadline (n = 23)

State	Started on	Completed	Time taken
Finished	2020/6/18 12:13	2020/6/18 12:44	31 mins 12 secs
Finished	2020/6/18 12:13	2020/6/18 13:02	48 mins 48 secs
Finished	2020/6/18 23:29	2020/6/19 0:10	41 mins 38 secs
Finished	2020/6/19 8:40	2020/6/19 9:29	48 mins 19 secs
Finished	2020/6/19 9:46	2020/6/19 10:29	43 mins 3 secs
Finished	2020/6/19 16:39	2020/6/19 17:29	49 mins 50 secs
Finished	2020/6/20 13:15	2020/6/20 13:57	42 mins 12 secs
Finished	2020/6/20 20:03	2020/6/20 21:18	1 hour 15 mins
Finished	2020/6/20 23:25	2020/6/21 0:14	49 mins 28 secs
Finished	2020/6/21 9:55	2020/6/21 10:32	36 mins 23 secs
Finished	2020/6/21 14:45	2020/6/21 15:38	52 mins 15 secs
Finished	2020/6/21 14:47	2020/6/21 16:29	1 hour 41 mins
Finished	2020/6/21 17:27	2020/6/21 18:31	1 hour 4 mins
Finished	2020/6/21 21:41	2020/6/21 22:21	40 mins 15 secs
Finished	2020/6/22 8:53	2020/6/22 10:12	1 hour 19 mins
Finished	2020/6/22 10:44	2020/6/22 11:15	30 mins 59 secs
Finished	2020/6/22 12:01	2020/6/22 12:43	42 mins 3 secs
Finished	2020/6/22 12:29	2020/6/22 13:20	50 mins 51 secs
Finished	2020/6/22 13:04	2020/6/22 13:28	24 mins 11 secs
Finished	2020/6/22 14:06	2020/6/22 15:06	59 mins 51 secs
Finished	2020/6/22 14:14	2020/6/22 14:51	37 mins 25 secs
Finished	2020/6/22 16:22	2020/6/22 17:06	43 mins 57 secs
Finished	2020/6/22 17:51	2020/6/22 17:59	8 mins 6 secs

We have seen the same trend at the Chinese Senior High School B. Photos of completed homework would storm into the WeChat Group right before the deadline.

Cultures impact on educational paradigms and peoples' anticipations toward education, hence, eventually influence online learning behaviors [11]. Although both are eastern Asian countries, cultural differences exist in online learning behaviors. Japanese students were quiet, sometimes silent online, while Chinese students were comparatively active; Japanese students usually need very specific instructions for online exam coverage, while sometimes Chinese teachers' instructions for exams were "purposefully" ambiguous.

3.4 Involvement of Students Family in Online Learning

The Covid-19 Pandemic created an urgent need of transition to online learning at most levels of education. As students as well as most parents were asked to stay within their homes, involving student family to remote learning seemed to be appropriate and necessary. At the Japanese University A, the Covid-19 Countermeasure Headquarter sent 3 letters to students' families informing the parents of actions that the university was taking and asked for their cooperation. With no face-to-face contact with their peers, teachers and university staff, many students asked for help from their parents when they had trouble at school.

As mentioned in previous sections, in Japan, any social media group created by a teacher with dozens of parents who are not familiar with each other in it seems to be impossible. The first author based in Japan for more than twenty years but has never seen any such social media groups. When the school needs to commutate with student parents, then telephone calls or emails are the preferred options.

However, in Chinese culture, it is acceptable and understandable that a class teacher creates a chat group for school-family communication. Parents do not mind to a certain extent sacrificing some of their privacy because they believe that only by joining the group can they receive timely information and such information is important for his/her child. They also realize that only through such a social media group families and families, families and the school can be connected. Consequently, through such a group that Chinese parents are much more aware of the status of their child's academic performance, class attendance…etc. in the school.

4 Findings and Discussion

Was urgent transition to complete online learning in the first half year of 2020 successful? Was the outcome of online inferior to face-to-face learning?

Data from two schools proved that online learning was in general as effective as face-to-face mode. The Test of English for International Communication (TOEIC for short) used as the final exam for an English online course at the Japanese University A reached the highest average score in the university history. The Chinese Senior School B also harvested good results in a unified examination in March and the entrance examination to college (Gaokao) in June, 2020. These facts proved that if managed properly, online learning can achieve similar outcomes compared to face-to-face education.

Experiences of online instructions during the Covid-19 Pandemic have changed the teachers' thinking toward online education. Before the Covid-19, of 22 faculty members in the department which the first author belongs to, only 3 teachers had experiences of using learning manage systems like Moodle. None had experiences of synchronous online instructions. However, half a year later, everybody in the faulty had courses residing in the university Moodle. One teacher spoke at a faculty development meeting: "I did not like Moodle before I used it. But now I found it has so many functions and it is very helpful in my teaching".

At the Chinese Senior School B, good changes also took place. At the beginning of the transition, teachers in the school were pressed to teach online, but afterwards most enjoyed this way of virtually interacting with students. Teachers agreed that online learning is not simply a remedial measure for the 2020 pandemic risk, but a very important part of school education. They consider online learning could be a norm during a special period of time and can largely replicate face-to-face learning at a time when needed.

As for school decision making, it is hard to judge in which way decisions are conveyed faster, in which way decisions were enforced more effectively. It might be just a matter of culture. Japanese university may rely more on decisions made by collective system, like "headquarter", while Chinese may prefer a strong leadership by leading individuals.

The number of web entries reflected frequencies of decision making. The Chinese Senior High School B had higher frequencies announcing its decisions on responding to online learning transition and Covid-19 prevention measures than the Japanese University A. This may suggest the Chinese culture of "concentrate on accomplishing major tasks".

As for communication tools, Chinese tend to use social media tools to convey urgent and demanding information, but Japanese students and their parents regard social media as a private tool and are not happy with its use for learning purposes. Instead of social medias, email is the most used communication tool at the Japanese University A. Indeed, email provides respondents time to think, permits excuses to "escape" and to pretend to "miss" the contact. By nature, email is less demanding and less oppressive than instant messages. However, as email is sent to individuals so that discussions are not easily activated. Therefore, email communication may lead to a delayed response.

Morning calls to individual students, uploading photos of students and students' homework to a class social media group would be most unlikely to happen in Japan. Chinese students have different perceptions from their Japanese peers concerning online privacy [12]. Uploading photos to WeChat group, or directly criticizing or parsing students in the group may sound very abrupt and personal to people in other cultures, but are naturally accepted by most Chinese students and their parents. Chinese students and their parents tend to think that teachers ought to discipline students in a strict way for the sake of the students' good.

Online disclosure sometimes has nothing to do with consciousness toward privacy, it may be merely a matter of culture.

The findings of students' submission rush near the deadline reminds us that just-before-the-deadline instructions may be very effective and meanwhile can increase submission ratio.

Another finding is that in China, especially at schools below university level, families get deeply involved in the school's everyday education. "Family-school collaboration" is a common-sense matter in China and is encouraged by the government. Parents report what the child does at home and class headteachers give feedback about students' behavior in school. Obviously, without the family's involvement, without "clock-in" to WeChat groups, the Senior High School B would have been unlikely to have a good academic outcome after the urgent transition to online learning in 2020.

5 Conclusion and Implications

In this paper, the authors reviewed transition to complete online learning due to outbreak of the Covid-19 Pandemic at two educational settings: a university in Japan and a senior high school in China. As these are two different types of educational contexts, only cultural factors were investigated for the purpose of identifying how culture impacted online learning transition, including policy makings, teachers' online instructions and students' online learning. Parents' role was also discussed.

The authors have no intention to judge which culture better influences online instructions and learning. We aim to remind online learning decision makers, online instructors and online learning system designers of how when starting an online program, one must consider culture elements: e.g. which online learning action is permitted or even encouraged by the culture, which online strategies may invite misunderstandings or uncomfortable feelings. For examples, in a Japanese educational setting, email should be used as the major communication tool as it is considered to be safe and less privacy intrusion. While, in China, a social media tool like WeChat would be most effective for a school to reach its students. More family involvement should be encouraged in Japan. While in China, a school needs to be cautious not to shift its own designated responsibilities and obligations to student families. As for online learning recourses, Japanese schools, especially schools below university level seem to need urgent investment.

The Covid-19 Pandemic will end some day and schools will return to their original face-to-face mode. However, the possible arrival of another pandemic, a serious natural disaster, a human-made crisis, etc. may impose an urgent transition from in-person to online teaching again. Furthermore, the transformation to technology-driven education is taking place with and will continue after the Covid-19 Pandemic. Thus, the findings of this research should be helpful for those online educators as a reference.

References

1. NHK. https://www3.nhk.or.jp/news/special/coronavirus/school-guideline/#mokuji2. Accessed 08 Mar 2021
2. Research Note powered by LINE. https://research-platform.line.me/archives/35015909.html#2. Accessed 11 Mar 2021
3. Trust, T., Whalen, J.: Should teachers be trained in emergency remote teaching, lessons learned from the COVID-19 pandemic. J. Technol. Teach. Educ. **28**(2), 189–199 (2020)
4. Borup, J., et al.: Supporting students during COVID-19: developing and leveraging academic communities of engagement in a time of crisis. J. Technol. Teach. Educ. **28**(2), 161–169 (2020)
5. Cirillo, M., et al.: An innovative early field experience for preservice secondary teachers: early results from shifting to an online model. J. Technol. Teach. Educ. **28**(2), 353–363 (2020)

6. Gerring, J.: Case Study Research – Principles and Practices, 2nd edn. Cambridge University Press, Cambridge (2007)
7. Baxter, P., Jack, S.: Qualitative case study methodology: study design and implementation for novice researchers. Qual. Rep. **13**(4), 544–559 (2008)
8. Japanese MOOC. https://www.jmooc.jp/institutions/. Accessed 13 Mar 2021
9. NHK. https://www.nhk.or.jp/school/ouchi/. Accessed 12 Mar 2021
10. Wang, S., Iwata, J., Jarrell, D.: Exploring Japanese students' e-learning habits. Jaltcall J. **14**(1), 211–223 (2018)
11. Jiang, M.: A study on chinese and foreign youth's online learning behavior. Life Opin. People **56**(5), 140–142 (2015)
12. Yang, F., Wang, S.: Students' perception toward personal information and privacy disclosure in e-learning. Turk. Online J. Educ. Technol. **13**(1), 207–216 (2014)

Implication on Perceived Usefulness of Open Educational Resources After a Rapid Switch to Online Learning Mode

Simon K. S. Cheung(✉)

The Open University of Hong Kong, Good Shepherd Street, Homantin, Kowloon, Hong Kong
kscheung@ouhk.edu.hk

Abstract. Evolved as open courseware, open online courses and tutorials, open access e-books and open source learning tools, open educational resources or OER are generally perceived as useful resources by university students. Over the last year, many higher education institutions have rapidly switched their usual classroom-based learning to online learning in order to accommodate the social distancing requirements arising from the outbreak of COVID-19. This paper investigates the implication on the students' perceived usefulness of OER after the switch to online learning. Based on two identical surveys conducted in a university in Hong Kong before and after the change, it is revealed that the students' perceived usefulness was generally increased, where the increase in perceived usefulness was more significant on open online complete courses, online tutorials, and open access e-books than other types of OER. It is also revealed that the students have become more aware of the shortcomings of OER, especially on accuracy and comprehensiveness. OER, especially open online courses, tutorials, and open access textbooks, are perceived to be useful for students to accommodate a rapid shift to online learning mode.

Keywords: Open educational resources · Open courseware · Online courses · Open access e-books · Learning tools · Online learning · Learning effectiveness

1 Introduction

Began in 2000's with an aim to make learning more accessible and equitable, open educational resources (OER) have evolved not only as an open source of learning resources but also as an agent to help transform teaching and learning [1–3]. According to the Organization for Economic Cooperation and Development, OER are formally defined as the digitized materials offered freely and openly for teachers and students to use and re-use for teaching, learning and research. They include learning content, software tools to develop, use and distribute content, and implementation resources such as open licenses [4]. Another definition given by the United Nations Educational, Scientific and Cultural Organization refers OER as teaching, learning and research materials in any medium, digital or otherwise, that reside in the public domain or have been released

R. Li et al. (Eds.): ICBL 2021, LNCS 12830, pp. 298–308, 2021.
https://doi.org/10.1007/978-3-030-80504-3_25

under an open license that permits no-cost access, use, adaptation and redistribution by others with no or limited restrictions [5].

Todays, OER are well available not only for higher education but also for K-12 [6, 7]. However, in many places such as Hong Kong, there are some specific curriculum requirements in primary and secondary education. Many OER may not be able to cater for these requirements, and therefore, adaptation of OER is required in order for them to be used in primary and secondary schools. Without adaptation, many primary and secondary school students may not find OER useful for learning, especially for self-learning. On the other hand, the majority of OER contents are targeted for higher education. As a result, OER are more popular in higher education than in primary and secondary education. The context of this paper is also placed on the usefulness of OER as perceived by university students.

OER for higher education can be generally categorized as open courseware and course materials, open online courses and tutorials, open e-books and e-journals, and open-source learning tools [8]. Open courseware are the course materials which are well organized and structured for a course of study, such as MIT open courseware or OCW [9] and OpenLearn [10]. Open online courses are online courses that are openly delivered through the Internet, including massive open online courses or MOOC, such as EdX [11] and Coursera [12]. Open e-books are by nature e-books, including both textbooks and reference books, that are openly accessible online or offline, such as OpenStar CNX [13] and Open Textbook Library [14]. Open-source learning tools cover online dictionaries, open software and tools that support learning, such as Wikipedia [15] and Google for Education [16].

For several years, the author has been actively investigating university students' perception on the usefulness of OER for learning purposes [17–19]. Starting from the academic year 2016–17, at the end of the first semester of each academic year, an online survey was conducted to the students in the Open University of Hong Kong. A number of general characteristics on the students' perception on how useful of OER for learning purposes were identified. First, the students often use OER for learning purposes. Second, more students consider OER useful for supplementing course textbooks, and doing assignments and projects than for preparing tests and examinations. Third, more students consider open courseware, open e-books and online dictionaries useful than other categories of OER. Fourth, the accuracy and comprehensiveness of OER contents are still the students' concerns.

Last year, owing to the outbreak of COVID-19, many higher education institutions have rapidly switched their typical classroom-based learning to online learning in order to accommodate social distancing requirements. The Open University of Hong Kong is not an exception. While the same online survey on the students' perceived usefulness of OER was conducted in 2020/21, the results are found different from those in the previous years. This paper reports the results of two identical online surveys conducted to the full-time students in the Open University of Hong Kong, one in 2019/20 (where the typical classroom-based learning is adopted) and the other in 2020/21 (where online learning is fully adopted). Based on the survey results, the implication on students' perceived usefulness of OER after a rapid switch to online learning would be discussed.

The rest of this paper is organized as follows. Section 2 describes the design of the above-mentioned survey. Section 3 presents the survey results, and highlights the changes between 2019/20 and 2020/21. Section 4 then discusses the key findings and implication so derived. Section 5 concludes this paper.

2 Survey on the Perceived Usefulness of OER

This section describes the design of an online survey on the perceived usefulness of OER conducted to the full-time students in the Open University of Hong Kong at the end of the first semester of 2019/20 and 2020/21. The Open University of Hong Kong offers full-time and distance-learning programmes in various disciplines, including arts, social sciences, business administration, education, nursing and health studies, science and technology [20]. Currently, there are about 10,800 full-time students and about 8,700 distance-learning students.

The online survey was separately delivered to the full-time students and distance-learning students of the Open University of Hong Kong through e-mail. As the scope of study is confined to full-time students, the survey results from full-time students were reported and analyzed in this paper. The survey contains questions, structured in three sections, each asking if the students agree on the usefulness of OER. In the typical Likert five-point scale, there are five choices, namely, strongly agree, agree, neutral, disagree, and strongly disagree.

In the first section, the students were asked if they agree that OER are generally useful for: (a) supplementing course textbooks and materials, (b) acquiring more knowledge as learning reference, (c) getting resources for doing assignments and projects, and (d) getting resources for preparing tests and examination.

In the second section, the students were asked if they agree on the usefulness of OER by four categories, namely, open courseware and course materials, open online courses, tutorials and forums, open e-books and e-journals, and open-source learning tools. Correspondingly, there are four subsections.

The first subsection focus on open courseware and course materials, asking if the students agree on the usefulness of: (a) openly shared complete sets of course materials, (b) openly shared lecture notes and class notes, (c) openly shared video clips of lectures and classes, and (d) other supplementary online learning materials.

The second subsection focus on open online courses, tutorials and forums, asking if the students agree on the usefulness of: (a) open online courses, (b) open online tutorials on specific topics, (c) small-scale mobile learning courses and applications, and (d) open online interactive help desks, and forums.

The third subsection focus on open e-books and e-journals, asking if the students agree on the usefulness of: (a) open access e-books which are self-contained text-books, (b) open access e-books which are self-contained reference books, (c) open access journals, magazines and periodicals, and (d) open access reports and other documentation.

The fourth subsection focus on open-source learning tools, asking if the students agree on the usefulness of: (a) open online dictionaries and encyclopedia, (b) online anti-plagiarism checker and grammar checker, (c) online learning software, such as mind-map and slide-builder, and (d) online learning platform for self and collaborative learning.

In the third section, the students were asked if they agree on the following shortcomings and concerns: (a) OER contents not being accurate, (b) OER contents not being up-to-date, (c) OER contents not being comprehensive, and (d) OER contents not being well organized.

3 Survey Results and Observation

This section reports the results of the two identical online surveys on the perceived usefulness of OER conducted to the full-time students in the Open University of Hong Kong, one in 2019/20 and the other in 2020/21.

For the survey conducted in 2019/20, an online questionnaire was delivered to the full-time students during 5 to 27 December 2019, and a total of 489 valid responses were received. For the other survey conducted in 2020/21, the same questionnaire was delivered to the full-time students during 28 January to 10 February 2021, and a total of 624 valid responses were received.

As mentioned in Sect. 2, students were asked with questions on their perceived usefulness of OER. For each question, there are five choices, namely, "strongly agree", "agree", "neutral", "disagree", and "strongly disagree". In this study, a weight is assigned to each choice, where 2 for "strongly agree", 1 for "agree", 0 for "neutral", -1 for "disagree", and -2 for "strongly disagree". The result of each question is expressed as a weighted sum, $(p_{sa} \times 2) + (p_a \times 1) + (p_n \times 0) + (p_d \times -1) + (p_{sd} \times -2)$, where p_{sa}, p_a, p_n, p_d and p_{sd} are the percentages of valid responses to the question, choosing "strongly agree", "agree", "neutral", "disagree" and "strongly disagree", respectively.

For example, given a question asking the students if OER are useful for getting more resources for doing assignments and project, there are 40% of the valid response choosing "strongly agree", 36% choosing "agree", 17% choosing "neutral", 5% choosing "disagree", and 2% choosing "strongly disagree". The result of this question is expressed as a weighted sum $(40\% \times 2) + (36\% \times 1) + (17\% \times 0) + (5\% \times -1) + (2\% \times -2) = 1.07$.

3.1 Usefulness of OER for Learning Purposes

Students were asked if they agree that OER are generally useful for different learning purposes, as reported in Table 1.

As shown in Table 1, for both surveys (2019/20 and 2020/21), OER were generally perceived to be more useful for supplementing course textbooks and materials, getting resources for doing assignments and projects, than for acquiring more knowledge as learning reference and getting resources for preparing tests and examinations. The perceived usefulness in 2020/21 is higher than that in 2019/20 for different learning purposes, but for supplementing course textbooks and materials, there is only a slight increase in the perceived usefulness.

Table 1. General usefulness of OER for different learning purposes.

Learning purposes	2019/20 (489 responses)	2020/21 (624 responses)	Difference
Supplementing course textbooks and materials	1.06	1.08	0.02
Acquiring more knowledge as learning reference	0.83	1.00	0.17
Getting resources for doing assignments and projects	0.97	1.07	0.10
Getting resources for preparing tests and examination	0.66	0.82	0.16

3.2 Usefulness of Different Categories of OER for Learning Purposes

Students were asked if they agree on the usefulness of each of the four categories of OER, namely, open courseware and course materials, open online courses, tutorials and forums, open e-books, e-journals and documentations, and open-source learning software and tools.

Table 2 reports the perceived usefulness of open courseware and course materials. For both surveys (2019/20 and 2020/21), openly shared complete sets of course materials, lecture notes and class notes are perceived to be more useful than openly shared video clips of lectures and classes and other supplementary course materials. The perceived usefulness in 2020/21 is generally higher than that in 2019/20, for all types of open courseware and course materials.

Table 2. Usefulness of different types of open courseware and course materials.

Types of open courseware and course materials	2019/20 (489 responses)	2020/21 (624 responses)	Difference
Openly shared complete sets of course materials	1.01	1.13	0.12
Openly shared lecture notes and class notes	0.99	1.13	0.14
Openly shared video clips of lectures and classes	0.95	1.09	0.14
Other supplementary online learning materials	0.86	1.05	0.19

Table 3 reports the perceived usefulness of open online courses, tutorials and forums. The survey in 2019/20 showed that the perceived usefulness of these open online self-contained courses, online tutorials, small-scale mobile learning courses and applications, online help desks and forums was not significant. The perceived usefulness on open online self-contained courses and online tutorials was higher than the others. The survey in 2020/21 also displayed similar characteristics, but the perceived usefulness was generally increased, and the increase was more on the open online self-contained courses and online tutorials than the small-scale mobile learning courses and applications, and help desks and forums.

Table 3. Usefulness of different types of open online courses, tutorials and forums.

Types of open online courses, tutorials and forum	2019/20 (489 responses)	2020/21 (624 responses)	Difference
Open online courses and self-contained courses	0.66	0.98	0.32
Open online tutorials on specific topics	0.56	0.85	0.29
Small-scale mobile learning courses and applications	0.27	0.35	0.08
Open online interactive help desks, and forums	0.23	0.39	0.16

Table 4 reports the perceived usefulness of open access e-books, e-journals and other documentations. The survey in 2019/20 showed that these open access e-books, e-journals and other documentations were generally perceived as useful, but the results were not very significant. However, for the survey in 2020/21, the perceived usefulness was generally increased. There was significant increase on the perceived usefulness of open access e-books which include both self-contained textbooks and reference books.

Table 4. Usefulness of different types of open access books, journals and other documentations.

Types of open access books, journals & other documentations	2019/20 (489 responses)	2020/21 (624 responses)	Difference
Open access e-books (self-contained textbooks)	0.79	1.11	0.32
Open access e-books (self-contained reference books)	0.75	1.04	0.29
Open access journals, magazines and periodicals	0.58	0.74	0.16
Open access reports and other documentations	0.78	0.93	0.15

Table 5 reports the perceived usefulness of open source learning software, tools and platforms. For both surveys (2019/20 and 2020/21), open online dictionaries and encyclopedia, and anti-plagiarism checker and grammar checker were perceived to be more useful than online learning software, and online learning platform for self and collaborative learning. For the survey in 2019/20, the perceived usefulness of open online dictionaries and encyclopedia was slightly higher than that of anti-plagiarism checker and grammar checker. This was reversed in 2020/21. Difference from other categories of OER, there was no significant change on the perceived usefulness between 2019/20 and 2020/21.

Table 5. Usefulness of different types of open source learning software, tools and platforms.

Types of open source learning software and tools	2019/20 (489 responses)	2020/21 (624 responses)	Difference
Open online dictionaries and encyclopedia	1.00	0.93	−0.07
Online anti-plagiarism checker and grammar checker	0.97	1.07	0.10
Online learning software (mind-map, slide-builder, etc.)	0.84	0.86	0.02
Online learning platform for self and collaborative learning	0.72	0.82	0.10

3.3 Concerns About the Shortcomings of OER

While OER are openly accessible by the general public, open contribution and sharing of OER contents are allowed. Like many open online resources in the Internet, OER also have shortcomings such as inaccurate, irrelevant and incomplete contents. The accuracy, readability, completeness, comprehensiveness and relevancy of the OER contents are the students' concerns [21, 22]. Some OER providers have established self-regulatory guidelines or measures for assuring quality of the contents before publishing in the Internet. These are usually found in open access textbook platforms, where quality assurance is essentially required [23–25].

Table 6 reports the students' concerns about the shortcomings of OER (such as on the accuracy, updatedness, comprehensiveness and organization of the contents) for learning purposes. For both surveys (2019/20 and 2020/21), the students' concerns were rather neutral (neither agree nor disagree). Students have more concerns about the accuracy and comprehensiveness than the updatedness and organization of the contents. Their concerns became more significant in 2020/21.

Table 6. Shortcoming and concerns about OER for learning purposes.

Shortcoming and concerns about OER	2019/20 (489 responses)	2020/21 (624 responses)	Difference
Some of the contents may not be accurate	0.30	0.48	0.18
Some of the contents may not be up-to-date	0.01	0.20	0.19
Some of the contents may not be comprehensive	0.29	0.39	0.10
Some of the contents may not be well organized	0.17	0.19	0.02

4 Key Findings and Implication

In both surveys (2019/20 and 2020/21), a number of general characteristics on the students' perceived usefulness of OER are identified, as follows.

- OER were generally perceived to be more useful for supplementing course textbooks and materials, getting resources for doing assignments and projects.
- Openly shared course materials, lecture notes and class notes were perceived to be more useful than other supplementary learning materials.
- Open online self-contained courses and online tutorials on specific topics were perceived to be more useful than small-scale mobile learning courses, and online help desks and forums.
- Open access e-books which are self-contained textbooks and reference books were perceived to be more useful than e-journals and other documentations.
- Open online dictionaries, encyclopedia, anti-plagiarism checker and grammar checker were perceived to be more useful than open source learning software, tools and platforms.
- Students' concerns on the shortcomings of OER were more on the accuracy and comprehensiveness than the updatedness and organization of the contents.

In comparing the results of the survey in 2020/21 with that in 2019/20, there are a number of changes which somewhat denote the implications on students' perception of OER arising from a rapid shift from the usual classroom.

- There was a general increase in the perceived usefulness of OER for different learning purposes, except for supplementing course textbooks and materials.
- There was a general increase in the perceived usefulness of different types of open courseware and course materials.
- There was a more substantial general increase in the perceived usefulness of open online courses, tutorials and forums, and the increase was more on the open online self-contained courses and online tutorials.
- There was also a more substantial general increase in the perceived usefulness of open access books, journals and documentations, especially on open access self-contained textbooks and reference books.
- Different from the other categories of OER, for open source learning software, tools and platforms, there was no significant change (increase or decrease) in the perceived usefulness.
- While there was a general increase in the perceived usefulness of different types of OER, the perceived usefulness was more significant on open online complete courses, open online tutorials on specific topics and open access e-books than other types of OER.

Teacher-student interactions and student-student interactions in the online learning mode are different from that in the classroom-based learning mode. After switching to online learning, students may seek further support in the learning process. As implied by the general increase in the perceived usefulness of OER for different learning purposes, the students consider that they need more learning resources to reinforce their understanding of the learnt concepts in order to accomplish assignments and projects, and prepare for tests and examinations.

Face-to-face instructions in the classroom-based learning mode are different from that in the online learning mode. In many higher education institutions, lectures and tutorials used in the classroom were delivered online via video-conferencing tools, on the same duration and without any change on the contents. After switching to online learning, the substantial general increases in the perceived usefulness of open online courses and tutorials, and open access textbooks and reference books imply that more instructions and materials are required. Learning effectiveness is inevitably affected by just a switch on delivery mode of lectures and tutorials without any changes on the contents and duration. To some extent, OER, especially open online courses, tutorial, open access textbooks and reference books, are perceived to be useful for students to accommodate a rapid shift to online learning mode.

5 Discussion and Conclusion

Free and openly available via the Internet, OER have been widely used by students at all levels, especially in higher education. For many years, university students have used to use OER for different learning purposes. These resources are typically used to supplement course textbooks and materials, do assignments and projects, and prepare for tests and examinations. As reported in the literature, university students generally found OER useful, despite to different extents. According to the recent studies, some specific forms or types of OER, such as openly shared course materials, lecture notes and open access textbooks, were perceived to be more useful than some others, such as small-scale mobile learning courses, video-clips and online interactive help desks and forums [17–19].

Last year, since the outbreak of COVID-19, almost all countries and regions have imposed different social distancing measures. In order to accommodate these social distancing requirements, many higher education institutions had to switch their usual classroom-based learning to online learning in a short span of time. This posed an unprecedented challenge for the institutions to ensure the continuity of teaching and learning while maintaining teaching quality and learning effectiveness after switching to online learning. Even though maintaining the same amount of contact hours and the same teaching and learning materials in online mode, this online learning experience is completely different from the traditional classroom-based learning experience. The students' learning process, learning styles and habits are inevitably changed. Their usage of OER as well as their perception of the usefulness of OER should also be changed. This paper studied the implication on the students' perceived usefulness of OER after a rapid switch to online learning.

In this paper, we reported two identical surveys recently conducted to the students in the Open University of Hong Kong. One was conducted in 2019/20 where the usual classroom learning was adopted, whilst the other in 2020/21 where online learning was adopted. In both surveys, a number of general characteristics on the students' perceived usefulness of OER are identified. These characteristics are consistent with a number of previous study [17–19]. Comparing the results of the survey in 2020/21 to that in 2019/20, the students' perceived usefulness was generally increased, where the increase was more significant on open online complete courses, open online tutorials on specific topics, and open access e-books than other types of OER. On the other hand, the students have become more concerned about the shortcomings of OER, especially on the accuracy and comprehensiveness of the contents. It is also concluded that OER are perceived to be useful for students to accommodate a rapid shift to online learning mode.

All these findings provide a useful reference that helps both researchers and practitioners better understand the implication on the students' perceived usefulness after a rapid switch to online learning.

References

1. Tuomi, I.: Open educational resources and the transformation of education. Eur. J. Educ. **48**(1), 58–78 (2013)
2. Miao, F., Mishra, S., McGreal, R., (eds.) Open Educational Resources: Policy, Costs and Transformation. UNESCO and Commonwealth of Learning (2016)
3. Hewlett Foundation, The Rich Global Landscape: An Overview of the Development of Open Educational Resources from 2002 to 2019, William and Flora Hewlett Foundation (2021). https://hewlett.org/wp-content/uploads/2019/05/The-rich-global-landscape-of-OER.pdf
4. OECD, Giving Knowledge for Free: The Emergence of Open Education Resources, Centre for Educational Research and Innovation, Organization for Economic Cooperation and Development (2007)
5. Website of UNESCO Open Educational Resources, United Nations Educational, Scientific and Cultural Organization. https://en.unesco.org/themes/ict-education/oer
6. Blomgren, C.: OER awareness and use: the affinity between higher education and K-12. Int. Rev. Res. Open Distrib. Learn. **19**(2), 55–70 (2018)
7. Ostashewski, N., Henderson, S.: Creating OER materials: perspectives of global instructors. In: Proceedings of E-Learn: World Conference on E-Learning in Corporate, Government, Healthcare, and Higher Education, pp. 644–648 (2017)
8. Cheung, Simon K.S., Li, K.C., Yuen, K.S.: An overview of open education resources for higher education. In: Lam, J., Li, K.C., Cheung, Simon K.S., Wang, F.L. (eds.) ICT 2013. CCIS, vol. 407, pp. 26–34. Springer, Heidelberg (2013). https://doi.org/10.1007/978-3-642-45272-7_3
9. Website of OpenCourseWare, Massachusetts Institute of Technology (2021). http://ocw.mit.edu
10. Website of OpenLearn, The Open University (2021). http://www.open.edu/openlearn
11. Website of EdX, EdX Inc. (2021). http://www.edx.org
12. Website of Coursera, Coursera Inc. (2021). http://www.coursera.org
13. Website of OpenStar CNX, OpenStar, Rice University (2021). http://www.cnx.org
14. Website of Open Textbook Library, Open Education Network, University of Minnesota (2021). https://open.umn.edu/opentextbooks
15. Website of Wikipedia, Wikimedia Foundation (2021). http://www.wikipedia.org
16. Website of Google for Education, Google Inc. (2021). https://edu.google.com
17. Cheung, S.K.S.: Distance-learning students' perception on the usefulness of open educational resources. In: Cheung, S.K.S., Kwok, L.-F., Ma, W.W.K., Lee, L.-K., Yang, H. (eds.) ICBL 2017. LNCS, vol. 10309, pp. 389–399. Springer, Cham (2017). https://doi.org/10.1007/978-3-319-59360-9_34
18. Cheung, S.K.S.: Perceived usefulness of open educational resources between full-time and distance-learning students. In: Cheung, S.K.S., Kwok, L.-F., Kubota, K., Lee, L.-K., Tokito, J. (eds.) ICBL 2018. LNCS, vol. 10949, pp. 357–367. Springer, Cham (2018). https://doi.org/10.1007/978-3-319-94505-7_29

19. Cheung, S.K.S.: A study on the university students' use of open educational resources for learning purposes. In: Cheung, S.K.S., Jiao, J., Lee, L.-K., Zhang, X., Li, K.C., Zhan, Z. (eds.) ICTE 2019. CCIS, vol. 1048, pp. 146–155. Springer, Singapore (2019). https://doi.org/10.1007/978-981-13-9895-7_13
20. Website of the Open University of Hong Kong, The Open University of Hong Kong (2021). http://www.ouhk.edu.hk
21. Tang, H.: A qualitative inquiry of K-12 teachers' experience with open educational practices: perceived benefits and barriers of implementing open educational resources. Int. Rev. Res. Open Distrib. Learn. **21**(3), 212–229 (2020)
22. Murphy, J.: Open Educational Resources: Question of Quality, Library Guide, Victoria University (2021). https://libraryguides.vu.edu.au/OpenEducationResources
23. Cheung, K.S., et al.: Open textbooks: engaging education stakeholders to share learning resources. Int. J. Serv. Stand. **10**(4), 225–239 (2015)
24. Cheung, S.K.S.: A review of open access textbook platforms. In: Cheung, S.K.S., Li, R., Phusavat, K., Paoprasert, N., Kwok, L. (eds.) ICBL 2020. LNCS, vol. 12218, pp. 114–125. Springer, Cham (2020). https://doi.org/10.1007/978-3-030-51968-1_10
25. Belikov, O., McLure, M.: A qualitative analysis of open textbook reviews authored by postsecondary educators. Int. J. Open Educ. Resour. **3**(2), 77–114 (2020)

Online and Collaborative Learning

COVID-19's Effects on the Scope, Effectiveness, and Roles of Teachers in Online Learning Based on Social Network Analysis: A Case Study

Yigang Ding, Xinru Yang, and Yunxiang Zheng(✉)

School of Educational Information Technology, South China Normal University, Guangzhou 510631, China

Abstract. The COVID-19 outbreak in early 2020 brought online learning to the forefront of education. Scholars in China and abroad have conducted many studies on online learning during the pandemic, but only a few have performed quantitative comparative analysis on this topic during and before the outbreak. The current paper presents social network analysis of a course hosted on China's MOOC platform "icourse163". Specifically, this study aimed to uncover (1) variations in the scale of online learning amid COVID-19; (2) the characteristics of online learning interaction during COVID-19; and (3) teachers'/teaching assistants' authority over online learning before, during, and after COVID-19. Results revealed that the scale of online learning interaction increased greatly during the pandemic but was not effectively maintained once the outbreak was under control. Online learning interaction became more frequent during the pandemic and more effective thereafter. The roles of teachers/teaching assistants in online learning during the pandemic were not as noteworthy as expected.

Keywords: COVID-19 · Online learning · Social network analysis · Learning interaction

1 Introduction

The COVID-19 outbreak has necessitated distance learning for more than 850 million students worldwide, disrupting school schedules in many countries along with traditional learning methods around the globe. Most schools have turned to online lectures or courses as a way to restore education. To meet the requirements of national pandemic prevention while maintaining a semblance of normal teaching and learning, China's Ministry of Education announced in February 2020 that it would vigorously support information-based education and teaching. The department proposed upholding the philosophy of "classes suspended but learning continues" by using network platforms [1].

However, a rapid increase in the number of online learners has illuminated several problems with online learning. Anwar and Adnan argued that, although online learning has been shown to help protect students' and teachers' health during the COVID-19 pandemic, it is less effective than traditional classroom learning [2]. The sudden shift from

R. Li et al. (Eds.): ICBL 2021, LNCS 12830, pp. 311–325, 2021.
https://doi.org/10.1007/978-3-030-80504-3_26

face-to-face to online learning has created an entirely different educational experience for students. Essentially, online learning comes with an array of obstacles to be analyzed and solved.

Bennett contended that comparative analysis of learning can likely explain causal mechanisms in the learning process and uncover universally effective learning strategies [3]. Chen posited that social network analysis (SNA) offers an effective method to study online collaborative learning. However, scarce educational research has applied social network analysis in China [4]. It is therefore necessary to carry out in-depth analysis and comparative studies of online learning during COVID-19. In this study, we selected a course hosted on www.icourse163.org (a large MOOC platform in China) with many participants. Next, we gathered data from several teaching terms before, during, and after the COVID-19 outbreak and then analyzed online learners' interaction via social network analysis. The pandemic's impact on the scale of online learners' interaction, the characteristics of such interaction, and the roles and functions of teachers/teaching assistants were visualized in Gephi and then discussed. Our findings offer valuable guidance for the development of online education under similar circumstances in the future.

2 Literature Review and Research Questions

Because COVID-19 is highly contagious, most of the world's teachers and students are currently separated by space and time to promote safety. Wu noted that this unforeseen shift to online learning could act as a yardstick to assess educational institutions' flexibility [5]. Many scholars and practitioners in China and abroad have conducted extensive research on online learning since early 2020. For example, based on fundamental principles and teaching theories in online learning, Xie systematically analyzed online teaching cases, identified pertinent problems in online education during the pandemic, and presented key mitigation measures [6]. Mahmood described a series of teaching strategies suited to distance learning to facilitate online teaching during the COVID-19 outbreak [7]. Zhu et al. proposed an "all media learning" ecological environment as a solution [8]. Yu assessed the current status of online learning organizations amid the pandemic and devised an online learning organization model based on activity theory [9]. Dhawan conducted an analysis of relevant journal articles and reports to study the strengths, weaknesses, opportunities, and challenges of the online learning model during COVID-19 [10]. Wang studied online teaching behavior, teaching models, and teachers' acceptance during the pandemic via questionnaire surveys and interviews [11]. Korkmaz and Toraman also collected data through online questionnaires and later used descriptive statistics to analyze the problems educators encountered in online learning during the pandemic [12]. In a similar vein, Hu gathered questionnaire data and then conducted structural equation modeling in SPSS17.0 to examine the associations among learners' information literacy, online learning investment, and learning performance [13]. Rouadi obtained questionnaire data through random sampling and network surveys to evaluate COVID-19's influence on middle school students' learning abilities based on a two-item table and frequency and percentage table [14]. In a university context, Kong visualized and analyzed log data from Tsinghua University's teaching and course selection system from multiple perspectives and discovered that college students' enthusiasm for their studies and work declined during the pandemic [15]. Alawamleh performed quantitative research using semi-structured online surveys and random sampling; results showed that students preferred classroom courses over online modes given the various obstacles they faced when learning online [16]. Mishra integrated quantitative and qualitative methods to analyze data from various sources regarding teachers' and students' views on the network teaching model, ultimately recommending its implementation [17].

As mentioned, the COVID-19 outbreak has inspired researchers in China and elsewhere to explore the online learning landscape; however, many relevant studies have neglected online learning's unique features in the case of the pandemic. Scholars have also seldom compared online learning prior to and during this outbreak. Although it is plausible to assume that differences exist in online learning before and during COVID-19, quantitative analysis of these potential discrepancies is lacking. To bridge this knowledge gap, we adopted SNA to analyze comment data from an online course on China's icourse163 MOOC platform, focusing on the following three questions:

(1) Variations in the scale of online learning based on COVID-19;
(2) The characteristics of online learning interaction during COVID-19;
(3) Teachers'/teaching assistants' authority over online learning amid COVID-19 (i.e., before, during, and after the pandemic).

3 Methodology

3.1 Research Object

To exclude the impacts of unrelated variables such as teaching activities in different courses, several teaching terms for one course with multiple rounds of teaching were taken as a case for experimental comparison. We intended to choose a course with a relatively large number of enrollees and sufficient learning activities (especially online interaction) that was held over the past 2 years (2019–2020). Among hundreds of course options on the icourse163 platform, we randomly selected a course with more than 10,000 participants. As indicated in Table 1, the chosen course had hosted many online learners and had been running on the platform for at least six terms between March 2018 and November 2020, covering three distinct periods (i.e., before, during, and after the COVID-19 outbreak). The course hosted a stable number of participants in every term except the fifth. We compared the number of participants across these six terms with the number of new COVID-19 cases over the same period in Fig. 1. Unsurprisingly, the curves were strongly coincident; Term 5 of the study period began in February 2020, the start of the COVID-19 outbreak. China has since strongly advocated for the policy of "classes suspended but learning continues"; accordingly, course enrollment peaked during Term 5 and then returned to a stable level in Term 6 once the pandemic was controlled. Table 1 and Fig. 1 show that the COVID-19 outbreak led to an increase in the number of students enrolled in online learning, whereas pandemic recovery caused enthusiasm for online learning to wane.

Table 1. Course overview

Period	Term	Number of participants
Before the outbreak (before Dec. 2019)	Term 1	6506
	Term 2	6118
	Term 3	7341
	Term 4	7342
During the pandemic (Jan. 2020 to July 2020)	Term 5	13858
After the pandemic (after Aug. 2020)	Term 6	6133

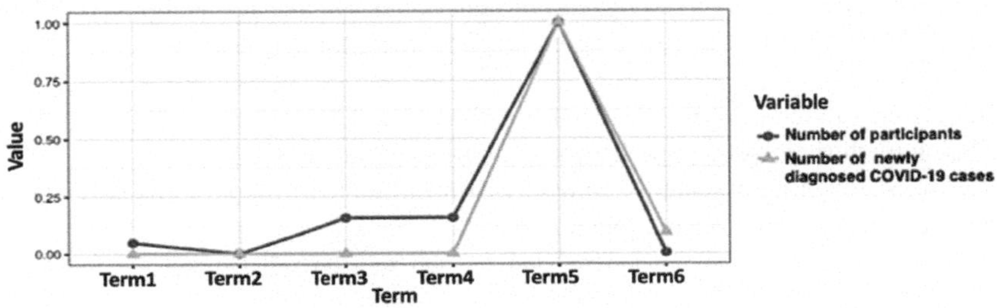

Fig. 1. Participants and newly diagnosed COVID-19 cases during the six study terms.

The teaching teams during Terms 4, 5, and 6 in this study were nearly identical, enabling us to consider the positions and roles of teachers/teaching assistants in the developed interaction network. The activity design of these three terms was also relatively consistent: teachers published posts to which students could respond or give a thumbs-up, contributing to the formation of a social network structure based on interaction. In addition, these three consecutive terms covered three phases of the pandemic, thereby allowing us to identify the pandemic's impact on online learning. Ultimately, we selected Terms 4, 5, and 6 as our research object for analysis and comparison. The resulting dataset contained a total of 1,132 themes and nearly 3,000 comments and thumbs-up interactions, representing participants' behavioral data.

3.2 Research Method

We transformed course participants' comments and thumbs-up into a network structure and used SNA for comparative research. M'Chirgui stated that network analysis is a powerful tool that provides a clearer understanding of networks through the use of sophisticated techniques to measure relationships between network actors [18]. Specifically, SNA can be used to describe underlying relationships between team members and to better understand their internal processes. Yang recommended integrating relevant SNA concepts to study performance [19].

To analyze Question 1, the number of degrees and nodes, diameter, and average path length within the network were taken as indicators to measure changes in network size. Social networks are generally depicted as graphs constructed of nodes and degrees. In network analysis, a graph's vertices are called "nodesit" and represent a network's spatial size. The number of nodes in the network indicates the sample size [20]. In Jan's study, the network size was determined by the number of nodes (i.e., students, lecturers, and tutors) [21]. In our research, network nodes represented the number of individual learners and teachers who participated in the course, with a higher number of nodes denoting more participants. The nodal degree indicates the connectivity of nodes, referring to an actor's number of direct connections with other actors in a network. The higher the nodal degree, the greater the node's influence on the rest of the network. The degree of interaction between two nodes can reflect the strength of a relationship [22]. According to He, the higher a student's degree of interaction, the more information and comments they receive [23]. In the current study, the degree of network interaction indicates whether each individual participated in an interaction; the higher this degree, the more frequent the interaction between individuals in the course. We also analyzed structural features at the network level, including diameter and average path length, which are commonly used to examine networks in SNA [24]. For each network, the average path length represents the average number of steps along the shortest paths for all possible network node pairs. Olivares found that when the average path length was smaller, the route from one node to another was shorter when graphed; that is, in an education context, all students tended to be more closely bonded [25]. The longest path between any two nodes in the network is called the network diameter. Diameter measures the maximum eccentricity of any node in a network, reflecting the maximum distance between any two nodes. A larger network diameter has been shown to enhance the spread of behavior [26]. Gašević transformed MOOC-related research citations into a network for analysis and discovered that a growing network diameter was more likely to spread innovative ideas about educational technology [27]. In other words, network diameter reflects a network's spatial size.

To address Question 2, we chose several indicators to represent network activity, such as the average degree, weighted average degree, and network density. The average degree is the average number of connections of each node in the network, thus indicating network density. Yihong Rong suggested that a network's average degree reflects network participants' extent of activity [28]. Hu found that, in the context of learning, higher average degrees indicate that more students are interacting directly with each other [29]. Average degree in our study refers to the average number of connections per learner: the larger the average degree, the more frequent the interaction between individuals in the network. The weighted average is computed by multiplying each degree by the corresponding weight and then taking the average (i.e., calculating the average degree based on the network's different weights). In work by Bydžovská, the weighted average degree was weighted by the strength of the relationship [30]. Maroulis calculated peer achievement by deriving the weighted value from friendship [31]. To obtain the weighted average degree in the current study, we calculated the specific number of interactions as the weight of the degree. The higher the weighted average degree, the more actively learners interacted with each other. The concept of network or graph density refers to the ratio of actual connections to potential connections. The more connections each group member enjoys with other members, the higher the network density. From an SNA perspective, network density is akin to group cohesion such that a denser network of strong relationships is deemed more cohesive [32]. Density captures the extent to which all network members are connected [33]. Wise used network density to represent whole-group cohesiveness to unearth the relationship between team cohesiveness and performance. In effect, network density can describe a network's overall features. Closeness centrality is another core concept in SNA; it measures how close a vertex is to all other vertices in the graph [34]. Opsahl stated that closeness centrality reveals how closely actors are connected to the entire social network [35]. Goran used closeness centrality as an indicator of social network–based engineering education and discovered that a student's closeness was significantly correlated with their grade [36].

Finally, for Question 3, we took the authority score as an indicator to measure teachers' roles in the network and to identify the teacher team's position in the network topology. Authority is the most basic definition of the hypertext-induced topic selection algorithm in network analysis [37, 41]. Taking the internet as an analogy, nodes with high authority are similar to high-quality web pages in a given field, such as Google and Baidu in the search engine domain. Young et al. transformed research topics in medical education into a network structure and analyzed trends in such research on the basis of the authority score; this score enabled the authors to extract major research topics based on mutual information between nodes in the network [38]. In our case, authority represents a key source of information that is frequently viewed, commented on, and given a thumbs-up by others in the interactive network. We used this indicator to quantify teachers' roles in the network: the higher the authority value, the more learners would view, give a thumbs-up to, or comment on a teacher's posts.

4 Results and Discussion

4.1 Scale of Interaction Expanded During COVID-19

By analyzing the number of nodes and degrees in our network, we found that the network's size was closely correlated with the development of the pandemic as illustrated in Fig. 2.

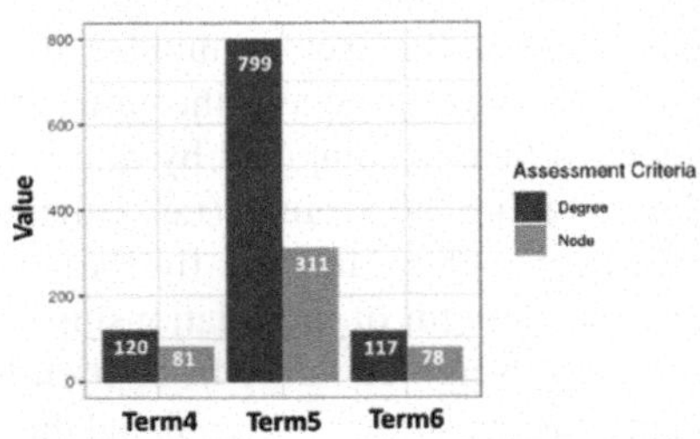

Fig. 2. Nodes and degrees of course network over Terms 4–6.

Figure 2 summarizes the number of nodes and degrees for the three chosen course terms. In Term 5, both the number of participants and the number of interactions were significantly higher than before COVID-19 and after the outbreak was under control. This phenomenon was tied to a rise in the number of participants in Term 5. By Term 6, learners' enthusiasm seemed to be waning along with their concerns about the pandemic. We also conducted a more detailed analysis of the interactive network, covering 8 months (i.e., Terms 5–6), displayed in Fig. 3.

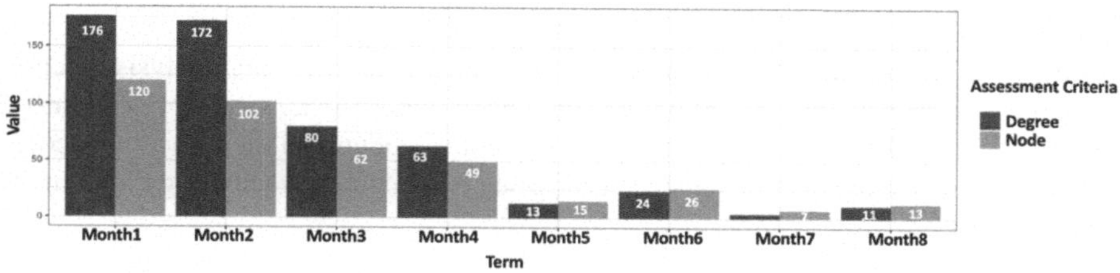

Fig. 3. Eight-month change in network nodes and degrees during COVID-19.

Early in the outbreak (Term 5), learners may have actively participated in comment-based interaction due to the pressure of online learning. Yet as the pandemic gradually came under control, especially during the 4 months of Term 6, the number of learners participating in course interaction declined substantially. As shown in Fig. 3, the number of nodes and degrees in the network decreased greatly compared with the outbreak period. The network scale thus expanded suddenly due to the impact of the pandemic, but this expansion was not effectively maintained. This "cooling" phenomenon was related to the control of the pandemic. In addition, the emergency policy introduced by China's Ministry of Education to promote online learning (and to call for more learners to participate in such learning) during the pandemic appeared to have gradually lost its effectiveness as students returned to school and work. We next analyzed the network diameter and average path length to evaluate the network's spatial size.

Table 2 shows that the social network size of courses after the pandemic was significantly larger than before the outbreak. The network diameter and average path length were largest early in the outbreak (Term 5). However, the increase in the average path length also had a negative effect; that is, interaction appeared limited to a small group with long-distance and multidirectional interaction seeming more difficult, consistent with our results in Sect. 4.2.

Figure 4 presents the monthly changes in network size during Terms 5 and 6 (i.e., after the outbreak) as a waterfall diagram. The size of the social network peaked in the first month, followed by a fluctuating and generally declining trend in the ensuing months. This trend may have arisen for several reasons. First, influenced by the number of participants and the development of the pandemic, learners' enthusiasm declined over time. Second, academic institutions have tended to concentrate on transferring educational content to digital platforms without focusing on effective strategies and methods. The lack of sufficient teaching activities to stimulate learning interaction has caused some

Table 2. Network diameter and average path length in Terms 4–6.

Term	Diameter	Average path length
Term 4	2	1.093
Term 5	11	4.231
Term 6	4	1.402

students to be left behind. Third, consistent with Zhong's research, our analysis of learners' home regions revealed that, although students in remote areas actively responded to China's call for online learning early in the pandemic, students in these locations could not continue to participate in distance learning due to inadequate technology later in the outbreak [39].

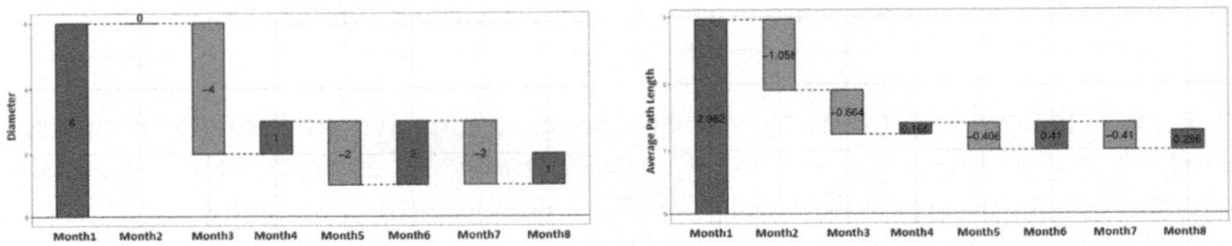

Fig. 4. Eight-month network diameter and average path length.

In the initial stage of the pandemic, the scale of the course's network and interaction frequency increased dramatically. However, after the pandemic was controlled, the scale of the course's interactive network did not remain consistently high in either its number of participants or its overall scale. We therefore recommend that organizers of online learning strive to capitalize on large-scale interactive networks amid the unique circumstances of the pandemic to enhance the impact of online learning.

4.2 Characteristics of Online Learning Interaction Amid the Pandemic

More Interaction During the Pandemic

As described above, at the start of the COVID-19 outbreak, the number of course participants increased along with the scale of the network and the intensity of interaction. Then, as the pandemic became better controlled, the scale of interaction returned to its pre-pandemic baseline. To further analyze the characteristics of this explosive growth in interaction during COVID-19, we examined our network's active properties based on its changing size. We referred to the network's average degree, weighted average degree, and other indicators to assess the number of learners participating in course discussions and their interaction.

Figure 5 depicts changes in the average degree and weighted average degree in Terms 4–6. Learner interaction was more frequent during the outbreak period, and overall activity after the pandemic returned to pre-pandemic levels. Figure 6 shows the network's evolution over 8 months of the study period based on network indicators. Network activity in the early stage of the outbreak was considerably higher than when the pandemic was under control. COVID-19 thus spurred an increase in students' online learning interaction, but this activity level was not maintained over time; as noted, learning interaction appeared to gradually drop to pre-pandemic levels.

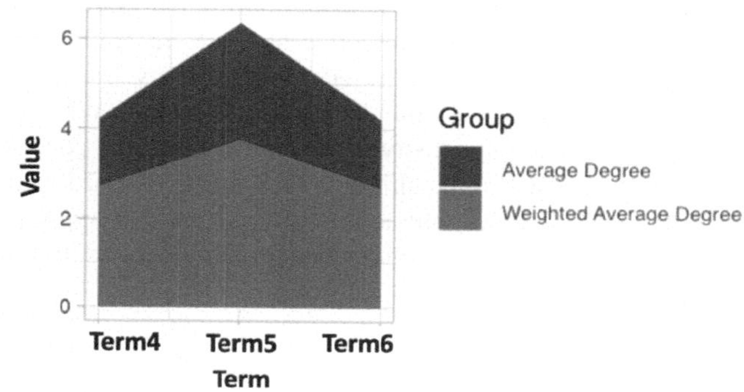

Fig. 5. Average degree and weighted average degree in Terms 4–6.

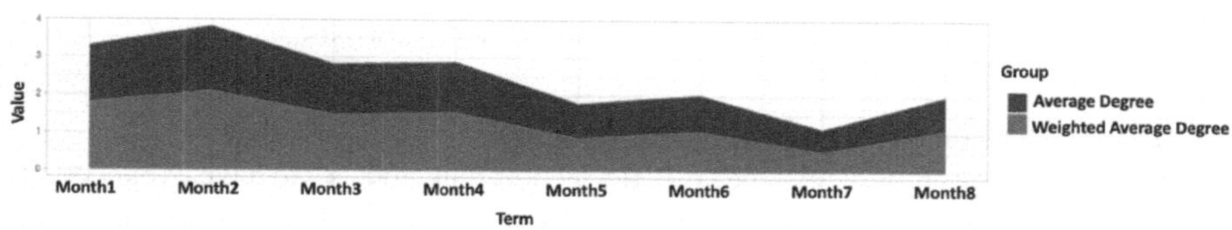

Fig. 6. Average degree and weighted average degree over 8 months.

We next took graph density as a macroscopic index to observe general learner interaction. Table 3 lists changes in graph density across the three focal course terms.

Table 3. Graph density of Terms 4–6.

Term	Graph density
Term 4	0.019
Term 5	0.008
Term 6	0.019

Different from the aforementioned trends in network size and average degree, graph density before and after the COVID-19 outbreak was relatively high. The number of learners increased during the outbreak, whereas the graph density declined (i.e., 0.008). Collectively, although the network scale of this course expanded along with the number of interactions during the pandemic, the connectivity of this large-scale network was loose. More specifically, information-based interaction was limited to a few groups and did not spread among all course participants. This finding aligns with Britt et al.'s conclusion that, because learners only engage in digital communication and seldom meet their peers in person during online learning, they lack a richer exchange of ideas [40].

Figure 7 compares graph density and network size (diameter and average path length) over 8 months of the pandemic. We previously observed that the size of the course's interactive network shrunk once the outbreak was under control, but graph density exhibited the opposite trend: as the scale of the interactive network decreased, the graph density increased once the pandemic was controlled. Graph density was lowest during the first month and then rose steadily over the 4 months of Term 5. When the pandemic was controlled, the network's graph density rose in waves and was consistently higher than earlier in the outbreak. Put simply, although the number of participants was large and interactions were frequent, these interactions did not seem to apply to all network participants; that is, online learning interaction appeared limited to certain small groups.

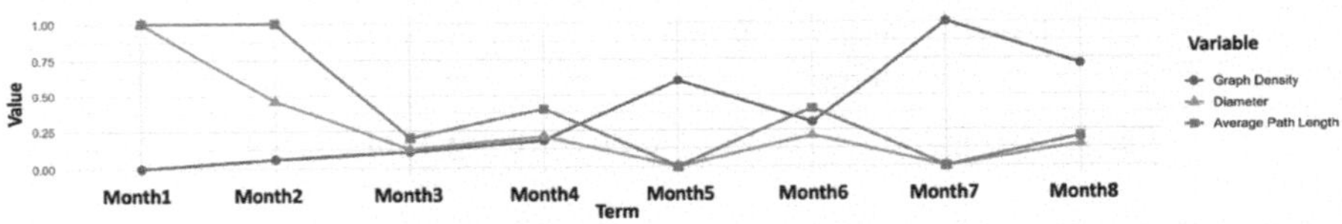

Fig. 7. Eight-month graph density and network size.

Interaction Was More Effective once the Pandemic Was Controlled

Based on the above comparisons, the COVID-19 outbreak appears to have expanded the course's scale and activity compared with pre- and post-pandemic levels. Superficially, the scope of the pandemic narrowed to pre-outbreak levels once the virus was controlled. Yet in fact, based on closeness centrality, this small network became more compact, interaction was more effective, and information was more likely to permeate the entire network once the outbreak was controlled. Figure 8 illustrates a comparison of the closeness centrality distribution by node for Terms 4–6.

Although the network's scale grew during the outbreak, no major differences emerged in the distribution of node centrality amid and before the pandemic. Once the virus was under control, even though the number of learners and network structure each shrank, the distribution of near centrality indicates that learners communicated more closely with others. Compared with Terms 4 and 5, learners in Term 6 had more frequent contact with other learners, and information could more easily reach the network edge. Furthermore, even though the number of participants and the network scale appeared to gradually return to a normal (pre-outbreak) state, interactive behavior in this course was in fact closer and more effective than in any prior term. Course developers should therefore aim to seize this trend in the subsequent design and implementation of online learning. Specifically, designers should emphasize interaction to enable learners to communicate more productively with others and immerse themselves in course content. At the same time,

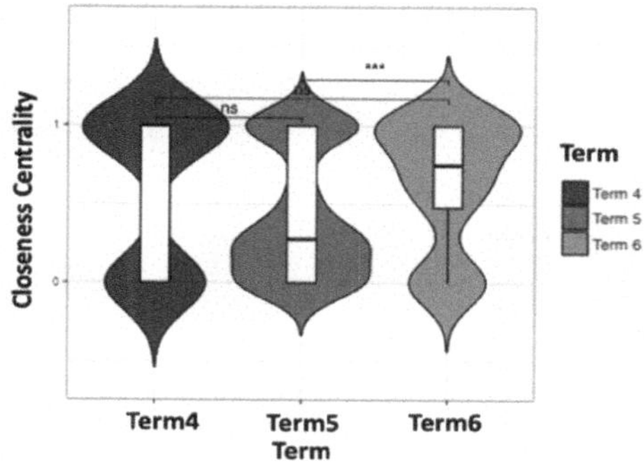

Fig. 8. Closeness centrality in Terms 4–6.

we noticed that information dissemination was largely limited to learners themselves. Therefore, in Sect. 4.3, we consider teachers' roles in information transmission.

4.3 Teachers' Roles During the Pandemic Were not as Noteworthy as Expected

We compared teachers' roles and positions in different periods based on the course network. In particular, we visualized the interactive network of Terms 4–6 as shown in Fig. 9. The larger network (the top right panel) displays the network topology of Term 5; the top left panel shows the topology of Term 4, and that of Term 6 appears in the bottom left panel. We used the community sniffing algorithm in Gephi to segment and cluster this network. In Fig. 9, different colors represent separate sub-community clusters: Terms 4 and 6 each contained six communities, whereas Term 5 included 14.

Fig. 9. Network topology of Terms 4–6.

Given the large increase in the number of sub-communities in Term 5 (due to a growing number of participants), we denoted the positions of the main course lecturer and two teaching assistants in Fig. 10. We also compared their authority within the interactive network as indicated in Table 4.

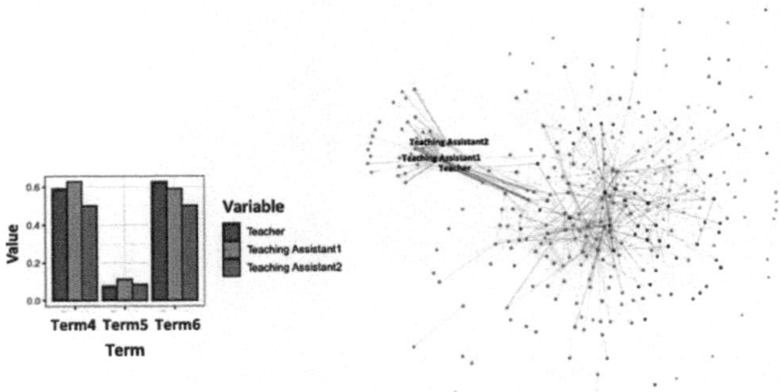

Fig. 10. Authority of teachers and teaching assistants and their position in Term 5.

Table 4. Teacher authority across Terms 4–6.

Role	Term 4	Term 5	Term 6
Teacher	0.591254	0.077376	0.628067
Teaching assistant 1	0.62818	0.112862	0.591324
Teaching assistant 2	0.502024	0.085354	0.503166

The three teachers' authority values were transformed into a histogram in the left part of Fig. 10. During the pandemic, given explosive growth in the number of learners, the teacher's and teaching assistants' authority declined. Therefore, these teachers' guiding roles should be further developed. The COVID-19 outbreak led to a sharp increase in the number of online learners. The network thus became larger, and teacher-provided information became more difficult for all learners to access. Additionally, Term 5 lacked a sufficient number of interactive themes and guiding strategies: the three teachers represented a small community cluster at the network's edge, and learners did not pay enough attention to them. As Zhong argued, a lack of adequate student–teacher interaction is a major problem in online learning. Learners in online settings generally communicate with their instructors via e-mail, comments, and similar modes, all of which require a certain response time. Teachers' low-authority interaction network can also likely influence the effectiveness of learning [39]. In light of these issues, we suggest that online courses include more teachers or teaching assistants to address unique circumstances (e.g., pandemics) that result in a sudden increase in the number of learners. Instructors should also plan effective online learning activities to enhance teachers' presence in online classrooms.

5 Conclusion

We took an online course on the MOOC platform "icourse163" as our data source. Using online learners' course comments as an entry point, we adopted the SNA method to conduct a comparative analysis of online learning before COVID-19, during the outbreak, and after the pandemic was controlled. Our results indicated that the size of online courses' interactive networks expanded but was not maintained during the pandemic. We also found that online learning interactions were more frequent amid the outbreak but more effective once the virus was controlled. As such, the pandemic appeared to positively influence interaction in online learning. We also discovered that teachers' roles were not as noteworthy as expected in terms of online learning interaction during the pandemic. These insufficiencies may be due to the delayed nature of long-distance interaction, teachers' limited number and finite energy, and a lack of sound interactive theme planning and guidance strategies. We thus proposed several targeted suggestions to enhance the effectiveness of online learning and enrich teachers' roles in this context.

In future work, we hope to integrate more courses during the pandemic into a dataset to perform a deeper quantitative comparison. Doing so will enable us to more fully uncover the impact and characteristics of online learning during the COVID-19 pandemic. It would also be intriguing to categorize different types of online courses. For example, might an engineering course held online be more rigid or less interactive than a literature course? This angle may be the focus of our next work. We are similarly interested in what students are discussing. In our study, we found that the content of learners' discussions during the pandemic differed from their pre-pandemic conversations. For example, the subjects of educational equity and flipped classrooms were pondered more frequently during the COVID-19 outbreak. Due to current space limitations, we will extend our content analysis in subsequent studies. Overall, the COVID-19 pandemic has reshaped online learning. To prepare to cope with similar crises, ongoing effort is needed to improve the effectiveness and adaptability of online learning, transform challenges into opportunities, and promote the sustainable development of this learning mode.

References

1. Shulian, Y., Lanjuan, L.: Research on online teaching practice in universities under the background of "non-stop teaching, non-stop learning" – taking Shanghai University of Finance and Economics as an example. Educ. Inf. China **482**(23), 63–67 (2020). (in Chinese)
2. Anwar, K., Adnan, M.: Online learning amid the covid-19 pandemic: students' perspectives. J. Pedagog. Res. **1**(2), 45–51 (2020)
3. Bennett, C.J., Howlett, M.: The lessons of learning: reconciling theories of policy learning and policy change. Policy Sci. **25**(3), 275–294 (1992)
4. Chen, X.: Research on online collaborative learning based on social network analysis. China Educ. Technol. **10**, 27–30 (2006). (in Chinese)
5. Wu, Z.: How a top Chinese university is responding to coronavirus. World Economic Forum: https://www.weforum.org/agenda/2020/03/coronavirus-china-the-challenges-ofonline-learning-for-universities/ (2020)
6. Youru, X., Yi, Q., Yulin, H., et al.: Characteristics, problems and innovation of online teaching method of "classes suspended but learning continues" during epidemic prevention and control. e-Educ. Res. (3), 20–28 (2020). (in Chinese)
7. Mahmood, S.: Instructional strategies for online teaching in covid pandemic. Hum. Behav. Emerg. Technol. **3**, 199–203 (2020)
8. Zhiting, Z., Hongchao, P.: Omnimedia learning ecology: a practical solution to the problem of schooling in the age of mass epidemic. China Educ. Technol. **3**, 1–6 (2020). (in Chinese)

9. Yu, S., Wang, H.: How to better organize online learning in extreme situations such as epidemics. China Educ. Technol. **400**(5), 12–20+39 (2020). (in Chinese)
10. Dhawan, S.: Online learning: a panacea in the time of covid-19 crisis. J. Educ. Technol. Syst. **49**, 1–18 (2020)
11. Jixin, W., Yitong, W., Min, Z.: The current situation, problems and reflection of online teaching for primary and secondary school teachers during a large-scale epidemic—based on the investigation and analysis of "Classes Suspended but Learning Continue" in Hubei province. China Educ. Technol. **400**(5), 21–27 (2020). (in Chinese)
12. Korkmaz, G., Toraman, Ç.: Are we ready for the post-COVID-19 educational practice? An investigation into what educators think as to online learning. Int. J. Technol. Educ. Sci. (IJTES) **4**(4), 293–309 (2020)
13. Xiaoyong, H., Huanyun, X., Zexuan, C.: The relationship between information literacy, online learning engagement and learning performance. China Educ. Technol. **3**, 77–84 (2020). (in Chinese)
14. Anouti, M., Rouadi, N.E.: The online learning experiment in the intermediate and secondary schools in Lebanon during the coronavirus (covid-19) crisis. Int. J. Adv. Res. Eng. Technol. **7**(7), 14466–14485 (2020)
15. Kong, X., Liu, N., Zhang, M., et al.: Analysis of online college teaching data before and after the COVID-19 epidemic. J. Tsinghua Univ. (Sci. Technol.) **61**(2), 19–31 (2021). (in Chinese)
16. Alawamleh, M., Al-Twait, L.M., Al-Saht, G.R.: The effect of online learning on communication between instructors and students during Covid-19 pandemic. Asian Educ. Dev. Stud. https://doi.org/10.1108/AEDS-06-2020-0131 (2020)
17. Mishra, L., Gupta, T., Shree, A.: Online teaching-learning in higher education during lockdown period of COVID-19 pandemic. Int. J. Educ. Res. Open **1**, 100012 (2020)
18. M'Chirgui, Z.: The economics of the smart card industry: towards cooperative strategies. Econ. Innov. New Technol. **14**(6), 455–477 (2005)
19. Yang, H.L., Tang, J.H.: Team structure and team performance in IS development: a social network perspective. Inf. Manag. **41**(3), 335–349 (2004)
20. Cela, K.L., Sicilia, M.Á., Sánchez, S.: Social network analysis in e-learning environments: a preliminary systematic review. Educ. Psychol. Rev. **27**(1), 219–246 (2015)
21. Jan, S.K., Vlachopoulos, P.: Social network analysis: a framework for identifying communities in higher education online learning. Technol. Knowl. Learn. **24**(4), 621–639 (2019)
22. Dawson, S., Bakharia, A., Heathcote, E.: SNAPP: realizing the affordances of real-time SNA within networked learning environments. In: Networked Learning (2010)
23. He, P.: Evaluating student's online discussion performance by using social network analysis. In: 2012 Ninth International Conference on Information Technology-New Generations, pp. 854–855. IEEE (2012)
24. Scott, J.: Social Network Analysis: A Handbook. Sage, London (2017)
25. Olivares, D., Adesope, O., Hundhausen, C., et al.: Using social network analysis to measure the effect of learning analytics in computing education. In: 2019 IEEE 19th International Conference on Advanced Learning Technologies (ICALT). IEEE (2019)
26. Centola, D.: The spread of behavior in an online social network experiment. Science **329**(5996), 1194–1197 (2010)
27. Gasevic, D.: Where is research on massive open online courses headed? Int. Rev. Res. Open Distrib. Learn. **15**(5), 134–176 (2014)
28. Rong, Y., Xu, E.: Strategies for the management of the government affairs microblogs in China based on the SNA of fifty government affairs microblogs in Beijing. In: 2017 International Conference on Service Systems and Service Management. https://doi.org/10.1109/icsssm.2017.7996282 (2017)
29. Hu, X., Chu, S.K.W.: A comparison on using social media in a professional experience course. In: International Conference on Social Media and Society (2013)

30. Bydžovská, H.: A comparative analysis of techniques for predicting student performance. In: International Educational Data Mining Society (2016)
31. Maroulis, S., Gomez, L.M.: Does "connectedness" matter? evidence from a social network analysis within a small-school reform. Teach. Coll. Rec. **110**(9), 1901–1929 (2008)
32. Wise, S.: Can a team have too much cohesion? The dark side to network density. Eur. Manag. J. **32**(5), 703–711 (2014)
33. Wasserman, S., Faust, K.: Social Network Analysis: Methods and Applications. Cambridge University Press, Cambridge (1994)
34. Okamoto, K., Chen, W., Li, X.-Y.: Ranking of closeness centrality for large-scale social networks. In: Preparata, F.P., Wu, X., Yin, J. (eds.) FAW 2008. LNCS, vol. 5059, pp. 186–195. Springer, Heidelberg (2008). https://doi.org/10.1007/978-3-540-69311-6_21
35. Opsahl, T., Agneessens, F., Skvoretz, J.: Node centrality in weighted networks: generalizing degree and shortest paths. Soc. Netw. **32**(3), 245–251 (2010)
36. Putnik, G., Costa, E., Alves, C., Castro, H., Varela, L., Shah, V.: Analysing the correlation between social network analysis measures and performance of students in social network-based engineering education. Int. J. Technol. Des. Educ. **26**(3), 413–437 (2015)
37. Kleinberg, J.: Authoritative sources in a hyperlinked environment. J. ACM **46**(5), 604–611 (1999)
38. Ji, Y.A.: Research topics and trends in medical education by social network analysis. BMC Med. Educ. **18**(1), 1–10 (2018)
39. Zhong, R.: The coronavirus exposes education's digital divide. The New York Times: https://www.nytimes.com/2020/03/17/technology/china-schools-coronavirus.html (2020)
40. Britt, R.: Online education: a survey of faculty and students. Radiol. Technol. **77**(3), 183–190 (2006)
41. Su, C., Pan, Y., Yuan, J.P., et al.: PageRank, HITS and impact factor for journal ranking. In: World Congress on Computer Science & Information Engineering. IEEE (2009)

Fading Scaffolds for Better Online Learning? A Comparative Analysis of Three Scaffolding Practices

Xu Han, Heng Luo(✉), Jiaxin Yang, and Siyi Jiang

Faculty of Artificial Intelligence in Education, Central China Normal University, Wuhan 430079, China
luoheng@mail.ccnu.edu.cn

Abstract. This study conducted a true experiment to investigate the effectiveness of three types of scaffolding practices (i.e., full scaffolding, fading scaffolding, and none scaffolding) on students' participating behaviors, learning outcomes, and overall experience during online discussion. A total of 107 participants from a graduate-level blended course were randomly assigned into three discussion groups that received three types of scaffolding. The comparative analysis results revealed that the effectiveness of fading scaffolding was inferior to that of full scaffolding, as the latter was associated with better online learning performance and experiences. The incorrect timing to remove scaffolds and misusage of scaffolding questions were two possible reasons behind the failure of fading scaffolding practice. Based on the research findings, four practical implications were drawn to guide the design and implementation of effective scaffolding for online learning contexts.

Keywords: Online scaffolding · Fading scaffolds · Participating behaviors · Learning outcomes · Learning experience · Online discussion

1 Introduction

Online learning has become an essential form of education for universities due to its convenience, flexibility, and cost-effectiveness [1, 2]. The current Covid-19 pandemic highlights the importance of online learning for sustaining education during disruptions. Despite its growing popularity, online learning is often criticized for its didactic, lecture-based nature [3], and many researchers called for more constructivist learning approaches in the online contexts, usually through the activity of online discussion [4, 5]. However, constructivist learning approaches place high demands on learners as their success is largely dependent upon learners' self-regulated and metacognitive skills [6]. As a result, it is particularly important for the instructor to provide adequate scaffolding in the online learning context to facilitate self-directed learning and guide the completion of constructivist learning activities.

Scaffolding is a pedagogical process that provides novice learners with guidance or assistance by instructors or experienced learners, in order to complete a task, solve

R. Li et al. (Eds.): ICBL 2021, LNCS 12830, pp. 326–337, 2021.
https://doi.org/10.1007/978-3-030-80504-3_27

a problem or achieve a goal [7]. Scaffolding can be used as an effective strategy to internalize thinking, develop higher-order thinking, promote students' knowledge construction and improve cognitive and metacognitive levels [8, 9]. The literature supports the effectiveness of scaffolding in brick-and-mortar learning environments as it can improve learners' learning performances, higher-order thinking skills, problem-solving strategies and self-regulatory behaviors [8, 10, 11].

One important yet often ignored feature of scaffolding is its fading nature. It is a process of gradual reduction of support: scaffolding is not constant but can be removed or withdrawn when students gain deeper understanding on teaching contents [12, 13]. While it is necessary to explore how and when to fade scaffoldings to support constructivist learning [14], empirical studies that compared fading scaffolding with constant scaffolding are scarce, and often produced contradictory findings. For instance, McNeill et al. found that learners with fading scaffolding gained greater learning experience and learning outcomes [15], whilst Bulu and Pedersen cautioned against varying scaffolding as it might lead to inconsistent learning effects [16]. Further, while Lee and Songer revealed the potential of constant scaffolding for promoting scientific explanation [17], Demetriadis et al. found that the invariance of prompt questions made students get bored and tired more easily [18]. Moreover, most studies on scaffolding were conducted in traditional learning contexts, little was known regarding its effectiveness and the optimal scaffolding strategies in the online learning settings.

To address this limitation in scaffolding literature, we conducted a true experiment to investigate the effectiveness of three types of scaffolding, full scaffolding, fading scaffolding, and none scaffolding, on students' participating behaviors, learning outcomes, and learning experience in a blended graduate level course. More specifically, we sought to answer the following research questions:

1. What are students' participating behaviors, learning outcomes, and learning experience in the blended course under three types of scaffolding?
2. Which type of scaffolding is most effective in improving students' participating behaviors, learning outcomes, and learning experience?

2 Methods

2.1 Participants

The participants of this study were 107 first-year graduate students (14 males and 93 females), from a research university in central China. The participants enrolled in a blended course named Instructional Design and Case Analysis which lasted 16 weeks. The course included two parts, offline class and online discussion. In offline class, the teacher taught the theories, methods, and procedures of instructional design. In online discussion, students applied what they have learned to analyze three real instruction design (ID) cases provided by the teacher. Before the online discussion, participants were randomly assigned into three groups. Group 1, 2, and 3 consisted of 36 students, 34 students, and 37 students, respectively. The three groups participated in three case discussion sessions and received different types of scaffolding during the process.

2.2 Procedure

The online case discussion was conducted on the Wolearn platform, a Moodle-based online learning platform. We provided three ID cases for learners to analyze ID problems and propose reasonable solutions in the discussion forum. Each case discussion session lasted for two weeks, the first week was for problem identification, and the second week was for problem solutions. After the two-week discussion, learners needed to complete a case study report to formulate their diagnosis of and solutions to the case problem.

At the end of the semester, all participants were asked to fill out an online discussion experience questionnaire to evaluate their online discussion experience in terms of cognitive presence, motivation, and overall experience. Participants rated each item on a 5-point Likert scale ranging from 1 ("strongly disagree") to 5 ("strongly agree").

2.3 Three Types of Scaffolding

In this study, we designed scaffolding questions to facilitate online discussion in which learners diagnosed and solved cases of ID collaboratively. The scaffolding questions were based on the problem-solving process and could be classified into two major categories: problem identification and problem solutions. The common guiding questions for each category were listed in Table 1. Based on the detail levels of scaffolding questions, scaffolding in this study was manipulated into three levels: detailed scaffolding, general scaffolding and no scaffolding.

Table 1. Common guiding questions for each category.

Major categories	Guiding questions (general scaffolding)
Problem identification	1. What are the main performance problems in this case? Why?
	2. What other key information is not mentioned in the case?
	3. What are the main factors causing this problem? Why?
Problem solutions	4. What solutions can be proposed to solve the problems in the case?
	5. What consequences may happen if the solution is implemented?
	6. What are the core logic and ideas of your proposed solution?
	7. Is there any evidence to support this solution you proposed?
	8. What are the advantages and disadvantages of your ID solution?
	9. Did you notice other solutions? How are they compared to yours?
	10. Is there anything that can be done differently?

Detailed scaffolding included those guiding questions as listed in Table 1, as well as various prompts associated with each guiding question. Taking the fourth guiding question "what solutions can be proposed to solve the problem in the case" as an example, it had three prompts to guide students proposing solutions from the perspectives of instructional strategies, resources, and process: (1) In terms of instructional strategies, what strategies are suitable for the staff training task in this case? (2) In terms of instructional resources, how to develop efficient and feasible teaching resources for teaching? (3) In terms of instructional process, how should training activities and processes be arranged? Contrarily, general scaffolding consisted of only the guiding questions, shown in Table 1, without prompts, and no scaffolding was absent of both guiding questions and prompts, simply asking students to freely discuss like "please discuss based on this case and propose some solutions to the problems".

Based on the three levels of scaffolding, we assigned three participant groups to three types of scaffolding correspondingly, named full scaffolding, fading scaffolding, and none scaffolding. As shown in Fig. 1, Group 1 received detailed scaffolding for all three case discussion sessions, indicating full scaffolding during the process. Group 2 received detailed scaffolding in the first case discussion session, general scaffolding in the second session, and no scaffolding in the last session, showing a trend of fading scaffolding. Group 3 received no scaffolding throughout, which was the group of none scaffolding. Additionally, in each case session, both Group 1 and 2 received the scaffoldings successively in four times (on Tuesday and Friday of every week), while Group 3 received only one reminder to participate in discussion at the very beginning.

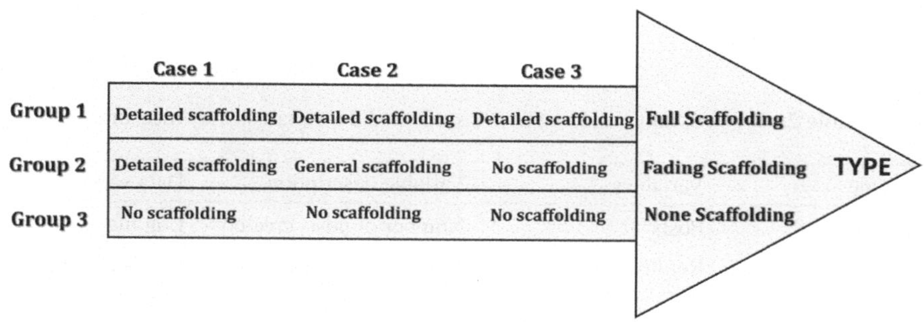

Fig. 1. The general sequence and the classification of scaffolding.

2.4 Data Collection and Analysis

We collected three types of data, students' participating behavioral data, learning outcomes and online discussion experience questionnaire. Table 2 shows all the variables, their definitions and the data sources in this study.

Participating behaviors reflected participants' engagement in online discussion, and were measured by the number of posts created, replied, and total words of posted content. The behavioral data were extracted from the logfile of the Moodle platform.

Learning outcomes were the evaluation on the learning effects, consisting of the quality of posts and quality of case study reports. Quality of post was measured by the average rating of post, which was the product of two types of ratings: relevance rating and cognitive level rating. Relevance rating refers to the degree of relevance of the posted content to the case problem. Cognitive level is based on the level of cognitive learning objectives proposed by Bloom, including recognition and understanding (high), analysis and application (medium), synthesis and evaluation (low). High, medium and low levels were assigned the cognitive ratings of 1–3 respectively. Quality of case study report was measured by the average rating of the completeness and reasonableness of the problem diagnosis and solution. We assigned the ratings of 1–3 respectively. Posts and reports were scored by two experts, with an acceptable inter-rater reliability (Spearman's Rho > 0.7). The average ratings of the two experts were used as the final scores.

Online discussion experience was evaluated by a questionnaire (Cronbach's Alpha = 0.863) comprising three constructs: cognitive presence, participation motivation and overall experience. Cognitive presence consisted of seven items adapted from the instrument developed by Arbaugh et al. [19]. Participation motivation included six items adapted from the instrument developed by Lin et al. [20]. Overall experience comprised only two items, which asked participants to rate their overall satisfaction towards online learning experience and performance.

In this study, the independent variable was the type of scaffolding, and the dependent variables were participants' online participating behaviors, learning outcomes and learning experience. To minimize the threat of diffusion, each group had its own independent discussion forum invisible to the other two groups. The statistical methods used in this study were mainly descriptive analysis and difference inferential statistics (e.g., non-parametric test).

Table 2. Types of data collected in this study and the variables they measured.

Data type	Variables	Variable description	Data source
Participating behaviors	Posts	Number of posts created	Log files
	Replies	Number of replying to others	Log files
	Total words	Number of words in all posts	Database
Learning outcomes	Quality of post	Average rating of all posts	Expert rating
	Quality of case study report	Average rating of case study reports	Expert rating
Online discussion experience	Online discussion experience	Average rating of all items in questionnaire	Questionnaire

3 Results

3.1 Participating Behaviors

The average number of posts generated by the participants were shown in Fig. 2(a). Group 1 outperformed Group 3 consistently in all three case discussion sessions, indicating the effectiveness of full scaffolding over no scaffolding. Interestingly, the posts generated by

Group 2 participants witnessed great fluctuation: they peaked in the second discussion session before a sharp decline in the last discussion session. Consequently, the posting behavior with fading scaffolding was similar to that with full scaffolding but ended weakly with the average number comparable to the no scaffolding group.

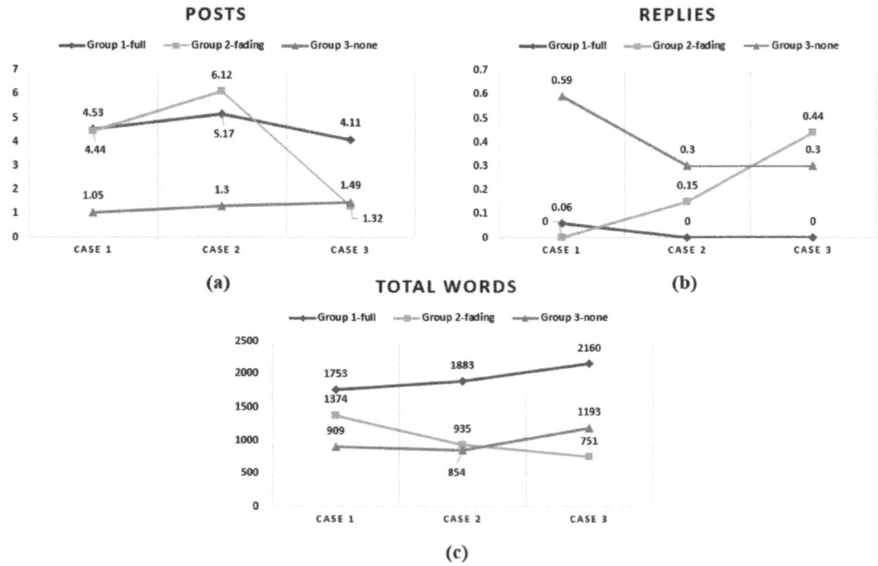

Fig. 2. The trends in students' participating behavior of three groups in online discussion based on three cases. (a): the average of posts created; (b): the average of replies; (c): the average of total words in all posts.

Figure 2(b) showed the trends of replies during the three discussion sessions. Compared to the behavior of posting, the behavior of replying was less frequent with the average number less than one for all three groups. The declining trends for Group 1 and 3 were similar featured by a sharp decline after the first discussion session, suggesting the same pattern of replying for students despite the presence of scaffolding. Fading scaffolding seemed to induce an opposite trend that was constantly upward, indicating that the gradual removal of scaffolding questions has promoted the peer interaction in the discussion forum featured by more replying behaviors among the participants.

The trends of total words of posted content were displayed in Fig. 2(c). Again, the participants with full and none scaffolding demonstrated similar upward trends while fading scaffolding seemed to produce the opposite pattern, with the length of posted content decreasing gradually from 1374 to 751, an approximate 45% decrease.

In addition to the descriptive statistics, we also examined the statistical significance of group difference, and the results were presented in Table 3. We calculated the mean differences of posts, replies and total words between every two groups in three discussion sessions, and used the statistical method of non-parametric test to compare the differences among the three groups. The significant results were most commonly found between

Group 1 and Group 3, indicating the substantially superior participating behaviors in students with full scaffolding. The fading scaffolding group started strong, producing comparable results with the full scaffolding group and outperforming those with no scaffolding in the beginning, but their participating behaviors decreased gradually, ended the weakest among the three groups.

Table 3. Results of difference inferential statistics of participating behavior.

	Case 1			Case 2			Case 3		
	Posts	Replies	Words	Posts	Replies	Words	Posts	Replies	Words
Group 1−2[a]	0.09	0.06	379	−0.95	−0.15	949**	2.79***	−0.44***	1410***
Group 1−3[b]	3.47***	−0.54***	844	3.87***	−0.3**	1030**	2.63***	−0.3**	967*
Group 2−3[c]	3.39***	−0.6***	465*	4.82***	−0.15	81	−0.16	0.14	−442*

Note: [a]Group 1 being the minuend and Group 2 being the subtrahend. [b]Group 1 being the minuend and Group 3 being the subtrahend. [c]Group 2 being the minuend and Group 3 being the subtrahend. ***$p < 0.001$, **$p < 0.01$, *$p < 0.05$

3.2 Learning Outcomes

The average scores of the posts submitted during the three case discussion sessions were presented in Fig. 3(a). Surprisingly, the quality of posts submitted by Group 3 students received the highest ratings in the first two discussion sessions before the final decline, suggesting the superiority of none scaffolding over full and fading scaffolding in earlier phases of online discussion. Although the ratings of the posts witnessed a gradual ascending trend in Group 2, its average rating scores were the lowest among the three groups consistently, indicating that fading scaffolding failed to promote the quality of online discussion. However, it is worth noticing that the average ratings were based on unequal number of posts submitted by partial participants from the three groups, therefore the validity of results were likely to suffer from threats such as selection and attrition. Our further analysis also revealed that Group 3 students tended to conduct holistic analysis and integrate different perspectives in one post, whilst students in Group 1 and 2 were in the habit of responding to the scaffolding questions and tended to answer one question in one post. The rating criteria favored the posts that were lengthy with integrated perspectives, which led to higher ratings scores for the posts in Group 3.

Compared to ratings of posts, ratings of case study reports might be a more proper measurement of learning outcomes as the submission of reports was mandatary as course assignment, and the participants completed the reports using the same template and under the same requirement. In contrast to the post rating results, the report rating results supported the strategy of full scaffolding with consistently higher ratings, and the difference increased over time. Fading and none scaffolding seemed to produce comparable results,

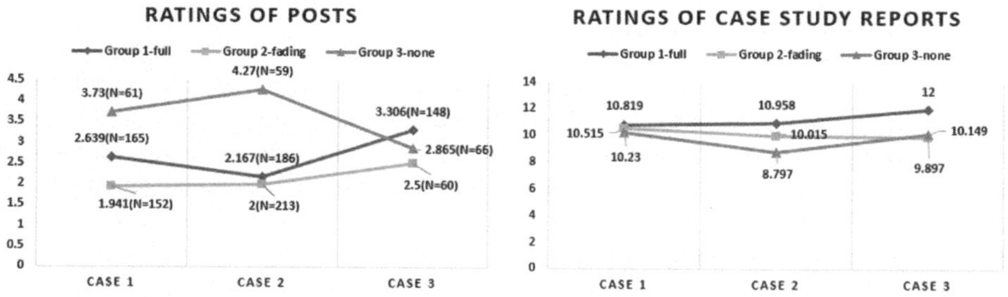

(a) (b)

Fig. 3. The trends in students' learning outcomes of three groups in online discussion based on three cases. (a): average ratings of all posts; (b): average ratings of case study reports; N stands for number of all posts in each group.

with the exception of Case 2 study report where the fading scaffolding was associated with significantly higher ratings.

We further examined the statistical significance of the rating difference among the three groups, and the results were listed in Table 4. In general, the learning outcomes of Group 1 were significantly greater than the other groups, as measured by the case study report ratings during the three case discussions, confirming the effectiveness of full scaffolding in promoting online learning outcomes. Fading scaffolding in Group 2 appeared to be increasingly ineffective compared to the other two groups, whose post ratings and case study report ratings ended up the lowest at the end of the study. A possible reason is that the fading of scaffolding happened too soon, bringing more issues rather than benefits to the online learning performance of Group 2 students.

Table 4. Results of difference inferential statistics of learning outcomes.

Learning outcomes	Group difference	Case 1	Case 2	Case 3
Post rating	Group 1–2[a]	0.698**	0.167*	0.806**
	Group 1–3[b]	−1.091**	−2.103***	0.441
	Group 2–3[c]	−1.789***	−2.27***	−0.365
Case study report rating	Group 1–2[a]	0.304	0.97*	2.103***
	Group 1–3[b]	0.589	2.188***	1.851***
	Group 2–3[c]	0.285	1.218*	−0.252

Note: [a]Group 1 being the minuend and Group 2 being the subtrahend. [b]Group 1 being the minuend and Group 3 being the subtrahend. [c]Group 2 being the minuend and Group 3 being the subtrahend. ***$p < 0.001$, **$p < 0.01$, *$p < 0.05$

3.3 Online Discussion Experience

The results of participants' online discussion experience questionnaires were indicated in the form of a bar chart in Fig. 4. We can find that Group 1 reported the highest ratings and Group 3 reported the lowest ratings in all three constructs of the questionnaire, which implied a positive correlation between online discussion experience and the level of scaffolding. Further analysis revealed that significant differences in online discussion experience were found between full scaffolding and none scaffolding in cognitive presence and overall experience, and between full scaffolding and fading scaffolding in overall experience. Nevertheless, there was no significant difference between the perceived experiences with fading scaffolding and none scaffolding.

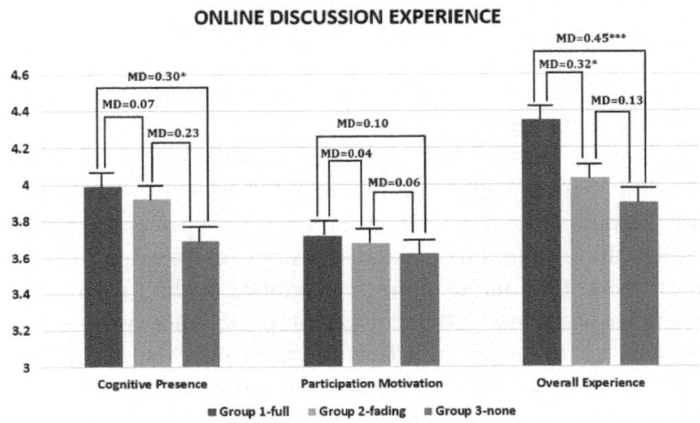

Fig. 4. Average ratings of online discussion experience of three groups in three constructs; MD stands for mean difference; ***p < 0.001, **p < 0.01, *p < 0.05.

4 Discussion and Conclusions

This study investigated the effectiveness of fading scaffolds on facilitating online discussion by comparing three different types of scaffolding practices. In general, the study results disapproved the practice of fading scaffolding during online discussion, as full scaffolding practice was associated with a greater number of posts, lengthier post content, higher assignment scores, and better evaluation ratings, which were indicators of superior learning behaviors, outcomes, and experience. Additionally, even students who received no scaffolding seemed to outperform those with fading scaffolds in terms of replying behavior and the quality of posts. As a result, it is fair to conclude that the effectiveness of fading scaffolds was largely unsatisfactory in this research context.

Two possible reasons were behind the failure of fading scaffolding practice in this study. First, the timeframe of fading was problematic. The fading of scaffolds started immediately after the first case discussion session, when most students were still familiarizing with the online discussion routine. The detailed scaffolds (i.e., guiding questions and prompt questions) that the students received in the previous session had little impact on their mental schema of problem solving. This speculation was supported by the upward trending patterns of Group 1 in both participating behaviors and learning outcomes, suggesting that students who received full scaffolding were getting used to it with improving learning performance. Second, the scaffolds were simplified as learning questions given by the teacher and the online discussion activity was reduced to answering questions in the discussion forum. Consequently, the removal of scaffolding questions has led to the inevitable decrease of online participation and cognitive engagement.

Moreover, this study has revealed two interesting findings. First, the behavior of replying was severely lacking in online discussion regardless of the scaffolding received. This finding is consistent with Zhang et al.'s argument that online discussion often suffers from insufficient reciprocity among the peers [21]. The reduction of scaffolds seemed to free students from the tendency of answering only the scaffolding questions and result in an increase of peer interactions. Second, even for the same scaffolding practice, its effects on online learning behavior and outcomes varied over time, susceptible to the confounding factors such as selection, attrition, maturation, task variance, and history. Caveats should be kept in mind when making conclusions regarding the efficacy of scaffolding practices.

Based on the study results, the following implication can be proposed: (1) For students who were new to online learning, we recommend using full scaffolding over a prolonged period for better participation and learning outcomes; (2) The absence of scaffolding allows for greater student agency and peer interactions and thus can be considered to enhance social constructivist learning; (3) The correct timing for the removal of scaffolding is important, and the instructor should make sure that the students were prepared both cognitively and emotionally; (4) The purpose of scaffolding should be explained to the students in the beginning to avoid being used as mere quiz questions.

Lastly, there are four limitations in the current study. First, the research study was conducted during a short time frame within one semester, students' preparedness for and familiarity with the scaffolding practices might affect their effectiveness. Second, the confounding factors that threaten the internal validity of the research findings cannot be ruled out in the natural context of a blended course. Third, there were over 30 students in each treatment group, which is not an ideal number for group discussion as many students might lurk during the discussion process. The lack of participation might confound with the impact of various types of scaffolding. According to Yang et al., small group size can increase student participation in online discussion [4]. Therefore, future research might divide each treatment group into sub-groups of 4–5, in order to promote active discussion and interaction. Lastly, the current study has drawn its research findings from the statistical results based on quantitative data, and lacked qualitative data for interpreting and sense making of the quantitative results. As a result, future researchers should consider conducting longitudinal studies with more rigid experimental design and a wider variety of empirical evidence.

Acknowledgement. This work was supported by the Basic Research Funding of Central China Normal University (CCNU20DC006) and the SEIT e-Learning Research Grant of Central China Normal University (CCNUSEIT202001).

References

1. Guo, F., Hong, X., Coates, H.: Accelerated transformation: designing global online higher education. High. Educ. Res. Dev. **39**(7), 1322–1326 (2020)
2. Rovai, A.P.: A constructivist approach to online college learning. Internet High. Educ. **7**, 79–93 (2004)
3. Luo, H., Koszalka, T.A., Arnone, M.P., Choi, I.: Applying case-based method in designing self-directed online instruction: a formative research study. Educ. Technol. Res. Dev. **66**(2), 515–544 (2018)
4. Yang, T., Luo, H., Sun, D.: Investigating the combined effects of group size and group composition in online discussion. Act. Learn. High. Educ. 1–14 (2020)
5. Wever, B.D., Keer, H.V., Schellens, T., Valcke, M.: Roles as a structuring tool in online discussion groups: the differential impact of different roles on social knowledge construction. Comput. Hum. Behav. **26**, 516–523 (2010)
6. Pisutova-Gerber, K., Malovicova, J.: Critical and higher order thinking in online threaded discussions in the Slovak context. Int. Rev. Res. Open Distance Learn. **10**(1), 1–15 (2009)
7. Lu, J., Lajoie, S.P., Wiseman, J.: Scaffolding problem-based learning with CSCL tools. Comput.-Support. Collab. Learn. **5**, 283–298 (2010)
8. Yelland, N., Masters, J.: Rethinking scaffolding in the information age. Comput. Educ. **48**, 362–382 (2007)
9. AK, S.: The role of technology-based scaffolding in problem-based online asynchronous discussion. Br. J. Educ. Technol. **47**(4), 680–693 (2016)
10. Simons, K.D., Klein, J.D.: The impact of scaffolding and student achievement levels in a problem-based learning environment. Instr. Sci. **35**, 41–72 (2007)
11. Devolder, A., van Braak, J., Tondeur, J.: Supporting self-regulated learning in computer-based learning environments: systematic review of effects of scaffolding in the domain of science education. J. Comput. Assist. Learn. **28**(6), 1–17 (2012)
12. Lajoie, S.P.: Extending the scaffolding metaphor. Instr. Sci. **33**, 541–557 (2005)
13. Pea, R.D.: The social and technology dimensions of scaffolding and related theoretical concepts for learning, education, and human activity. J. Learn. Sci. **13**(3), 423–451 (2004)
14. Tawfik, A.A., Law, V., Ge, X., Xing, W., Kim, K.: The effect of sustained vs. faded scaffolding on students' argumentation in ill-structured problem solving. Comput. Hum. Behav. **87**, 436–449 (2018)
15. McNeill, K.L., Lizotte, D.J., Krajcik, J.: Supporting students' construction of scientific explanations by fading scaffolds in instructional materials. J. Learn. Sci. **15**(2), 153–191 (2006)
16. Bulu, S.T., Pedersen, S.: Scaffolding middle school students' content knowledge and ill-structured problem solving in a problem-based hypermedia learning environment. Educ. Technol. Res. Dev. **58**, 507–529 (2010)
17. Lee, H.S., Songer, N.B.: Expanding an understanding of scaffolding theory using an inquiry-fostering science program. J. Learn. Sci. **15**(2), 153–191 (2004)
18. Demetriadis, S.N., Papadopoulos, P.M., Stamelos, I.G., Fischer, F.: The effect of scaffolding students' context-generating cognitive activity in technology-enhanced case-based learning. Comput. Educ. **51**, 939–954 (2008)
19. Arbaugh, J.B., et al.: Developing a community of inquiry instrument: test a measure of the community of inquiry framework using a multi-institutional sample. Internet High. Educ. **11**, 133–136 (2008)

20. Lin, L., Ginns, P., Wang, T., Zhang, P.: Using a pedagogical agent to deliver conversational style instruction: what benefits can you obtain? Comput. Educ. **143**, 1–11 (2020)
21. Zhang, J., Skryabin, M., Song, X.: Understanding the dynamics of MOOC discussion forums with simulation investigation for empirical network analysis (SIENA). Distance Educ. **37**(3), 270–286 (2016)

An Assessment Framework for Online Active Learning Performance

Caixia Liu[1,5], Di Zou[2(✉)], Wai Hong Chan[1], Haoran Xie[3], and Fu Lee Wang[4]

[1] Department of Mathematics and Information Technology, The Education University of Hong Kong, Tai Po, New Territories, Hong Kong, China
waihchan@eduhk.hk

[2] Department of English Language Education, The Education University of Hong Kong, Tai Po, New Territories, Hong Kong, China

[3] Department of Computing and Decision Sciences, Lingnan University, Tuen Mun, New Territories, Hong Kong, China

[4] School of Science and Technology, The Open University of Hong Kong, Ho Man Tin, Kowloon, Hong Kong, China
pwang@ouhk.edu.hk

[5] Institute of EduInfo Science and Engineering, Nanjing Normal University, Nanjing, China

Abstract. Under the influence of COVID-19, online learning has become the primary way for students to continue their education. At all stages of online learning, active learning is a useful strategy promoting optimal understanding. However, there is a lack of relevant research on how to evaluate students' active learning performance. This paper presents an online active learning assessment framework based on the learning pyramid and learning dimension theory. After the division of course modules according to the learning pyramid theory, the active learning assessment is performed from five dimensions: (1) positive attitudes and perceptions about learning; (2) acquiring and integrating knowledge; (3) extending and refining knowledge; (4) using knowledge meaningfully, and (5) productive habits of mind. By identifying patterns from each online course module's weblog data, instructors can assess students' active learning conveniently from the beginning to the end of the online course. This study helps instructors understand learners' learning situations and adopt corresponding strategies to adjust teaching activities to ensure high-quality teaching activities. Simultaneously, learners can also actively change their learning status according to active learning assessment to improve the learning effect.

Keywords: Active learning · Assessment framework · Learning pyramid · Learning dimensions

1 Introduction

Recently, the COVID-19 pandemics have swept through the world and affected many aspects of our life, from the decline of economics to re-adjustments of the academic

R. Li et al. (Eds.): ICBL 2021, LNCS 12830, pp. 338–350, 2021.
https://doi.org/10.1007/978-3-030-80504-3_28

calendar and teaching modes of educational institutions [1]. To prevent and control COVID-19, China's Ministry of Education has proposed postponing the school year's opening and conducting online education through online platforms [2]. The same thing is happening to Latin American countries, European countries, Australasia, and so on. Undoubtedly, this pandemic has utterly changed the education system [3], and online learning boomed in recent years, is having its moment in the sun.

Online learning requires learners to have a strong active learning ability for achieving good learning outcomes. Active learning covers activities where the learners are entitled to a high degree of autonomy and control over the course activity. The activities involve problem-solving and research, which can be individualized or cooperative [4]. In order to understand learners' active learning behaviors, online assessment is necessary. The assessment includes systematic and continuous evidence collection, analysis, and interpretation to estimate how well a learner's performance meets the course's standards and expectations [5]. According to the assessment and feedback, on the one hand, teachers can make appropriate suggestions or advice to help learners find out their drawbacks and weaknesses. On the other hand, learners also can make a personal scheme for themselves to continue their study and practice by evaluations of the assessment model.

A practical assessment framework plays a vital role in education within this perspective, and the big data and relevant mining techniques provide strong support for active online learning assessment. This paper aims to present a web-based assessment framework for assessing active learning performance. We first introduce teaching content design based on five learning dimensions and the learning pyramid. Then, we determine the variables that can describe a learner's performance from a weblog. After that, we assess active online learning from five learning dimensions using the deep learning technique and statistical method.

2 Related Work

Assessment is an essential part of online learning, and many researchers have analyzed and explored assessment models. The research can be divided into two classes: one is general assessments, and the other is specialized assessments.

The general assessment usually focuses on the assessment itself, such as types, efficacy, accuracy, and paradigm. For example, Reeves [6] discussed the major directions for integrating alternative assessment methods into an online learning environment. Graff [7] argued that there were some relationships between cognitive styles and online learning and assessment, and presented the correlations between each attitude component and the total attitude score in the online assessment results and displayed participants' assessment ratings. Mateo and Sangrà [8] analyzed limitations to the classic educational assessment model and presented an online learning assessment approach, where they shifted the paradigm in assessment, such as from written examinations to coursework, from tutor-led assessment to student-led assessment, and from implicit criteria to explicit criteria. Gaytan and McEwen [9] proposed online assessment strategies of using a descriptive research method to maintain instructional quality. Unmoderated peer assessment results usually lack credibility. To deal with this issue, Suen [10] investigated the peer assessment for MOOCs and analyzed methods for improving peer assessment results' accuracy. Guerrero-Roldán and Noguera [11] investigated the assessment of competency-based and student-centered learning in online learning and proposed an e-assessment mode based on competence and learning activities.

Specialized assessment pays attention to the assessments on online learning's particular aspects, such as learning outcomes, collaborative activity, discussions, assignments, and games. Swan et al. [12] gave rules for evaluating discussion in an educational computing course and argued that online courses' collaborative learning assessment was critical to its success. Vonderwell et al. [13] employed the case study method to examine the assessment in online asynchronous discussions. James et al. [14] presented a performance assessment framework by graphing direct and indirect outcomes of courses. They concluded that the online group's performance was substantially greater than or equal to that of the face-to-face group. Formanek et al. [15] conducted a massive online peer assessment using an analysis of an astronomy MOOC to assess the role of peer-graded assignments in such courses and how they contribute to student learning and motivation. [16] developed a game-based formative assessment tool for online learning courses to assess the affects of gaming modes on the effectiveness of knowledge acquisition and participants' perceptions. Ikejir et al. [17] evaluated students' learning effects of a history MOO from two perspectives: historical knowledge and historical thinking skills.

Students' active learning ability is one of the important factors for the success of online courses. Although many researchers had investigated the online learning assessment, limited studies examine active learning in online education and gave a framework for assessing active learning performance quantitatively. Therefore, our study aims to provide a framework to assess the active learning effects of online learning effectively.

3 Evaluation Framework of Active Online Learning Performance

Assessment is closely related to teaching and learning [18]. Thus, before making a learning assessment, teachers should first hierarchically design their teaching contents to meet students' learning needs. "Deep" learning occurs when learners have time to participate in increasingly high "level" investigations and content explanations, with each level bringing new insights and new learning [19]. From this perspective, we can evaluate the performance of students from various levels and dimensions. Teachers can find the student learning performance in different levels and dimensions, too, which helps them adjust their teaching arrangement and teaching design. At the same time, students can also identify weaknesses in their learning and take appropriate measures.

Marzano et al. [18] proposed a learning-dimension framework (Fig. 1(a)) for student performance assessment. D1 emphasized learning attitudes and perceptions. For D2, an important aspect of learning is acquiring new knowledge and combining it with what is already known. For D3, it is a critical learning ability for learners to expand and refine their knowledge. For D4, learners can use knowledge to solve practical problems or use knowledge meaningfully. D5 concerns the mind habits used by critical, creative, and self-regulated thinkers. According to the learning-dimension framework (LD) [18] and hierarchical teaching design, teachers first divided the teaching content into different layers (levels). For example, the lower level shows the basic concepts, knowledge, properties, and some simple, practical examples and the higher level contains deeper knowledge providing opportunities for students with better ability to study further.

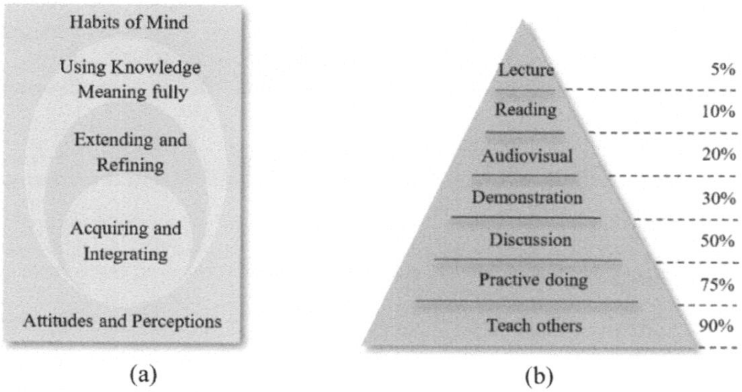

Fig. 1. The theoretical basis of the assessment framework. (a) Five learning dimensions; (b) Learning pyramid.

Learning pyramids (LP) [20] shown in Fig. 1(b) is widely publicized within-subject didactics, and it also enjoys an alarmingly high level of recognition [21]. According to Sousa [22], the average rates of material retention 24 h after instruction are 5%, 10%, 20%, 30%, 50%, 75%, 90% from lectures, reading, audio and visual media, demonstration, engaging in a group discussion, practice, and teaching someone, respectively. Even if there is disagreement about this percentage, there is little dispute about the effectiveness of teaching methods that require students to participate actively rather than absorb material passively [23]. According to the above theory, the layers of the learning pyramid can be divided into two groups: passive learning (the first four layers) and active learning (the last three layers) [24].

In the following, we discuss the method of active online learning assessment.

3.1 Preparation

Before assessing the online active learning, we design the course content and teaching modules according to the learning pyramid, determine the indicators used for performance assessment,

Course Content and Teaching Module Design. In our study, each knowledge module (e.g., J1, J2, J3) is divided into seven different forms according to the learning pyramid, see Fig. 2(a) for a reference. The first three forms (v1, v2, v3, v4) belong to passive learning, and the last three forms (v4, v5, v6) belong to active learning. However, because all the learning is through an online learning system, students must log in to attend the course. In some sense, the login manifests a kind of active learning behavior of students. Accordingly, in addition to the last three learning forms, the first three forms also reflect a certain amount of student initiative, even though they account for a smaller proportion in the following active learning evaluation.

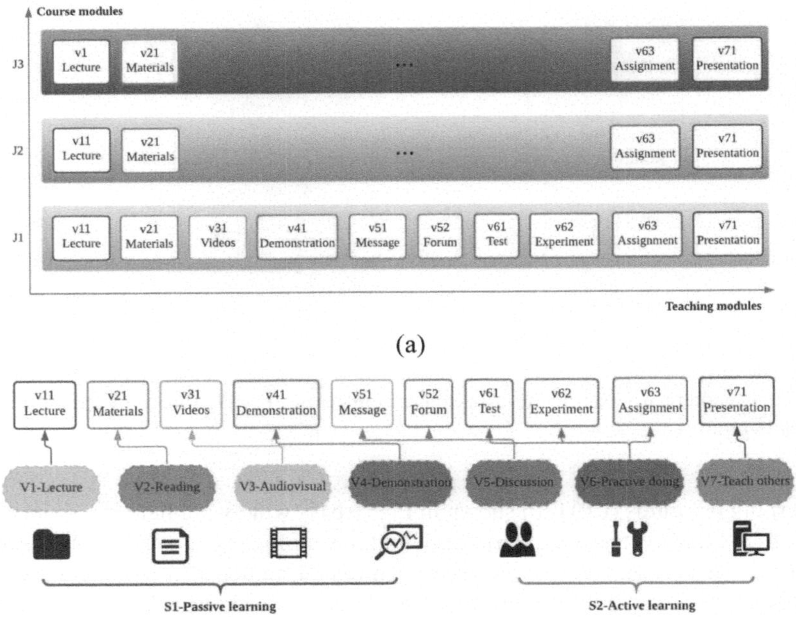

(a)

(b)

Fig. 2. An example of course content division (a) and teaching modules (b)

Table 1. Indicators for assessing students' online learning performance (C: learning content, K: clicks, T: time, O: content, G: grade, N: number, P: pages, ID: student number)

C	K	T	O	G	P	N	ID
Lecture: v11		√				√	√
Meterials: v21		√			√		√
Video: v32		√				√	√
Demonstration: V41		√				√	√
Message: v51			√				√
Forum: v52	√					√	√
Test: v61				√		√	√
Experiment: v62				√		√	√
Assignment: v63				√		√	√
Presentation: v71						√	√

Indicators for Performance Assessment. Students' online learning is recorded in detail in the weblog, such as stay time, click numbers, interaction times, etc. The records in weblogs, combined with students' scores, forum text, and messages, are considered the indicators or data resource for assessing students' online learning performance. The indicators are shown in Table 1. The corresponding data are collected from weblog and website.

Assign Indicators for LD. We assess active learning using the learning dimensions (LD) Model and assign LD indicators shown in Table 2.

Table 2. Assing indicators for five learning dimensions.

Dimention	D1	D2	D3	D4	D5
Description	Positive attitudes and perceptions about learning	Acquiring and integrating knowledge	Extending and refining knowledge	Using knowledge meaningfully	Productive habits of mind
Content module	J1–J3	J1	J2	J3	J1–J3
Indicators	v51:O v11–v41: T/N, P v52–v71: N, K	v11–v71: N	v11–v71: N	v11–v71: N	v61–v62: G

3.2 Online Active Learning Performance Assessment

In this section, online active learning will be assessed from five dimensions D1–D2.

D1 Assessment. Research shows that positive emotions (e.g., happiness, pride, and hope) are the essential components of learning motivation [25]. In the following, D1 is assessed with a text semantic analysis approach for positive attitude assessment and a student participation model for participation assessment.

Semantic Emotion Analysis. Semantic emotion analysis, one of the most important branches of artificial intelligence (AI) [26], involves theories and algorithms in statistics, linguistics, psychology, and other fields. The general semantic analysis process is depicted in Fig. 3 [27]. Practically, a semantic analysis model based on LSTM [28] can be applied to track learners' emotional tendencies and evaluate positive attitudes from a Chinese dataset. Similarly, the research [29] proposed sentiment analysis models for English reviews. The dataset comes from the student's feedback text extracted from the message platform (v51). The final result, SE, is calculated according to the average probability of positive emotion (x%) in a learning period.

Participation Assessment. Chan et al. [30] proposed a student participation model consisting of a set of components, such as pages viewed and forum questions read and posted, and associated weights. Here, the model is adjusted to evaluate the participation of passive learning and active learning, respectively. Here, the indicator T, N, and P can be taken as measures. For example, in the passive learning module, the indicator set

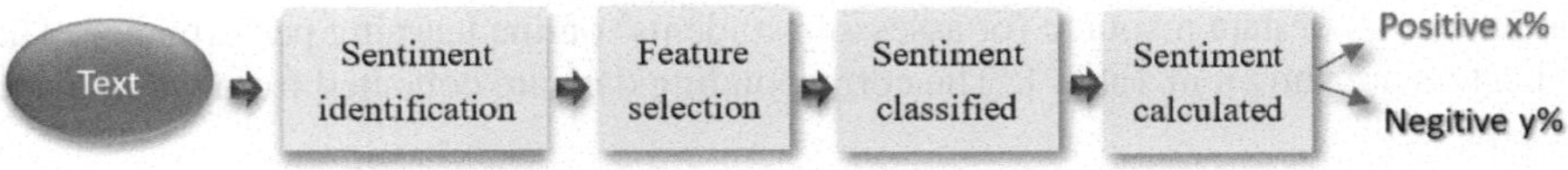

Fig. 3. The semantic emotion analysis process

(v11-T, v21-T, v31-T, v41-T) or (v11-N, v21-P, v31-N, v41-N) can be used to calculate the passive learning participation (S_{PI}). the indicator set (v52-N, v61-T, v62-T, v63-T) can be used to calculate the active learning participation (S_{AI}).

Table 3. Constitution and formula of the student PLP index (S_{PI}).

Item	Variable	Weight	Score
Lecture: v11-T/N	X1	7.7%	Score (X1) = 7.7% × X1/Max (X1)
Materials: v21-T/P	X2	15.4%	Score (X2) = 15.4% × X2/Max (X2)
Video: v31-T/N	X3	30.8%	Score (X3) = 30.8% × X3/Max (X3)
Demonstration: v41-T/N	X4	46.1%	Score (X4) = 46.1% × X4/Max (X4)
Total score	Score (X1) + Score (X2) + Score (X3) + Score (X4) + Score (X5)		
S_{PI}	100 * Total score/Median score		

Table 4. Constitution and formula of the student ALP index (S_{AI})

Student actions	Variable	Weight	Score
Forum: v52-N+K	Y1	23.3%	Score (Y1) = 23.3% × Y1/Max (Y1)
Test: v61-N	Y2	11.6%	Score (Y2) = 11.6% × Y2/Max (Y2)
Experiments: v62-N	Y3	11.6%	Score (Y3) = 11.6% × Y3/Max (Y3)
Assignment: v63-N	Y4	11.6%	Score (Y4) = 11.6% × Y4/Max (Y4)
Presentation: v71-N	Y5	41.9%	Score (Y5) = 41.9% × Y5/Max (Y5)
Total Score	Score (Y1) + Score (Y2) + Score (Y3) + Score (Y4) + Score (Y5)		
S_{AI}	100 * Total score/Median score		

The passive learning participation is assessed according to the time spent on lectures, materials, videos, and demonstrations. The score of each action items is calculated according to (1):

$$Score(X_i) = \alpha_i \times \frac{X_i}{\max(X_i)}, \quad \sum \alpha_i = 1 \tag{1}$$

The weights, α_i, for v11, v21, v31, and v41 are set according to the average rates of material retention 24 h after instruction in the learning pyramid. In practical application, they can also be assigned by corresponding teachers.

Then, all the scores of S_{PI} are added up, and the S_{PI} is obtained according to (2):

$$S_{PI} = 100 \times \sum Score(X_i)/Median(Score(X_i)) \tag{2}$$

where $Median(Score(X_i))$ refers to the median score in all of the scores.

The detailed calculation processes of participations S_{PI} and S_{AI} are depicted in Tables 3 and 4.

Finally, the participation score, S_P, is calculated according to the following equation:

$$S_P = \beta_p \times S_{PI} + \beta_a \times S_{AI}, \quad \beta_p + \beta_a = 1 \tag{3}$$

The calculation of S_{AI} is the same as S_{PI}. According to the learning pyramid, β_p and β_a can be assigned 0.23 and 0.77, respectively.

Assessment of D2–D4. In this section, the active learning performance assessments on D2–D4 are performed on J1, J2, and J3 modules, respectively. TOPSIS (Technique for Order Preference by Similarity to Ideal Solution) [31] is a commonly used and effective multi-objective decision analysis method. Taking D2 as an example, we first define the evaluation variables for each student. As mentioned above, the passive learning module is also a part of our assessment, and we assess D2 with the modules of active learning (AL). The corresponding variables in each module are listed in Tables 5 and 6, respectively.

Table 5. AL assessment in D2

ID	v11	v21	v31	v41	v52	v61	v62	v63	v71	Score2
Weight	0.02	0.03	0.07	0.11	0.18	0.09	0.09	0.09	0.32	
Stu1	x_{11}	x_{12}	x_{13}	x_{14}	x_{15}	x_{16}	x_{17}	x_{16}	x_{18}	
Stu2	x_{21}	x_{22}	x_{23}	x_{24}	x_{25}	x_{26}	x_{27}	x_{26}	x_{28}	
…	…	…	…	…	…	…				
Stun	x_{n1}	x_{n2}	x_{n3}	x_{n4}	x_{n5}	x_{n6}	x_{27}	x_{26}	x_{28}	

In Table 5, the score is calculated according to the TOPSIS method. The main steps are described in the following:

Suppose there are n objects to be evaluated, and the positive matrix constituted by m evaluation indicators is as follows:

$$X = \begin{bmatrix} x_{11} & x_{12} & \cdots & x_{1m} \\ x_{21} & x_{22} & \cdots & x_{2m} \\ \cdots & \cdots & \cdots & \cdots \\ x_{n1} & x_{n2} & \cdots & x_{nm} \end{bmatrix} \tag{4}$$

(1) Matrix normalization

$$y_{ij} = x_{ij}/\sqrt{\sum_{x=1}^{n} x_{ij}^2} \tag{5}$$

(2) Weighted matrix

$$z_{ij} = w_j \cdot y_{ij} \tag{6}$$

where w_j is determined according to the learning pyramid.

and we have

$$z = \begin{bmatrix} z_{11} & z_{12} & \cdots & z_{1m} \\ z_{21} & z_{22} & \cdots & z_{2m} \\ \cdots & \cdots & \cdots & \cdots \\ z_{n1} & z_{n2} & \cdots & z_{nm} \end{bmatrix} \tag{7}$$

(3) Determination of the best and worst project

Define maximum:

$$Z^+ = \left(Z_1^+, Z_2^+, \cdots Z_m^+\right) = \begin{pmatrix} \max\{z_{11}^+, z_{21}^+, \cdots z_{n1}^+\},\ \max\{z_{12}^+, z_{22}^+, \cdots z_{n2}^+\}, \\ \cdots,\ \max\{z_{1m}^+, z_{2m}^+, \cdots z_{nm}^+\}, \end{pmatrix} \tag{8}$$

Define minimum:

$$Z^- = \left(Z_1^-, Z_2^-, \cdots Z_m^-\right) = \begin{pmatrix} \min\{z_{11}^-, z_{21}^-, \cdots z_{n1}^-\},\ \min\{z_{12}^-, z_{22}^-, \cdots z_{n2}^-\}, \\ \cdots,\ \min\{z_{1m}^-, z_{2m}^-, \cdots z_{nm}^-\}, \end{pmatrix} \tag{9}$$

(4) Calculation of distance

Define the distance between the $i(i = 1, 2, \cdots n)$ evaluation object and the maximum value:

$$D^+ = \sqrt{\sum_{j=1}^{m} \left(Z^+ - z_{ij}\right)^2} \tag{10}$$

Define the distance between the $i(i = 1, 2, \cdots n)$ evaluation object and the maximum value:

$$D^- = \sqrt{\sum_{j=1}^{m} \left(Z^- - z_{ij}\right)^2} \tag{11}$$

(5) Approximation degree calculation

Calculate the approximation degree between each evaluation object and the optimal scheme

$$c_i = \frac{D_i^-}{D_i^+ + D_i^-} 0 \le c_i \le 1 \tag{12}$$

c_i synthesizes the comprehensive level of a number of evaluation indexes, and the bigger it is, the better the evaluation object is. Take c_i as the score obtained in the dimension.

With the same method, we can assess the dimensions D3 and D4, noted as S_3 and S_4, respectively.

Evaluation of D5. We encourage the formation of good habits, and thus, we assess the D5 from two aspects: first, whether the student always gets a high score in each test. Second, whether the student with low scores gradually becomes a one with high scores? In the assessment, in an interval of [t_0, t_n], if the fitting curve is always high with little fluctuation or monotone increasing (see the two curves, C1 and C2, in Fig. 4), the assessment score is high. In other cases, the assessment is low.

Here, we focus on the scores, including Test (St), Experiment (Se), Assignment (Sa) in active learning. For example, assume the test score sequence is Test, we assess the St according to (13):

$$S_t = e^{\frac{1}{|P-L|}} \times \frac{1}{N}\sum_{i=0}^{N}(Test)_{t_i} \times \frac{1}{N-j+1}\sum_{i=j}^{N}(Test)_{t_i} \quad (13)$$

where P and L are the peaks and valleys of the corresponding fitting curve, respectively. $e^{\frac{1}{|P-L|}}$ stands for curve fluctuation, and the bigger the $e^{\frac{1}{|P-L|}}$, stabler the habit. $\frac{1}{N}\sum_{i=0}^{N}(Test)_{t_i}$ is the mean value of TT. $\frac{1}{N-j+1}\sum_{i=j}^{N}(Test)_{t_i}$ indicates that the TT achieves a high score after a period of study.

Similarly, Se and Sa are calculated according to (13).

Active Online Learning Performance Assessment. The assessment of active online learning performance (AOLPA) can be taken as a multi-attribute decision-making problem. The purpose of decision-making is to find the best solution from the group of alternative options or to comprehensively evaluate and rank this group of solutions and reflect the decision maker's intention via the ranking results. Here, we assess the performance divergence with TOPSIS (the weights are 1 s) in students' active learning and help teachers decide for those with poor performance (Table 6).

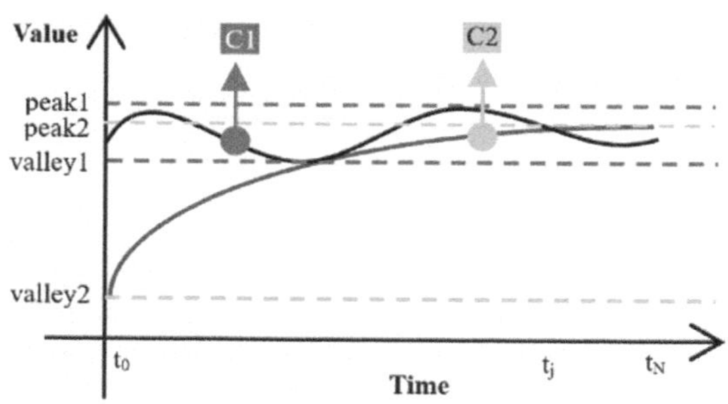

Fig. 4. The sustainability of active learning activity

Table 6. Assessment of active online learning performance

Student	D1		D2	D3	D4	D5			AOLPA
	$V_1(S_E)$	$V_2(S_P)$	$V_3(S_2)$	$V_4(S_3)$	$V_5(S_4)$	$V_6(S_t)$	$V_7(S_e)$	$V_8(S_a)$	
Stu1	x_{11}	x_{12}	x_{13}	x_{14}	x_{15}	x_{16}	x_{17}	x_{18}	
Stu2	x_{21}	x_{22}	x_{23}	x_{24}	x_{25}	x_{26}	x_{27}	x_{28}	
...	...	...	...	...	...	...	...	...	
Stun	x_{n1}	x_{n2}	x_{n3}	x_{n4}	x_{n5}	x_{n6}	x_{n7}	x_{n8}	

4 Discussion

In this article, an assessment framework for active online learning performance was presented to help teachers assess student performance in online learning and adopt effective countermeasures accordingly. The assessment framework are flexible and extendible. For example, the modules can be redesigned according to the arrangement of teaching content. For example, the lack of lectures in the online courses will not affect the calculation of AOLPA. In addition, D1–D5 can be calculated individually according to the institutors' needs. For example, if the institutor only wants to focus on students' positive attitudes, they can select the D1 dimension. Finally, the framework can derive many other evaluations for online learning.

Nevertheless, many limitations of the study are noted. First, this study lacks an experimental design. It is worthy of conducting more quantitative tests about the framework's effect. Future research will collect corresponding data from more online learning websites and perform detail empirical research with the assessment framework on students' active learning performance. Second, qualitative research can help us explore both students' and teachers' perceptions and understanding of the assessment strategies that promote active learning performance. Accordingly, future research will collect questionnaire data to assess students' active learning in online environments.

5 Conclusion

Due to the uncertain development of the pneumonia epidemic, classes' full resumption is pending, and online education may continue. Online learning during the epidemic is both a challenge and an opportunity for education. For example, online learning is a significant opportunity to improve students' active learning ability and improve their learning methods. Through assessment of online active learning performance, teachers and students are provided with feedback on students' active learning ability, which contributes to increase the efficiency of learning and teaching and help teachers deal with students' learning differences.

References

1. Demuyakor, J.: Coronavirus (COVID-19) and online learning in higher institutions of education: a survey of the perceptions of Ghanaian international students in China. Online J. Commun. Media Technol. **10**(3), 1–9 (2020)
2. Li, Z.: With the suspension of classes, online education is facing new challenges. People's Daily Overseas Edition. http://paper.people.com.cn/rmrbhwb/html/2020-02/18/content_1971524.htm. Accessed 1 Dec 2020
3. Li, C., Lalani, F.: The COVID-19 pandemic has changed education forever. This is how. The World Economic forum COVID action platform. https://www.weforum.org/agenda/2020/04/coronavirus-education-global-covid19-online-digital-learning/. Accessed 1 Dec 2020
4. Kiryacu, C.: Temeljna nastavna umijeća. https://www.azoo.hr/images/razno/TEMELJNA_NASTAVN.pdf. Accessed 1 Dec 2020
5. Timmerman, B., Lingard, R.: Assessment of active learning with upper division computer science students. In: 33rd Annual Frontiers in Education, vol. 3, p. S1D-7 (2003)
6. Reeves, T.C.: Alternative assessment approaches for online learning environments in higher education. J. Educ. Comput. Res. **23**(1), 101–111 (2000)
7. Graff, M.: Cognitive style and attitudes towards using online learning and assessment methods. Electron. J. e-Learn. **1**(1), 21–28 (2003)
8. Mateo, J., Sangrà, A.: Designing online learning assessment through alternative approaches: facing the concerns. Eur. J. Open Distance E-Learn. **10**(2), 1–7 (2007)
9. Gaytan, J., McEwen, B.C.: Effective online instructional and assessment strategies. Am. J. Distance Educ. **21**(3), 117–132 (2007)
10. Suen, H.K.: Peer assessment for massive open online courses (MOOCs). Int. Rev. Res. Open Distrib. Learn. **15**(3), 312–327 (2014)
11. Guerrero-Roldán, A.E., Noguera, I.: A model for aligning assessment with competences and learning activities in online courses. Internet High. Educ. **38**, 36–46 (2018)
12. Swan, K., Shen, J., Hiltz, S.R.: Assessment and collaboration in online learning. J. Asynchronous Learn. Netw. **10**(1), 45–62 (2006)
13. Vonderwell, S., Liang, X., Alderman, K.: Asynchronous discussions and assessment in online learning. J. Res. Technol. Educ. **39**(3), 309–328 (2007)
14. James, P.A., et al.: Performance assessment framework for measuring online student learning outcome. In: Proceedings of the 120th Annual Conference, Atlanta, Georgia (2013)
15. Formanek, M., Wenger, M.C., Buxner, S.R., Impey, C.D., Sonam, T.: Insights about large-scale online peer assessment from an analysis of an astronomy MOOC. Comput. Educ. **113**, 243–262 (2017)
16. Tsai, F.H., Tsai, C.C., Lin, K.Y.: The evaluation of different gaming modes and feedback types on game-based formative assessment in an online learning environment. Comput. Educ. **81**, 259–269 (2015)
17. Ikejiri, R., Oura, H., Fushikida, W., Anzai, Y., Yamauchi, Y.: Evaluating learning in the MOOC about the study of history. Educ. Technol. Res. **41**(1), 77–89 (2019)
18. Marzano, R.J., Pickering, D., McTighe, J.: Assessing student outcomes: performance assessment using the dimensions of learning model. Association for Supervision and Curriculum Developmen, Alexandria (1993)
19. Jaques, E.: The development of intellectual capability: a discussion of stratified systems theory. J. Appl. Behav. Sci. **22**(4), 361–383 (1985)
20. Letrud, K., Hernes, S.: The diffusion of the learning pyramid myths in academia: an exploratory study. J. Curric. Stud. **48**(3), 291–302 (2016)
21. Dale, E., Nyland, B.: Cone of learning. Educ. Med. (1960)
22. Sousa, D.A.: How the brain learns, 3rd edn. Corwin, Thousand Oaks (2006)

23. Baranowski, M.: Single session simulations: the effectiveness of short congressional simulations in introductory American government classes. J. Polit. Sci. Educ. **2**(1), 33–49 (2006)
24. Peng, H., Chen, Y., Hu, H.: Research and exploration of online to offline (O2O) blended teaching for talent cultivating. In: 2020 International Conference on Advanced Education, Management and Information Technology (AEMIT 2020), pp. 191–194. Atlantis Press, French (2020)
25. Pekrun, R., Goetz, T., Titz, W., Perry, R.P.: Academic emotions in students' self-regulated learning and achievement: a program of qualitative and quantitative research. Educ. Psychol. **37**(2), 91–105 (2002)
26. Wang, L., Hu, G., Zhou, T.: Semantic analysis of learners' emotional tendencies on online MOOC education. Sustainability **10**(6), 1–19 (2018)
27. Medhat, W., Hassan, A., Korashy, H.: Sentiment analysis algorithms and applications: A survey. Ain Shams Eng. J. **5**(4), 1093–1113 (2014)
28. Sentiment Analysis. https://github.com/Edward1Chou/SentimentAnalysis. Accessed 1 Dec 2020
29. Al Amrani, Y., Lazaar, M., El Kadiri, K.E.: Random forest and support vector machine based hybrid approach to sentiment analysis. Procedia Comput. Sci. **127**, 511–520 (2018)
30. Chan, A.Y.K., Chow, P.K., Cheung, K.S.: Student participation index: student assessment in online courses. In: Liu, W., Shi, Y., Li, Q. (eds.) ICWL 2004. LNCS, vol. 3143, pp. 449–456. Springer, Heidelberg (2004). https://doi.org/10.1007/978-3-540-27859-7_58
31. Hwang, C.L., Yoon, K.: Multiple Attribute Decision Making: Methods and Applications. Springer, New York (1981). https://doi.org/10.1007/978-3-642-48318-9

Relationships Among Online Teaching Design, Experience, and Perception of College Teachers During the Pandemic

Shiqian Gu[1], Xiaotong Yang[2(✉)], and Wei Li[1(✉)]

[1] Academic Affairs Office of Undergraduate School, Jinan University, Guangzhou 510632, China

[2] College of Education, Florida State University, Tallahassee 32306, USA

Abstract. The outbreak of COVID-19 forced many higher education institutions worldwide to transfer from dominantly off-line teaching to online teaching mode in a short time. Instructors' online teaching design is critical to learning achievements of undergraduate students during and even after the pandemic. The current study investigates the relationships between college teachers' online teaching design, online teaching experience, and perceptions. A total of 1, 318 instructors (645 females, 673 males) from a Southeastern university in China completed an online survey and statistical analyses were conducted to compare their online teaching design across experiences and perceptions of online teaching. Results showed that college teachers designed online teaching differently across genders and ages. Additionally, teachers' perception and prior experience of online teaching might also affect their online teaching design . The implications and suggestions for improving teachers' online teaching design practice from the institutional perspectives are discussed.

Keywords: Online teaching design · College teachers · Relationships · Pandemic

1 Introduction

COVID-19 has posed an unprecedented challenge to global universities and colleges. Many higher education institutions worldwide have to transfer from dominantly offline teaching to online teaching mode (i.e., emergency remote teaching, ERT) [1]. Unfortunately, it is challenging to transfer smoothly and effectively for some colleges and universities, especially those without adequate technical and human resources. One of the most important factors that may affect online teaching effectiveness is teachers' online teaching design abilities.

The shift to ERT requires university instructors to "take more control of course design, development, and implementation process." Eric Fredericksen, vice president for online learning at the University of Rochester, posits that the pandemic would affect teaching in an incremental approach rather than a revolutionary one. It is foreseeable that even when COVID-19 is eradicated, teachers and students will likely become more accepting and accustomed to online instruction. Teachers may continue to carry out

R. Li et al. (Eds.): ICBL 2021, LNCS 12830, pp. 351–366, 2021.
https://doi.org/10.1007/978-3-030-80504-3_29

online instruction for the long term. Therefore, it is important to improve teachers' online teaching design practice to make online instruction sustainable even after the epidemic.

Current studies on education and teaching during the COVID-19 have been primarily focused on topics such as changes in the family in education [2, 3], developing new suggestions on how curriculum as the essence and core of all educational systems [4], boosting students' online learning engagement [5], factors influencing both teaching/learning effectiveness and general human comfort and wellbeing [6], the effectiveness of intergenerational learning during the COVID-19 pandemic [7], and teachers' online teaching perceptions [8]. Research on teachers' online teaching design and influencing factors during the pandemic is scarce. Only by clarifying the influencing factors of online instructional design can we find an anchor point for improving the level of teachers' online instructional design. Taking a university J in southern China as an example, the current study examines the faculty's online teaching design status during the pandemic and how the design varied across teachers' online teaching experience and perceptions. This study can shed light on the design of online teaching professional development programs for higher education administrators. Moreover, teachers can gain some insights on how to analyze and improve their online teaching design abilities.

2 Literature Review

2.1 Teachers' Online Teaching Design in Higher Education

Instructional design was a process, according to the level and requirements of educating objects, based on settling down the reasonable starting and ending point of education, reorganizing and transforming the content, arranging instructional elements systematically and ordinary, then to form the instructional plan. During the pandemic, some teachers in higher education have to adopt online teaching. The challenge for instructors and instructional designers is knowing which forms of instructional interactions and conditions best support student learning [9]. Relevant research has been focusing on improving online teaching effectiveness by optimizing instructional design, strategies, and models. For example, Jennifer Maddrell proposed a set of instructional design considerations for the effective and efficient facilitation of service-learning experiences in both campus-based and online courses: (a) goal examination, (b) the nonprofit partnership, (c) project design and management, and (d) assessment [10]. Betul and colleagues proposed a culminating instructional design framework: E-Learning Engagement Design, based on an extensive literature review on student engagement. This framework included four stages, i.e., identify instructional needs, define instructional goals and objectives, develop learning environments, and summative Assessment.

Moreover, some research has investigated instructional design aimed at improving students' online learning performance. For example, Trespalacios and colleagues [11] have argued that a small group strategy has great potential to help students analyze case studies and consequently enhance learning. The implications of these findings for instructional designers and online instructors are discussed.

In summary, research on online teaching design mainly focuses on need analysis, teaching objectives, environments, activities, and evaluation. These related studies provide some guidance on how teachers can do a good job of online instructional design during the epidemic. The key elements of instructional design are also helpful in designing research dimensions for analyzing teachers' online instructional design's effectiveness during the epidemic. Suppose teachers borrowed these instructional design frameworks or models or conducted their own online instructional design based on their perceptions and experiences during the epidemic. How did they examine the effectiveness of their own instructional design? And what factors have an impact on online instructional design? Research on the above topics is warranted in terms of ensuring teachers' online teaching performance.

2.2 Influencing Factors of College Teachers' Online Teaching Design

What factors in online teaching are related to teachers' instructional design? Through literature analysis, we found that there are quite a few studies on factors affecting college teachers' online instructional design from two perspectives: instructional design and students' learning outcomes.

Hong Xie and colleagues [12] argued that the basic elements to be considered during the online course instructional design were instructional objective, preparation, content, structure, learning method, and learning evaluation. Afsaneh Sharif [13] investigated the effect of cultural differences (i.e., different contexts and backgrounds) on instructional designers' perspectives of quality in online environments. This study shows that these differences do not impact the designers' views on the quality of online courses and the key elements. Designers found all eight categories, including proper course overview, alignment of learning objectives, assessment strategies, current instructional materials, effective learner interaction, proper use of course technology, learner support, and accessibility important for quality design. Choi and colleagues [14] indicated that students perceived instructional design and organization as a part of teaching presence were positively related to students' perceived challenge in an online course. Also, students perceived instructional design and organization were positively related to persistent intention but were not significantly related to students' achievement. Finally, challenge mediated the relationship between students' perceived instructional design and organization and persistent intention, and the relationship between students' perceived instructional design and organization and students' achievement as well. Moreover, one survey study [15] explored which instructional design components (e.g., course content, transactional interaction between student and content, structure/organization, assessment) influence learner control, sense of progress in the achievement of learning goals (sense of progress), and perceived effectiveness in a large-scale MOOC course called "Learning How to Learn" hosted in Coursera, a MOOC learning platform. One survey study [16] indicated that the three proposed external factors, including technical support, instructional design, and perceived self-efficacy, significantly influenced students' use of learning management systems.

In conclusion, factors that influence college teachers' online teaching include teaching objectives, teaching preparation, cultural background, teaching content, teaching strategies, interaction with students, teaching evaluation, etc. Based on the existing research, we believe that there are five key elements of online teaching design during COVID-19: teaching environment/tools, teaching content, teaching methods, teaching interaction, and teaching evaluation. In the current study, we do not emphasize the teaching objectives. One reason is that the Chinese Ministry of Education proposed to ensure that online teaching and offline teaching during the pandemic should be "homogeneous and equivalent". That is, the teaching objectives of online teaching should be the same as those of traditional offline teaching and cannot be lowered or adjusted. Moreover, teaching objectives and teaching evaluation is interactive, and we can understand teaching objectives through teaching evaluation. Based on the existing research, we propose that teachers' basic characteristic factors, understanding of online teaching, and existing online instructional design experience may influence their online instructional design.

Online teaching during COVID-19 is quite different from regular online teaching or offline teaching. During the pandemic, most teachers, who may lack prior experience, are forced to carry out online teaching. Teachers' understanding and attitudes towards online teaching may also vary greatly. Teachers of different ages and different subjects have different acceptance and competence levels for online teaching.

In the current study, we examine college teachers' online teaching design status and factors that may influence their teaching design. Specifically, we will answer the following research questions:

1. What is the status quos of the online teaching design of college teachers during the pandemic?
2. Do college teachers' characteristics (i.e., gender, age, title) correlate with their online teaching design?
3. Does college teachers' perception of online teaching correlate with their online teaching design?
4. Does college teachers' online teaching experience correlate with their online teaching design?

3 Methods

3.1 Participants

This study takes university J as the research case. University J is a comprehensive university with 2,684 full-time faculty members and full-time undergraduate students worldwide. In 2020, there are 28,628 full-time undergraduate students, with one-third from Hong Kong, Macau, Taiwan, and overseas. In this study, 2,684 questionnaires were distributed to the faculty members through the academic administrators on March 13, 2020 (the third week after the start of the school year), and 1,318 valid questionnaires were returned in two weeks, with a response rate of 49.1%.

Among all participants, cover all colleges and majors, 49% were female, while 51% were male. A total of 42.79% of teachers who participated in the survey were between 35–45 years old. Most of the teachers (41.05%) were associate professors. Regarding the geographical distribution, 87% were in Guangdong.

3.2 Measurements

We developed an electronic questionnaire, then distributed and collected it through an online platform. We first developed a preliminary survey framework and specific survey questions based on existing instructional design theories with literature analysis. We then sent the first draft of the questionnaire to instructional design experts, instructional managers, and teachers for comments. The finalized questionnaire consisted of 19 items: questions 1–5 were about teachers' characteristics, questions 6 and 7 were about teachers' experience and understanding of online teaching, question 8 was about teachers' choice of teaching platform, question 9 was about teachers' teaching content processing, question 10 was about teachers' teaching style, questions 11 and 12 were about teachers' teaching interaction style and length, question 13 was about teachers' teaching evaluation method. The rest of the questions are about teachers' satisfaction with the school's online teaching arrangement and suggestions for improvement. It took two weeks to develop the questionnaire and two weeks to distribute and collect surveys. Data that teachers filled in by clicking the link was automatically collected on the "Questionnaire Star" platform. We exported the raw data to the SPSS software to conduct further analyses.

4 Results

4.1 Descriptive Analysis

We first conducted a descriptive analysis regarding teachers' online teaching perception, experience, and design. Since all variables are categorical variables, we computed the frequency and percent of each category within each variable. Table 1 presents a descriptive analysis regarding teachers' online teaching perception and experience.

Table 1. Descriptive analysis regarding teachers' online teaching perception and experience

Variable	Categories	n	% within variable
Online teaching perception	A good opportunity for creative teaching	534	40.5
	Tasks assigned by the university	77	5.8
	I prefer the traditional face-to-face teaching method	46	3.5
	An effective way to accomplish the teaching tasks	661	50.2
Online teaching experience	Have no online teaching experience	822	62.4
	Have blended teaching experience	355	26.9
	Have MOOC development and application experience	81	6.1
	Have flipped classroom teaching experience	60	4.6

As shown in Table 1, 50.2% and 40.5% of teachers perceived online teaching as "an effective way to accomplish the teaching tasks" and "a good opportunity for creative teaching," respectively. Only 9.3% of teachers held a negative perception towards online teaching (e.g., "Tasks assigned by the university," "I prefer the traditional face-to-face teaching method"). Additionally, 62.4% of teachers did not have online teaching experience before the pandemic. Among teachers with such experience, most of them have taught in the blended mode; others have developed and applied MOOCs in their teaching or have conducted flipped classrooms.

RQ1— Online Teaching Design Status Quos. To answer the RQ1 (i.e., the status quos of teachers' online teaching design during the pandemic), we computed the frequency and percent of each category within each online teaching design variable. Results are shown in Table 2.

Table 2. Descriptive analysis regarding teachers' online teaching design

Variable	Categories	n	% within variable
Preparation	None	50	3.8
	Slightly changed teaching content	509	38.6
	Fragmented teaching content	84	6.4
	Redesigned teaching content	675	51.2
Teaching method	Self-study	11	.8
	MOOC/SPOC	78	5.9
	Live lecture	721	54.7
	Recorded lecture	74	5.6
	Tutoring	37	2.8
	Combined	350	26.6
	Others	47	3.6
Interacting method	Collective Q&A	148	11.2
	Group discussion	34	2.6
	Synchronous video/audio interaction	535	40.6
	Asynchronous textual/audio interaction	473	35.9
	Sign-in/vote	47	3.6
	Others	81	6.1
Interacting time	None	75	5.7
	<10 min	480	36.4
	10–20 min	445	33.8
	>25 min	318	24.1

(continued)

Table 2. (*continued*)

Variable	Categories	n	% within variable
Evaluation method	Assignment	395	30.0
	Test	286	21.7
	Teacher evaluation	232	17.6
	Comprehensive evaluation	211	16.0
	Participation	108	8.2
	Survey/vote	52	3.9
	Others	34	2.6

In the current study, we focused on five elements of teachers' online teaching design, i.e., preparation, teaching method, interaction method, interaction time, and evaluation method. As shown in Table 2, most teachers either slightly changed or redesigned their teaching content in the preparation phase. Only 3.8% of teachers did not adjust their teaching content at all before the online teaching during the pandemic. The most adopted teaching method was live lecture (54.7%), followed by a combination of different methods (26.6%), MOOC/SPOC (5.9%), recorded lecture (5.6%).

Similar to the teaching method, the most popular interacting method was synchronous video/audio interaction (40.6%), followed by asynchronous textual/audio interaction (35.9%) and Collective Q&A (11.2%). And 57.9% of teachers spent more than 10min interacting with students in each class, while 5.7% did not interact with students at all. Regarding evaluation method, 30.0% of teachers adopted assignment only, 21.7% test only, 17.6% teacher evaluation only, and 16.0% combined different evaluation methods together.

RQ2— The Relationship Between Individual Characteristics and Online Teaching Design. Regarding RQ2 (i.e., the relationship between teachers' individual characteristics and their online teaching design), we computed the Chi-Square Test of Independence to test the association between teachers' online teaching design and gender age, and title respectively. The cross table with percent and chi-square statistics are shown in Tables 3, 4 and 5.

Table 3. The association between online teaching design and gender

Online teaching design variable	Category	Gender (%)		Chi-square statistics
		Female	Male	
Preparation	None	2.6	4.9	X^2 (3) = 14.52 $p = .002$
	Slightly changed teaching content	35.7	41.5	
	Fragmented teaching content	5.6	7.1	
	Redesigned teaching content	56.1	46.5	

(*continued*)

Table 3. (*continued*)

Online teaching design variable	Category	Gender (%)		Chi-square statistics
		Female	Male	
Teaching method	Self-study	0.6	1.0	X^2 (6) = 30.99 $p < .000$
	MOOC/SPOC	4.2	7.6	
	Live lecture	51.9	57.4	
	Recorded lecture	4.7	6.5	
	Tutoring	3.4	2.2	
	Combined	32.4	21.0	
	Others	2.8	4.3	
Interacting method	Collective Q&A	9.0	11.4	X^2 (5) = 22.79 $p < .000$
	Group discussion	2.2	3.0	
	Synchronous video/audio interaction	45.0	36.4	
	Asynchronous textual/audio interaction	33.5	38.2	
	Sign-in/vote	2.6	4.5	
	Others	7.8	4.6	
Interacting time	None	3.3	8.0	X^2 (3) = 48.00 $p < .000$
	< 10min	29.6	42.9	
	10—20min	38.8	29.0	
	> 25min	28.4	20.1	
Evaluation method	Assignment	31.8	28.2	X^2 (6) = 30.47 $p < .000$
	Test	22.3	21.2	
	Teacher evaluation	13.6	21.4	
	Comprehensive evaluation	19.8	12.3	
	Participation	6.7	9.7	
	Survey/vote	3.1	4.8	
	Others	2.8	2.4	

Table 3 indicated significant associations between gender and online teaching preparation (X^2(3) = 14.52, p = .002), teaching method (X^2(6) = 30.99, p < .000), interacting method (X^2(5) = 22.79, p < .000), interacting time (X^2(3) = 48.00, p < .000), and evaluation method (X^2(6) = 30.47, p < .000). Compared to male peers, more female teachers tended to redesigned teaching content, combined multiple teaching methods, prefer synchronous interacting method, have longer interacting time, and evaluate their students by assignment.

Table 4. The association between online teaching design and age

Online teaching design variable	Category	Age (%)				Chi-square statistics
		<35	35–45	46–55	>56	
Preparation	None	2.1	4.3	2.2	11.1	X^2 (9) = 30.44 $p < .000$
	Slightly changed teaching content	32.4	37.6	43.1	40.7	
	Fragmented teaching content	6.7	6.7	5.6	6.5	
	Redesigned teaching content	58.8	51.4	49.0	41.7	
Teaching method	Self-study	0.4	1.1	0.5	1.9	X^2 (18) = 21.41 $p = .259$
	MOOC/SPOC	5.0	7.4	3.9	7.4	
	Live lecture	58.4	50.0	57.6	60.2	
	Recorded lecture	5.0	5.7	5.9	5.6	
	Tutoring	3.8	2.7	2.7	1.9	
	Combined	23.9	29.8	26.0	17.7	
	Others	3.4	3.4	3.4	5.6	
Interacting method	Collective Q&A	8.4	10.5	12.0	18.5	X^2 (15) = 25.88 $p = .039$
	Group discussion	2.1	3.4	1.5	3.7	
	Synchronous video/audio interaction	46.6	39.5	39.2	38.0	
	Asynchronous textual/audio interaction	36.1	37.4	35.0	30.6	
	Sign-in/vote	4.2	3.0	3.7	4.6	
	Others	2.5	6.2	8.6	4.6	
Interacting time	None	5.0	4.1	7.4	9.3	X^2 (9) = 37.09 $p < .000$
	< 10min	29.0	34.4	39.0	53.7	
	10—20min	37.8	34.8	33.8	19.4	
	>25min	28.2	26.8	19.9	17.6	

(*continued*)

Table 4. (*continued*)

Online teaching design variable	Category	Age (%)				Chi-square statistics
		<35	35–45	46–55	>56	
Evaluation method	Assignment	29.8	30.0	28.4	36.1	$X^2(18) = 15.71$ $p = .613$
	Test	21.8	21.6	23.3	15.7	
	Teacher evaluation	19.3	16.0	18.1	20.4	
	Comprehensive evaluation	13.0	17.6	15.9	14.8	
	Participation	10.1	7.4	8.6	6.5	
	Survey/vote	4.6	4.8	2.5	3.7	
	Others	1.3	2.7	3.2	2.8	

Table 4 indicated significant associations between gender and online teaching preparation ($X^2(9) = 30.44$, $p < .000$), interacting method ($X^2(15) = 25.88$, $p = .039$), and interacting time ($X^2(9) = 37.09$, $p < .000$). However, results showed that age was not significantly correlated with teachers' teaching and evaluation method.

Younger teachers made more efforts preparing for online teaching during the pandemic. For example, the younger the teachers, the more likely they redesigned teaching content. Moreover, younger teachers prefer the video/textual/textual interacting method, while older peers tended to have students submitted their questions first and adopted collective Q&A sessions. And older teachers, especially those older than 56-year-old, tended to have less interaction with their students than younger peers.

RQ3— The Relationship Between Online Teaching Perception and Design. Regarding RQ3 (i.e., the relationship between teachers' perception of online teaching and their online teaching design), we computed the Chi-Square Test of Independence. The cross table and chi-square statistics are shown in Table 5.

As shown in Table 5, results indicated significant associations between teachers' perception of online teaching and their online teaching preparation ($X^2(9) = 52.14$, $p < .000$), teaching method ($X^2(18) = 42.52$, $p = .001$), and interacting time ($X^2(9) = 29.85$, $p < .000$), and evaluation method ($X^2(18) = 55.81$, $p < .000$). Viewing online teaching as "a good opportunity for creative teaching" and "an effective way to accomplish teaching tasks" was categorized as a positive perception regarding online teaching. And we categorized views that online teaching was mandatory tasks or preferring face-to-face teaching as negative perception. Results showed that teachers with a positive perception of online teaching tended to redesign teaching content to adjust the online environment and use multiple teaching and evaluation methods than those with negative perceptions.

Table 5. The association between online teaching design and perception

Online teaching design variable	Category	Online teaching perception (%)				Chi-square statistics
		Good opportunity for creative teaching	An effective way to finish tasks	Tasks assigned by the university	Prefer face-to-face	
Preparation	None	3.0	4.5	2.6	4.3	X^2(9) = 52.14 $p < .000$
	Slightly changed teaching content	28.7	43.6	59.7	47.8	
	Fragmented teaching content	7.1	6.1	2.6	8.7	
	Redesigned teaching content	61.2	45.8	35.1	39.1	
Teaching method	Self-study	0.6	0.9	1.3	2.2	X^2(18) = 42.52 $p = .001$
	MOOC/SPOC	5.8	6.1	5.2	6.5	
	Live lecture	51.7	56.0	59.7	63.0	
	Recorded lecture	3.4	7.1	7.8	6.5	
	Tutoring	1.7	3.3	2.6	8.7	
	Combined	33.5	23.1	16.9	10.9	
	Others	3.4	3.5	6.5	2.2	
Interacting method	Collective Q&A	9.2	13.8	6.5	6.5	X^2(15) = .25.20 $p = .047$
	Group discussion	3.0	2.3	3.9	0.0	
	Synchronous video/audio interaction	43.6	38.1	39.0	43.5	
	Asynchronous textual/audio interaction	34.1	36.9	36.4	41.3	
	Sign-in/vote	2.6	4.1	7.8	0.0	
	Others	7.5	4.8	6.5	8.7	
Interacting time	None	3.4	7.0	7.8	10.9	X^2(9) = 29.85 $p < .000$
	<10 min	31.5	39.9	39.0	39.1	
	10–20 min	36.1	33.1	24.7	30.4	
	>25 min	29.0	20.0	28.6	19.6	

(*continued*)

Table 5. (*continued*)

Online teaching design variable	Category	Online teaching perception (%)				Chi-square statistics
		Good opportunity for creative teaching	An effective way to finish tasks	Tasks assigned by the university	Prefer face-to-face	
Evaluation method	Assignment	27.0	32.1	32.5	30.4	X^2(18) = 55.81 $p < .000$
	Test	26.2	20.1	14.3	4.3	
	Teacher evaluation	13.7	19.7	18.2	32.6	
	Comprehensive evaluation	19.9	13.9	13.0	6.5	
	Participation	5.8	9.2	13.0	13.0	
	Survey/vote	4.3	3.3	3.9	8.7	
	Others	3.2	1.7	5.2	4.3	

RQ4— The Relationship Between Online Teaching Experience and Design. Regarding RQ4 (i.e., the relationship between teachers' online teaching experience and their online teaching design), we computed the Chi-Square Test of Independence. The cross table and chi-square statistics are shown in Table 6.

As shown in Table 6, results indicated significant associations between teachers' online teaching experience and their online teaching preparation (X^2(9) = 53.88, p < .000), teaching method (X^2(18) = 108.73, p < .000), interacting time (X^2(9) = 39.49, p < .000), and evaluation method (X^2(18) = 42.23, p = .001). However, online teaching experience was not significantly associated with the interacting method they adopted.

Results showed that teachers with online teaching experience tended to make more efforts in preparation than those without such experience. Teachers without online teaching experience or with blended teaching and MOOC experience preferred teaching via live lecture. Still, those conducted flipped classroom before were more likely to adopt multiple teaching methods together. Additionally, the latter were more likely to use multiple evaluation methods and had a longer interacting time than the former.

Table 6. The association between online teaching design and experience

Online teaching design variable	Category	Online teaching experience (%)				Chi-square statistics
		None	Blended teaching	MOOC	Flipped classroom	
Preparation	None	4.6	3.1	1.2	0.0	X^2(9) = 53.88 $p < .000$
	Slightly changed teaching content	45.0	29.9	25.9	20.0	
	Fragmented teaching content	4.9	8.5	8.6	11.7	
	Redesigned teaching content	45.5	58.6	64.2	68.3	
Teaching method	Self-study	0.7	0.8	0.0	3.3	X^2(18) = 108.73 $p < .000$
	MOOC/SPOC	4.9	3.9	19.8	13.3	
	Live lecture	59.5	51.8	46.9	16.7	
	Recorded lecture	5.7	6.8	2.5	1.7	
	Tutoring	2.9	2.8	2.5	1.7	
	Combined	22.6	29.0	28.4	63.3	
	Others	3.6	4.8	0.0	0.0	
Interacting method	Collective Q&A	12.2	9.9	11.1	6.7	X^2(15) = 10.04 $p = .817$
	Group discussion	2.7	2.3	2.5	3.3	
	Synchronous video/audio interaction	39.8	42.0	44.4	38.3	
	Asynchronous textual/audio interaction	36.0	34.6	35.8	41.7	
	Sign-in/vote	3.9	3.4	0.0	5.0	
	Others	5.5	7.9	6.2	5.0	
Interacting time	None	6.8	3.7	6.2	1.7	X^2(9) = 39.49 $p < .000$
	<10 min	40.3	33.2	24.7	18.3	
	10–20 min	32.1	36.3	39.5	33.3	
	>25 min	20.8	26.8	29.6	46.7	

(*continued*)

Table 6. (*continued*)

Online teaching design variable	Category	Online teaching experience (%)				Chi-square statistics
		None	Blended teaching	MOOC	Flipped classroom	
Evaluation method	Assignment	32.0	27.6	21.0	28.3	X^2(18) = 42.23 $p = .001$
	Test	19.6	23.4	30.9	28.3	
	Teacher evaluation	19.3	14.6	21.0	6.7	
	Comprehensive evaluation	13.5	20.3	12.3	30.0	
	Participation	9.4	6.2	8.6	3.3	
	Survey/vote	3.5	4.8	4.9	3.3	
	Others	2.7	3.1	1.2	0.0	

5 Discussion and Implications

The study explores the relationships among online teaching design, online teaching experience, and perception of online teaching of college teachers during the pandemic. Results indicated that college teachers designed online teaching differently across genders and ages. Additionally, teachers' perception and prior experience of online teaching might affect their online teaching design.

Results indicated that most college teachers, although did not have sufficient online teaching experience, tended to hold positive perception of such teaching method during the pandemic. However, there were many teachers designed online teaching as moving the offline teaching to the internet, that is, relying too much on synchronous lecture and interacting. However, there are many differences between online teaching and offline teaching. In the online teaching mode, teachers and students are in a state of separation, so that the interaction between teachers and students is more complicated and difficult to control. At the same time, the teaching content suitable for offline teaching is not completely suitable for online teaching. Teachers in the online teaching model need to adjust the teaching content to adapt to the Internet. Therefore, the requirements of the online teaching model for teachers' teaching experience are different from those of offline teaching. Teachers need to clearly recognize this point, conduct more online teaching practice, accumulate online teaching experience, and improve the quality of online teaching.

We found that teachers with online teaching experience tended to make more efforts in preparation and spend more time in interacting with students than those without such experience. One explanation is that experienced teachers are more likely to beware of the different nature between online and offline teaching than un-experienced ones. Therefore, colleges and universities need to create an online teaching community where teachers are free to share their online teaching experience and learn from each other. For example, universities and colleges can set up "online teaching week" every semester, where teachers can carry out online teaching classroom demonstrations, online teaching research, and online teaching expert lectures.

Moreover, teachers' perceptions towards online teaching might affect their teaching design. Teachers with a positive perception of online teaching tended to redesign teaching content to adjust the online environment and use multiple teaching and evaluation methods than those with negative perceptions. Therefore, professional development is needed to not only improve teachers' knowledge and skills of how to design online teaching, but also help them see the value of online teaching design.

Furthermore, consider that teachers' online teaching design ability might vary across ages, special attention should be paid to older teachers as they may need more time to accept and learn new things than younger teachers. For example, in professional development, experienced younger teachers can be teamed up with older teachers and build small learning groups.

References

1. Hodges, C., Moore, S., Lockee, B., Trust, T., Bond, A.: The difference between emergency remote teaching and online learning. Educause Rev. (2020). https://er.educassuse.edu/articles/2020/3/. Accessed 26 February 2021
2. Cynthia, B., Martha, S.: Covid-19 shocks to education supply: how 200,000 U.S. households dealt with the sudden shift to distance learning. Rev. Econ. Household **19**, 1–28 (2021). https://doi.org/10.1007/s11150-020-09540-9
3. Margaret, M., Cher, H.: The educational impact of the Covid-19 rapid response on teachers, students, and families: insights from British Columbia, Canada. Prospects 1–15 (2021). https://doi.org/10.1007/s11125-020-09527-5
4. Sümer, A.: Waking up to the dawn of a new era: reconceptualization of curriculum post Covid-19. Prospects 1–13 (2021). https://doi.org/10.1007/s11125-020-09529-3
5. Dave, E.: Transforming student engagement in COVID-19 remote instruction: a research perspective. Edu. Technol. Res. Dev. **69**, 1–4 (2021). https://doi.org/10.1007/s11423-020-09919-6
6. Naddeo, A., Califano, R., Fiorillo, I.: Identifying factors that influenced wellbeing and learning effectiveness during the sudden transition into eLearning due to the COVID-19 lockdown. Work **68**(3), 1–23 (2021)
7. Keyi, L., Ying, X., Hao, C., Jiacheng, L.: The implementation and effectiveness of intergenerational learning during the COVID-19 pandemic: Evidence from China. Int. Rev. Educ. **66**, 1–23 (2021). https://doi.org/10.1007/s11159-020-09877-4
8. Zheng, H., Xie, Z., Wang, J.: Investigation and research on college teachers' attitudes towards online teaching in post-pandemic era. J. East China Normal Univ. (Educ. Sci.) 38(07), 54–64 (2020)
9. Abrami, P., Bernard, R., Bures, E., et al.: Interaction in distance education and online learning: using evidence and theory to improve practice. J. Comput. High. Educ. **23**(s 2–3ss), 82–103 (2011). https://doi.org/10.1007/s12528-011-9043-x
10. Jennifer, M.: Service-learning instructional design considerations. J. Comput. High. Educ. **26**(3), 213–226 (2014). https://doi.org/10.1007/s12528-014-9085-y
11. Trespalacios, J.: Exploring small group analysis of instructional design cases in online learning environments. Online Learn. **21**(1), 189–200 (2017)

12. Hong, X., Yanwen, R.: Instructional design of individualized online courses based on the characteristics of learners. In: 4th International Conference on Social Science and Higher Education (ICSSHE 2018), Advances in Social Science, Education and Humanities Research, vol. 181, 4 (2018)
13. Afsaneh, S., Merce, G.: The impact of culture on instructional design and quality. Int. J. Instr. **8**(1), 143–156 (2015)
14. Choi, K., Lee, S.: A relationship among instructional design and organization, students' perceived challenge, and learning outcomes in an online science gifted education program. J. Learn.-Cent. Curric. Instr. **16**(8), 617–639 (2016)
15. Eulho, J., Dongho, K., Meehyun, Y., Sang, H., Barbara, O.: The influence of instructional design on learner control, sense of achievement, and perceived effectiveness in a supersize MOOC course. Comput. Educ. **128**, 377–388 (2018)
16. Alshammari, S.: The influence of technical support, perceived self-efficacy, and instructional design on students' use of learning management systems. Turk. Online J. Distance Educ. **21**(3), 112–141 (2020)

Implementation of an Online International Exchange Project for an Official University Lecture

Shinichi Sato(✉) and Makoto Kageto

Nihon Fukushi University, Tokai, Aichi, Japan
satoshin@n-fukushi.ac.jp

Abstract. The authors have been organising the World Youth Meeting (WYM), an international collaborative project for more than two decades. Students in the authors' university host the WYM in a faculty's official lecture. Formerly, presentations during the event were face-to-face at the faculty's official lecture room; however, the 2020 WYM was conducted online due to COVID-19 restrictions. In this study, the authors report on how the online WYM and the project-based learning (PBL) to host it were implemented in the context of COVID-19 restrictions. The impacts and challenges of PBL are discussed by analysing the data collected through the reflection form prepared by the teachers. Results show that meaningful events can be implemented and their core aims can be achieved. However, the quality of collaboration in PBL should be improved with limited and discretional use of face-to-face settings. It is also challenging to conduct the informal and casual parts of the event.

Keywords: International collaborative project · Project-based learning · Higher education

1 Introduction

1.1 Background

Student-centred learning is one of the key concepts for implementation in universities [1]. Project-based learning (PBL) is one way to realise this learning style. In PBL, students collaborate to address ill-structured and meaningful problems that have no single solution. It helps students develop flexible knowledge, effective problem-solving skills, self-directed lifelong learning skills, effective collaboration skills, and intrinsic motivation [2].

The authors' university provides PBL through a formal class, wherein students host the World Youth Meeting (WYM), which is an international exchange event. Through this class and the project, students are expected to gain practical experience in English communication and in the facilitation and utilisation of information and communication technologies (ICT) [3]. The core activity of the WYM involves presentations in English by mixed teams of students from Japan and overseas. The presentation event is held

R. Li et al. (Eds.): ICBL 2021, LNCS 12830, pp. 367–378, 2021.
https://doi.org/10.1007/978-3-030-80504-3_30

annually for two days in August. However, due to the COVID-19 pandemic, the 2020 WYM (WYM2020) was held online. Earlier studies have discussed the impacts of e-learning or differences between online and face-to-face settings (e.g., [4–6]). With prior face-to-face events increasingly moving online, this is a good opportunity to re-formulate this knowledge for sustainable learning and improved blended learning.

1.2 Purpose

This study aims to share how an international exchange event was implemented online and determines the impact of PBL on students for hosting the event online compared to PBL for hosting it face-to-face. The authors outline the online WYM and how PBL was organised. They also discuss students' perception of their PBL experience.

Although earlier studies propose PBL for effective online learning (e.g., [4]) and experiential learning (e.g., [7]) very few studies describe how face-to-face international events can be shifted online. Studies analysing the impact of PBL for hosting an event that is forced to shift online are also scant. Therefore, this paper aims to provide future directions of PBL to host events online.

2 Methodology

The event studied is WYM2020. While previous WYMs were held face-to-face on the event days in previous years, it was held online in 2020.

First, there is a PBL lecture under the regular curriculum on hosting the WYM; therefore, the authors focus on students who have enrolled for this lecture. The teachers request the students to answer the reflection form after the WYM has been conducted. The students' answers to the form are used as sources for the analysis. Since the lecture is part of the regular curriculum, teachers enquire about various issues for improving the WYM and the class. The authors focused on some items, which are provided below:

- Single choice (1: strongly agree, 2: agree, 3: disagree, 4: strongly disagree)
  - English presentation: I understood how to deliver an English presentation effectively
  - Communication 1: I communicated deeply with classmates from another grade
  - Communication 2: I communicated deeply with classmates from the same grade
  - Utilization of Abilities: I thoroughly utilize my abilities
  - Contribution: I contributed to the WYM
- Freewriting
  - Reflection (e.g., Good points, what I learnt, what I discovered, future challenges)

The items of the 2020 reflection form are the same as items in the previous years, except for 'Communication 2'. In the past, students from the same grade knew each other well and communicated well too; therefore, teachers did not ask about communication among the same batch. However, in 2020, first-year students were not very familiar with each other due to limited opportunities to meet face-to-face. Therefore, the teachers decided to add the final item, and the questionnaire was conducted after WYM2020. Students' answers in 2020 are compared to those from 2019 to analyse similarities and differences between the face-to-face and online event.

To summarise, we extracted the keywords from the freewriting results and analysed the differences between a face-to-face international collaborative project and an online international collaborative project. The text analysis system KH coder [8, 9] was used for this purpose.

3 The International Collaborative Project

3.1 Implementation of the World Youth Meeting

The WYM is a two-day event held annually in early August for university and high school students. The core activity of the WYM is presentations in English by mixed teams of students from Japan and overseas based on the theme of the year. The theme of WYM2020 was 'Quality Education, Goal 4'. In addition to the joint presentation as a core activity, it involved several other activities, such as homestays and visitation to historical sites [3]. As mentioned above, the faculty offered a formal preparatory class for the WYM where students worked on all the tasks related to hosting the event. Instructional design theories are used for PBL for hosting the WYM [10]. Some students collaborate with overseas students for the English presentation, and others host and administrate the event.

Approximately 50 schools from both Japan and overseas participate in the two-day event, with around 500 participants. In 2020, students from twelve countries, mainly Asian, joined the WYM, and 42 teams made presentations. All students, both overseas and Japanese, joined online. More students than observed usually joined from overseas in 2020 because of easy access to the event. Depending on each country's or school's policy, they joined an online room either from their school or home. The WYM is usually held around the beginning of August; however, in 2020, it was postponed to the end of September to prepare for hosting the event under the unprecedented situation. The start of the first semester was also postponed from the beginning of April to May, which also impacted the decision to postpone the WYM.

This year's program was conducted entirely online, and the critical difference was that there was no face-to-face collaboration. There was no possibility of presentation practice through collaborative work in Japan. All presentations at the venue, homestays, and sightseeing were cancelled. Usually, two types of presentations are conducted over two days. One presentation is held in front of large audiences, and the other is with small groups. In the latter presentation, each team is expected to make an interactive presentation based on the former presentation, and the audiences are also expected to ask questions and give comments. Through such a program, participating students are expected to gain skills for speaking formally and interacting in English. They usually also get opportunities to share snacks and meals.

Since all programs were shifted online this year, the steering committee acknowledged that it would be difficult to be online for long hours. Therefore, they decided that presentations would only occur once. Furthermore, presentations were held in three online rooms concurrently to finish the program on the first day.

At the beginning of the second day, the presentations selected by the judges were introduced to improve the students' English and presentation skills. All students, including those who did not make a presentation, are expected to learn about delivering effective English presentations. After this, casual programs were held to compensate for the relaxed exchange that is usually held during break time when the event is hosted face-to-face. The first program was 'Discussion Fair', where volunteer students prepared a video sharing their standpoint about a problem. After watching the video, they discussed and exchanged opinions. It is difficult for participants, especially Japanese students, to discuss the topics freely in English. Hence, we decided on this format. In the second program, 'Entertainment Session', participants gave performances such as singing a song, traditional dancing, and playing a musical instrument. The third program, 'Café Talk', was the last program before the closing ceremony. Here, a high school student's room, a university student's room, and a teacher's room were prepared. Although it is challenging to have a free conversation with many people in English, especially for most Japanese students, participants were expected to talk freely and reflect on the event and deepen their friendship.

Zoom and Microsoft Teams were used to host the WYM online. In one participating country, the use of Zoom was not approved officially; hence, the committee decided to use Microsoft Teams. Zoom was still used because some countries are not familiar with other tools. We also used YouTube Live for the plenary session to increase capacity. The detailed itinerary of WYM2020 is shown in Table 1

Table 1. Detailed itinerary of WYM2020.

<table>
<tr><td colspan="5">Day 1</td></tr>
<tr><td>13:00</td><td colspan="4">Opening ceremony (Teams + YouTube Live)</td></tr>
<tr><td rowspan="2">13:30–17:00</td><td colspan="4">Collaborative presentations</td></tr>
<tr><td colspan="2">Room1 (Teams)</td><td>Room2 (Zoom)</td><td>Room3 (Teams)</td></tr>
<tr><td colspan="5">Day 2</td></tr>
<tr><td>10:00</td><td colspan="4">Review of good presentations (Teams + YouTube Live)</td></tr>
<tr><td>11:30</td><td colspan="4">Lunch break</td></tr>
<tr><td rowspan="2">12:30</td><td colspan="4">Discussion fair</td></tr>
<tr><td>Room1 (Teams)</td><td>Room2 (Teams)</td><td>Room3 (Teams)</td><td>Room4 (Zoom)</td></tr>
<tr><td>13:20</td><td colspan="4">Entertainment session (Teams + YouTube Live)</td></tr>
<tr><td rowspan="2">14:00</td><td colspan="4">Café talk</td></tr>
<tr><td colspan="2">Room1 for high school students (Teams)</td><td>Room2 for university students (Zoom)</td><td>Room3 for teachers (Teams)</td></tr>
<tr><td>14:40</td><td colspan="4">Closing ceremony (Teams + YouTube Live)</td></tr>
</table>

3.2 Student Steering Committee

The WYM is organised by a steering committee composed of teachers from participating schools. Students from Nihon Fukushi University compose a student steering committee and host the program based on the policy set by the WYM steering committee. The faculty offers a formal preparatory class for the WYM. Students enrol in this class and prepare for the WYM. Second-year students fulfil the central roles in the project. Three leaders and the chief of each group are selected from second-year students. First-year students contribute to the project under the instruction of second-year students. In 2020, students were divided into ten groups. The roles and their tasks are shown in Table 2.

Table 2. Role of the students

Roles for 2020	Tasks/Remarks
Leaders	Leaders manage tasks for each team and promote collaboration among teams
Presenters	Presenters make a presentation team with foreign university's student(s) and make a presentation for the theme of the year
MCs	MCs host and manage the proceedings of the presentation on event days
Proceedings organisers	Proceedings Organisers collect necessary documents and compile and issue them as the WYM proceedings
Hall keepers	Hall Keepers manage the presentation facilities. Usually, their tasks include setting up microphones and preparing presentation PCs. Here, their main task was to prepare online rooms and support presenters in using the web conferencing tools appropriately
Foreign affairs	Usually, they help issue visas. Here, they collected and managed information about the participants from foreign countries' universities
Recording	Recording members were expected to record the entire activities of the WYM with photos and videos, including the preparation and what it was like on the event days
Website administrator	The Website Administrator was expected to publish information necessary for the participants
Writers	Writers were expected to collect data about the activities toward the WYM and to report them to the enrolled students. We expected their reports to promote cooperation with other groups and help students understand the total movement toward the WYM. This role was newly assigned for this year
SDG4	Based on the theme of the year (Quality Education, Goal 4), members worked to support education in Cambodia and shared their experiences with other students

3.3 Implementation of the Class and the Event

Four teachers oversaw the class, and they had a weekly meeting with the student Leaders. Eighty-nine first-year students and 86 s-year students enrolled in the class. The regular class for first- and second-year students met weekly, and students voluntarily gathered to perform tasks that they deemed necessary as per their role. As it was a university class, all students were not necessarily highly motivated; hence, the teachers oversaw the basic direction of the event and managed the students' activities considering typical pitfalls that tend to happen in PBL [11].

In 2020, the first semester started at the beginning of May and ended in the first week of August; the second semester started at the beginning of September and ended at the end of December. The class was held weekly for 90 min. It started as an online class using the Zoom web conferencing system. The class was held in a face-to-face setting on campus for a month in July after the government lifted the state of emergency. However, the university requested teachers to move all classes to the online setting again, although the campus was not completely closed. Teachers could enter the campus anytime, and so could students who obtained approvals from teachers.

Students learned about the general information of the participating countries and basic knowledge related to the theme of the year from the beginning of the semester (May) until the end of June. They also learned about useful English expressions for discussion, deepening friendship, and so on. They started to work on their tasks in full pursuit, including during class, from July; some had already started their tasks outside the class.

3.4 Practice of the Event

As per the university's policy, we allowed but did not compel the students to come to the campus on the event days. Those who came were Leaders, Presenters, MCs, Hall keepers, some Recording staff, and Writers.

The Presenters and MCs were allowed to secure a stable network and collaborate as team members. The Hall Keepers administrated the online conference rooms stably and collaborated quickly in case of an emergency because no program could proceed without stable online rooms. As for the Recording staff and Writers, only those who were assigned to record and write about the members who worked at the university were allowed to enter the campus. The two-day event proceeded generally well and according to the program; however, there were some difficulties, such as low quality of audio and echo.

4 Students' Responses in the Reflection Form

4.1 Results of the Students' Self-assessment

Table 3 shows the results of the t-test conducted to compare the students' answers on the reflection form in WYM2020 and WYM2019.

A significant difference was noted only for the item regarding communication with students from another grade; challenges in such communication were also observed.

Table 3. Comparison of the students' self-assessment between WYM2020 and WYM2019

	2020			2019			t-value
	M	SD	N	M	SD	N	
English presentation	3.06	0.55	155	3.06	0.75	165	0.03
Communication 1	2.82	1.27	155	3.18	0.89	165	3.08*
Utilization of abilities	3.21	0.65	155	3.19	0.78	165	0.26
Contribution	3.26	0.67	155	3.19	0.67	165	0.70

$^{*}p < 0.05$

However, generally speaking, the PBL objectives were achieved through engagement in an online event.

We compared the students' responses in 2020 in further detail. As described above, only some students were allowed on the campus on the day of the event. Therefore, we conducted a t-test for comparing responses of students who came to the campus on either or both of the event days and the students who joined the event from their home on both days. For the item 'English presentation', we excluded the responses provided by students who conducted the joint presentation since they would have learned English presentation better than other students because they focused on it; additionally, most (25 out of 26 students) joined from the campus, which would have hindered accurate comparison. Table 4 shows the results.

Table 4. Comparison of the students' self-assessment based on whether they were on campus on the event day

	Home			Campus			t-value
	M	SD	N	M	SD	N	
English presentation	2.94	0.58	82	3.04	0.52	47	0.76
Communication 1	2.71	1.13	83	2.94	1.41	72	1.30
Communication 2	3.02	0.63	83	3.50	0.48	72	3.94*
Utilization of abilities	3.04	0.74	83	3.42	0.47	72	3.01*
Contribution	3.05	0.75	83	3.50	0.48	72	3.55*

$^{*}p < 0.05$

There were no significant differences in English presentation and communication among same-grade students. However, there were significant differences in students' communication with those in another grade (first-year students communicating with second-year students, and second-year students communicating with first-year students), utilization of their abilities, and contribution to the WYM. The students who joined and worked from their campus scored higher on these items.

4.2 Freewriting for Reflection

Text analysis was conducted using the KH coder for the students' freewriting for reflecting on the event. The extracted keywords are shown in Table 5, in descending order of the frequency with which these appeared in the freewriting. The keywords that did not appear on the top 20 in the other years are shaded.

Table 5. Top 20 keywords used in students' freewriting for reflection reports

Freq.	Keywords: WYM2020	Freq.	Keywords: WYM2019
140	オンライン Online	124	自分 Me
117	自分 Me	105	参加 Participation
95	英語 English	91	先輩 Older student
95	参加 Participation	91	仕事 Task
64	対面 Face-to-face	83	英語 English
59	仕事 Task	61	反省 Reflection
56	先輩 Older student	54	海外 Overseas
55	グループ Group	54	準備 Preparation
50	反省 Reflection	44	発表 Presentation
41	開催 Holding (an event)	37	交流 Exchange
38	海外 Overseas	36	情報 Information
37	経験 Experience	36	経験 Experience
35	活動 Activity	35	グループ Group
32	不安 Worry	35	改善 Improvement
31	協力 Cooperation	31	練習 Practice
30	準備 Preparation	30	本番 Actual event
29	学生 Student	29	観光 Sightseeing
27	先生 Teacher	27	人数 Number of people
26	コロナ Coronavirus	27	定例会 Regular meeting
25	コミュニケーション Communication	24	先生 Teacher

The keywords used frequently are similar for 2019 and 2020. Common keywords reflecting the essence of the WYM, such as 'English', 'reflection', and 'experience', were seen frequently. Keywords such as 'task', 'group', 'preparation', and 'reflection', related to hosting the event and PBL, were also common.

However, some differences were also noted. New keywords, such as 'online', 'face-to-face', and 'Coronavirus', appeared in 2020 considering the ongoing pandemic.

Nonetheless, the context of freewriting must be analysed to determine why other different keywords were used.

5 Discussion

5.1 Conducting the Project Online

Comparison of the students' self-assessment between 2020 and 2019 showed that there was no significant difference for items about English presentation, utilization of their abilities, and contribution to the WYM. This result indicates that, through PBL, the students understood what they should do and had developed a sense of fulfilment, even though the event was held online. Thus, as long as the tasks are clear and meaningful, it is possible to implement meaningful PBL through an online event.

However, the comparison among students in 2020 showed that those who came to the campus on either or both of the event days scored themselves higher for items regarding the utilization of their abilities and contribution to the WYM. This result implies that having a sense of being together may have positively influenced their participation in the event. Although no guideline has been established yet, it will be necessary to carefully design a face-to-face setting for PBL even if participants from other schools cannot come to the venue. We need to identify ways in which students joining remotely can also experience the same atmosphere as the others.

5.2 Collaboration with Project Members

Although PBL through an online event was effectively developed, we need to pay attention to how students worked with this. Collaboration is one of the key issues in PBL and is considered an important skill in the 21st century [11]. There was a significant difference in communication with students from another grade. The comparison among students in 2020 showed that those who came to the campus on either or both of the event days scored themselves higher for items regarding the utilization of their abilities and contribution to the WYM.

The comparison among students in 2020 also shows that those who came to the campus on either or both of the event days scored themselves higher for the item regarding communication with same grade students; however, there was no significant difference in the item regarding communication with another grade students. This may imply that since same grade students meet face-to-face, it does not take long for them to establish good communication. However, being exposed to a face-to-face setting during the event for merely one or two days is not enough for improving communication with unfamiliar students.

It seems to be challenging for students to collaborate with unfamiliar members, which indicates that online communication was somewhat more difficult for them. This may also imply that they hesitated to communicate with other students with whom they do not have a close relationship. This resulted in communication with students whom they were already familiar with. Students should be allowed some time to become more familiar with each other before asking them to perform team tasks. This result also implies that establishing better communication and collaboration between first- and second-year students will take more time.

The importance of casual exchange was explored from the perspective of social presence, using the Community of Inquiry (CoI) framework [4, 13]. CoI is a framework proposed generally for e-learning; however, we can refer to it to deal with such problems. Incorporating this concept with social media, which is popular among the youth, may also help to deal with this challenge [14]. It will also be crucial to remember that students' sociability would be different depending on whether they are presented with a face-to-face or online setting [15].

5.3 Consideration of the Potential Differences of Online Events

Although some features of PBL were discussed in the context of hosting an online event, there are other issues that will need to be considered when the event cannot be hosted in a face-to-face setting. We preliminarily consider the differences identified from the analysis of the students' freewriting for constructing a better project design in the future under such circumstances.

As shown in Table 5, we can find both similarities and differences. The keywords 'online' and 'face-to-face' were not observed in freewriting in 2019, although the students worked online in a preparatory stage to communicate with participants from other schools and had a face-to-face event in the past WYM. They became conscious of these notions for the first time during the pandemic in 2020. The keyword 'holding' (an event) was used 41 times in 2020, but it was used only twice in 2019. Another similar reason for this was that they were supposed to be more conscious about hosting the event when they faced the possibility of event cancellation. We would like to observe if these keywords decrease after the online event was hosted.

The keywords 'presentation', 'exchange', 'practice', and 'actual event' were noted more in 2019—the frequencies for these were about 50% or less during 2020. These keywords seem to be related to the distinction between the preparatory stage and the actual event days. This distinction might become blurred during an event that does not have a face-to-face setting. This implies that it is important to raise awareness about the event to ensure that students perceive it as a real event.

In previous years, students who managed the event communicated with overseas participants to support them in the campus, and could also communicate with them during breaktime and casual exchange. In the online event, the students could not have, or had far less, such opportunities. Due to operational difficulties in interaction, instructions were mainly prepared as documents, and participants were requested to read them prior to the event. This lead to the decrease of the keyword 'exchange'. Although some casual programs were created, further consideration is necessary to facilitate informal communication through an online event.

6 Conclusion and Future Challenges

In this paper, the authors introduced an annual international collaborative project that was held online for the first time in more than 20 years, and discussed the effects of PBL on hosting the event.

The purpose of the project was achieved. The students felt a sense of fulfilment while hosting the event both in online and face-to-face settings. We have identified the challenges involved in collaborating with other members, especially when students need to collaborate with new members. The facilitation of informal communication is also a potential challenge in the case of an online event. We also reveal the importance of designing face-to-face settings for students. Appropriate designing of a face-to-face setting, as long as students can enter the campus, may lead to better online collaboration. Such issues would be important even during a face-to-face event. As more students than usual years joined the event this year, it can be said that there are some benefits to hosting the event online. To fully utilize such benefits, we should pursue hosting an event that has a mixed (both online and face-to-face) setting. When designing such an event in the future, we believe that the findings of this study will facilitate instructional designs.

However, the analysis of the event and PBL is still preliminary. In this research, the authors analysed from the viewpoint of students who hosted the event. The quality of the event itself, which is also an important aspect to assess the quality of PBL, was not addressed. The feedback from the participants from other schools, including Japanese and non-Japanese students and teachers, were not considered in this paper, although they were read by teachers. In the future, a multi-faceted assessment should be performed. We also aim to provide further knowledge for implementing and hosting a better event with better PBL.

Acknowledgements. This work was supported by JSPS KAKENHI Grant Numbers JP18K02841, JP15K01097.

References

1. Reigeluth, C.M., Beatty, B.J., Myers, R.D. (eds.): Instructional-Design Theories and Models, Volume IV: The Learner-Centered Paradigm of Education. Routledge, New York (2016)
2. Hmelo-Silver, C.E., Chinn, C.A., Chan, C. (eds.): The International Handbook of Collaborative Learning. Routledge, London (2013)
3. Kageto, M., Sato, S.: An international collaborative project based on constructivism. In: Siemens, G., Fulford, C. (eds.) Proceedings of Ed-Media 2009–World Conference On Educational Multimedia, Hypermedia and Telecommunications, pp. 1615–1620. Association for the Advancement of Computing in Education (AACE), Honolulu (2009)
4. Garrison, D.R.: E-Learning in the 21st Century: A Community of Inquiry Framework for Research and Practice. Routledge, London (2016)
5. Kang, M., Liew, B.T., Kim, J., Park, Y.: Learning presence as a predictor of achievement and satisfaction in online learning environments. Int. J. E-Learn. **13**(2), 193–208 (2014)
6. Johnson, S.D., Aragon, S.R., Shaik, N.: Comparative analysis of learner satisfaction and learning outcomes in online and face-to-face learning environments. J. Interact. Learn. Res. **11**(1), 29–49 (2000)
7. Kolb, D.: Experiential Learning As The Science of Learning and Development. Prentice Hall, Englewood Cliffs (1984)
8. Koichi, H.: A two-step approach to quantitative content analysis: KH coder tutorial using Anne of Green Gables (Part I). Ritsumeikan Soc. Sci. Rev. **52**(3), 77–91 (2016)
9. Koichi, H.: A two-step approach to quantitative content analysis: KH coder tutorial using Anne of Green Gables (Part II). Ritsumeikan Soc. Sci. Rev. **53**(1), 137–147 (2017)

10. Kageto, M., Sato, S.: Rethinking the university learning environment: how to enrich students' education through a constructivist learning environment. Int. J. Educ. Media Technol. **4**(1), 67–78 (2010)
11. Kirschner, P.A., Sweller, J., Clark, R.E.: Why minimal guidance during instruction does not work: an analysis of the failure of constructivist, discovery, problem-based, experiential, and inquiry-based teaching. Educ. Psychol. **41**(2), 75–86 (2006)
12. Griffin, P., McGaw, B., Care, E.: Assessment and teaching of 21st century skills. Springer, Dordrecht (2012). https://doi.org/10.1007/978-3-319-65368-6
13. Ling, L.: Community of inquiry in an online undergraduate information technology course. J. Inf. Technol. Educ. Res. **6**(1), 153–168 (2007)
14. Sato, S., Kageto, M.: Analysis of informal use of social media in formal project-based learning. Int. J. Educ. Media Technol. **7**(1), 26–37 (2013)
15. Tufekci, Z., Brashears, M.E.: Are we all equally at home socialising online? Cyberasociality and evidence for an unequal distribution of disdain for digitally-mediated sociality. Inf. Commun. Soc. **17**(4), 486–502 (2014)

Author Index

The manufacturer's authorised representative in the EU is Springer Nature Customer Service Centre GmbH, Europaplatz 3, 69115 Heidelberg, Germany. If you have any concerns regarding our products, please contact ProductSafety@springernature.com

Printed and bound by CPI Group (UK) Ltd, Croydon, CR0 4YY
22/09/2026
02220983-0002